To Joyce,
who shared
some of this history

Cynthia Bowman

DAWN CLARK NETSCH

To my Rockford
Holmbergs
with fond memories
+ love
Dawn

DAWN CLARK
NETSCH

————A Political Life————

CYNTHIA GRANT BOWMAN

NORTHWESTERN UNIVERSITY PRESS

EVANSTON, ILLINOIS

Northwestern University Press
www.nupress.northwestern.edu

Printed in the United States of America

10 9 8 7 6 5 4 3 2 1

Library of Congress Cataloging-in-Publication Data

Bowman, Cynthia Grant, 1945–
    Dawn Clark Netsch : a political life / Cynthia Grant Bowman.
        p. cm. — (Chicago lives)
    Includes bibliographical references and index.
    ISBN 978-0-8101-2411-0 (trade cloth : alk. paper) 1. Netsch, Dawn Clark. 2.
Legislators—Illinois—Biography. 3. Women legislators—Illinois—Biography.
4. Illinois—Politics and government—1951– 5. Politicians—Illinois—Biography.
6. Women politicians—Illinois—Biography. 7. Illinois. Comptroller's Office—
Officials and employees—Biography. 8. Democratic Party (Ill.)—Biography.
I. Title.
F546.4.N48B69 2010
977.3'043092—dc22
[B]
                                                                2009032427

∞ The paper used in this publication meets the minimum requirements of the
American National Standard for Information Sciences—Permanence of Paper for
Printed Library Materials, ANSI Z39.48-1992.

CONTENTS

Photographs follow page 120.

PREFACE

Dawn Clark Netsch is an extraordinary woman. She has played an important role in the politics of Chicago and of Illinois. As a woman in the legal profession, legal academy, and politics, she has also been a pioneer. I was lucky enough to have been her colleague at Northwestern University School of Law from 1988 to 2006, and I was honored to be asked to write her biography for Northwestern's Chicago Lives series.

Dawn is a warm and charming woman of many contradictions—a schoolmarm who drinks and smokes, a powerful woman who has never learned to drive, a feminist who thought of herself as one of the boys, a well-to-do woman who is frugal to a fault. Michael Holland, a former student who worked on Dawn's many political campaigns, including her 1994 campaign for governor of Illinois, fondly recalls:

> In late 1993, probably September, leading up to the primary, four or five of us . . . were in the campaign office on Grand. What I was doing was outlining how much money we could raise from labor organizations and who could best make those requests and set up the meetings. We discussed what the ask [was] going to be and who's going to make the ask. We were talking about $400,000 to $500,000. Suddenly Dawn comes in all by herself. And she's carrying a paper sack. "I brought these for the campaign," she says, and opens the sack—and there are hundreds of rubber bands that she has saved for who knows how many years. She was as proud as a peacock. We were all stunned, sitting there talking about raising thousands.[1]

Dawn is not only frugal but also a pack rat. She saves everything—old correspondence, school report cards, newspaper columns from high school, her undergraduate papers, campaign literature and speech notes, yellowing newspaper clippings, baseball scorecards, and funeral programs. Had she not done so, much of her remarkable history—and fascinating parts of the history of Chicago, of Illinois, of the Democratic Party, and of women—might have been lost.

Dawn Clark Netsch has been involved in the ongoing fight for racial equality since her undergraduate years at Northwestern University, when she joined the campaign to integrate the school's dormitories after World War II. She graduated first in her class from Northwestern University School of Law, the only woman to graduate in the spring of 1952. She participated in Adlai Stevenson's campaigns for president in 1952 and 1956 and was one of a group of young, liberal Democrats whose careers he inspired. Although she practiced law for a time, her ambition was always to be involved in political life. She was an early and very active member of the Committee on Illinois Government, a group of Stevenson-inspired liberals who contested the dominance of the Chicago Democratic "machine" in Illinois politics. She served as aide to Governor Otto Kerner and then joined the law faculty at Northwestern in 1965, as one of the first group of women law professors in the United States. In 1970, she played an influential role as a delegate to the constitutional convention that produced a new constitution for Illinois.

In 1972, Dawn's first political campaign, for the Illinois state senate, brought her a hard-won victory against the candidate supported by the Regular Democrats. After they fought hard to unseat her in 1974, she served with distinction, virtually unopposed in the primary elections, until 1990. In 1990, when she was elected state comptroller, she became the highest-ranked woman in Illinois state government—indeed, the first woman ever to serve in a statewide executive office. She was also the first woman to run for governor of Illinois, after winning a hotly contested four-way race for the Democratic Party nomination in 1994. Now emerita professor of law at Northwestern, Dawn Clark Netsch continues to advocate for a variety of progressive causes, including affordable housing, tax reform to fund public education, merit selection of judges, governmental ethics and campaign reform, and the equal treatment of gays and lesbians. Her story—full of firsts for women, the law, and the state of Illinois—begins in Cincinnati, Ohio, more than eighty years ago.

DAWN CLARK NETSCH

—— *Chapter 1* ——

Growing Up in Cincinnati

WHEN PATRICIA DAWN CLARK was born in Cincinnati on September 16, 1926, the city was a bustling metropolis of more than four hundred thousand people, with almost twice as many in the greater metropolitan area.[1] Situated on a bend in the Ohio River, Cincinnati was a river town that had boomed during the age of steamboat commerce as the port midway between Pittsburgh and New Orleans. When that traffic declined at the end of the nineteenth century, merchants, bankers, and industrialists developed a new city. German and Irish immigrants had swelled the city's population in the 1800s, but in the prosperous 1920s, Cincinnati industry drew new groups of migrants from the hills of Kentucky and West Virginia.[2] While these groups settled in the downtown area along the river, suburbs sprang up on the hills rising above the river, incorporating the numerous separate communities that had existed before.

A 1943 guide to Cincinnati written by the talented writers of the Works Progress Administration's Federal Writers' Project describes the city as it looked at that time, when Dawn, as she is now known, was in high school:

> The Queen City gives the impression of enormous size and variety. It rises from the riverbank in a series of terraces that lead to a broad alley shelf known as the Basin. Here are the narrow streets and massed buildings of the downtown district, with skyscrapers, church spires, and chimney pots on red brick houses forming a jagged sky line. Reaching down into this valley like thick fingers from all directions except the south, where the river winds, are the wooded hills on whose tops and sides most of the city's people live. . . .

Cincinnati is largely composed of scores of suburbs, each of which was once a separate community isolated from its neighbors by steep hillsides, deep valleys, and thick ravines. As the city grew it annexed these towns. Roads and streets were cut among the thickets, streetcar inclines hammered to the hillsides, and viaducts threaded from hilltop to hilltop. These and the automobile drew the suburbs together but failed to erase their insularity. Even today each suburb is different from its neighbors in its architecture and in the economic and social levels of its people. When Cincinnatians are asked where they live they do not reply "Cincinnati . . ." but "Hyde Park."[3]

The Clark family lived in Pleasant Ridge and later in Hyde Park, middle-class suburban communities in the hills overlooking the river. But the family was not native to the region. Indeed, its origins were far more venturesome. George W. Clark, Dawn's great-grandfather, was a captain in the Indiana cavalry; his first wife, Dawn's great-grandmother, was an Osage Indian. Their son, William Henry Clark, left the Midwest to become surveyor general of Colorado, surveying most of the western part of the state in the late nineteenth century. Dawn and her brother, Keith, remember their grandfather as an imposing man—tall, with a big mane of white hair—but very gentle and kindly.

Dawn's paternal grandmother, Mary Frances Clark, was born in Ohio but accompanied her surveyor husband to Meeker, Colorado, a town that grew out of an army fort in the 1880s, soon after the last big Native American uprising and "pacification." The couple lived in a log cabin, where Dawn's father, William Keith Clark (known as Keith), was born on April 18, 1897; he was the couple's seventh child (although only four survived). Dawn remembers her grandmother as small but tough, "from handling things out in the mountains of Colorado."[4] Her children joked later in life that she had invented frozen foods as a way of surviving through the long winters there.

Dawn's father was an exceptional athlete, playing football especially well and competing in track-and-field events. At Colorado College, where he met Dawn's mother, Hazel Dawn Harrison (also known as Dawn), he was renowned for his physical prowess. One article in a local newspaper described how he could lift 455 pounds with ease and predicted, "His record will not be equaled in any educational institution of the Rocky mountain region."[5] Keith Clark's college career was interrupted, however, by World War I. Serving in the American Expeditionary Force as a first lieutenant in the field artillery, Clark was exposed to mustard gas and suffered from its effects long after. He nonetheless played on the force's football team and won a football scholarship to Harvard, which he attended after his discharge in July 1919.

Dawn's maternal grandparents died before she was born, and she knew little about them. Her mother was born in Fort Smith, Arkansas, but moved to Colorado as an infant, where her father was a schoolteacher and principal of the schools in two towns. She lived in the state until she graduated in 1917 from Colorado College, with a major in philosophy, and went to Washington, D.C., to work during World War I.

Hazel Dawn Clark's three living siblings remained in the West. An unmarried sister, Coy, a schoolteacher in Ogden, Utah, with whom she was particularly close, often traveled to Ohio to visit her sister. Dawn's maternal uncle, DeWitt, also lived in Utah, where he worked as a representative of a rifle company. He was a crack shot and often won marksmanship contests in the area. Dawn's father's siblings lived out west as well, where Dawn and her brother visited them when they were children. Their aunt Peg lived in Yuma, Colorado. A big-boned woman, she reminded Dawn of the frontier. An uncle had a ranch in a remote part of the Colorado mountains, which impressed Dawn with its lack of indoor plumbing.

After Dawn's father left Harvard (after some dispute about credits, he later received his degree), he returned for a while to Colorado, where he married Hazel Dawn Harrison on July 14, 1922. Their first child, William Keith Jr. (known as Keith, like his father), was born there in 1924. The family moved to St. Louis, where a job beckoned, and then to Cincinnati when Keith Clark Sr. bought a business there. After helping to develop a type of cinder block that was a particularly good building material, Clark set up a plant in Cincinnati to produce it. Hence Patricia Dawn was born in Cincinnati, three years after her brother's birth in Colorado.

The Clarks built a colonial-style house out of Keith Sr.'s cinder block material; painted white, the house stood on a large corner lot on Briarcliff Avenue in Pleasant Ridge. The layout of the house was typical of an upper-middle-class home of this type: a large living room with built-in bookcases; a dining room, kitchen, and room with a bath for the maid on the first floor; three bedrooms and a bath on the second floor; a full basement; and a large yard for the children to play in. Dawn's mother stayed at home, although there was also household help, including an African American caretaker of whom the children were very fond. The family lived a very comfortable life.

By the 1930s, however, the Clark building materials business was doing badly. No one was building in the early years of the Depression; and although Clark hung on for a while, his business did not survive the economic downturn. He went from job to job, mostly in the construction industry, and worked for a time as the night supervisor in a division at Procter and Gamble, a large Cincinnati employer that survived the Depression.

The family's life changed substantially when Dawn's father's business failed. The family was forced to sell their house and move into a more modest one, which they rented, close enough to the Pleasant Ridge elementary school that the children did not have to change schools. It was smaller, older, and in a less desirable neighborhood, but the children still had their own rooms and a yard. This was the first of many moves, as the family moved down the economic scale. They moved into ever-more-modest homes in Cincinnati, and for a year when Dawn was eleven or twelve, to Nashville, Tennessee, where her father had bought a paint business. After that business also failed, the Clarks returned to Cincinnati.

Throughout all this upheaval, Dawn's parents protected their children from knowing what a catastrophe the Depression was for them. They acted as though it were completely normal to move from house to house repeatedly and never expressed their financial worries in front of the children. After all, unlike others at that time, the family did have a decent home and food to eat, even if there was no money to spare. As adults, both Clark children realized how hard the economic disaster of the 1930s had been for their parents. "There is no way of understanding what it did to their psyche and emotions; it was a major factor in my father's being," says Dawn.[6]

Dawn's father was virtually destroyed by the Depression. The loss of his business, coupled with the effects of mustard gas and trauma from the war, left him with deep psychological scars. His physical and mental health were unstable for the rest of his life. Yet both children remember him as charming, intelligent, and an amazing talker. Dawn adored him while she was growing up. Both children recognized that he had major flaws as well. He was not a very present parent at the best of times. Sometimes he would toss a ball with his son on weekends, but most of the time he was preoccupied with his unstable work situation and absent except at dinner.

Dinner was sacred in the Clark household. Dawn's mother, a good middle-class mother of her time, had strong convictions about how to take care of her family and raise her children to be good citizens. Rules were strictly enforced, and all members of the family had to be there for dinner every night and at 1 P.M. on Sunday. Until they reached high school, neither Dawn nor Keith missed a meal, and that was allowed only if they had been granted permission in advance. Conversation at the dinner table focused both on what the various family members had done that day and on what was going on in the world. Hazel Dawn Clark was a strict disciplinarian, and both parents believed in and practiced corporal punishment, a fact that appears to have affected the life of Keith but not to have touched Dawn at all, because she rarely needed to be punished.

The Depression brought another major change to the family's life: Dawn's mother went to work. She found employment as a social worker, a profession in which she continued for her whole adult life. During the Depression, Hazel Dawn Clark worked with people in desperate circumstances and must have seen many grim things. She was known for her intelligence and compassion, and her coworkers loved her. Yet Dawn's mother's employment meant that, from an early age, Dawn came home every day to a maid or caretaker. She remembers a black woman named Marie who stayed with them for a long time and whom she adored.[7] Other household help disappeared from the Clarks' life.

The two Clark children were quite different from each other. Keith liked sports and the out-of-doors. After school he joined his own friends— all boys—in cowboy or soldier games when he was young and later played organized sports. His grades were barely passing. Dawn, by contrast, was a very good student, regularly earning top marks in every subject except for household arts in elementary school and typing and gym in high school. She was more of an indoor type. Keith remembered her trying to roller-skate a few times with him and other friends, but she soon gave up. Instead, Dawn read a lot, helped with housework, and listened to Cincinnati Reds games on the radio, starting her lifelong love affair with baseball. Because of economic constraints, she hardly ever made it down to the big ballpark on the river, but often her father would take her to watch a friend's son play on a community team at a field across the river in northern Kentucky. Dawn was also a fan of football—her father's and brother's sport—but as the years passed, she became intensely hooked on baseball for its combination of individual skill, grace, and team effort.

Dawn's lifelong passion for opera also stems from this period. When Aunt Coy would come east for a visit, she and Dawn's mother would go to the opera, and they took Dawn a number of times. When Dawn grew older, she went with friends who shared her interest. Cincinnati also had summer opera performances at the zoo, which she would attend with her friends. Sometimes sea lions or other animals would blend their voices with those of the singers; and when pigeons flew overhead, it was occasionally necessary to beat a speedy retreat.

From the time she was a young girl, Dawn was assertive. Keith and Dawn would get into brother-sister spats over things like the size of their respective portions of cake. Keith knew that Dawn made better grades than he did and that his parents would have liked it if he had done better in school. He wondered why he did not do better than his younger sister, when she, after all, could get married and have a husband support her.[8]

The year the family spent in Nashville made a deep impression on both Clark children. Nashville was the Deep South, and although blacks and whites lived close to one another, they were segregated. The family lived in the second story of a duplex, and Dawn attended a whites-only school with an outdoor bathroom. Keith remembered that the neighborhood kids let him know he was a "damn Yankee" and didn't belong there, although he did succeed in making friends.[9] One day, Dawn was looking out her window and saw some young black girls of about her age, perhaps eleven years old, on their way home from the school they attended. White children were following them and throwing stones at them. Dawn sensed that the black girls were trembling, but she did not dare intervene. She formed a strong conviction that the whole situation was simply not right, and she felt bad about her inability to help the girls. This incident marked the beginning of Dawn's deep attachment to racial equality and to the improvement of race relations in the United States.

That ugly incident in Nashville also influenced Dawn's choice of schools after she returned to Cincinnati. Her godmother taught Latin at Walnut Hills, the preeminent college preparatory school in Cincinnati, and Dawn was under pressure to take the admission exam to enroll there. Although she would certainly have earned a spot at the prestigious school, she stubbornly insisted on going to Withrow for secondary school instead. Withrow, an excellent public school, was a veritable melting pot for the times. Perhaps as many as 15 percent of the students were African American. (Ohio was a Free-Soil state before the Civil War, and Cincinnati, a stop on the Underground Railroad, had a large African

American population.) The school was also diverse economically. Dawn wanted this diverse setting for herself, so she enrolled at Withrow in junior high school.

Visitors entered Withrow High School, built in 1919, by a footbridge across a small ravine. The school was housed in an imposing castlelike building on a twenty-four-acre campus, with a 114-foot clock tower at its center offering beautiful views across a valley.[10] Four thousand students were enrolled there in the early 1940s. Although each class was large, the students were instructed in groups of about thirty, and the faculty was outstanding. The students were not formally streamed, but those who would clearly be going on to college had classes together and the best teachers. Dawn remembers one especially good English teacher, Dorothy Atkins, who, by calling students' attention to events in the world at large, contributed to her developing interest in politics. Dawn's classmate Bob McGrath described Miss Atkins as "a firebrand" who encouraged female students to get involved in campus politics.[11]

There was also a memorable Latin teacher at Withrow, Ruth Grove. Miss Grove may have been short, fat, and unattractive, but she bubbled over with love of Latin language, culture, and archaeology, contributing to Dawn's love of Latin and the ancient world. One year Miss Grove wrote and produced an operetta about Catiline, the classical Roman politician and rival of Cicero, with Latin lyrics set to contemporary popular songs. Dawn appeared on stage in a toga. Dawn's experience with excellent teachers in a large, diverse public school had a great deal to do with her subsequent support for quality public education: she wanted all children to have an experience like hers.

Although she was scholarly and obviously very bright, Dawn also appears to have been quite popular during high school. Bob McGrath reports that Pat Clark—she later adopted the name Dawn in college—was a great deal of fun to be with and had many friends. She dated some as well, although she did not go steady. Dawn does remember having a passion for one young man in particular. There were dances, and sometimes young people from the high school would take a boat called the *Island Queen* on the river to Coney Island for music or dancing or just to go to the amusement park.

Dawn also stepped into a leadership role during high school, participating in student council, French club, Latin club, various literary clubs, and the school newspaper, among other activities. By senior year, Dawn and her best friend Martha Larsen were coeditors of the school newspaper and wrote a column called "Et Cetera"; each column began with the statement "We grow by mental shocks." "Et Cetera" contained some fairly radical ideas about national and international politics. Some targets of their wrath were the Dies Committee (predecessor of the House Un-American Activities Committee) and J. Edgar Hoover, head of the Federal Bureau of Investigation. Dawn and Martha were called into the principal's office concerning one of their columns. In it they had advocated a temporary federal takeover of schools throughout the country to equalize the education received in different states. "Is it equality of opportunity," they asked, "that there is not an accredited high school in the city of Nashville, Tennessee, while every high school in Cincinnati, Ohio, is accredited?" They concluded by proclaiming, "Education is the starting point in a race for better living—a race in which there should be no handicaps."[12] The local board of education contacted the Withrow principal with complaints about this column, and he suggested to the two editors that they were in danger of being tossed out of school.

By the end of Dawn's sophomore year in high school, the United States was at war. With the U.S. entry into World War II at the end of 1941, Dawn's father, who had been at loose ends since the Depression struck, reenlisted in the armed services—this time, the U.S. Air Force—and was sent overseas in July 1942. He was stationed initially in North Africa, where he participated in the invasion and the Tunisian campaign. Later he flew cargo missions from India to China over the "hump," the eastern end of the Himalayas, to resupply the Chinese armies fighting the Japanese, and he subsequently helped set up air bases in the Marshall Islands. He was discharged in 1945 with the rank of major. When Dawn's brother, Keith, also went into the service, only two members of the family were left in Cincinnati. With their belts tightened, Dawn and her mother moved into a one-bedroom apartment in a house across the street from Withrow High School.

To contribute to the war effort, Dawn organized a school project to buy an ambulance for the Red Cross. Bob McGrath describes her as having almost single-handedly raised the money for it. In addition to the predictable bake sales, she solicited donations from businesses close to the high school, asked parents for contributions, and auctioned off ration stamps to raise money. When the ambulance was finally purchased, Dawn made the presentation during halftime of a Withrow football game, marching onto the field to rousing cheers to hand the keys to a representative of the Red Cross.

Depression and world war were a somber background to childhood. In her senior year of high school, Dawn and a girlfriend founded a canteen where lower-income youths could go on weekends to keep them out of trouble. They located a boarded-up former grammar school in Oakley, a working-class neighborhood of the city, obtained permission from the board of education to use it, and then cleaned and painted it themselves. They asked local business owners in the Oakley area for money and furnishings, gathered donated pool and ping-pong tables and jukeboxes, and set up a counter for soft drinks and snacks. The first floor held the snack bar, a lounge, and two dance halls; two large game rooms occupied the second floor.[13]

There was a good deal of publicity at the time the canteen opened. After that, interest dropped off, and Dawn was left to run it virtually alone. She was there to open up and close every Friday and Saturday night from about five o'clock to midnight, kept track of the till, and generally supervised the operation. Running the canteen gave Dawn more exposure to young people from economic classes other than her own, and she learned from them. Among other things, she learned how to play pool. A young man who came to the canteen frequently was a fine pool player and helped her perfect her game. Her exceptional skill at pool became a theme during her campaign for governor of Illinois many years later.

Dawn also met a diverse group of people at her summer jobs during high school. One job was at a large wartime defense factory on an assembly line making radio sets for the signal corps. With almost no experience working with her hands, she was all thumbs with the wires at the beginning. The other workers on the line, mostly women during the war, recognized that Dawn was only doing the job temporarily and would be going to college, but they were patient and supportive of her while she learned. Dawn later worked another factory job in a small plant, making plastic containers. Most of the workers there were from the mountains of Kentucky, rural people who were recent immigrants to Cincinnati. Dawn enjoyed listening to them sing hill-country music as they worked. She became friends with the supervisor, a man who had no legs and used a wheelchair, and he would tell her about what life had been like in the Kentucky hills before the war.

Her year in Nashville, influential teachers, and the people she met in the canteen and factories all doubtless contributed to Dawn's developing political consciousness. Her parents were Republicans, although both children are sure that their mother actually, or eventually, voted for

Democrats. There was no local Democratic Party in Cincinnati in any case; there were only Republicans and Charterites. The Charter Party originated as a political reform movement in 1924, when a multipartisan committee was organized to campaign to amend the city charter.[14] In the late nineteenth and early twentieth centuries, a Republican political machine, led by George B. "Boss" Cox, had dominated Cincinnati politics. Boss Cox set up a powerful patronage system and essentially ran the city for his own profit. Embezzlement and extreme corruption resulted in a virtual breakdown of public services by 1923. The Charterites proposed changing to a city manager form of government, with a city council elected by proportional representation at large rather than by geographic units, so as to ensure representation of diverse groups.[15] Voters would rank candidates for a nine-member city council as their first and second choice, and so on; votes cast for a first choice would be transferred to the second choice if the first choice candidate did not win a seat, and down the list of preferences, so that the majority still ruled but minority voters were guaranteed representation.[16] In November 1924, the new city charter passed in a landslide.

Dawn's first directly political activity was to go door to door raising money on weekends for the Charterites when she was in junior high school, even though this may have opposed her parents' political leanings. There is a certain fitness to this. The Charter Party took on and deposed machine politics in Cincinnati, just as Dawn was later to challenge the powerful Daley machine in Chicago. Moreover, when Dawn was first elected to state office, Illinois also had a type of cumulative voting that enabled minority interests to obtain some representation. Independent Democrats who were Dawn's allies used the system to obtain seats in the Illinois House of Representatives in the late 1960s and 1970s.

By the time she was in high school, Dawn focused on a career in politics. She told everybody that she wanted to be president, or at least a U.S. senator. People laughed and thought she was nuts. Dawn also considered going into the diplomatic service, even though it was closed at that time to women. That did not strike her as an unalterable obstacle. Rules of exclusion did not deter her.

Chapter 2

Northwestern University

ONE OF DAWN'S BEST friends in high school was a young man named Clarke Stayman. Bob McGrath remembers Clarke Stayman as weird, sort of effeminate, and with a biting tongue, but Dawn could be sharp tongued as well.[1] Clarke shared Dawn's love of opera and had a marvelous sense of fun. So when Stayman decided to go to college at Northwestern University, although Dawn had never heard of it before, that was recommendation enough. Her family wanted her to go to school in Ohio, perhaps at Miami University, where her godmother and many of her mother's friends had gone, but Dawn was determined not to continue her education in her home state. Miami University was too close to home, and she had begun to find Cincinnati too conservative and confining. The only other place she seriously considered was Radcliffe, because it was the closest she could get to Harvard at a time when it did not admit women. Because she planned to spend most of her life in a field dominated by men, however, Dawn thought that it made more sense to attend a coeducational university. Northwestern also had a good program in political science. So she followed her friend Clarke Stayman to Evanston, Illinois, in 1944.[2]

When Dawn first arrived at Northwestern, she settled into Willard Hall, the relatively new women's residence named for Frances Willard, founder of a women's college that had merged with Northwestern in the late nineteenth century. Willard was a strong proponent of women's rights and a founder of the Women's Christian Temperance Union. The WCTU is remembered for its prohibitionist stance toward alcohol, but it was also a more broadly based movement for reform—for women's suffrage, prison reform, and the abolition of prostitution. The hall dedicated in 1938 in honor of Francis Willard was a large gray stone building with mullioned windows on an expansive residential quadrangle in Evanston. Dawn made friends quickly and soon pledged to the Chi Omega sorority, moving the following year into the sorority house—a low gray stone building on the same quadrangle and built in the same Collegiate Gothic style. Twenty-four of the eighty to ninety sorority sisters lived in the house, along with a housemother, eating three meals a day there—sit-down meals served by waiters.

A photo of Dawn with several sorority sisters shows a tall, stylish young woman with long dark hair, dressed in a suit with shoulder pads and a cinched waist; she looks more mature than her sorority sisters do. Dawn was in fact different from them in many ways. Although most of the members of Chi Omega were politically conservative, Dawn's liberal views were clear; and the others appear to have respected her. One friend from that time remembers her as warm, genuine, and funny.[3] Dawn was sociable and fit in easily, although the other women recognized that she was different from them. For one thing, Dawn was exceptionally bright; for another, she had ambitions the others did not have. Most coeds at Northwestern at that time expected to get married, even if they worked for a while in teaching or some other job "suitable" for a woman. By contrast, Dawn was oriented toward politics and a career from the start, her friend remembers, the only woman in her group who was career minded. Dawn told them she was going to be the first woman president of the United States.

Northwestern University in 1944, like other colleges and universities, was radically changed by the war. Undergraduate enrollment in the college of liberal arts was reduced to 1,768 from a prewar total of 2,706.[4] A place that had been known for its fun-and-games atmosphere became something quite different, as most social activities—dances and theater performances, for example—were eliminated or curtailed, and fraternity houses were turned over to the military, which trained on campus. When the war ended, the football games, dances, and parties that had gained Northwestern its reputation as a country-club school started up again, and returning veterans crowded the campus. Quonset huts were set up in front of the library to house them all. Yet although campus life revived with the cessation of hostilities in August 1945, the men who returned to school were more mature and sobered by what they had seen. Concern about national and international politics was high.

Dawn did not experience Northwestern as the country club it was reputed to be, in part because she was accepted into the first class of 104 students in an ambitious new curriculum that Northwestern had introduced in 1944. The new bachelor of arts program was an innovative and interdisciplinary course of study that covered all four years, with each year and each course building on those that preceded. Some of Northwestern's finest professors, such as Bergen Evans and Melville J. Herskovits, were instructors in the program. The intent of the new program was to resist specialization and give students a broad grounding in the disciplines regarded as necessary for a civilized person while requiring them to integrate their understanding through the set progression of required courses.[5]

In the first two years, students all took virtually the same courses. In the first year, they enrolled in Use of English, Introduction to Science and Mathematics, a foreign or classical language, and Bases of Social Life, which emphasized understanding cultures historically in light of the natural environment, psychological forces, customs, institutions, and the beliefs that produced them. In the second year, a higher-level unit of the same or similar area of study (e.g., literature, a particular physical or biological science or math, and the second year of a foreign language) succeeded each of the first-year courses, in addition to the course called Modern Society, which emphasized the economic, social, and political forces shaping contemporary society. Both Bases of Social Life, in the first year, and Modern Society, in the second, were team-taught by prominent faculty from a variety of departments—history, philosophy, economics, anthropology, and political science, for example—who would attend one another's lectures. Discussion section leaders were also drawn from different disciplines, thus exposing each student to different perspectives each quarter. In the third year, students were allowed to develop a field of special interest in one of their four course areas, but they were still required to take a course in arts or philosophy, another in social science or philosophy, and an elective from outside their field of special interest. Only in the final year were students allowed to work almost entirely in their field of special interest; they were also required to take a tutorial reading course in a correlative subject.

One of the faculty members who put together this innovative program was the celebrated American anthropologist Melville J. Herskovits, who had a deep influence on Dawn. Herskovits, a student of Franz Boas at Columbia, founded the Department of Anthropology at Northwestern in 1927 and the Program of African Studies in 1948.[6] He did extensive field-work in Africa at a time when the continent did not attract much academic attention in the United States, and he was responsible for building the most extensive library of Africana in North America at Northwestern.

Herskovits was particularly interested in exploring the cultural links between Africa and black people in the Americas; in his 1941 master-piece, *The Myth of the Negro Past*, he argued that West Africa and the New World formed a single cultural area as a result of the slave trade. He wrote about African history and culture from the perspective not of the colo-nizer but of the colonized, and about African American culture. In the process, Herskovits formed close links with African independence move-ment leaders, soon to become presidents of newly independent nations, and with luminaries such as W. E. B. DuBois, Ralph Bunche, and Zora Neale Hurston, who was his student at Northwestern.[7] He was politically active both on the national scene, supporting African independence and racial justice in the United States, and locally, campaigning against racial segregation of the hotels in Evanston, where Northwestern's campus is located.

Dawn remembers Herskovits as a man of extraordinary, indeed intim-idating, intelligence and energy, who "moved very quickly, somewhat like a terrier" and "gave off sparks."[8] He devoted immense amounts of energy to his students. According to Herskovits's daughter Jean, her father was also an early-days feminist, and he explained to her that he put as much energy into his female students as his male students because "you can't afford to overlook the talents of half of the human race."[9] Certainly one young woman responded to his efforts. At the time of the centenary cele-bration of Melville Herskovits's birth, Dawn proclaimed, "He opened up worlds for me, [especially] the social and cultural strength in the African community."[10]

Herskovits so impressed Dawn that she wanted to share his intel-lectual power and enthusiasm with friends outside the classroom. Soon after arriving on campus, she had become involved in the YWCA student chapter, an influential student organization at that time, and by her soph-omore year, she had been elected its vice president.[11] She organized a program for the YWCA at which a larger audience could hear her hero. The meeting was held at the John Evans Center, a large but gracious Victorian building in mock Tudor design, and everyone sat on the floor of the living room. Herskovits talked with great enthusiasm about a variety of African nations, emphasizing their sophisticated cultural and societal structures, at a time when most of his audience still probably thought of Africans as uncivilized, if they thought of them at all. His talk, Dawn remembers, was "breathtaking" and "absolutely mesmerizing." Herskovits made an enormous impression on the young Dawn Clark.

As a student, Dawn continued to pursue her interest in racial justice, inculcated early in life and developed through her exposure to Herskovits. An experience during the summer after her sophomore year helped her see the effects of American racism. That summer, Dawn participated in the Washington Student Citizenship Seminar, a program sponsored by the National Intercollegiate Christian Council for college students from all over the country. A group of about thirty students from different states and schools were taken to Washington, D.C., for a ten-week program, during which they worked in low-level government jobs and lived together, dormitory-style, in a big mansion in Georgetown. Dawn's job was at the Veterans Administration. Several times a week, the group had seminars with speakers who addressed the students about issues ranging from atomic energy to national housing problems to the issues facing legislators.

The students were a diverse group geographically and ethnically, both male and female, and included a number of African Americans. Washington was still a segregated city at that time, so the simple fact that they were all living together was remarkable. The group also went together to a different church each Sunday, and it is etched on Dawn's memory that at least one church told the group that they were not welcome.

Returning to Northwestern, Dawn and her fellow editors on the Northwestern student newspaper decided to launch a campaign against racial segregation on campus. Dawn had joined the staff of the *Daily Northwestern* as a freshman and, by her second year, was one of two campus editors. As she began to write editorials, she wrote one that was in hindsight a real blooper. In an editorial titled "Marshall Choice Diplomatic Blunder," Dawn opposed the appointment of General George Marshall as secretary of state in early 1947, on the grounds that he was a military man and lacked diplomatic skills at a time when such experience was important. When Marshall later distinguished himself as author of the Marshall Plan, the extravagantly effective plan for the reconstruction of postwar Europe, Dawn laughed at her earlier and obviously mistaken opinion.

As a junior, Dawn was a member of the *Daily Northwestern* editorial board, which began a campaign to integrate the university dormitories. She already had some experience lobbying the university's administration on similar matters, having gone with a group of students to a meeting with the dean of students to protest what the students alleged were admissions quotas applied to restrict the number of Jewish students. The administrators told the group, "We don't do that." This bald assertion appeared to be a misrepresentation, and the students in essence called the administration liars in response. Although the administration's comeback has been lost to history, Dawn recalls veiled threats directed at the protesting students. But this did not deter them from pursuing the cause of racial justice on campus.

Racial segregation at Northwestern was a problem of long standing. The administration considered it unfeasible to house black and white students together; thus black students were denied on-campus housing and forced to find whatever living arrangements they could in Evanston or Chicago. The housing situation was even worse for black women because black men could live at the segregated YMCA on Emerson Street; however, both would have had difficulty finding places to eat out. Although the Student Interracial Commission, formed in 1940, began to raise such issues, Northwestern's president Franklin Bliss Snyder affirmed the exclusionary policy because, he said, "the racial factor makes it impossible to divert rooms used by other students."[12] The only member of the administration to oppose the policy was Ruth McCarn, the dean of women, who urged better treatment of minorities on campus, especially with respect to housing. McCarn's advocacy brought her into conflict with the central administration; as a result, she was asked to resign in 1948.

On January 24, 1947, the editors of the *Daily Northwestern* announced, under the headline "Our Aim: To Correct Negro Housing Evils," that they were launching a campaign to address the housing situation, through investigation, education, and advocacy.[13] The following week they published multiple articles on the subject, culminating with a proposal that the *Daily* editorial staff survey black students about their attitude to an all-black dorm, which some had suggested.[14] The response came back from the black students group, the Quibblers, the following week: "We believe that there should not be a separate dormitory for Negroes."[15] A column next day pointed out that, although the university denied having any policy limiting admission of black students, the unavailability of housing accomplished the same goal.[16] By February 12, in the third week of the *Daily*'s campaign, the editors urged the Student Governing Board to take action by circulating student petitions.[17] The dean of students responded with a vigorous defense of the university's so-called selective housing policy, saying that parental objections to interracial housing left them with no choice: "if a sizeable group of Negroes had to be intermingled with white students the housing office would face an impossible task."[18] Ultimately, the men's Interhouse Council and the

Women's Student Government Association took a poll of student attitudes on the subject.[19] The results were discouraging. Of some nine hundred students surveyed, 72.8 percent said that they would refuse to live with a Negro roommate; 42 percent said they would not live in the same house or even share facilities with a Negro student. These results caused the Student Governing Board to declare, "Unrestricted housing is not feasible on this campus."[20] However, 76.4 percent of students did favor separate on-campus housing for Negro students, and 67 percent favored establishing an International House that would be open to students of all races, though only 34.7 percent said they would be willing to live there themselves. On the basis of these latter statistics, the Student Governing Board modified its position to say that, although completely unrestricted housing was not feasible, unrestricted housing in one house was. Given that almost five hundred students had said they would live in the same house with Negroes, and that there were only twenty Negroes who would be affected, the Student Governing Board declared itself in favor of an International House—rather an odd title for a house designed for African Americans.[21] Another *Daily* column commented that those who refused to live in a house open to all races could still live in dorms, "where they may continue without molestation their peculiar concepts of democracy and fair play."[22]

The university leaped at this solution, buying property for an international house for women during the summer of 1947.[23] The house opened the following September, and seven women students—five black, one white, and one Asian—applied to live there.[24] In short, the first big racial justice campaign in which Dawn was involved culminated in the establishment of what essentially became a segregated dorm for black women. Yet the university president continued to insist that there was not a "race problem" at Northwestern.[25]

Perhaps to deepen her understanding of the forces that underlay the situation at Northwestern and their seeming intractability, Dawn decided to read and to write a major paper on Gunnar Myrdal's *An American Dilemma* in the senior tutorial required by her B.A. program. Her group of four students was assigned to Bergen Evans, a well-known English professor, and met once a week to discuss the readings they had chosen. *An American Dilemma*, a 1,500-page tome, resulted from a five-year, Carnegie Foundation–funded research project to examine the history and characteristics of race relations in the United States. Myrdal—a Swedish economist who subsequently won the Nobel Prize—was chosen as the project's director-author on the theory that American biases on the subject would influence him less than they would an American author.[26] After describing at length the history and characteristics of race relations in the United States, Myrdal concluded that white Americans' prejudicial treatment of blacks was responsible for the disadvantaged state in which African Americans found themselves. The "dilemma," according to Myrdal, was created by the coexistence of liberal American ideals of equality, on the one hand, and the dire situation of black Americans, on the other.

Dawn took this lesson to heart. She wrote in her paper, "We must recognize in the first place that the political problem, that is the denial of political equality to Negroes, cannot be solved in and of itself. It is merely a part of a much greater problem, one that is imbedded in every phase of American culture."[27] But, she argued, this did not provide an excuse for doing nothing. Among the actions she advocated were the passage of federal anti–poll tax legislation, the use of federal grants-in-aid to improve equal educational opportunity, federal antilynching legislation, and federal leadership in the area of nondiscriminatory employment practices. What is particularly impressive about the paper is that Dawn, a senior in college, presented in it persuasive analyses of the unconstitutionality of white primaries and the constitutionality of anti–poll tax legislation— legal arguments beyond the ability of most students who have not been to law school. The paper clearly indicates that law school is the direction in which this young woman was headed and reflects her attraction to law as an instrument of social justice. It also demonstrates Dawn's continuing commitment to racial equality, the influence of Melville Herskovits, and a penchant for the use of government, especially government on the federal level, to bring about racial justice in America.

If race and inequality were the problems, and law the solution, Dawn had also clearly decided by that time that politics was the route to change, as her active extracurricular life illustrated. During her sophomore year, Dawn took an active part in the model United Nations held at Northwestern, an event intended to demonstrate to students the workings of the new international organization (the United Nations had been founded only the previous year) and to cause them to think concretely about the international problems of the day.[28] The final model UN session, held in the Tech building, attracted a good deal of attention at the school and in the community and media, because both Senator Claude Pepper of Florida and Ralph Bunche addressed the assembly. Senator Pepper's address was titled "Blueprint for World Peace," while Bunche, who was then in charge of the UN Trusteeship Council, spoke about "Colonies, Empires, and Trusteeships."[29] Bunche had done postdoctoral research at Northwestern under Herskovits; and in 1947, the year after the model UN, he became involved in the United Nations' negotiations in Palestine, for which he ultimately won the Nobel Peace Prize in 1950.

Dawn represented Egypt at the model UN on behalf of her sorority house.[30] Indeed, a picture of her in this role appeared in the *Chicago Daily News;* she was entirely veiled in a chadorlike garment made of a large white sheet wrapped around her body, with only her eyes peeping out. In February, the nations represented elected delegates to the Security Council and to four commissions; Egypt was elected both to the Security Council and to the "trusteeship and colonies commission."[31] The small nations, at the instigation of Egypt and Ethiopia, also formed a bloc to protect their interests from being swamped by those of the great powers, to strengthen the United Nations as a peacekeeping instrument, and to provide a body through which economic aid could be obtained without the great powers' political strings attached.[32] The delegations, the commissions, and the blocs held frequent meetings during March and April, and both the General Assembly and Security Council met, culminating in a final session during the week of April 22–26, 1946.[33] After "fiery debates," the model UN adopted resolutions in favor of the eventual formation of a federal world government; called for the lifting of trade barriers and the immediate independence of Syria, Lebanon, Indochina, Indonesia, and India, and passed recommendations calling for equal educational opportunity without regard to race or sex.[34]

Dawn participated actively in the model UN, where she got to know Newton Minow, with whom she would work politically in the future. Her role as a delegate of Egypt submerged her deeply in that country's problems; she was particularly interested in desalinization and future water resources, as well as the harnessing of nuclear energy for peacetime uses. She enjoyed the conference so much that she worked on planning similar conferences in her later years at Northwestern.

In the beginning of her junior year, Dawn made a foray into national student politics as well. From August 30 to September 7, 1947, the founding convention of the National Student Association took place in Madison, Wisconsin. The NSA grew out of the organizing efforts of students in colleges throughout the nation immediately after World War II; many members were veterans returning to university after service abroad. The association's goal was to establish a national organization to represent students' rights and needs and to press for an end to segregation in higher education. The meeting convened at the University of Wisconsin Memorial Union in the fall of 1947 drew some seven hundred delegates from more than 350 colleges and universities all over the United States.[35] Dawn attended as one of four delegates from Northwestern; Bill Branch, a prominent spokesperson for the African American students at Northwestern, was another.

The NSA convention voted to set up a permanent organization located in Madison; the members were the student bodies or student government organizations at the affiliated universities. Given that the delegates came from all over the country, including from colleges in the southern states, the most difficult resolution was that committing the organization to the elimination of discrimination in education. The delegates finally reached a compromise that committed the group to the goal but set forth a policy to take action on a local or regional level "with regard to the legal limitations involved," a phrase added to accommodate schools in southern states where segregation was still de jure.[36]

Following the convention, the student government organizations at all the potential member universities were required to decide whether to join, usually after some sort of campuswide referendum. Dawn and her comrades returned to Northwestern to submit the matter to the Student Governing Board there. An all-student vote on whether to affiliate was held the following March. Northwestern refused to join the new organization, though its rival on the South Side, the University of Chicago, did.[37] An editorial in the *Daily Northwestern* counseled a no vote, apparently because of suspicion that the group would be some kind of communist front ("until . . . we have more time to see how NSA shapes up, what schools join it, and how far the Communist influence infiltrates").[38] The NSA's commitment to racial equality may also have been too radical for the students and the administration in Evanston.

The extracurricular event of most direct relevance to Dawn's subsequent life was the 1948 mock political convention, which she chaired. A tradition at Northwestern since 1920, mock conventions were held at the school every presidential election year, with Greek houses and unaffiliated groups of students representing all fifty states and campaigning to nominate various national political figures for president of the United States. During the spring of her senior year, Dawn chaired the steering committee that organized and ran the convention that year.[39]

Primary nominations for the convention elicited some controversy, as did other aspects of planning. Groups supporting most of the major Republican candidates quickly formed, but the incumbent Democratic president, Harry Truman, was initially without support.[40] Rumors circulated that the steering committee added Truman's name even though he had not attracted enough votes to qualify as a nominee, a charge that Dawn vigorously denied.[41] The steering committee was committed to a bipartisan convention, however, and without a Democrat on the ballot, they could not invite any Democratic candidates to speak. Ultimately the following were nominated, perhaps, Dawn now admits, after some bending of the rules: Thomas E. Dewey, Douglas MacArthur, Wayne C. Morse, Harold E. Stassen, Harry S. Truman, Arthur Vandenberg, Henry A. Wallace, and Earl C. Warren. A number of houses (representing states) then broke off and formed a bloc that refused to back any candidate.[42] After creating headaches for the steering committee, the bloc soon disintegrated, and its members distributed their support among the candidates.[43]

Controversy also erupted over the choice of speakers at the convention. Dawn and other students very much wanted to have Henry Wallace, the Progressive Party candidate for president, speak at the convention. Wallace was running on a platform that emphasized ending segregation, extending full voting rights to blacks, and passing universal health insurance legislation. The university objected to inviting such a left-winger to campus. The organizers then asked the Progressive Party to send them a substitute for Wallace; Johannes Steel, a refugee from Nazi Germany who had become a news analyst and author, was sent instead.[44] The irony was that Steele, while not as well known, was far to the left of Wallace himself, and he gave what Dawn describes as a "pretty wild, left-wing speech."

The organizers were determined to have Harold Stassen speak at their convention. Stassen, a liberal Republican, was very popular on campus. The year 1948 marked the first of his nine attempts to gain the Republican nomination for president. Polls at the time showed that he would beat Truman if nominated (he lost the nomination to New York governor Thomas Dewey, and Truman won the election). Dawn and the steering committee tracked down Stassen's speaking schedule, and a group, including Dawn, followed Stassen to a not-very-fancy hotel in a small town in Wisconsin, where they managed to get in to see him. The group of students sat around Stassen's hotel room and told him why he should come to Northwestern, ultimately obtaining his agreement to address the mock convention.

Stassen was the star attraction. Indeed, the board came under attack when it refused to move Stassen's speech from Patten Gymnasium to an outside location in Deering Meadow to expand from the limited seating capacity in the gym. Dawn, as chair, responded to the criticism by saying that the board wished that all Northwestern students could hear Stassen speak but that it would be impossible to move the event because broadcasting facilities had already been set up in the gym.[45] With Senators Wayne Morse of Oregon and Samuel Jackson of Indiana, as well as senatorial candidate Paul Douglas, all addressing the mock convention, the event attracted a great deal of attention in the Chicago press, on national wire services, and on the radio.[46]

What Dawn remembers with particular pleasure was leading Harold Stassen down to the speaking platform. Stassen and Vandenberg led the field when the balloting began, but as the balloting went on, Stassen picked up votes. Because of curfew rules set by the administration, however, the mock nominating convention resulted in a tie between the two candidates at 1:45 A.M. in the middle of tabulating the sixth ballot.[47] The editors of the *Daily Northwestern* were convinced that Stassen would have won on the next ballot.[48] The mock convention was different from the real-world conventions and election that took place later that year in another significant way as well: Harry Truman received hardly any votes.

The *Daily Northwestern* described interviewing a "tired but happy" Miss Dawn Clark when the convention was over. "We were greatly surprised and flattered at the tremendous enthusiasm shown by the student body as a whole," she said. "It just swept us off our feet." She added, "All of us connected with the convention had a lot of fun. . . . And I feel we all learned a lot, too . . . something intangible perhaps, but something very valuable."[49] The lessons learned were not so intangible for Dawn, who went on to attend numerous Democratic National Conventions in the future, once cochairing the Illinois delegation.

It is ironic that the first real convention Dawn ever attended, soon after graduation, was the 1948 Republican National Convention; she had identified as a Democrat since she was a teenager. One of her political science professors at Northwestern recognized how passionate Dawn was about politics and arranged at the last minute for her to have a position as a page at the Republican National Convention held in June in Philadelphia; indeed, the convention's organizers added an extra page position for her after Professor Kenneth Colegrove interceded on her behalf and, as the letter appointing Dawn said, because she was a Chi Omega.[50] So the candidate Dawn actually saw nominated for president in 1948 was New York's Governor Dewey. The Republican governor of Illinois, Dwight Green, was the keynote speaker at the convention and invited Dawn to a preconvention dinner he was hosting. When she returned to Illinois, however, she volunteered for his opponent, Adlai E. Stevenson II, who was elected governor of Illinois in 1948 in a record landslide.

——— *Chapter 3* ———

The Law

DAWN GRADUATED FROM NORTHWESTERN in June 1948, having been elected to Phi Beta Kappa for her academic prowess. Her parents came to graduation, but after the ceremony was over, her father told her that she had thirty days to become self-supporting. She had never really assumed otherwise, nor had she planned to return to Cincinnati. She wanted to be away from her family and be herself in a way that distance made possible, and she wanted an active urban scene with a Democratic Party. Chicago fulfilled these requirements.

With the assistance of her political science mentor, Kenneth Colegrove, Dawn had scrambled during May to find a position related to politics. Colegrove wrote laudatory letters on her behalf to the Democratic National Committee and to the senators from Illinois and Utah, describing both Dawn's academic record and the administrative ability she had demonstrated by chairing the mock political convention at Northwestern.[1] He also wrote to the Stevenson-for-Governor Committee and suggested that she write to the campaign manager for Paul Douglas's senatorial campaign (his first of many).[2] None of the inquiries turned up anything of the sort Dawn was seeking, although one senator did write back asking whether she could type.

Colegrove also wrote to someone he knew at the League of Women Voters of Illinois.[3] The League of Women Voters was founded in 1920 as a nonpartisan organization that emerged from the struggle for women's suffrage. Its focus was not so much women's issues as the education of the electorate. In addition to voter education, the LWV studies issues and lobbies both political parties and legislatures for reform after the organization has reached a consensus position. The LWV's 1920 program, for example, included items relating to child welfare, education, women's employment, and public health, among other things, and its first legislative success was the passage of the act providing federal aid for maternal and child-care programs. In the 1930s, the group worked to enact Social Security, the Food and Drug Act, the Tennessee Valley Authority, and a merit system for government employees. The LWV has also been responsible over the years for candidate questionnaires and debates. In the years after World War II, just before Dawn sought employment, it was one of the preeminent American organizations leading the drive to establish the United Nations and for the United States to participate in it.[4]

The LWV of Illinois offered Dawn her first political job. She was hired as the sole paid staff person assigned to the LWV of Cook County, which had its office at 225 North Michigan Avenue in Chicago. She typed newsletters, handled correspondence, and did whatever other jobs were to be done.[5] At that time, the local LWV was involved in a variety of projects having to do with governmental reform, including the drive for a new constitution for Illinois, mental health reforms, and some types of protective legislation. While working at the LWV, the importance of state and local government became clear to Dawn for the first time. Previously focused, as most young people were, on the federal government, she realized that what happened in the city of Chicago and the state of Illinois could have a greater influence on the day-to-day lives of many people.

For her services at the LWV, Dawn received a minimal salary. She survived on it by sharing an apartment at 1001 North Dearborn Street with three or four other young women, at least one of whom she knew from college; they split the expenses among them. Although the job at LWV did not pay much, Dawn was glad to get the job and wrote to a friend, "I considered myself most fortunate. I've always respected the League and could not have found a better place to begin, for their interests are, like mine, in better government and better citizens."[6]

Through her position at the LWV, Dawn began to meet some of the people involved in reform politics in Illinois. She spent her spare time in her first months at the new job working for Democrats running in the November 1948 election, doing both low-level office work and research as a volunteer at Adlai Stevenson's headquarters. This service merited a letter of thanks after the election from the Women's Division of the Stevenson-for-Governor Committee, for Dawn's "substantial contribution of time and effort to Mr. Stevenson's great victory which resulted in the largest total vote ever given a state candidate for any office in the history of Illinois."[7] The letter that pleased her most, however, was one directly from Stevenson himself, in which he recounted, "The Women's Division has told me of the several ways in which you have contributed to the success of my campaign—of your faithful office work at our headquarters, and your corralling helpful information and statistics for our use," and he expressed his gratitude in effusive terms.[8] On the outside of the envelope, which she put away with her many keepsakes, Dawn wrote "Oh Boy!!" in her neat handwriting.

Dawn also appears to have adopted early on the politicians' habit of writing congratulatory letters to one another. After Paul Douglas won his first race for senator from Illinois, she wrote to him on November 6, 1948:

> As a political scientist of sorts and a budding politician of ideals—which Heaven help me, they won't take away from me—I am always overjoyed when a man of your high standards will make the sacrifices necessary to enter public life. It happens all too seldom. That it did happen in this state, and for a number of high offices, is a tribute to the Democratic party and an effective lesson to its opposition that the American voters are maturing politically.[9]

She reminded Douglas that she had chaired Northwestern University's mock political convention earlier that year and had introduced him as keynote speaker. Douglas wrote back to thank her and said that he remembered her well.[10]

Dawn's interest in national and international politics remained keen, and she continued to try to know and understand as much as she could. In the late summer and fall of 1948, Alger Hiss was accused before the House Un-American Activities Committee of being a member of the Communist Party and of having given State Department documents to a Soviet agent in 1938. Charged with perjury because the statute of limitations for espionage had run out, Hiss was convicted at his second trial (the first having resulted in a hung jury) and served almost four years in prison. He contended that he was innocent until his death in 1996.

In December 1948, Dawn wrote to Jo and Herbert Abraham, the Quaker couple who had been in charge of the Washington program for undergraduates she had participated in during the summer of 1946. The Abrahams were friends of Alger Hiss and had invited him to speak to the group that summer, where he had made a deep impression on young Dawn. She wrote to express her shock at the accusations leveled at Hiss, a protégé of one Supreme Court justice (Felix Frankfurter) and clerk to another (Oliver Wendell Holmes) who had been such an articulate spokesperson for international cooperation and peace. Dawn asked whether the Abrahams believed the charges to be true and, if so, what would make a man like that turn to communism and betray his country.[11] Jo Abraham wrote back immediately, though she was recovering from surgery in hospital, to say:

> We firmly believe Alger is innocent, as do most people who knew him. There is something about him—his honesty, integrity, and devotion to duty which just don't square with the charges. I have no doubt that Alger was interested, in the 30's, in exploring communist philosophy (what thinking person was not?) and I've no doubt he talked to many communists, befriended some, may have attended meetings, but I do not believe that he ever betrayed a trust.[12]

Dawn also described her thinking about the future to the Abrahams, writing of her continuing dedication to a career in politics. "My League work is most enjoyable," she wrote in late 1948, "but not my permanent future." She had decided to enter law school and make that her path of entry into politics. Most politicians, legislators, and government personnel seemed to be lawyers, so law school seemed to be a plus, if not a sine qua non, for the future she wanted. Dawn wrote to Jo Abraham:

> My life is still dedicated to governmental service and still—until the lessons become too bitter—through the medium of politics. I am proud of my Democratic party in Illinois, and in many other states. But both parties need young and trained leadership, young people with some serious and sensible ideals who will begin early enough to have time to develop into statesmanlike stature. Indifference has always been the greatest internal enemy of democracy. That will probably still be my battlecry when I die a poverty-stricken, disillusioned old party hack. But they will have to sit on me hard to make me disavow it.[13]

This was indeed a determined young twenty-one-year-old woman.

Although Dawn was determined to go to law school, the question remained as to how to make that happen, given her penurious state. In the summer of 1948, she was walking on the beach in Evanston with a friend and met a young man, Jim Clement. Clement had gone to Northwestern's law school; as soon as he heard that Dawn was thinking about law school, he encouraged her to do the same, arranging for her to meet a woman from his class to talk about it. Dawn did not need encouragement; she just needed to figure out how to do it.

She applied for admission to Northwestern University School of Law in 1949. It was the only school to which she applied. Dawn thought Harvard might be a good place to study, given her father's connection with it; but Harvard Law School did not admit women until the following year. Northwestern Law School was highly regarded at the time. Although there were no published rankings back then, as there are today, it was generally considered among the top five schools in the country and was clearly ahead of the University of Chicago Law School. The school had the added advantage that Dawn knew people at Northwestern's under-graduate college who might have connections that would enable her to get financial assistance. Scholarships were rare in those days, and Dawn wanted to take her best shot at getting one.

In March 1949, Harold Havighurst, the dean of Northwestern Law School, notified Dawn that she had been admitted and would receive a full tuition scholarship. Havighurst suggested that Dawn look into employ-ment opportunities at the dining hall in Abbott Hall (a student residence) to support herself, saying, "Several of our best students have worked in the dining room without any bad effects on their work in the school."[14] There were also opportunities to work in the library at the rate of $0.50 per hour, he said. Dawn responded, thanking him for the scholarship and his suggestions and asking to speak with him further about possible ways to finance her education.[15] Northwestern continued its support during Dawn's years in law school, with a $520 scholarship in 1950–51, an allo-cation of $35 from a grantor to purchase books for "needy students," and a $750 scholarship in 1951–52. After exhausting a small fund left to her by her Aunt Coy, which allowed her not to work during her first semester, Dawn paid for her living expenses with money from a variety of unusual odd jobs.

Dawn entered Northwestern Law School during its "age of the giants." The faculty included Willard Wirtz, who later became secretary of labor under Presidents Kennedy and Johnson; Francis Allen, later dean of the University of Michigan Law School; Walter Schaefer, who became a member of the Illinois Supreme Court; along with other scholars of repute, such as Nathaniel Nathanson, James Rahl, Philip Kurland, Willard

Pedrick, and others. The faculty was quite small and extremely close knit. Faculty members lived near one another, drove to work together, had lunch together on a daily basis, and socialized outside of work. Unlike today, however, their relationships with students were, with few exceptions, quite distant and formal.

Dawn remembers each of those faculty members with fondness and respect. Rahl, she remembers, slowly and methodically brought his students to think things through; he was a strong believer in antitrust laws and in spreading risk, and he was skeptical of traditional monopolistic price-fixing laws. Schaefer was more of a formalist, serious and methodical. Kurland, who arrived in Dawn's second or third year, was very lively, a bachelor who invited students to his apartment and enjoyed living well. He was also a keen baseball fan, which endeared him to Dawn, and he would sometimes stop class early on a sunny afternoon to go to Wrigley Field, the major league ballpark on Chicago's North Side, home of the Chicago Cubs. Pedrick, who taught taxation, was "a good old South Texas country guy, with an accent, a twang, and a great sense of humor."[16] The standard joke about Nathanson was that only two people in the class understood what he was talking about. One of them was Nathanson himself; the other was Dawn. He was the absentminded professor who lived in a world of abstraction, but he was a lovely human being in Dawn's opinion.

The law school building, a gray Gothic affair, was located at Chicago Avenue and Lake Shore Drive, overlooking Lake Michigan. It was housed at that time in one four-story building with large, formal classrooms, one of which was modeled after the British House of Commons. Students, who were typically instructed in large groups—up to 150 students—sat on rather uncomfortable wooden benches with attached desks, and often had to share them with another student in the larger classes. If the professors, all of whom were men, had had women's voices, they would have had trouble being heard in some of these cavernous spaces. This was not a problem, for all of the faculty were men. Faculty offices were distributed throughout the halls, which were decorated with portraits of old English (and some American) jurists and courthouses, most of which the peripatetic former dean John Henry Wigmore had selected on his travels, along with reproductions of historical documents and memorabilia of Abraham Lincoln, Illinois' favorite-son lawyer. The library featured the same oak paneling found throughout the school, busts of the ancients, and long tables at which students could sit facing one another to study. On the grassy plot of land toward the lake was a separate building, Thorne Hall, used for large gatherings and commencements.

The curriculum at the time Dawn attended Northwestern Law School left little choice for students. Most courses were required—all of them during the first year, when everyone took the usual common law courses in contracts, torts, property, criminal law, civil procedure, and constitutional law, along with legal writing. Everyone took most of the other fundamental courses (evidence, corporations, administrative law, tax law, labor law, antitrust law) during the second year, even though the courses were not required. Compared to a place like Harvard Law School, Northwestern was relatively small, and students in the same entering class got to know one another quite well. There were few extracurricular activities apart from the student-edited law journal. There was nowhere to eat, and just one bathroom accommodated women students.

Most of the law students at Northwestern, like the faculty, were male. There were about six women students enrolled over the three years Dawn was there. Three of them entered with her class in September 1949, but she was the only one who graduated in June 1952. Many of her fellow students were returned veterans, whose studies the government financed under the GI Bill, and were in a hurry to reconstitute their lives and careers. Courses were therefore held all year long, and the other two women students followed that accelerated program. Dawn, however, needed her summers to make money.

Dawn was not only an exceptional student but also popular, forming close friendships that lasted through the decades after graduation. She made quite an impression on her male colleagues. The first thing they all noticed about her was her unusual voice. Harold Shapiro, who became a lifelong friend, remembered the first time he noticed her: "She was in the U part and I was over at the side [of Lincoln Hall, which is shaped like an elongated U]. Havighurst called 'Clark,' and I heard this baritone voice. It was female and I was sitting on the top row and I said 'What the hell was that?'"[17] Jack Coons remembers her as having what appeared to be a fake English accent—which was "an object of curiosity in someone from Cincinnati."[18] Everyone speculated about whether it was an affectation.

Perhaps the most nuanced description of Dawn at that time came from Coons, who was in the class behind her. He had come to Northwestern from a Catholic, working-class background in the upper Midwest and from a nonelite, nonresidential college. To him, all the other students were objects of some wonder because they were so different from people he had known before. Looking back in 2006, he recalled:

> She was positively, by which I mean in a healthy way, she was odd. She was different. She was not somebody that you would put in the middle of the bell-shaped curve. She was at some point toward the end of some spectrum, but I wasn't sure what it was at first. She had an odd voice, not odd, but odd for her, odd for a young woman; she didn't have a young woman's voice. It was mannish, deep. In addition, it had a certain quality that had something special about it. It was a certain form of diction and a certain pitch that was to me quite unique.[19]

Dawn denies that she ever spoke with a phony British accent, opining that students jumped to that conclusion simply because she enunciates carefully, never elides words, and has no Midwestern drawl. Her deep voice and distinct manner of speech still strike people.

Dawn also impressed the other students in her class because she was so smart. She spoke up in class, was always well prepared, and had good answers in the play of Socratic dialogue that dominated legal pedagogy at that time. Indeed, when Dean Havighurst, who taught contracts, had a distinguished English visitor attend his class, he called on Dawn because he knew she would do a good job. By the end of a semester or two, all her classmates knew that she was at the top of the class. She was the first woman to win the Scholar's Cup award for having the highest standing in the first-year class.[20]

So why didn't Dawn's classmates resent her as an oddball, a teacher's pet, or a "gunner" for top grades? The answer appears to be that she was always good natured, outgoing, approachable, and friendly to everyone. She was clearly brilliant but also attractive, with a great sense of humor. These qualities went a long way to assuage any resentment on the part of her classmates because she outdid them or because she was a woman. They remember her instead as "one of the boys." One former classmate, now-judge Jim Richards, commented, "She had a lot of interests guys had, would watch football or hockey games, and basketball."[21] Her male classmates seem to have recognized that she was out of the ordinary as well. Coons confesses that he was a little bit afraid of her, in part because of her intensity:

She looked very focused and not in the kind of unhealthy way of some people who are obsessed. She was listening intently to what was going on around her whatever it was. She was very intent. And as a consequence one was a little bit more careful than average at first in what you said to her because you knew she would listen. It really mattered what you said.[22]

In short, Dawn's fellow students recognized her uniqueness and valued it, even though another woman student might not have had an easy time being accepted during that period.

Women law students were a rare breed in the early 1950s. They did not enter legal education in large numbers until the Civil Rights Act of 1964 and ensuing lawsuits in the 1970s forced schools to accept them. Substantial prejudice against women in the legal academy, from both professors and fellow students, greeted female law students.[23] Yet Dawn denies that she ever felt prejudice as a law student. If it existed, she says, laughing, "I was too dumb to figure it out." She confesses that she was "a pretty obnoxious student," always speaking out in class and not being intimidated by anyone, but she thinks everyone just got used to it. Willard Wirtz, one of her professors, remembers her in this way: "Characteristically a woman coming to law school at that time would take a pretty passive role. Not Dawn. She was never passive; she was always outspoken. She would initiate a point of view, which was not characteristic of women in law school at that time."[24] Although women law students were rare, Wirtz described them as having been treated with "tolerance and grudging acceptance" at Northwestern, not with actively negative behavior. Of course, most women law students were not like Dawn.

Did Dawn perhaps refuse to see any resentment toward her? It is clear that she had very close friendships with the brightest men in her class. Perhaps because they were so bright, they loved her for her intelligence. Many of them were older and had seen combat in World War II, a maturing experience. Whatever the reason, they appear to have accepted her as one of them, and she related to these men rather than to the two women in her class. This might have created some problems for her fellow students' wives and girlfriends, who were excluded from the intense life their husbands and boyfriends shared with Dawn, a pretty woman. Problems of jealousy or sexual tension were eased, Jack Coons's wife, Marilyn, remembers, because many of her classmates were newlyweds and Dawn was open and friendly with their wives.[25] Perhaps more important, Dawn may have become less threatening when she developed a close relationship with one of the male students in her class, someone everyone described as the best-looking man in class and one of the smartest.

If the men in her class all accepted her, there is some indication that some of those in the class before her might not have. Dawn's outstanding first-year grades qualified her for law review, the student-edited journal that provides a hierarchy among law students. After election to the review, students were assigned to write comments on various topics before they could become editors. The previous year's editors made the assignments and edited the other students' work. Dawn was given a topic that she rapidly gleaned from her research was not worth a comment, and she brought this to the attention of the editors who had assigned it to her. They ignored her complaints and repeatedly told her to keep working and to try to make something of it, until she finally outright said that she could not. By the time the student editors agreed, not very nicely, that the topic should be ditched, Dawn had put in a great deal of time that was wasted and had to start over again on a new topic. This delayed her ascent in the law review hierarchy—to the board of editors—by at least a semester. Even Dawn wonders whether prejudice against her as a woman played any role in such treatment.[26]

Although Dawn spent a great deal of her time on law school activities and studies, after exhausting her limited funds, she also had to spend a good deal of time supporting herself. For her first summer while in school, she found a truly unique job as an inspector of restaurants and restrooms throughout the nation for the Greyhound bus company. At that time, Greyhound owned a series of post houses, or rest stops. One of the college friends with whom Dawn had been sharing an apartment had a brother-in-law who was president of the post house operation and needed someone to visit and inspect them. Dawn leapt at the job, in part because it would give her, in addition to pay, both lodging and board for the entire summer. From June 12 to August 29, 1950, she gave up her apartment and slept either on the bus or in a motel en route and ate Greyhound food.[27]

It was physically difficult to sit on a bus most of the day, and the overnight accommodations were sometimes not very comfortable. The summer was hot and air-conditioning not yet available. Dawn remembers her stay in Flat River, Missouri, in particular, because it was one of the few times in her life she ever had food poisoning. Nonetheless, Dawn liked the job because it gave her a chance to see a substantial part of the United States. She traveled ten thousand to twelve thousand miles in three months, from New England to the Florida Keys, through the South, and into the Dakotas, Washington, and Oregon, inspecting some 130 post houses along the way. She would chat with the passengers; observe the drivers; and then go into the post house to see how the customers were treated in the restaurant, to inspect both the restroom and the kitchen, and to talk with the resident manager. At the end of the summer, she wrote up a detailed report for the corporate managers, who had not sent an inspector out on the road for a few years.[28]

That summer—the summer of 1950—added to Dawn's experience of America and its people. She saw the immense diversity of the nation and the diversity of the people who rode the bus or worked at Greyhound. At one point, in South Carolina, she had to find someone to "translate" for her because she could not understand the thick regional accent. (The locals probably had a hard time understanding her "English" accent as well.) But she enjoyed hearing the different dialects and perspectives and listening to the post house workers, who were open with her about what they needed to do their jobs well. The summer was undoubtedly good training for Dawn's later travels as a political candidate.

To keep her expenses low, Dawn moved from rooming house to rooming house while in law school. She needed quiet to study, so continuing to share quarters with four girls would not do. She lived alone for a while in a room in a former mansion on Lake Shore Drive. During her last year in law school, she stayed in a rooming house on Dearborn Street, a grim place with no private bath and only a tub in the shared bathroom. Her male classmates worried about her living alone and walking back to her apartment alone late at night, so they often insisted on walking her home.

Dawn ate on a shoestring as well. She would stop to buy a doughnut as she walked to school in the morning, but she ate the rest of her meals for free at Passavant Hospital (a pavilion that then formed part of Northwestern Hospital). She and a number of other students worked at Passavant delivering meals to patients in return for their own meals; that is, instead of being paid, they received meal credits. Judge Richards recalls that if you worked for one hour, you would get dinner; for forty-five minutes, lunch; and for thirty minutes, breakfast.[29] Dawn generally worked weekdays from 4 to 7 P.M. and alternate weekends, distributing trays to rooms and then going to collect them after eating her own meal.

Dawn worked a number of other jobs at the hospital during law school as well. One semester she worked as a waitress in the dining room for

interns and residents. She found the job interesting because she could hear
Edward R. Murrow's news broadcasts on the radio as she worked, and they
showed movies of surgical operations during dinner. "I remember seeing
a hysterectomy during dinner. I've always had a very strong stomach, so
it didn't bother me," she says.[30] One year, Dawn also worked the hospital
switchboard from about 5 P.M. to midnight on Saturdays and Sundays.
When she was first on the job, it reminded her of her first week as an inexperienced worker on the assembly line at the wartime plant in Cincinnati:
she was all thumbs and kept mixing up calls.

The pinnacle of success in law school is to become editor in chief of the
law review. The post went to Dawn's best friend, Harold Shapiro ("Hal," as
he was called), though Dawn was first in the class. Jack Coons thinks that
today the editor would have been Dawn, even though Shapiro had many
wonderful qualities that endeared him to one and all. Shapiro's fun-loving
nature was particularly well displayed, for example, in the student skit he
wrote, produced, directed, and choreographed during their final year of
law school. It was called *Die Shystersingers,* "a series of operatic put-ons and
put-downs." Dawn remembers that the arias, all of which Shapiro wrote,
were hilarious. Because she cannot sing, her role was to dance the cancan,
in red petticoats, to music by Jacques Offenbach, kicking her legs, bending
over backward, and throwing up her skirt. Hal and Dawn remained close
friends until he died in December 2005. He supported Dawn in multiple
ways throughout their friendship—from finding legal work for her during
law school to providing financial support for her campaigns for political
office later in life.

For example, after Shapiro became editor in chief of the law review
in the spring of their second year, he was offered a plum job as a summer
associate at Covington & Burling, a large and politically connected law
firm in Washington, D.C. Although it has now become standard for law
firms to offer summer positions to second-year law students as a way to
recruit them, this practice was just beginning when Dawn and Hal were
in law school. Shapiro, who was married, had a job with a law firm in town
and recommended to Covington that they hire Dawn in his stead. The
firm went along with his suggestion, and so Dawn was the first woman
summer associate at the firm, and possibly the first in the whole country.
Thus Dawn set out for her first well-paid job, one that made use of her
developing legal skills.

Jack Coons remembers driving from Chicago to Washington with
Dawn that summer in another friend's car. The two men came in a small

coupe to pick up Dawn at her apartment early one morning in June 1951. She came out of the apartment building in several trips, carrying bag after bag of clothing, adding them to those the men had already stashed in the backseat, until it was entirely full. As a result, the three had to sit jammed into the front seat together for the three-day trip. It was hot, and much of the thousand-mile journey, marked by traffic jams and flat tires, was on two-lane roads. Coons remembers the trip as great fun, despite the discomforts. The three friends sang and joked and talked nonstop "about civil rights and religion, Democrats and Republicans, the faculty. We would incessantly rate the faculty."[31] Along the route they stopped for the night, saw a movie at an outdoor theater in Pennsylvania, and drank a lot of Coca-Cola and an occasional beer. Coons's lasting impression of Dawn from this trip, apart from how much fun she was, was that she was also very good at adjusting to other people's needs—and it took a lot of adjusting to make that trip together in a small car.

Dawn enjoyed her summer experience at Covington & Burling. She lived in a large townhouse off Connecticut Avenue with another woman who was working at the firm, although not as a lawyer. They lived in the home of the woman's uncle, a senior partner who spent summers in Virginia and let them live there for free. Often Dawn had the house to herself, sharing it only with the bats who flew in the unscreened windows. Her work at the law firm, like that of any summer associate, consisted of researching and writing memos related to cases that the firm's lawyers were working on. Fitting right in with her background representing Egypt in the model United Nations as an undergraduate and her focus then on water resources, she was assigned to an international law project concerning water rights in the Jordan River. She also worked for two of the main partners who were known to be difficult, but she got along well with both of them. Dawn's other projects involved antitrust law and food and drug law for one partner, and a project for the National Association of Securities Dealers for another. Apparently her work was of high quality, for the firm made her an offer of permanent employment the following year, at a time when major law firms employed virtually no women lawyers.[32]

Dawn returned to Northwestern for her final year, to her studies and heavy extracurricular work schedule. (When asked by a student interviewing him later in life what extracurricular activities students in his class participated in, Hal Shapiro curtly said, "Work.")[33] The exhausting schedule took its toll, for Dawn, normally very hardy, came down with mononucleosis during the spring of her final year and was hospitalized at

Northwestern. She talked hospital staff into placing her in a private room, allegedly because of contagion, but really so that she could continue to study. Luckily the week coincided with spring break, because she found it hard to function at all. Another friend from law school, Jim Otis, remembered visiting Dawn in the hospital, with a group of five of her male classmates. Dawn was in bed, and they all began teasing her about having "the kissing disease" (the common explanation for how one got mononucleosis). Dawn was a good sport about their jokes.

After a week in the hospital, Dawn was released, but she had a hard time coping with the extreme exhaustion of mono, which typically lasts for three or four weeks. Even after the week of bed rest, she was so weak that she could not manage to walk back and forth from her rooming house to school. Friends helped by giving her rides for a time. Having been in the hospital paid a bonus to cash-starved Dawn, though. The combination of student health insurance and her parents' Blue Cross coverage resulted in her receiving a refund of $85 for her hospital stay. She lived on it for the rest of the semester and took her friends out to dinner to boot.[34]

Friends were a plentiful commodity for Dawn. One of the most remarkable things about her experience of law school was the extremely tight network of friends that she formed there, a network that continued long after graduation. Hal Shapiro organized weekly luncheons at the Chicago Bar Association for a group of the graduates of the class of 1952, and the table was reserved for decades. After that, the informal reunions transmuted into a New Year's Eve party held at lunchtime on December 31, with Shapiro as its host up through 2004, fifty-two years after they had graduated. Dawn and Hal Shapiro's friendship was important to both of them, as was their connection with Northwestern Law School, where both of them taught on a part-time basis in later years. In 2005, the two collaborated for the *Northwestern University Law Review* on an article that traced the history of the review for a hundredth-anniversary commemorative issue.[35]

Chapter 4

Adlai Stevenson, 1952

Dawn graduated from Northwestern Law School in June 1952, first in her class and armed with a job offer from a premier Washington law firm, Covington & Burling. In December of her third year of law school, the firm had written Dawn to ask whether she was interested in working there permanently after graduation, and she had replied that she was.[1] Covington immediately responded by making her a job offer, as an associate (new lawyers work in law firms as associates for a number of years before being considered for partnership status), at a salary of $4,000 a year. Covington & Burling had wanted her to start work the day after Labor Day or before.[2]

But this was 1952, another election year. Although Dawn was planning to take the Illinois Bar Exam that summer, she also wanted to work with Adlai Stevenson's campaign for reelection as governor of Illinois. She didn't respond to the job offer from Covington & Burling for some time. On March 1, 1952, she finally wrote to explain her long silence:

> I think it best that I let you know what my plans are to get your reaction to them. . . . The heart of it is a desire of long standing to work full-time in Governor Stevenson's campaign for re-election. It would be a labor of love—he personified what I think a public servant should be. . . . It would mean that I could not come to Washington until about November 15, which is later than you had expected. It is, however, something I would like very much to do, if it is not too inconvenient for the firm.[3]

Dawn explained, as well, her plan to take the Illinois Bar Exam, which would also qualify her for admission later in the District of Columbia. The firm wrote back, agreeing to her proposal and saying, "Inasmuch as

41

most of us here, whether Democrat or Republican, are admirers of Adlai Stevenson, we are willing to postpone your arrival until the middle of November."[4]

To understand Dawn's later life in politics, it is important to understand the tremendous influence that Adlai Stevenson had on her and an entire generation of young people who were attracted by him, either as governor of Illinois or as presidential candidate. Many of these individuals—such as Carl McGowan, Willard Wirtz, Arthur Schlesinger Jr., Bill Blair, Newton Minow, and Dawn, to name just a few—went on to play substantial roles in the political life of the United States.

Adlai Ewing Stevenson II, born in 1900, came from an Illinois family with an impressive history of public service. His grandfather, Adlai Ewing I, had come to the state as a teenager with his parents in 1852 and settled in Bloomington, Illinois. He subsequently served two terms in the U.S. Congress and as vice president under Grover Cleveland.[5] Stevenson's maternal ancestors were just as impressive, including Jesse Fell, an associate of Abraham Lincoln who founded many of the towns in central Illinois, as well as the first newspaper in Bloomington. When that newspaper failed, he bought the *Bloomington Pantagraph* with his son-in-law.[6] Fell was also instrumental in getting the state normal school (or teachers' college) established in a part of Bloomington that later was renamed Normal; that college is now Illinois State University.[7]

Stevenson grew up in Bloomington, where his father managed numerous farms and was active in public affairs, and his family lived well.[8] After school in Bloomington, Stevenson attended the Choate School, Princeton University, and Harvard Law School for two years, then returned to Bloomington to help run the *Pantagraph* for more than a year.[9] He then graduated from Northwestern University Law School and went into practice in Chicago. By the time he ran for governor of Illinois in 1948, Stevenson had served in several New Deal agencies in Washington and, during World War II, as assistant to the secretary of the navy, for whom he wrote speeches, among other duties. From 1945 to 1947, he was a special assistant to the secretary of state and played an instrumental role in the founding of the United Nations.[10]

In 1948 Stevenson ran for governor of Illinois. Dwight Green, the Republican incumbent, had come into office in 1940 as a reformer, but his administration had been marked by a series of scandals and the corruption that was endemic to Illinois politics.[11] Undertaking the campaign against

Governor Green, Stevenson took to the road to meet the people of the state and explain to them his plans for change.

The first time Stevenson produced a campaign speech, his supporters realized that they were hearing something new and special. Stevenson's speeches were extraordinary. Although he typically asked staff members for a draft to start from, he was a gifted writer and speaker, with a background as a journalist. Even if he started from a draft, as he did during his subsequent presidential campaigns, Stevenson labored over it until it was something uniquely his own. The speeches were so eloquent, and spoke to people's longing for change so directly, that those from 1952 were published as a best-selling book. He was also elected governor by a record margin.

When elected governor, Stevenson began by recruiting a group of outstanding young men to come to Springfield. Walter Schaefer accompanied him from Northwestern Law School, to be succeeded by Carl McGowan the following year. Stevenson convinced Walter Fisher, a prominent Chicago lawyer, to take over the scandal-ridden Illinois Commerce Commission and Willard Wirtz to head the corrupt Liquor Control Commission. William McCormick Blair Jr. became Stevenson's appointments secretary. By the end of his four-year term, Stevenson had also succeeded in recruiting Abner Mikva and Newton Minow, young lawyers straight out of clerkships with the U.S. Supreme Court, to work for him.[12] All those involved in this period remembered it as one of hard work but also great fun.

Stevenson began by taking on many of the areas most plagued by crime and corruption. He transformed the state police from a major source of political patronage into an institution of the civil service, convinced the retired head of purchasing for Sears, Roebuck to become the purchasing agent for the state, and talked nationally recognized economists and businesspeople into taking on other high-level state jobs.[13] Together with those he had recruited, Stevenson accomplished a great deal over the four years he was governor. In addition to restoring integrity to state government, he rebuilt state roads, substantially increased funding to education, overhauled welfare services, put the state on a sound financial basis, desegregated the Illinois National Guard, and vetoed a state loyalty oath in the midst of the McCarthy era.[14] Governor Stevenson also had some major failures, primarily because he rigidly opposed trading favors for the votes of legislators. As a result, one of his major commitments, to convene a constitutional convention to rewrite the antiquated Illinois Constitution, did not come to fruition, and he failed to establish a fair employment practices commission. Neither of these reforms, about which Stevenson felt very strongly, occurred until many years after he had left office.[15] Yet in the opinion of Mikva (later federal judge and counsel to President Bill Clinton), "To this day you can't turn anywhere in Illinois without seeing his mark. . . . He was ahead of his time. . . . It's hard to think that he was only Governor for four years. He had a profound influence."[16]

One of Stevenson's most important legacies for Illinois was the network of young people he either brought into or inspired to enter public life. Although Dawn had already decided that public life was to be her future, she heeded his call to service in Illinois. In the spring of 1952, she had lined up a summer job with the campaign to reelect Stevenson as governor. Because she needed to take the "cram" course for the bar exam, however, she was unable to begin work full-time until after the exam was over at the end of July. By that time, her job had been redefined.

After President Truman decided not to run for reelection in 1952, he began to try to recruit Stevenson as the Democratic candidate. Stevenson was reluctant to run, for a number of reasons, including his devotion to his job in Illinois, which he regarded as only half finished, and the fact that his sons were young. He was also genuinely committed to the two-party system and thought that it was time for a change after two decades of Democratic control.[17] He also thought, at least initially, that Dwight D. Eisenhower, former commander of the troops in Europe during World War II, whom the Republicans nominated in June, would not be a bad president.

Throughout the period that Dawn was completing her last semester of law school and studying for the bar exam, rumors about Stevenson's possible future distracted her. The matter was determined only at the Democratic National Convention, which took place in Chicago from July 21 to 24, 1952, the week before the bar exam. "Draft Stevenson" forces had been organizing for months without the candidate's official approval, and the crowd went wild during Stevenson's fourteen-minute welcome speech. Some think that the nomination was a foregone conclusion after that exceptional speech.[18] Stevenson was nominated as the Democratic Party's candidate for president on the third ballot, and the gubernatorial campaign for which Dawn had signed up was transformed into a presidential campaign. Stevenson's acceptance speech, one of his finest, set the campaign's theme. In it he proposed:

Let's talk sense to the American people. Let's tell them the truth, that there are no gains without pains, that we are now on the eve of great decisions, not easy decisions, like resistance when you're attacked, but a long, patient, costly struggle which alone can assure triumph over the great enemies of man—war, poverty and tyranny—and the assaults upon human dignity which are the most grievous consequences of each. . . .

Better we lose the election than mislead the people; and better we lose than misgovern the people. Help me to do the job in this autumn of conflict and of campaign; help me to do the job in these years of darkness, doubt and of crisis which stretch beyond the horizon of tonight's happy vision, and we will justify our glorious past with the loyalty of silent millions who look to us for compassion, for understanding and for honest purpose. Thus we will serve our great tradition greatly.[19]

Porter McKeever, who worked for Stevenson in this campaign and later wrote his definitive biography, sums up what Stevenson meant to the young people who responded to his call:

They were the young, the idealistic, the emerging postwar generation groping for a just and better America. He was a promise of what politics might be, and a call to enter political life. He sounded themes they wanted to hear: the responsibilities of freedom, the discipline of democracy, and the necessity of recognizing that the first and last issues of democracy are moral issues.[20]

Dawn and many others responded to this call. As soon as the bar exam was over, Dawn reported for full-time work at the national Volunteers for Stevenson headquarters at 7 South Dearborn Street in Chicago. This was the center of the campaign in Chicago, but Stevenson had decided to establish his overall campaign headquarters in Springfield, with other matters run out of the Democratic National Committee offices in Washington. At the Elks Club in Springfield, he assembled a staff of policy analysts and speechwriters that included, among others, Carl McGowan, Arthur Schlesinger Jr. (already a Pulitzer Prize–winning historian), Willard Wirtz, John Kenneth Galbraith, John Bartlow Martin, and a number of other renowned writers, academics, and journalists. The speeches that emerged from this group and Stevenson's own pen became best-selling books years after the election.[21] John Bartlow Martin also wrote an overtly political biography of Stevenson that had made it onto the *New York Times* best-seller list by October 12, 1952.[22]

The office in Chicago, where Dawn worked, was charged with publicity, fund-raising, and coordination of the thousands of volunteers who were offering their services to Stevenson. Porter McKeever, whom Stevenson had known from McKeever's role as director of information for the U.S. Mission to the United Nations, was recruited to become the national publicity director of Volunteers for Stevenson. Dawn was his deputy and served as executive director of the publicity office. Extremely talented people worked at the office as volunteers, including Eugene W. "Debs" Myers, who later became managing editor of *Newsweek,* and Ralph G. Martin, then thirty-two years old, who went on to write numerous popular books of nonfiction, including biographies of Golda Meir, John F. Kennedy, Franklin D. Roosevelt, and Winston Churchill's mother, Jennie.

Dawn's work for Volunteers for Stevenson consisted of both research and supervision of the office in general, including staffing.[23] In this capacity, she hired a woman who was to become a lifelong friend, Connie Chadwell (later Koch). Walter Johnson, a professor at the University of Chicago whom Connie had assisted during that July and August with his book *How We Drafted Adlai Stevenson* (published in 1955), referred Chadwell to Dawn. Connie remembers going to the office and meeting Dawn for the first time. Dawn, she recalls, seemed very smart, very efficient, and very nice. Dawn told Connie that she was afraid they could pay her only $56 a week, but this was almost twice what she had been making in her last job as a script typist for WGN, and Connie said, "Oh, it's fine." Dawn herself worked for Volunteers for Stevenson almost around the clock from late July until a few days after the November election for a total of $809.72, according to her W-2 tax form for that year. The volunteers worked twelve hours a day and sometimes more. Dawn only dimly remembers the place she was living at the time (an apartment she was sharing at 10 East Elm Street) because she was not home enough to have formed any distinct memories of it. But Connie Chadwell remembers working for Dawn at Volunteers for Stevenson as having been great fun. "We all worked hard and we produced some pamphlets. Dawn was very fair, nice, efficient. I don't remember any controversies; we were all having a fabulous time."[24]

What did the volunteer publicity brigade produce? Much of their product looks quaint by the standards of present-day glossy campaign materials.[25] The pamphlets and brochures stick very much to matters of substance, relying especially on Stevenson's record as governor of Illinois. The group drafted and distributed biographies of their candidate and detailed histories of his administration. It also put out a series of small brochures, all with the theme "Let's Talk Sense to the American People," with different versions focusing on civil rights, farm policy, labor, foreign policy, and political morality. Excerpts from Stevenson speeches and endorsements from influential people in the area under focus filled each brochure. Another publication theme was "Why I Switched to Stevenson," and some of the well-known people who had made the switch in allegiance wrote those materials. The one by author Herman Wouk, for example, consists of seven double-spaced typed pages:

> Adlai Stevenson had begun his campaign with a stunning acceptance speech that was recognized at once as a classic American document; a great sunlit statement of democratic aims and faith, shadowed with a sober awareness of our period, and clearly based on deep religious faith and personal humility. He was following it up with speech after speech of unbelievable literary brilliance and oratorical force, full of plain common sense about the issues, utterly honest, and addressed to the best in people's minds and hearts. The American people were beginning to stir and say to each other in plain words, "This is the man."[26]

Perhaps the most astonishing feat pulled off by the writers at Volunteers for Stevenson was the book volunteers wrote in a weekend and published commercially within two weeks because they had little money for more brochures. The publisher Bennett Cerf said that his publishing company would consider bringing out a paperback if they could get a manuscript to him by Monday. Debs Myers and Ralph Martin solicited a foreword from John Steinbeck, to be written overnight, collaboratively wrote a biography of Stevenson, edited twenty speeches to be included in the 128-page volume, and delivered the manuscript on schedule. The book used a standard brochure photo for its cover and included Stevenson's speeches up through September 27, 1952.[27] It was published by Random House and was selling like hotcakes at newsstands and in bookstores within two weeks.[28]

In addition, the group provided materials and advice to volunteers eager to help win votes and raise funds for Stevenson. One plan revolved around getting women to throw house parties using either a film or a set of records called *The Stevenson Bandwagon,* which supporters in Hollywood had developed. The handout volunteers distributed advised that, for a "platter party,"

> The hostess should invite as many women as her home can accommodate. The records will not have great appeal to die-hard Republicans, but they will help convince the independent-minded voter, and rouse the enthusiasm of Stevenson supporters. The plan can and should operate within all economic, social and ethnic groups. Skillful coordination would permit the record to be used twice, or even three times daily.[29]

Volunteers were also provided with a sample speech as a model for them to use at public meetings or on the radio. This text emphasized, first, Governor Stevenson's integrity and courage, then launched into a detailed comparison of Stevenson's and Eisenhower's experience, and closed with a synopsis of Stevenson's views on civil rights, free economy, foreign affairs (especially the war in Korea), McCarthyism, and political morality, describing his views more generally as "an intelligent and balanced mixture of the conservative and the liberal."[30]

While Volunteers for Stevenson toiled in Chicago, Stevenson toured the country to bring his message to the people. At the end of the three-month campaign, brief by modern standards, he returned to Illinois for a closing rally in Chicago, at which he made his exceptionally moving "I See America" speech. He told the crowd, "No American could travel the long road I have traveled and not find his faith renewed, his faith in his country and its future." But, after eloquently describing the inspiring sights he had seen, Stevenson went on to say:

> But, we have much to do in this century in this country of ours before its greatness may be fully realized and shared by all Americans.
>
> As we plan for change let us be sure that our vision is high enough and broad enough so that it encompasses every single hope and dream of both the greatest and the humblest among us.
>
> I see an America where slums and tenements have vanished and children are raised in decency and self-respect.
>
> I see an America where men and women have leisure from toil—leisure to cultivate the resources of the spirit.

I see an America where no man is another's master—where no man's mind is dark with fear.

I see an America at peace with the world.

I see an America as the horizon of human hopes.

This is our design for the American cathedral, and we shall build it brick by brick and stone by stone, patiently, bravely and prayerfully. And, to those who say that the design defies our abilities to complete it, I answer: "To act with enthusiasm and faith is the condition of acting greatly."[31]

The audience cheered and wept, and the speech appeared on the front page of the next day's *New York Times*.[32]

The following Tuesday, November 4, 1952, however, Eisenhower received 55 percent of the popular vote, and Stevenson carried only nine states.[33] Although America was ready for a change of party, it apparently also longed for a rest, not the honest self-reflection and challenge that Stevenson offered.

Dawn thinks there was no way Stevenson could have won in 1952 against Eisenhower, the national war hero. By election night, she says, many of the volunteers and staff realized that he was not going to win. "We didn't accept it necessarily because we were all really committed to Stevenson, and with good reason. He was not perfect, but a glorious role model for public service, and we felt so strongly."[34] Willard Wirtz has described Stevenson's most compelling attributes as his "total honesty," "total independence of mind," and "introducing of the moral dimension of political issues, the values dimension." After reflection, he concluded, "Dawn's attractions were like his. She too I think of as somebody who would have been totally honest in what she said. Totally principled and totally effective, a pretty good combination."[35]

The Volunteers for Stevenson office closed, and the staff disbanded a few days after the 1952 election. There is a wonderful photo of them all, with Porter McKeever, Ralph Martin, Connie Chadwell, and Dawn smiling broadly and posing in front of a poster that reads ADLAI IN 1956. Soon after, they all went their separate ways. Porter McKeever went to his job as executive director of the Chicago Council on Foreign Relations, and took Connie Chadwell to work for him there. Debs Myers left for the world of writing and publishing in New York City, and Dawn, of course, to her law firm job in Washington, after being sworn in to the Illinois bar on November 6. Debs Myers wrote to her in Washington at the end of January 1953, urging her to come visit and saying that he had a feeling from her general silence that she was "in the dumps and feeling miserable."[36] This was not an unlikely surmise, whether as a result of the lost election or the comedown from politics to law practice. In fact, however, Dawn had simply gone on with her life and was very busy.

Chapter 5

Covington & Burling, 1952–1954

WHEN DAWN BECAME AN associate at Covington & Burling in November 1952, she was a rare breed—a woman lawyer hired by a major law firm. Although women had been admitted to practice in every state since 1920, there were few women working at preeminent law firms. A few had been hired during World War II, when the big firms had lost men to the armed services and were desperate for lawyers, but as soon as the men returned, veterans replaced the women.[1] With one or two exceptions, none of the women that the firms hired in the 1930s, 1940s, and 1950s was admitted into partnership status at the firms, and most women lawyers employed by firms were in fact working as legal secretaries or librarians. Studies of law firms' hiring during the 1950s and 1960s show rampant discrimination against women attorneys, with law firms defending their practice of not hiring women on the grounds that their clients would not like it or that women lawyers would just marry and have children.[2]

In the 1950s, law firms turned downed numerous women who have since become prominent, or if firms offered them jobs, they paid women less than men.[3] Firm after firm rejected both of the women who later became the first female justices on the U.S. Supreme Court. Sandra Day O'Connor graduated in the top ranks of her class at Stanford Law School in 1952, but the only employment a law firm offered her was as a legal secretary. Ruth Bader Ginsburg graduated first in her class at Columbia Law School in 1959, but every New York City firm to which she applied rejected her.[4] The pattern persisted during the 1960s, when major law firms in New York, Florida, and Colorado rejected Geraldine Ferraro, Janet Reno, Patricia Schroeder, and Elizabeth Dole.[5] Judith Kaye, later chief judge of the New York Court of Appeals, eventually did receive an offer in 1962 but only after "scores of rejections."[6] The stories of these women were only the tip of the iceberg, and law firms continued to fill their ranks with male attorneys.

Moreover, according to Dawn's classmate Howard Kane, now a successful big firm lawyer, 1952 was not a good time to be seeking a law firm job. The firms had done a great deal of hiring immediately after the war, from 1945 to 1952, but by the year he and Dawn graduated, they were uncomfortable with the large numbers that had been hired and had a kind of "depression mentality." Kane himself had difficulty finding employment with a law firm after graduation, despite having been an editor on the law review with Dawn. Kane did finally get a job in 1952, at a salary of $3,600.[7] All of this makes it even more unusual that Dawn had an offer from Covington & Burling long before graduation, at a salary of $4,000 per year.

The difference was certainly not that Covington was the most enlightened law firm with respect to sex equality. The first woman ever hired at the firm was Amy Ruth Mahin, whose employment was a direct result of the lawyer shortage during World War II. Edward Burling wrote to the dean of Northwestern University Law School in 1942 to try to recruit younger professors to work for the firm. The dean responded that there were no faculty available but suggested that they hire Mahin, who was articles editor of the law review.[8] She began work at Covington & Burling on July 1, 1942, and eight other women lawyers joined her during the war. Soon after hostilities ended, however, Mahin was the only woman left as an attorney at the firm; and though she worked there until her retirement in 1974, while round after round of male associates was admitted into partnership, she never made partner.

In 1952, when Dawn began work at Covington, she was one of three women the firm hired that year, a bumper crop. One of those three, Virginia Watkin, eventually became the first woman partner at the firm, but not until two decades later, after resigning in 1958 and being recruited to return as a partner in 1974. Although other women who had begun to work in small numbers as lawyers at the big firms were consigned to work in estates and trusts, this was not the case for Dawn and Watkin. They both worked on big corporate litigation from the beginning. Dawn was soon doing a good deal of work in the antitrust field, and Watkin eventually specialized in tax law. In this and other respects Dawn and Watkin were different from the other women at Covington. For example, the other women lawyers there kept to themselves and never lunched with the male lawyers. Virginia Watkin reports that she was not about to put up with this herself, nor would Dawn:

None of [the other women] had lunch with the fellows. I was used to having lunch with the fellows. . . . So I wasn't about to go to lunch with just women all the time. Fortunately we shared offices and my office mate was Al Sacks, who later became dean of Harvard Law School. So I'd ask him, can I go to lunch with you? . . . And as soon as I established that I insisted on paying for my own lunch there was no problem. I said, "Look, you guys have families, kids in school, mortgages to pay; you're not going to pay for me." . . . Dawn would have been the first woman who, as I would put it, sort of thought like I did.[9]

Lunching with the men only went so far, though, because many of the clubs where male lawyers ate and held important meetings, such as the Metropolitan Club, did not allow women.

Dawn and Ginny, as Virginia Watkin is called, both went to work on the Texas City disaster litigation (Dalehite v. United States). On April 16, 1947, a ship loaded with fertilizer bound for the depressed postwar economies of Europe exploded in the harbor at Texas City, Texas, killing almost six hundred people, injuring thousands, destroying the port facility, and setting fires throughout the city. The fertilizer had been produced according to specifications by the federal government from ammonium nitrate that had been used for explosives during the war. The program to convert it into fertilizer and send it to aid the war-torn European countries was developed at the highest levels of government. Thus, when the explosion caused so much damage to people and property at Texas City, the people injured sued the U.S. government for negligence in the manufacture and shipment of the fertilizer. Although the government, as sovereign, had historically been immune from suit, Congress had passed the Federal Tort Claims Act in 1946, waiving sovereign immunity in certain types of suits alleging negligence.

The plaintiffs succeeded in having the trial court recognize their claims under the FTCA, but the court of appeals reversed that decision. When the case reached the U.S. Supreme Court, as a case to test the reach of the new statute, Covington & Burling was called in to write the brief and make the oral argument on behalf of some three hundred consolidated claimants. The issue was whether the victims' claims fell within the discretionary function exception to the FTCA, which provides that the federal government cannot be sued for actions, even if negligent, that are taken in its policy-making capacity, involving choices among a variety of alternatives. The claimants argued that the series of errors that led to the disaster at Texas City were instead garden-variety negligence, for which a private person would be liable.

As a newly arrived lawyer at Covington & Burling, Dawn was assigned to research the science of ammonium nitrate. The claimants wanted to show that the government was fully aware, or should have been aware, of the dangerous properties of the fertilizer and specifically of its potential for spontaneous combustion. With no background in science, Dawn found herself assigned to work with an eminent scientist from the Massachusetts Institute of Technology who was serving as an expert to advise the plaintiffs on their petition to the Supreme Court. She spent long hours with him, poured over the trial court testimony, and did additional research, in order to understand the characteristics of ammonium nitrate. Watkin says Dawn "was a terror. She really would get into something like a bulldog and work at it. And she wound up knowing about as much as [the expert] did about it."[10]

Dawn found this introduction to work at a big law firm fascinating, even though her assigned task was only a very small part of a large case staffed by many lawyers:

> In the briefs and everything, it ends up being a terribly small part, but the case was so important that each of us [was] sort of like the roust-abouts who used to set up the circus tents; each one had our own stakes to pound in, which is why it could all happen so fast. . . . Each of the young guys, anyway. Each of us had little segments that we were responsible for. Then we would get brought in and see some of the rest of the stuff happening or do it by talking to some of our peers who were working on other parts of the case.[11]

The case was argued in the U.S. Supreme Court on April 6, 1953, and all those who had worked on it attended the argument, part of which was presented by Howard Westwood, the partner for whom Dawn had worked during the previous summer.

When the decision was announced on June 8, however, the parties on whose behalf the lawyers from Covington & Burling had argued lost by a vote of four to three, with two justices not participating (Douglas and Clark), and Justices Jackson, Black, and Frankfurter dissenting. Writing for the plurality, Justice Reed found that the alleged negligence involved decisions that "were all responsibly made at a planning rather than operational level and involved considerations more or less important to the practicability of the Government's fertilizer program," and the government was therefore immune from suit.[12] In short, the federal court, as one branch of the government, simply would not second-guess the decisions taken by the executive branch, even though in retrospect they appeared negligent. (In 1956, Congress passed a special act to settle the more than three thousand lawsuits arising out of the Texas City disaster.)[13]

Watkin tells an interesting story about working on the Texas City disaster team with Dawn that illustrates the difficulties under which women lawyers labored at that time. The firm often had meetings at the Metropolitan Club, which did not admit women except on weekends or in the evening if accompanied by a man. Howard Westwood wanted to have a meeting of the Texas City disaster team at the Metropolitan Club but found himself with a team whose members would not all be admitted to its confines. Thinking himself particularly liberal and accommodating of the two women, he scheduled a meeting there on a Saturday, when women were allowed. But Watkin had a small child and lived in Baltimore, so she told him she just could not make it. Westwood, she says, "was very disappointed because he made these plans just so Dawn and I could be there."[14] Yet in attempting to evade outright discrimination (the exclusive club), he had unknowingly bumped into the more difficult and more lasting burdens under which women labor in law firms— their responsibilities to families in a work environment that demands total commitment.

After the Texas City disaster case was over, Dawn worked primarily for Tommy Austern, a workaholic partner who indeed required total commitment, making excessive demands on those who worked for him and checking the sign-in and sign-out charts in the evening to see how many hours young lawyers were working. Austern, according to Dawn, was the "certified ogre" of the firm; Watkin describes him as a "short, somewhat rotund, foul-mouthed, hard-driving powerhouse" who would treat the lawyers who worked for him abusively. Associates of both sexes lived in terror of him. Dawn did a great deal of work for Austern on antitrust cases and researched speeches he would give on matters relating to antitrust law. Ginny surmises that Dawn was able to get along with Austern, despite his abusiveness, simply by standing up to him and feeding it right back, with humor. That is probably true. Dawn herself says, when asked to explain her spunkiness as a young woman, that she has simply never been easily intimidated.

An anecdote serves as an example of her sangfroid. One Sunday morning soon after she had started working at Covington, Dawn received a phone call at her apartment from Austern. He told her that he needed help looking something up and asked her to come down to the office that morning. "Oh," she said, "Mr. Austern, I'm very sorry. I just can't come down this morning; I have a croquet match scheduled." (Dawn was indeed planning to play croquet at the house of a friend that morning.) "There was a sort of silence at the other end of the line, and then [Austern] said 'Oh, all right.' Nobody had ever done that to him before. Or maybe they had, but he was at least stunned that I did it, because I was still pretty new around there."[15] In short, Dawn had the guts to stand up to Austern from her first days at the firm, and perhaps he respected her for it.

In addition to working on antitrust matters for Austern, Dawn became Covington's in-house expert on immigration law, a field in which the firm practiced only as a favor for clients. For example, the wife of one of the managers of American Can Company, one of Austern's big clients, was detained in New Orleans when trying to return to the country from her husband's previous posting in South America. She was not a U.S. citizen but had apparently never realized it because her parents moved from her birthplace in Canada when she was only two years old. The woman quickly became hysterical about being held in detention. Her husband and his employer called in the big guns at Covington, and the case was assigned to Dawn. With no prior immigration law experience, she managed to get the woman out of detention. After that success, Dawn stepped into the role of resident immigration expert at Covington & Burling. As a result, she had to immerse herself in the repressive, anti-immigrant McCarran-Walter Act. The act, passed in 1952, created an immigration quota system based on race and national origin. It also contained provisions aimed at "subversion."[16]

One of the firm's pro bono clients was caught up by the provision about subversion. He had been born in Canada and was a naturalized U.S. citizen, but the authorities were trying to strip him of his citizenship and deport him because he had refused, as a conscientious objector, to go into the military in a combat role. The client was a Mennonite, a member of one of the traditional peace churches, and thereby entitled to exemption from combat duty as a conscientious objector.

Dawn's research into the McCarran-Walter Act revealed, as she recalls, that the "provision having to do with conscientious objectors was probably the only semi-compassionate thing in the McCarran-Walter Act, which was a very anti-immigrant, regressive act. It did provide that genuine conscientious objectors could be admitted to citizenship even though they would not serve in the military, so long as they did some public service."[17] The client had worked in a hospital for two years as alternative service. Yet the judge before whom his case was tried prided himself on being superpatriotic and was determined not to allow the man to be a citizen if he were unwilling to fight for his country. He was about to be deported when the American Civil Liberties Union gave the case to Covington & Burling to argue in the Supreme Court.

Dawn was a member of the small team preparing the brief for the Supreme Court and was working hard on it when Dean Acheson returned to the firm. Acheson had been a partner at Covington & Burling before serving in the Roosevelt administration and ultimately as secretary of state under Truman. When he first came back to law practice in 1953, he did not have much to do. As a result, he took a look at the brief they were constructing on behalf of the conscientious objector. He turned it into an entirely different document—no longer a dull legal argument but a moving narrative of the role of the peace churches in the United States and the historic role of the Mennonites at the heart of this nonviolent group—and wove the client's tale into that context.

To Dawn, Acheson was an awesome personage, and she was thrilled to be working with him on this brief. One day she was in the library, exhausted from having had little sleep for many nights in a row as they were finishing the brief. All of a sudden she became aware of an imposing presence standing beside her chair. A voice she describes as "magnificent" said, "Ms. Clark, you took my footnote out!"[18] She looked up to see Acheson standing over her. Dawn was so tired that she could not even remember what footnote he was talking about. She had obviously removed some piece of the brief in which Acheson took particular pride, probably because she had found that it was not sustainable factually on some ground. She defended her action but made some accommodation so that the footnote went back in, in a more sustainable form.

Dawn and the others working on the conscientious objector case were eagerly looking forward to seeing Acheson argue it in the Supreme Court. Unfortunately, the brief constructed under his supervision was so persuasive that the government simply confessed error, and the argument never took place.

The pinnacle of Dawn's practice as an immigration lawyer was the case of Ian McHarg. McHarg, a Scotsman, had studied landscape architecture and urban planning at Harvard and was teaching at the University of Pennsylvania, where he founded the Department of Landscape Architecture. He was already quite well known when the United States denied him a reentry visa because he had scar tissue on his lungs. Dawn put on her scientist cap again. She got McHarg's X-rays and learned how to read them. Her research showed that almost anyone who grew up during World War II in Europe had some scar tissue on his or her lungs. And she entered into negotiations with someone at the State Department who eventually cleared McHarg for admission into the United States. Near the end of her time at Covington & Burling, Dawn got a call from McHarg in Philadelphia, expressing his gratitude. "He had this glorious Scottish brogue," she recalls. "It was enough to send shivers up and down your spine, it was so beautiful."[19] McHarg went on to become very prominent, even hosting his own program, *This House We Live In*, on CBS in 1960. His 1969 book *Design for Nature* was a pioneering work in ecological planning and continues to be a much-studied classic in courses on land-use planning.

Dawn regularly worked ten to twelve hours a day and weekends during the two years she spent at Covington & Burling, which left little time for anything else in her life. For much of the time, she shared a house with a woman named Casey Colvin, who worked at the Central Intelligence Agency, and the two occasionally gave parties. Jack Coons, her friend from law school, was working at the Pentagon during this period and remembers going out with Dawn to nightclubs a couple of times to listen to music. Dawn had no serious romantic relationships in Washington.

Dawn's relationship with the man from her law school class continued during her first year in Washington; they telephoned back and forth on a regular basis and saw each other occasionally. Friends from Chicago kept half-humorously, half-seriously nudging Dawn toward marriage. Marriage, however, was something she did not want. Ginny Watkin remembers that Dawn was determined not to relent, because marriage, at least to that man and at that time, would have meant giving up her career. In the early 1950s, the postwar era of domesticity, it was an unusual man who was supportive of his wife working, particularly in a job that might pose a threat to his own sense of self. Working for a while, as a teacher or nurse or in some "female" occupation, might have been tolerated, but a high-powered career was not. So after a while the long-distance romance ended, and her friend of many years soon married someone else. Friends from Chicago wrote to express their sadness. One college friend told her, "I probably won't ever forgive you for permitting that to happen. But it's your life and you have to live it and enjoy it. Only you can decide what's best for you."[20]

Dawn says that she never wanted to get married, that she knew it would tie her down and interfere with the freedom and independence she enjoyed. "I didn't want to get married. . . . I had other things to do. And also, I think, perhaps because it was still at a time you thought that you might be sort of taken out of the context in which you wanted to be if you got married."[21] Dawn was not inclined in that direction, bucking the statistics on early marriage in the 1950s: not marrying after college, when all her classmates were getting married; not in law school, when many already were married; and certainly not when she was forging a career for herself in a field few women had entered. Indeed, when Dawn finally did marry Walter Netsch in 1963, at the age of thirty-seven, she felt rather embarrassed about doing so. "I just considered that it was sort of a badge of dishonor almost. It meant that I was going to shut down some part of my life that I was much more interested in. So I absolutely did not want to get married."[22]

Dawn and Hal Shapiro, who had been married since the end of his first year in law school, remained fast friends across the miles separating Washington from Illinois. Hal had gone to work in the Stevenson administration in Springfield after graduation and started work at the Sonnenschein law firm in Chicago in 1953. By later that year, Shapiro and his wife, Bea, were expecting their first child, and his letters to Dawn with news about mutual friends reported ripples from the 1950s baby boom all around. Shapiro virtually demanded Dawn's presence at parties in June of each year and at year's end. He also shared with her the life of a junior associate at a big law firm, writing that he was "currently saddled with the research for unquestionably the dullest case that has ever been filed in the State of Illinois. . . . [But] I am not really discontent. . . . It's just that at the moment I'm dealing with ennui, the profitable end of the business[,] and I think I shall cry."[23] Shapiro's letters were often illustrated, and some included mock recipes or mock newspaper reports good-naturedly satirizing all the weddings his friends were going to at the time. In the same letter about his boring case, he drew a picture of his new business card, with his own name in tiny print and the firm name very large: "This, I guess, makes them easier to use for the next guy." In fact, Shapiro practiced at Sonnenschein for fifty-three years and was chair of the firm from 1985 to 1990.

In 1954 Hal Shapiro told Dawn that a newly appointed federal judge in Chicago needed a judicial clerk and suggested that she apply. This presented a dilemma for her, because she loved her work at Covington & Burling. "Covington was a fun place to be, and in fields of law in which I was interested, government one way or another. If I had intended to practice law the rest of my life, I never would have left," she says.[24] But Dawn was still determined to make her mark as a politician, and Illinois was the turf she had chosen and where she had connections. So she applied for the clerkship, was offered the job, and accepted it as "a quick and dirty way to make the break." She went in to talk to Tommy Austern about it, but he said that if she had made up her mind, she should not stay around and prolong it, so she left rather soon.

Before leaving the firm, Dawn went to tell Amy Ruth Mahin, the first woman hired there, that she was going. Amy said that she felt very sorry about this, because she thought the firm would have made Dawn their first woman partner, though it was not ready yet. She knew that she would never become partner herself, and indeed she never did. Perhaps Mahin's prediction would have come true. Yet if Covington & Burling had made Dawn a partner in the 1950s, they would have been well in advance of other firms. As it was, the firm waited until it was under quite a bit of public pressure in 1974 to name its first woman partner. An excerpt entitled "Oink, Oink, Oink, Oink, Oink" had appeared in the October 1973 issue of *Washingtonian* magazine about the firm's problems with respect to women, specifically, its policy of holding weekly firm luncheons at the all-male Metropolitan Club. It was only at that point that Covington & Burling contacted Ginny Watkin, who had left the firm almost two decades before, finished raising her four children, and reentered practice in Boston, and asked her to return to Washington as Covington's first woman partner.

Chapter 6

Back to Chicago and the Committee on Illinois Government

IN THE SUMMER OF 1954, Dawn returned to Chicago and to a two-year position as judicial clerk to Judge Julius Hoffman, who had been appointed the previous year to the U.S. District Court for the Northern District of Illinois. Hoffman had been the speaker at Dawn's law school graduation and had a close relationship with the law school at Northwestern, where a hall is named for him. As a new judge, he had been given an enormous workload, including old cases that had been on the docket for a long time, and he badly needed Dawn's services. So she went to work in the old Beaux-Arts federal courthouse building with a huge dome on the corner of Dearborn and Adams in downtown Chicago. The grand spaces of the interior were of a different epoch. Dawn was given a huge office between the judge's courtroom and the secretary's area.

Judge Hoffman, who was a stickler about clearing up the backlog and moving cases along, was on the bench most of the day, while Dawn worked in his chambers researching and drafting opinions about past cases, motions by parties in current cases, and documents related to discovery disputes. Discovery is the process by which parties demand information from the other side before trial, through written questions, requests to produce documents, and depositions (the sworn testimony of witnesses). Disputes about discovery take up a good deal of time on the docket of a district court judge, and judges and clerks typically consider them pains in the neck. Hoffman gave Dawn almost total freedom to work on such disputes. She became convinced that the process was being abused and discovery used to harass or delay, and she received leeway to write some opinions that required parties to be precise about the information they needed and to proceed to trial in a timely fashion. In this respect, she and Hoffman were on the same page.

On other issues, Dawn differed from Hoffman. He was, for example, particularly tough on draft dodgers, those who refused to serve in the military or fled to Canada to avoid service. This was not an area in which he respected, or even sought, his clerk's advice. Hoffman was also hard on crime, though he did think that drug offenders who were genuine addicts belonged in treatment rather than in jail. He could be hard on attorneys he thought were abusing the process by prolonging cases either because they were unprepared or because their clients stood to gain from delay. Attorneys surveyed in Chicago reported that he treated them abusively.[1]

Personally, Dawn found Judge Hoffman to be a good boss, pleasant to be around, and generous to his employees. When he and his wife returned from one of their frequent trips to Europe, for example, he brought Dawn a Gucci handbag before anyone in the United States had ever heard of Gucci. He entertained his staff several times a year with elegant meals at the Standard Club, a private club close to the federal building (the "Jewish club" at a time when the nearby Union League, to which most judges belonged, discriminated against Jews).[2] He filled the chambers in which his clerk and secretary worked with fresh flowers and gave Dawn the freedom to get on with her work.

Julius Hoffman became notorious fifteen years later as the judge in the famous Chicago Seven Trial. Eight political activists were tried for conspiracy to incite a riot at the time of the 1968 Democratic National Convention in Chicago, when the streets were filled with antiwar protesters challenging Mayor Richard J. Daley's refusal to give them permits to march and to camp out in the city's parks. Daley called out the police and National Guard in large numbers; the protesters taunted them; and the police responded with tear gas and truncheons. The Walker Report to the National Commission on the Causes and Prevention of Violence described what happened as, at some points, a "police riot."[3]

The assignment of the Chicago Seven Trial in 1969 to Hoffman was doomed from the start. The case was a political trial that verged on theater of the absurd, as Hoffman treated the defendants and their lawyers abusively and the defendants acted out their rage at him, the war, and the system. Hoffman would not delay the trial so that the main defense attorney could recover from surgery and then refused to allow Bobby Seale, the Black Panther leader who was a defendant, to defend himself. When Seale objected noisily, calling Judge Hoffman a "fascist dog," a "pig," and a "racist," the judge ordered him bound and gagged.[4] Hoffman made no pretense about his dislike of the defendants and their lawyers. The feeling was mutual.

In the end, the jury acquitted all the defendants of conspiracy but convicted five of the seven (Seale's case had been severed by that time) of crossing state lines to incite a riot; the judge also sentenced each of the defendants and two of their lawyers to lengthy terms for contempt of court. In 1972, the Court of Appeals for the Seventh Circuit reversed all the convictions, because of, among other things, the judge's "deprecatory and often antagonistic attitude toward the defense."[5] As a result of his conduct in the trial of the so-called Chicago Seven, Judge Hoffman became known as the epitome of an irrational and unjust judge.

Dawn remembers him differently, yet understands how the trial played out "like a Greek tragedy." As soon as she and some colleagues at Northwestern Law School, where she was then teaching, heard that Hoffman had been assigned to the case, they tried to talk to him. They told the judge that the trial would be extremely trying, that the defendants would try to provoke him and show disrespect for the system, and that "it was very important for him to keep his cool and not let them get under his skin, which is exactly what they wanted to do." At the end of the conversation, Dawn and her colleagues sensed that Hoffman had not been able to hear what they were saying. In Dawn's opinion, "It was clear he . . . never understood the defendants and absolutely fell into their trap. That's what they wanted to have happen, and they couldn't have found a better candidate for it. It was just like a Greek tragedy."[6] She rues that this is what Judge Hoffman is now known for and tries to explain his reaction to the Chicago Seven and their attorneys:

> It really grew out of this enormous sense of respect and reverence and awe he had for the integrity for the judicial system. What he saw were people who were thumbing their nose at it, who were blatantly abusing it; this is in his mind. And he just could not live with that. . . . When you combine that with his feeling that here were people who did not appreciate, respect and revere the importance of the judiciary and its role in this great democracy . . . , you just had two things coming together which could not have been avoided.[7]

But, she also confesses, Hoffman "was not quite the same person at the time of the conspiracy as he was when I worked for him."

The reason Dawn had returned to Chicago in 1954, however, was not the clerkship with Hoffman, though it enabled her to support herself back in Illinois. She came back to get involved in the efforts to build a Democratic Party of substance and principle in the state. While she was still in Washington, a group of people, many of whom had worked in Adlai Stevenson's administration in Springfield, started to organize to continue the Stevenson tradition of government in Illinois. A number of them had met with Stevenson after his term had expired to discuss, over dinner, what had been going on in state government since he left office. This dinner laid the germ of an idea that became the Committee on Illinois Government (CIG), organized in March 1953.

Many of CIG's organizers were graduates of Northwestern Law School, including Jim Clement, the man Dawn had met on the beach who encouraged her to apply to law school. Jim Otis was also a founder of the group. Otis had been in the law school class ahead of Dawn, and he and his wife, Peg, would invite Dawn's group of friends over to their apartment for an occasional home-cooked meal during their law school days. Dan Walker, also a Northwestern graduate (and future governor of Illinois); John Hunt, a lawyer-friend of Otis's; Frank Fisher; and Manly Mumford were among the principal organizers of the group. Dick Nelson, who had been an aide to Governor Stevenson, became the first chair. Otis, Clement, Hunt, and Walker had all worked in the Stevenson administration. All but Fisher were graduates of Northwestern University School of Law.

A conversation that Otis and Hunt had with Walter Fisher sometime in 1953 led to CIG's initial activities. Fisher had served as chair of the Illinois Commerce Commission under Stevenson but had left office rather than serve under Stevenson's successor, the Republican governor William G. Stratton. Fisher suggested to the two men that they "start keeping book" on the Stratton administration, perhaps by clipping and organizing newspaper articles, to monitor whether Stratton was honoring his campaign promises and whether he was maintaining the important reforms Stevenson had initiated.[8] So the new group did just that: they subscribed to newspapers from downstate Illinois as well as Chicago, divided them up among themselves, and started clipping, thereby assembling a great deal of information. Other liberal-minded Democrats joined them as time went on, including Jim Alter, Walter Dahl, Angelo Geocaris, Willard Lassers, Abner Mikva, Jim Moran, Newt Minow, Hal

Shapiro, and of course Dawn Clark, who was the only woman for most of the time.

A key question the group had to face at its inception was what its relationship to the Democratic Party would be. Should it function in a supportive role or strike out on an independent course that would at times be at odds with the party? After discussion, the members decided to focus on the things they could do best. As a group of talented young lawyers, this was to develop materials for use in drafting legislation or in campaigns for Democratic candidates. The new organization met with Adlai Stevenson again; he encouraged them in their activities and helped them raise money by passing the word to a few of his friends and supporters, such as Ben Heineman, a lawyer who was soon to become president of the Chicago & North Western Railway. Stevenson also spoke to Mayor Daley, with whom he had always been on good terms, telling Daley, in effect, that CIG members were good people and that he should help them out. So, over the years, one source of CIG's income was the Cook County Democratic Committee.

Just as Dawn returned to Chicago, CIG published its first pamphlet, *The Stratton Record*.[9] The back of the pamphlet bears a statement of purpose for the organization that also describes its relationship to the Democratic Party:

> The Committee on Illinois Government works with the Democratic Party of Illinois for good state government by helping to provide the public with information about how the State is being run.
>
> The Committee investigates and publicizes shortcomings in state laws and administrative practices. Constructive suggestions concerning legislation and administration are also studied and distributed from time to time.

The group was operating only out of a post office box. It was some time before it opened an office and hired a staff member, Victor de Grazia.

The Stratton Record is an interesting piece of propaganda. Forty-eight pages long and four inches by seven inches in size, *The Stratton Record* is organized by wryly styled topic areas—corruption, pay-rollers, political roads, and the like—and composed entirely from the clipping files that CIG maintained. According to Otis, its composition—quotes from newspapers with a bit of independent writing to introduce and conclude each section—was primarily the work of John Hunt. On each issue, Stratton's campaign promises were measured by what had happened during the first two years of his gubernatorial administration, portrayed as a return to the corruption, cronyism, and patronage of the Green administration. Cartoons of Stratton by an unidentified artist illustrate the pamphlet. CIG members distributed *The Stratton Record*, its first publication, by hand before the 1954 election to various groups and people who might be interested in it, as well as to ward committee members and other Democratic Party workers. A year later, in October 1955, CIG issued an updated and more thorough critique of the Stratton administration, *The Stratton Record: Part II*, which dealt with key issues in a narrative format instead, drawing on both the clipping files and some independent research.

By the time Dawn returned to Chicago from Washington, CIG had grown enough that its members gathered in one another's homes to clip newspapers. Twenty-five or so lawyers might gather, clipping and drinking into the wee hours, dividing the work both geographically and topically. Dawn's special area was mental health, and she was responsible for reviewing the *Quincy Herald-Whig* newspaper. The group's mission was to keep an eye on things Governor Stevenson had started in Illinois state government. What bound the group together was the members' common dedication to the model of state government he had begun—a completely honest government in which well-qualified people of high integrity would be glad to serve. As Dawn saw it, CIG was committed to standing up for issues that required courage, as Stevenson had done. The group did this, for example, by preparing research papers for Democratic candidates advocating constitutional reform, cleaning up the mental health system, and instituting a state income tax as a fairer way to distribute the costs of government. Their vision was to change the way things were done, "to stand up and be counted" on things that needed to be done or changes that needed to be made, however unpopular.

In pursuit of this mission, CIG began to draft legislation and prepare memoranda for legislators on issues in which it was interested. It attempted to get the Democratic Party to pay attention to substantive issues rather than just to politics, power, and patronage. The Cook County Democratic Organization, or "the machine," which focused its attention primarily on elections and the patronage that both followed and enabled elections, controlled the Democratic Party. Moreover, in the 1950s, legislators in

Springfield had very little staff assistance; they shared offices and had no secretaries. Although the Legislative Research Council existed, it was rare for legislators to seek its help. To some extent, CIG attempted to fill these gaps as a way of putting forward the issues in which it was interested. For example, when the Democratic Party met in Chicago in September 1954 to adopt a statewide platform, the committee submitted eleven suggested reform planks dealing with reapportionment, mental health services, judicial reform, civil service, disclosure of political contributions, labor, publicity of records, revenue, a code of procedure for legislative investigations, schools, and highways. Five of the planks (mental health, civil service, revenue, code of procedure for legislative investigations, and highways) appeared virtually without change in the party's final twenty-two-plank platform, causing the committee to conclude that the enormous amount of work members had devoted to the task was well worth it. "Our members can feel justly proud of the fact that they have supplied the text for a substantial portion of the 1954 platform. . . . This project represented a constructive contribution to the Democratic Party and to the cause of good government in Illinois and was well worth the time and effort expended."[10] The committee also drafted twenty-one bills and resolutions for the General Assembly's 1955 session, most of them accompanied by detailed statements, and circulated them among Democratic legislators.

In December 1956, CIG submitted to Senator William J. Lynch, then minority leader of the Illinois Senate, a complete legislative program for the Democratic Party, along with twenty-three bills, amendments to eighteen bills, and three resolutions for constitutional revision; again, detailed memoranda accompanied most of these. The committee also held meetings with legislators and circulated memos analyzing other legislative proposals.[11] After hiring Victor de Grazia as executive director in 1956, more lobbying was possible in Springfield, against, for example, construction of the lakefront McCormick Place convention center. The *Chicago Tribune* was pressing the location at least in part, CIG believed, because it held money in railroad bonds and would profit if that were the site. The committee supported the construction of a convention center, but not in a place that gobbled up a large slice of the remaining lakefront area in the city.

Another obvious route for importation of CIG's ideas into state government was the election of sympathetic candidates for high office. When

Cook County Treasurer Herbert C. Paschen was nominated to run for governor against the incumbent Stratton in 1956, he asked CIG to provide him with background research and ideas for his campaign. A confidential memorandum dated February 7, 1956, circulated by Jim Clement, then chair of the committee, set forth an outline of campaign issues proposed for submission to Paschen, prepared by Frank Fisher and Hal Shapiro from reports submitted by issue committee chairs; it was circulated for members to check the parts related to their assigned fields. The document included sections on abolition of the loyalty oath, economic development for depressed areas in southern Illinois, construction of nontoll highways, judicial reform (though not coming out for merit selection of judges lest this "deny the people the right to vote directly for the members of their courts"), a minimum wage, legislation concerning job discrimination, factory health laws, property tax reform, and aid for education, among others. Dawn's section on mental health reform was long in relation to the others and advocated, among other things, increasing the budget to reduce overcrowding in state hospitals and strengthening community programs to help people before they needed institutional care.

Over the months of Paschen's candidacy, CIG members in fact drafted much of his campaign literature, speeches, and press releases. Unfortunately, by the fall of 1956, the *Chicago Sun-Times* revealed the existence of a fund in the treasurer's office made up of contributions from banks where county money was on deposit. Paschen insisted that the fund had been used solely for welfare purposes, specifically to buy flowers to send to funerals or to sick people. The so-called flower fund led to further investigation by federal and local authorities, however, and to the release of records showing that the fund had been used for political purposes. At the mayor's insistence, Paschen withdrew from the ticket and, in late September, Judge Richard Austin replaced him.

The substitution of a new candidate so close to the election was not as bad a development as it might have been, however, because Governor Stratton confronted a much larger scandal of his own: embezzlement in the state auditor's office. Orville Hodge, the state auditor, had been making out false state checks, endorsing them, and cashing them through a banker in Chicago. In June 1956, George Thiem, a reporter for the *Chicago Daily News*, began sniffing out the story. He acquired definitive proof (micro-filmed checks) by early July, and the governor persuaded Hodge to resign as soon as the story broke on July 7.[12] This clearly put Governor Stratton on the defensive. Indeed, he ultimately confessed that he had not even reviewed the obviously inflated figures (by $2.5 million) that Hodge had submitted for inclusion in the previous state budget. This scandal offered the Democrats an opportunity to retake the governorship.

Judge Austin, however, knew almost nothing about state government when he became the Democratic Party's new candidate for governor (basically by Mayor Daley's fiat). Knowing his weakness, Austin asked CIG for a crash course, which it immediately put together—a full day's intensive course at the Italian Village restaurant, with speakers like Walter Fisher from the Stevenson administration filling him in on the workings of state government. Austin had hardly ever been in any other part of the state than Cook County. He asked the illustrious group of ex-Stevenson aides what the people were like in the rest of the state. According to Jim Otis, Fisher replied that they were "the salt of the earth," good people, and told Austin you could talk with and to them.[13]

Members of CIG helped Austin in numerous other ways. On October 1, 1956, a memo went around to all members saying that Judge Austin needed to be prepared for a television interview in Decatur in a few days, asking them all to contribute, by noon the next day, questions in their fields of special expertise that he might expect at the interview and to suggest questions Austin might direct to Stratton.[14] In addition, CIG prepared a large loose-leaf binder for Austin called the bible; it consisted of background briefings and possible positions on a range of major issues, all prepared by the busy young professionals who belonged to the group. In addition, CIG composed a polished twenty-three-page document portraying the Hodge scandal as a failure of Stratton's oversight and a dereliction of his constitutional responsibilities. At the same time, the document used the scandal as an opportunity to push a variety of proposals for legislative and constitutional change on the grounds that they would make such problems less likely in the future. The proposals included shortening the ballot so that the only executive officials to be elected were the governor and lieutenant governor, transferring a number of regulatory powers from the auditor to other state agencies, strengthening state fiscal policies in a number of detailed ways, and increasing publicity and disclosure about the conduct of state government.[15] The document was exceedingly well researched and well written, and the arguments were set forth in persuasive detail, backed up by substantial knowledge of the workings of state government in Illinois.

Austin's unfamiliarity with the state remained a weakness. He was rather vague about state geography, and the Republicans and the press played this to the hilt. Abner Mikva remembers a *Chicago Tribune* reporter asking Austin in Springfield during one of his campaign "fly-arounds" what he thought about the problems of Van Buren County. There is no Van Buren County in Illinois. Nonetheless, Austin expressed his concern for the problems the citizens experienced there.

Despite his weaknesses as a candidate, with CIG's help, Judge Austin ran a good campaign. Yet Stratton pulled out a close election win on late returns from downstate. In a March 1958 CIG brochure, Austin is quoted as saying, "I feel certain that the efforts of your group were largely responsible for our coming so close to victory at the polls."

By 1958 Dawn was treasurer of CIG, and Jim Otis its chair. The group met fairly often, around a big long table at the cafeteria in the YMCA that was then downtown on LaSalle Street. Abner Mikva, who had already been elected to the state legislature, remembers Dawn from this period:

> She was very energetic. She would smoke a cigarette at the end of a long holder; we'd tease her that she picked that up from our hero FDR. She was mostly very concerned that because we were progressives, liberals, our work must be beyond reproach, with no excessive statements or positions. Victor de Grazia was executive director of the group. He painted with a broad brush, and she was always pulling back. She was very precise, and very determined.[16]

The CIG's main accomplishment in 1958 was the publication of *A Democratic Challenge*, a fifty-page, nine-inch-by-twelve-inch booklet setting forth a challenge for the Democratic Party to carry out much-needed reforms in Illinois state government. It was divided into the following topical sections: mental health, schools, revenue, the people's right to know, commission to study state government, constitutional changes, labor, strengthening state financial management, bond issues, highways and toll roads, housing, administrative investigations, hiring and firing, public aid, civil liberties, juvenile delinquency, conservation, agriculture, southern Illinois, and insurance. Each section, contributed by the CIG member charged with keeping up in that area, included a brief critique of the status quo in relation to that issue and then devoted attention to explaining, in numbered paragraphs, detailed reforms that should be instituted. Many of the reforms were progressive ideas for the period, such as open housing legislation and an act guaranteeing equal opportunity in employment (though the proposal omitted sex as a forbidden basis for discrimination), performance-based budgeting, and campaign finance reform requiring disclosure of contributions to all candidates and monies that lobbyists spent. Illinois did not have an income tax at the time, and the group reiterated its demand that one be instituted, though a flat rate rather than a progressive tax, to replace the state's heavy reliance on sales taxes for revenue.

Dawn's section on reform of the mental health system came at the beginning of the document and was the longest section. It showed how her expertise in this area had developed over the years she had worked with CIG. From clipping newspapers in 1954, she had advanced to following and reporting on all legislation introduced in this area and circulating "information bulletins" about developments throughout the state and the inadequate attention that both Governor Stratton and the legislature paid to funding, staffing, and facilities for mental health. By the time of the 1956 gubernatorial campaign, she was producing at least one major memo per month on the topic, critiquing, for example, Governor Stratton's expenditures on mental health, exposing overcrowding in facilities like the Tinley Park State Hospital in Cook County and the insufficiency of psychiatric personnel throughout the state, and setting forth a nine-page proposal for community mental health services.[17] The contribution of her expertise on this issue to the gubernatorial campaign is evident in articles that appeared in the *Chicago Daily News* and *Chicago Tribune* describing attacks by candidate Paschen on incumbent Stratton for his "indifference" to conditions in state mental health.[18]

By 1958, Dawn had honed her program of reform for the mental health system in Illinois. Nonetheless she circulated drafts of the section that was to appear in *A Democratic Challenge* to Fred K. Hoehler, who had been Stevenson's director of social welfare, and to Howard R. Sacks, for comment; each wrote back with detailed comments and praise for the excellence of her memo.[19] The final product proposed the establishment of a separate Department of Mental Health, raising the funding for mental health in Illinois, vigorously recruiting psychiatrists and other employees, providing facilities for forty-eight thousand inpatients, investing in outpatient treatment centers, and separating treatment of alcoholics and the elderly who did not, in fact, require inpatient treatment in the mental hospitals where they were being housed.[20] Many of the themes would reverberate throughout Dawn's subsequent years of work in the executive and legislative branches of government.

A Democratic Challenge was a major production, and it required funding. The group decided that Dawn and Jim Clement should approach the mayor, so they made an appointment to do so. The encounter with the often-impassive Richard J. Daley, boss of the Cook County Democratic machine, was a memorable one. Dawn remembers:

> It's as though you are sitting in front of the great Buddha; there is no sign of anything that passes across his face. It's literally as if it were a statue almost. And so of course you start talking faster and louder because you don't know whether you are getting your point across or not. What we were saying was that we were doing something that would be available to all Democrats and that it was something that needed to be done. . . . We were probably talking about some of the things we were proposing. Then I remember at some point, either Jim or I mentioned the words "printing costs." For the first time there was a flicker of something across the mayor's face. That's something he knew and understood. Party organizations, award committees, whatever it might be, had to be able to print literature, print palm cards, whatever it might be. He really responded to that. . . . I think we got as much as $1,500 or something like that to cover printing expenses.[21]

And so the Cook County Democratic Organization funded production of *A Democratic Challenge* by the group of independent Democrats who would later successfully challenge its dominance.

Money came in from progressive supporters as well. Adlai Stevenson, who was then practicing law in Chicago, continued to help the group in this respect. By the late 1950s, his son Adlai Stevenson III had also joined CIG and was on the Finance Committee, which Jim Alter, one of the few nonlawyers in the group, headed. Dawn was chair of CIG that year, and they needed to raise a few thousand dollars to keep going. Adlai Stevenson III suggested that they get his father to open up his farm in Libertyville for a fund-raiser. This was an exciting prospect because the public had never been in that house and people were curious about it. When Stevenson agreed, Alter and Dawn put together a fund-raiser that turned out to be much bigger than anyone expected. The invitation read as follows:[22]

COMMITTEE ON ILLINOIS GOVERNMENT

Autumn Cocktail Party

Sunday, October 18, 1959 · 3 to 7 p.m.

at the

FARM OF ADLAI E. STEVENSON

St. Mary's Road · Libertyville, Illinois · (see directions)

Contribution
$5.00 per person at door
$4.00 if mailed in advance   Cash Bar

The fund-raiser was a smashing success. It was a perfect fall day, with sunlight glinting on the golden leaves surrounding the ex-governor's estate. Hundreds of people attended. Photographs show a stylishly dressed Dawn Clark with a broad smile on her face standing next to Adlai Stevenson, with his son Adlai on her other side. Stevenson was a charming host, even though Alter says that a guest managed to break the chair he used in his library.[23] The event raised several thousand dollars for CIG, and in subsequent years the group held several more fund-raisers at the Libertyville farm.

The Committee on Illinois Government survived until 1969, although Dawn's own participation waxed and waned depending on whether she was located in Chicago or Springfield. The persons involved in it went on to illustrious careers, not only as lawyers but also as public servants, including federal judges (Jim Moran and Abner Mikva) and a U.S. senator (Adlai E. Stevenson III). The people involved also formed strong bonds that continued not just as political collaboration but also as strong personal friendships. Nancy Stevenson, Adlai Stevenson III's wife, recalls that while the CIG folks "were all very serious, engaged and hard-working, there were also gatherings which were wonderfully fun, get-togethers with spouses. Dawn was always right there, being part of the nonserious as well as the serious."[24] Adlai Stevenson III and others tried to reconstitute the group in the early 1980s but found that it was no longer possible for young lawyers to devote that kind of energy to a political cause with law firms insisting on their billing excessive numbers of hours.[25] The firms contribute money to public interest groups instead, but the body politic is the poorer.

—— *Chapter 7* ——

Starting to Take On the Machine

WHEN DAWN'S CLERKSHIP WITH Judge Hoffman ended in the summer of 1956, she did not seek a new job in law. Instead she went to work, once again, for the Stevenson-for-President campaign. After winning the primaries in Florida and California, Adlai Stevenson was the frontrunner by the time of the nominating convention. The Democratic National Convention was held in Chicago from August 13 to 17, 1956, and Stevenson won the nomination on the first ballot.

The ensuing campaign was quite different from that of 1952. For one thing, it was run out of Washington rather than Springfield. For another, the decision was made to take overall control out of the hands of the intellectuals close to Stevenson and give the national politicos more say. The egghead vote was Stevenson's for the asking, so the focus shifted to attracting the regulars. Willard Wirtz, who was on the road with Stevenson during the 1956 campaign, reported that the quality of Stevenson's speeches suffered as a result:

> The practical thing to do was to try to increase the vote from people who would be attracted by plainer ways of talking. Therefore the speeches lost the grand flavor that they had in '52. . . . If there was an elegant way of putting it or a commonplace way of putting it, in '52 we did it the elegant way, and in '56 we took the commonplace way.[1]

Unfortunately, this strategy was not consistent with Stevenson's own style, and did not allow him to emphasize his strong points. Moreover, the pace of the campaign, designed to display a vigorous candidate in contrast to an elderly president recovering from a heart attack, left Stevenson exhausted and often out of sorts.[2]

Dawn began to work for Stevenson early that summer in Chicago, doing research at a rented office in the Loop. She produced research papers—one, for example, criticizing Eisenhower's policy on Native Americans—and was so busy that she never had time to go to the convention at the International Amphitheatre. After the convention, she moved with the campaign to Washington, working out of a small office at 1025 Connecticut Avenue.[3]

Before arriving, Dawn called Barbara Lamberton, a cousin she had not seen since childhood, to inquire whether she could stay with her in Falls Church until she found a place to live. Neither was enthusiastic about the arrangement, for fear they would not like living with a relative they hardly knew. Barbara and her husband, Jim, who was an associate at a law firm, also had three very young children and lived in a modest home. As it turned out, they all liked one another tremendously, and Dawn stayed in Falls Church throughout the campaign. She took the bus into the District early in the morning with Jim Lamberton and a taxi home in the wee hours, after the last bus had left.[4]

Everyone at the campaign worked twelve to fourteen hours a day, seven days a week. Dawn's job was to do research and fact-checking for the speechwriters. In theory she was to check the accuracy of every speech before Stevenson delivered it, but his tendency to work on speeches up until the last minute made doing so rather difficult. In addition, the team traveling with the "Governor," as they called him, might call at any time with a request for some odd fact. Dawn remembers one call at 1 A.M. from Willard Wirtz, who wanted to know how much an aircraft carrier cost.[5] She found the answer, though she cannot recall how she managed to do so in the middle of the night, when the Congressional Budget Office and Library of Congress were both closed.

The campaign group with whom Dawn worked also produced documents that could be useful to the candidate in both putting forth his own positions and responding to attacks from the Republicans.[6] For example, Stevenson was on the defensive about issues of race and desegregation, so the group produced a lengthy document detailing Stevenson's civil rights record as governor of Illinois and another compiling his statements on the subject over the period from 1949 to 1956. They put together a tabbed folder of Stevenson's views on topics ranging alphabetically from agriculture to youths of the Democratic Party (mentioning, under the last, the young senator from Massachusetts, John F. Kennedy). And they responded to emergencies. On October 28, for example, Dawn sent a lengthy telegram to the Stevenson campaign party, then in Boston, alerting it to questions put to both candidates by the Veterans of Foreign Wars, which Eisenhower had already answered and Stevenson had not. Because the questionnaire was to be released to the press immediately, Dawn had composed a suggested response for Stevenson to each question, noting that "the proposed reply is a little vague and skirts some of the points," presumably deliberately.[7]

On one occasion, Dawn went on the road with the Stevenson campaign party, on a whistle-stop train journey from West Virginia through Kentucky to Cincinnati and on to Chicago by plane. She was excited to be going with the presidential campaign to her hometown. A major foreign policy speech was scheduled for Cincinnati, and Dawn was one of the people charged with getting media coverage for it. After stopping for a campaign fish-fry event in northern Kentucky, however, Stevenson kept reworking the speech as they crossed the river to Cincinnati. Dawn ran around the city trying to find some kind of duplicating machine (in an era before the Xerox revolution) to get the speech run off for the press. They finally found something and made the best copies they could, but Stevenson had delayed so long that the speech was clearly not going to make the national news.[8] Dawn was devastated because Stevenson's tendency to work on things until the last minute deprived them of major media coverage of a very good speech. This was a typical failing of Stevenson, who thought it more important to make just the right statement than to accommodate the schedule that staff and media demanded. This frustrated those who worked for him.

After the stop in Cincinnati, the campaign party flew on a twin-engine plane to South Bend, Indiana, for a Notre Dame football game. This trip was the occasion for Dawn's most interesting encounter with Stevenson, at least in retrospect. As the plane bounced up and down, Dawn ended up in the bathroom in the back, throwing up. When she had finally cleaned up and put herself to rights, she opened the door, only to find Stevenson on the other side. "I must have been every shade of green and yellow. He was very solicitous, asking 'Are you all right? What can I get for you? Can I get you a glass of water? Can I get you a cold towel?' He did go get me a cold towel. It was rather embarrassing."[9] After the football game, there was another challenging flight to Chicago, with fog down to a few feet from the ground. The candidate's plane was allowed to land at Midway Airport, and everyone on board applauded in relief when the plane touched ground. But it was impossible to find the way in from the runway, and trucks with spotlights had to be sent out to guide the plane in.[10]

By election night, Dawn and the speechwriters were back in Chicago, preparing speeches for victory or concession. They were fairly certain by then that it would be a concession speech. It had been an uphill battle against a popular incumbent president who was a war hero. Stevenson's chances were not helped by two international military events on the eve of election: the Soviet Union's invasion of Hungary to put down a popular insurrection and Israel's invasion of the Sinai Peninsula after Nasser closed the Suez Canal. At times of national crisis, the American people tend to rally around the leader they already have. The result was a landslide for Eisenhower and Nixon over Stevenson and Kefauver, who carried only seven states, losing even Illinois, and earned just 73 electoral votes to Ike's 457. Dawn spent election night running around fact-checking a concession speech and trying to find someone to type it.

After the election, Dawn worked out of Stevenson's law office for several weeks putting together a volume of speeches from the 1956 campaign. She was chosen for the task because she had done the research for the speeches and knew them better than anyone else. She agrees with Willard Wirtz that the 1956 speeches did not have the wonderfully unique quality of the speeches from 1952. "The way he spoke in '52 was something you never heard from a presidential candidate except maybe Lincoln," she says. Yet a publisher was waiting, so Dawn worked to get the best available version of each speech and compile them for submission. By working in his law offices, Dawn came to know Stevenson better than she had before. He was in and out of the office on a regular basis, and she accompanied him to dinner on a number of occasions. She remembers him as "utterly charming [with] a wicked sense of humor . . . at times a self-deprecating sense of humor."[11]

After finishing her work for Stevenson, Dawn did not seek legal work in Chicago right away. What she wanted to do instead was to go to the Middle East. The area had fascinated her since college because of its millennia of history and the tensions there. While clerking for Judge Hoffman, she even took an evening course in ancient civilization at Northwestern to feed her continuing interest. She very much wanted to visit the ancient monuments and understand more about the area first-hand, but because she did not have money to travel, she needed to find work there. Before leaving Washington, she had gone to various associations involved in Middle Eastern or Arab affairs trying to locate a position. One of Stevenson's speechwriters had worked for the Arabian American Oil Company and tried to use his connections to find something for her. He also talked to the American University campuses in Beirut and Cairo, to no avail. "Dawn," he finally said, "people who have been there for eons are pulling their people out [because of the Suez crisis]. Why would they send you? You don't speak the language; you have no background."[12]

Dawn did not give up for some time after the campaign was over. She persisted in trying every avenue she could think of to get herself to the Middle East. She asked a law school classmate to contact a friend of his who worked for an oil company in Beirut, but his efforts bore no fruit (the contact suggested she write to the legal department of Socony in New York, but Dawn was not interested in practicing law).[13] Professor William L. Cary at Columbia Law School, who had been a professor at Northwestern when Dawn was a student, tried to help her get a position as assistant to a colleague who was leading an exchange program to Turkey.[14] Despite Dawn's determination, none of the efforts was successful. Eventually she had to face the fact that her time in the Middle East was not going to happen, and by late winter, her money was running out. So when she got an offer to join the Chicago law firm of Snyder, Chadwell, Keck, Kayser & Ruggles, Dawn accepted. (She hired a private tutor to instruct her in Arabic while she worked there nonetheless.)

The firm was located in the Field Building at 135 South LaSalle Street, the heart of the financial district, one of the finest art deco office buildings in the city. It was the preeminent antitrust firm in Chicago, the one to which New York firms referred business. One of the named partners was the father of Connie Chadwell, Dawn's friend from the 1952 Stevenson campaign, but Dawn's job came through the good offices of Jim Rahl, her antitrust professor at Northwestern Law School, who was of counsel at the firm. "Networking and connections [are] what life is about," says Dawn. "I can't imagine a life in which persons you know are a crime to hire."[15] Of course, Dawn also had experience in the antitrust field from her work for Tommy Austern at Covington & Burling.

The Snyder, Chadwell firm was small but experiencing a burst of growth at the time it hired Dawn. John Chadwell was an outstanding trial lawyer and had become well known after litigating several large antitrust cases. As that area of the practice exploded, the firm hired ten new lawyers in two or three years. Nonetheless, the firm remained quite small, with fewer than twenty partners and even fewer associates, so that the junior and senior lawyers worked closely together. The younger lawyers lunched together and socialized frequently, but Richard Rhodes, an associate with Dawn, does not remember her participating in the socializing, probably because she spent all her spare time on politics. The other lawyers liked her. Rhodes remembers her as "a very proper lady, almost British; she would use proper language rather than slang. At the same time she was very warm and friendly. You always respected her intelligence and knowledge, her ability to think. Working with her on cases was a pleasure."[16] Another young lawyer at the firm remembers that he would talk a lot about baseball with Dawn, who was by then a Chicago White Sox fan. Once she told him that she had three major interests—"the Chicago White Sox, the Democratic Party, and the law, in that order."[17]

There was not a lot of time left over for socializing. Both Rhodes and Dawn worked long hours every day, often coming in on weekends and putting in an occasional all-nighter when a brief was due. Some of the work that paralegals do today was then performed by junior associates, who might end up at the printer's office in the middle of the night proofing briefs to be filed the next day and later taking them to the courthouse to file. Dawn typically ran down to a restaurant on the first floor or to a nearby fast-food counter to get meals to bring back to the office.

With her background in antitrust law from Covington, Dawn was immediately put on the case challenging the merger of Owens-Illinois and National Container. In October 1956, Owens-Illinois Glass Company, the leading glass container maker in the United States, had acquired National Container Corporation, the third-place maker of paper containers. In mid-December, the Justice Department filed an antitrust suit, claiming that the merger gave Owens-Illinois a decisive competitive advantage over smaller companies and increased the tendency toward monopoly in the container field. Dawn was assigned to the team working under Chadwell to defend Owens-Illinois, which had its headquarters in Toledo. The associates on the case drafted memos about the law and the facts, trying to fit the two together to develop a defense. One of Dawn's tasks was to construct a long and detailed legislative history of just-revised section 7 of the Clayton Act, which prohibits mergers and acquisitions when the effect may be to lessen competition or create a monopoly.[18] In connection with gathering facts, Dawn also flew down to Georgia to see how paper was produced from the fast-growing pine trees planted for that purpose. After seeing how many trees it took to make paper, she became stingy about using paper from then on.

Snyder, Chadwell had never hired a woman before, but the year Dawn started it hired two, followed quickly by a Jew and a Catholic, at a time when other major firms in Chicago hired no women, Jews, Roman Catholics, or African Americans.[19] Other Midwestern firms were thus not accustomed to seeing a woman lawyer playing a role in a big anti-trust case. When Dawn went to Toledo to learn about the business at the Owens-Illinois headquarters, the senior partner of the Toledo firm with which Chadwell was cooperating was upset that a woman was working on his case. At early team meetings, he would refuse to look at Dawn or acknowledge her presence. Over time, Dawn's intellect and knowledge of the case brought him to like and respect her. Indeed, a number of years later, Jean Allard, now a prominent Chicago attorney, moved to Toledo and interviewed with that same firm for a job, only to be told by the same attorney, "If you're anything like Dawn Clark, you can't be all bad."[20] So it was that Dawn broke paths for other women who followed. She considers this evidence that once you work with people who are hostile—even old-school, conservative types—barriers come down. This certainly seems to have worked for her, but other women and African Americans have not always had the same experience.

While waiting for the barriers of discrimination to fall, a thick skin is necessary—to sit through meetings where a leading participant will not even acknowledge your presence, as happened to Dawn in Toledo, for example. Sex discrimination interfered in other ways as well. While the associates working on the Owens-Illinois case were regularly included in team meetings, sometimes discussions took place over lunch, usually at the Midday Club, which excluded women. On an ordinary day, Dawn did not mind being left behind at lunchtime; she assumed that the male attorneys were talking about golf, and she could get a lot of work done while they were gone. But one day the group was gone for a very long time and made some major decisions about the case at lunch without her input. This infuriated Dawn, especially because she had been doing the investigation of facts and knew more about the issues involved than the men. She told John Chadwell that in no uncertain terms, explaining how the decision they had reached did not fully reflect the facts. In summary, all parties could lose because of the exclusionary measures toward women.

The only other major problem Dawn had at Snyder, Chadwell arose out of the necessity for her to record her hours. Law firms bill their clients on the basis of the amount of time put in on a case, thus requiring all personnel to record exactly how much time they spend on each matter.

Dawn hated this practice, which made her feel regimented, and did not submit her time records regularly. The bookkeepers were always after her. Finally Chadwell himself called, begging, "You're driving the bookkeepers crazy; we can't send out any bills."[21] After that, Dawn tried to do somewhat better, but she was still terrible about submitting her time sheets.

Nonetheless, Dawn enjoyed her work at Snyder, Chadwell, even though it was sometimes burdensome and dull. She liked the people and the intellectual stimulation, although she was putting in hours that were too long for most human beings. She loved doing research, especially on legislative history; learning about how industries work; trying to come up with theories; and having input into decisions about cases. Before she left the firm, Dawn was told that they wanted to make her partner but did not know what to do because there was another woman and they felt they could not make one of them partner and not the other. (Of course, law firms have no trouble making one man a partner and not another.) But Dawn's heart was in government and things political. She had made every effort not to go back to practicing law and had never intended to practice law for her whole career. If she had, she says, she would have stayed at Covington & Burling, where the practice was more oriented toward government work.

In the meantime, Dawn poured herself into her after-hours political activities. The Committee on Illinois Government was a continuing commitment. But Dawn also began to get involved as an activist and organizer in her neighborhood. When she returned from Washington to her clerkship, Dawn had wanted to live in one of the twin brick apartment towers that were being built—the first new buildings to go up after World War II—at 1350 and 1360 North Lake Shore Drive, where Potter Palmer's immense nineteenth-century mansion had stood. The Palmer mansion was demolished in 1951, but the new buildings were not finished for several years, so Dawn lived in a studio apartment in the Streeterville neighborhood, at 201 East Delaware Place (now the Raphael Hotel), while waiting. Eventually she moved into a one-bedroom unit on the fourth floor of 1350 Lake Shore Drive. The two twenty-two-story luxury buildings stood, as their address suggests, right on the drive bordering Lake Michigan, between Schiller and Banks streets.

In the spring of 1958, Dawn helped organize the Schiller-Banks Democratic Club, which was open to any residents of the Twenty-third or Thirty-sixth precincts of the Forty-third Ward, which comprised the two buildings. Its constitution, which Dawn appears to have drafted, provided that the club's objectives were the following:

1. To support the Democratic Party and its principles;

2. To encourage and support Democratic candidates for public office who are dedicated to the achievement of good government;

3. To inform the voters of the record, programs and ideals of the Democratic Party and its candidates;

4. To encourage more active participation in and support of the program of the Democratic Party.[22]

Unlike CIG, which was primarily a research group, Schiller-Banks was an explicitly political and activist organization. It decided in January 1959 to affiliate with the Democratic Federation of Illinois, a movement of independent Democrats that Dan Walker and others had organized as a confederation of clubs throughout the state. Victor de Grazia was now DFI's executive director and Walker its president. In 1958 and 1959, DFI was very active, holding highly publicized statewide conventions with keynote speakers such as Eleanor Roosevelt.[23]

The Schiller-Banks organization began to hold meetings and bring in speakers, typically either state or national politicians. When they invited Senator Paul Douglas to come, it was clear that a large apartment would be necessary to hold all the people who would want to meet him and hear what he had to say. Dick Lobel, a member who was an architect, often made his apartment available but for some reason could not for this particular event. He recommended that Dawn call and ask another architect he knew if they could use his apartment, the penthouse at 1360 North Lake Shore Drive. That architect was Walter Netsch. Dawn thought this was a good idea because people would come not only to hear the speaker but also to see the interior of the penthouse, where Netsch was reputed to have a great deal of interesting art.

Netsch, a tall, skinny, bespectacled man in his late thirties, was already a well-known architect by the late 1950s. When Dawn went to call on him, she found him with an associate down on the floor sketching out the stained glass window for the Air Force Academy Chapel, an extraordinary building designed by Netsch in Colorado Springs, Colorado. Netsch described his first meeting with Dawn:

> She knocked on the door and came in. I had my Mies [van der Rohe] chair and stools. She sat on the Mies stool, got out a cigarette, and looked out at the little garden. The cigarette holder startled me; it had a filter in it. She explained that a man in the

penthouse in her building told her to get in touch with me, that she wanted to hold a Democratic Party event here. She had a sort of English accent; I noticed that. She saw the art, big paintings, and she said, "People will love to come here to see it." I said, "Sure, I'll let you have it; I'll let either party have it." She gulped.[24]

When the event took place, Walter was out of town and simply gave Dawn the key to his apartment. The meeting was so successful that the club kept on holding meetings there, and Netsch himself gradually got involved, both with the Democratic Party and with Dawn.

The Schiller-Banks Democratic Club was located on the edge of the Forty-third Ward, run by its notorious old-style party boss, Mathias "Paddy" Bauler. Bauler held court on a daily basis in his brother's saloon at North and Sedgwick avenues and is best known for his pronouncement "Chicago ain't ready for reform." He was not particularly interested in the welfare of the Democrats living along the lakeshore rim of his ward. In 1959 Frank Fisher, a CIG member and son of Walter Fisher from the Stevenson administration, decided to challenge Bauler for his aldermanic seat. Dawn and her friends from both Schiller-Banks and CIG threw themselves into Fisher's campaign, trying to work the whole ward, parts of which were rough at that time. The contest captured the attention of the media, as they focused on the Ivy League socialite lawyer taking on tough old Paddy Bauler, who had controlled the territory since 1933. Fisher, thirty-two years old, declared that the ward had "had enough of Paddy and his do nothing attitude after 24 years. . . . Deterioration in the ward must be stopped thru [sic] conservation and proper zoning and I think I can do it."[25] Bauler, sixty-eight years old, shot back, "I've seen them come and I've seen them go. It will be win or go broke for me this time and I don't think the people will forget me."[26] Though clearly relying on his dispersal of patronage jobs and favors to get him reelected, the *Chicago Tribune* reported that Bauler also "went to the mayor's office with a group of women who were protesting the closing of a school damaged by fire. He supported the protests wholeheartedly, something he has seldom done."[27]

Dawn was president of the Schiller-Banks Democratic Club in 1959 and was in charge of running the Fisher campaign in the two precincts it encompassed, assigning campaign workers to floors and apartments. They worked the precinct just as the machine did, going out with lists of registered voters, knocking on doors to talk about Fisher's virtues, and coming back to report the likely plus and minus votes. William McCormick Blair, Governor Stevenson's aide and, at that time, his law partner, chaired the Fisher campaign and joined in the efforts at 1350 Lake Shore Drive, where he lived. When other volunteers had trouble getting residents of the high-rise apartments to open their doors, Bill Blair, the attractive young scion of two socially prominent Chicago families, never had a whit of difficulty. Walter Netsch got involved in the campaign as well.

The Frank Fisher campaign printed and distributed brochures reminis-cent of many used in the Stevenson campaigns, trained and deployed poll watchers, held coffees and open houses, placed ads in the local Spanish-language newspaper, and gained the endorsement of the *Chicago Daily News*.[28] In his campaign, Fisher emphasized the number of dilapidated or substandard housing units in the ward, the crime rate, and the general deterioration of the community in the face of Bauler's longtime inaction. By contrast, Paddy Bauler's literature simply emphasized his long tenure as alderman and the open-door policy at his saloon-headquarters. When the polls closed on February 24, 1959, Bauler had won. But the polling places at 1350 and 1360 Lake Shore Drive came in for Frank Fisher by a vote of 724 to 28. Maybe Chicago wasn't ready for reform, but it was coming.

In 1960 there were two major electoral races—for president of the United States and for governor of Illinois. The 1960 Democratic National Convention in Los Angeles that July was the first that Dawn attended as an active participant, though she was not a delegate. Numerous Draft Adlai committees had formed throughout the year, although Stevenson himself refused to state outright that he was running for president. He appeared to want a genuine draft, however.[29] Dawn thought the like-lihood of this happening was low, because by the time of the conven-tion, John F. Kennedy had received commitments from a large number of delegates; but she went out to California at the last minute nonetheless. Dawn and other friends from the previous Stevenson campaigns, from CIG, and from DFI launched a last-ditch attempt to persuade delegates to nominate Stevenson again. Paul Butler, chair of the Democratic National Committee, assigned the Stevenson group to a small suite while Kennedy had an enormous one; according to Jim Alter, everyone called their quar-ters the "Butler's pantry."[30] Adlai Stevenson III was placed in charge of convincing his father, who was on the Illinois delegation but sequestered somewhere, to accept if he got the nomination. Victor de Grazia was in charge of strategy and assigned volunteer troops to different states, giving

them a list of potentially friendly delegates to visit and convince. Because
the delegates were spread out at different hotels in the Los Angeles area,
the taxi fares were expensive.

Dawn did her part:

> We found delegates in their delegation offices or, if you had
> some identified to go see, you'd look for them. You'd introduce
> yourself, say you're there working for Governor Stevenson, and
> say why you thought he ought to be the nominee—and that he
> could win election in a way Kennedy could not. You were looking
> not for a firm "yes" or "no" but what we call in Chicago the pluses
> and minuses when you go door to door to get a sense of where the
> person was. . . . My recollection was that a lot would either say,
> "Nope, I'm for Kennedy" or weren't about to say. You can usually
> pick up a sense of where they were.[31]

The sense Dawn was getting was that a Stevenson nomination was a lost
cause. Her reports to this effect served to isolate her from others in the
delegation headquarters who were absolutely convinced that Stevenson
would be nominated and did not want to hear anything to the contrary.

The efforts of Stevenson's friends, of course, were ultimately unsuccessful, as John F. Kennedy received the nomination for president on the
first ballot and chose Lyndon B. Johnson as his running mate. Numbers
of Dawn's friends from Illinois absented themselves from the convention
during Kennedy's acceptance speech, distancing themselves by going to a
party at a swimming pool in Beverly Hills. Dawn reluctantly went along
but left early. When she returned to Illinois, she worked to elect Kennedy
that November. Stevenson was honorary chair of Illinois Lawyers for
Kennedy, and Dawn was on the committee for Cook County. Illinois
turned out to be a decisive state that year.

Dawn's lasting memories from the 1960 convention involve encounters
with Eleanor Roosevelt and John F. Kennedy. Roosevelt was Stevenson's
most loyal supporter and was intensely involved in the lobbying efforts
on his behalf. One day she visited the little headquarters to which the
Stevenson staff had been assigned. "You had the feeling that you were in
the presence of someone very, very special," remembers Dawn. "It wasn't
because she was so good-looking or charismatic in today's sense of the
term; she just was a presence—in part because you read into it all the
things she had stood up for all of those years."[32]

The encounter with Kennedy, by contrast, was amusing. The Stevenson headquarters was next door to an office where the South Carolina delegation had been having a caucus about whom to support. Kennedy had met with the delegation and was trying to escape through a side door to avoid the press. The side door led right into the office where Dawn was, startling them both. "He looked around and didn't know where he was. I said 'Hello, Senator Kennedy, welcome to the Stevenson Headquarters; you're always welcome to come in,' and I showed him the way to get out safely," sneaking past the press who were lying in wait.[33]

The Illinois gubernatorial election had more of an impact on Dawn's life. As early as February, the Schiller-Banks Club hosted an informational session about the three declared candidates for the Democratic nomination: Otto Kerner, formerly the U.S. attorney for the Northern District of Illinois and then a state court judge; Joseph D. Lohman, a sociology professor at the University of Chicago who had been Cook County sheriff and state treasurer; and Steve Mitchell, a former Stevenson aide and Democratic Party national chair from 1952 to 1955.[34] The members of the Committee on Illinois Government were split among the three candidates. Dawn supported Kerner and worked in his campaign, helping, among other things, to organize Career Women for Kerner. The members of CIG met with Kerner during this period to give him some of their research and ideas. When he succeeded in unseating the Republican Governor Stratton in November, there was at last a possibility for change. But Kerner had come out of the machine, the son of one of former mayor Anton Cermak's Czech supporters, and the CIG was not sure what to expect from his administration.

This feeling intensified after Kerner took office in January 1961. One day, a group was sitting around the CIG office, one room with some hand-me-down furniture at 30 North Dearborn Street. Jim Otis was there, as were Adlai Stevenson III, Jim Moran, and Dawn. They were discussing their feeling that nothing substantive was coming out of the new Democratic administration in Springfield and concluded that they needed someone there to do something about it. As Dawn describes, "Everyone looked around the room. Who was going to go to work for Kerner? It ended up with all eyes on me, because most of them had families and budding careers. I was single and had no family responsibilities, so I was the one who could pack up and move to Springfield."[35]

This made sense to Dawn. CIG had spent a great deal of time and effort generating ideas and programs, and now it needed someone in the new governor's administration to make sure that some of the things were accomplished. "My station in life was to go to Springfield as a representative of liberal progressive government."

———— *Chapter 8* ————

Springfield and Governor Kerner

DAWN CLARK WORKED AS one of Governor Otto Kerner's chief aides for four years, from early 1961 to early 1965. Kerner was the grandson of immigrants from what was to become Czechoslovakia. His father, Otto Kerner Sr., was an upwardly mobile lawyer, and the ascendancy of Mayor Anton Cermak in Chicago Democratic politics had facilitated his career. Cermak, also a Czech, put together Chicago's disparate ethnic groups into a powerful multiethnic coalition and built a disciplined and centralized party through the use of patronage.[1] Otto Kerner Sr. was elected first as Democratic alderman, later as judge on the Cook County Criminal Court, then as Illinois attorney general; and in 1938 he was appointed to a seat on the U.S. Court of Appeals.[2] Otto Kerner Jr. was sent to Brown University and Cambridge, then returned to Chicago for law school at Northwestern. He married Helena, daughter of the recently assassinated Mayor Cermak. After service in the military during World War II, his rise within the Democratic Party in Chicago was meteoric—U.S. attorney by 1947 and a Cook County judge in 1954. He made a name for himself in the late 1950s as a champion of both adoption reform and reform in the mental health system. He was also very handsome—"the state's first ready-made television candidate"—ideal for slating as the machine's candidate for governor in 1960.[3]

When Kerner defeated Stratton in 1960, this brought the potential for a good deal of change to Springfield. He also brought one large incubus—his longtime friend (and ultimately his downfall) Theodore Isaacs. Isaacs and Kerner had been close ever since they had served in the National Guard together, and Kerner trusted Isaacs implicitly. He was Kerner's closest aide while he was governor. Others have described Isaacs as "a Rasputin or Svengali-like character in Kerner's life who exploited his undue influence over the governor and led him astray."[4] Kerner named Ted Isaacs director of revenue in 1961, although Isaacs continued to solicit private law clients who did business with the state, seemingly a conflict of interest.[5]

Kerner knew little about the workings of the Illinois legislature and executive agencies when he took office, so when someone from CIG suggested that he engage Dawn Clark as his assistant to help with such matters, he agreed. Dawn left her job at Snyder, Chadwell and was in Springfield by late February (Kerner was inaugurated in January), taking a big cut in pay. Armed with a legislative program that her CIG buddies put together, she arrived before the new governor delivered his State of the State address, which would be given somewhat late that year. She joined a relatively small staff, with the title of assistant to the governor, and was given a large office that had once been the governor's office.[6] It was close to the current governor's office on the third floor of the immense state capitol.

Setting aside the problem of Ted Isaacs, Dawn liked working for Kerner; she liked him as a person as well:

> He was very gentlemanly, perfectly nice, cordial, accessible, not a go-for-the-jugular politician. He was willing to listen. When we were putting together the legislative program, he went along with us on a very enlightened program, especially on the bill review process. There were a couple of places he wasn't going to tread, like the income tax, but on civil rights and civil liberties he was very good. He was easy to work with.[7]

Tasks that an army of personnel performs today were executed by a handful of people at that time. Among Dawn's many responsibilities were developing legislation and reviewing the legislative program; reviewing all bills at the end of the legislative session to determine whether the governor should sign or veto them; reviewing legislative proposals from state agencies; recommending appointments to unpaid boards and commissions; and, by the second half of Kerner's first term, reviewing recommendations from the pardon and parole board. Because one person could not possibly do all of these things, Dawn pulled in people from outside to help, such as friends from CIG and scholars attached to the University of Illinois and its Institute of Government and Public Affairs.

Legislative Program

The Illinois legislature met in biennial sessions, so that most legislation was introduced between January and June of 1961, 1963, and so on. The governor put forth his program in the State of the State address typically in February and submitted a budget in March. Dawn helped introduce many of the measures she had advocated as a member of CIG, such as the establishment of a fair employment practices commission and of a capital development board for long-range planning and budgeting and mental health reform. She also worked to establish a board of higher education to integrate the various branches of the state university that were competing for funding. Although the capital development board failed to pass, the other initiatives were successful.

Kerner was very receptive to the legislative proposals Dawn put forward. On some things, they had been thinking along parallel lines. The poor condition of the public mental health system in Illinois had long been a concern of both—of Kerner from his experience as a judge doing commitment proceedings in Cook County and knowing the terrible conditions in the institutions to which he was sending people, and of Dawn from her expertise as the CIG specialist in that area.[8] The Kerner administration quickly replaced Governor Stratton's director of public welfare and began the work of reform. Legislation to create the Department of Mental Health was passed, and Francis Gerty, a prominent psychiatrist, was persuaded to undertake the reform of the system, assisted by Lowell Sachnoff, a young lawyer who was a CIG member.[9] In short, Dawn was able to see some of the ideas she had advocated for a long time come to fruition.

Illinois set up the Fair Employment Practices Commission during Kerner's first two years in office as well, among the last of the northern industrial states to do so. This was the first civil rights legislation in Illinois. Dawn worked hard to come up with the right mix of people to appoint to the first FEPC, and she describes Kerner as having made some "very gutsy" initial appointments to this board. The Illinois Senate rejected one of them, Earl Dickerson, a prominent African American lawyer and businessman, in committee because they perceived him as too much of a leftist. Dawn felt badly when that happened. Dickerson, a wonderful human being, comforted her that day. "Oh, Dawn," he said, "don't worry about it. They can't hurt me. Their vote can't take away from me what I know I've done and what I am."[10] Even though Kerner was liberal on many issues, the Illinois General Assembly was not, and it refused to pass the open housing legislation introduced in the next session as well, despite Dawn's literally begging legislators to vote for it.

Votes in the Illinois legislature divided, in part, along party lines, with Republicans dominating both downstate and in the collar counties, the areas around Cook County. Moreover, the Cook County Democratic Organization largely controlled the votes of the Democratic Party members. Interesting situations would arise where the governor's position and that of Mayor Richard J. Daley differed. On important issues, Dawn remembers Kerner as willing to stand up to the mayor, telling his followers in the legislature that he was the governor of the whole state and that the mayor of Chicago represented only one part of it.

In other cases, divisions in the legislature arose simply because legislation affected various areas and interests differently. The bill to establish the board of higher education, for example, succeeded because the expansion of Southern Illinois University, whose president was influential with the legislature, had threatened the main campus of the University of Illinois at Urbana-Champaign. An independent board to plan and coordinate the growing system of universities and colleges in the state seemed a better approach than simply expanding in response to regional or political pressure and ending up with duplicative programs. It was important that the first board be composed of people who would garner respect. In her role of overseeing appointments to boards and commissions, Dawn labored to put together a balanced first board, going so far as to draw up a huge chart with columns for candidates' geography, age, sex, background, and public-private diversity, and then selecting persons to fit the blanks. She advocated appointing Ben Heineman, the lawyer who had been close to Stevenson, as its first chair and Dick Nelson, Stevenson's aide and a CIG member, as second in command. Fortunately both men accepted with little persuasion.

To succeed in passing most measures, it was important to attract Republican votes. Although it was Dawn's job to focus on the substance of legislation (another staff person was the official liaison with the legislature), from time to time she was directly involved with legislative relations because she was the person most familiar with the substance of a bill. Part of the administration's program, for example, was the escheat bill, under which any unclaimed property would revert to ownership by the state. The questions for decision included what types of property would be included, the length of time before property would escheat, and what the property would then be used for. Dawn became heavily involved in this issue, which required dealing with W. Russell Arrington from Evanston, the Republican leader of the state senate. Arrington was notorious for being hard to get along with, arrogant, and condescending. Dawn was a match for him, though, just as she had been for Tommy Austern at Covington & Burling. Arrington quickly realized he was dealing with someone who was very intelligent, knew what she was talking about, and—probably most important—would stand up to him. They had what she describes as "a great in-your-face working relationship."

Arrington was not opposed to the escheat bill in general, but he represented the interests of banks, which wanted the period during which the money sat in their vaults before reverting to the state to be as long as possible. The administration started from the position that this period should be five years but compromised at seven. The issue remained as to how to spend the money. There was no way to know how much would come in, and Arrington thought the accumulation would be very large. Dawn thought the amount would be much less and was adamantly opposed to building it into the revenue base, when it would not recur at the same level after the first year. She and the people she was consulting at the University of Illinois' Institute of Government and Public Affairs came up with the idea of putting the escheated funds into the state's unfunded pension liability (the cost of future retirement payments to current state employees for which adequate funds had not been set aside), and that was the happy resolution. Dawn discovered that she loved getting involved in figuring out, and negotiating solutions to, dry public policy issues like this one, in part because she knew that dry issues often had important consequences for individual human beings.

Dawn's involvement in Governor Kerner's legislative program was not without problems. For one thing, Kerner met weekly with the Democratic Party leaders in the executive mansion to go over the legislative agenda so that they could prepare a list of administration bills. Dawn was never invited to these meetings, in part because Helena Kerner objected to her presence. By this period, Helena Kerner had become a disturbed personality and was known to be an alcoholic. She was exceedingly jealous of others who spent time with her husband, including Ted Isaacs, but her irrational fears about Dawn appear to have been especially severe.[11] "I avoided her," Dawn says, "and everyone agreed I should stay out of her path as much as possible." A crisis arose when Kerner took Dawn along to a governors' conference out of town in 1962. Helena made an incoherent phone call to Dawn's hotel room at 2 A.M. Her erratic behavior convinced Kerner to have his wife admitted to a hospital for evaluation.[12]

Old-style politicians like Paul Powell, a Democratic leader in the Illinois House from southern Illinois, also did not want Dawn to attend the weekly meetings for some reason. Sex discrimination is a possible explanation. Powell was also a politician who later was found to have been on the take; after his death in 1970, shoeboxes filled with $800,000 in cash were found in his Springfield hotel room. So perhaps Powell did not want Dawn there because she was too honest. The presence of a woman in a position of great influence close to the governor elicited resistance from other quarters as well, including from female secretaries and staff members, who found Dawn an alien being, with her formal way of talking and her cigarette holder.[13]

Kerner, however, was supportive of Dawn's relationship to the legislature and even sent her to the National Conference of State Legislative Leaders' meeting in Nevada. While there, Dawn improved her relationship with Paul Powell by teaching him how to play blackjack at the gaming tables, and he stayed up all night obsessed with the game. Dawn displayed her well-known integrity after the conference. On the plane home, lobbyists accompanying the group told her to give them her bills so they could pay them, as they were obviously doing for some of the legislators. Dawn refused and reported this to the governor after she had turned in her own receipts for reimbursement by the state. Kerner told her that she was absolutely right to do so.[14]

Veto Messages

After the legislative program was prepared early in the first year of the legislative session, bills were submitted to the General Assembly by a deadline, usually at the end of March. Any bill then was required to go through committee hearings before going to the floor, and to survive second and third readings in its house of origin before the same process was repeated in the other house of the legislature. Almost all the most important legislative work was accomplished in the last several weeks of the legislative session, which ends on June 30 of each year. (If the legislature has not completed its work, the clock is stopped at midnight on June 30 until it does.) After the legislature adjourned, some 1,400 to 1,600 bills that both houses passed at the end of the session were sent to the governor, who had to decide whether to sign them or to veto them. The constitution provided ten days within which he was to do so.

There was no established procedure for how to review all these bills and make careful decisions about them in such a short time. Dawn devised a plan that took advantage of the skills of her old colleagues at CIG and others. She approached Jim Otis, who was then involved in a heavy litigation practice at a big law firm, and told him she needed help. She asked whether he could come down to Springfield for a period. Otis agreed to approach his firm to see whether he could take time off for the project. Even though the firm was predominantly Republican and some senior partners were reluctant, they ultimately decided that it was a good opportunity to learn about state government at the highest level and gave him permission.[15]

Dawn approached other friends and allies and managed to recruit a team of lawyers—Willard Lassers, Claude Soule, Harry Golter, Jim Moran, and Harold Katz (a labor lawyer she did not know but whom members of the governor's staff had recommended). She talked them into coming down to Springfield for periods ranging from long weekends to a week or more, paying them minimal expenses and putting them up in double rooms in a cheap hotel. Moran, later a federal judge, describes the terms of engagement:

> I'd take a train down, get down there about 9:00. Go to the Capitol, work until about midnight, then Jim Otis and I were sharing a room at the—I can't even remember the name of the hotel; it was a dump. We shared a bath with some salesman who had an adjoining room. The wallpaper, I remember, was peeling off the walls. But it didn't really make much difference because we were hardly there anyway. So at midnight we'd go back to the hotel. On Friday we'd be back at the capital at 8:00, work through lunch, break for about an hour and a half in the late afternoon. We'd all get together for a couple of drinks and supper, then go back till about midnight, and do the same thing on Saturday and then on Sunday until about 4:00 in the afternoon, and then catch the train and get home at about 11:00 at night. Then I'd go to work at Bell Boyd the next day and sleep at my desk.[16]

Otis also remembers that it was hot and humid as they worked during the summer months, in an era when there was little air-conditioning.

He remembers leaving the capitol one night at 2 A.M. and noticing as he walked in front of the rotunda that the big marble columns holding up the dome were dripping from the humidity.[17]

Dawn worked out an elaborate plan for reviewing the bills. She set up a comprehensive filing system with a folder for each bill that had passed; the folder contained all the amendments and any significant correspondence about the bill, including any attorney general's opinion as to its legality. The ten-day period the governor has to act on a piece of legislation after the session has ended starts to run only when the bill has been sent over to the governor's office by the relevant officials in the legislature. The practice was to send the bills once the governor said he was ready for them. Dawn arranged for the bills to be sent over in groups when she called for them, specifying which ones she wanted in each batch and grouping together different bills on the same or similar subjects.

Before calling for the bills to be sent, Dawn divided them up among her staff of friends for review, so that the work of review would be done before the veto period began to run. Each of her lawyer friends would receive a packet of bills. For each bill, they would do independent research; consult key interested people, such as the director or legal adviser for an agency and often the bill's sponsor or sponsors; and then dictate a memorandum describing the bill, discussing the issues, and recommending, with an explanation, whether the governor should or should not veto it. If the recommendation was to veto, they also drafted a several-paragraph veto message for the governor to send to the secretary of state.

Subject areas were divided among the team helping Dawn review the bills. Otis, for example, drew bills about horse racing and the regulation of trucks (because of his background at the Illinois Commerce Commission), and Moran did all the agricultural and civil rights bills. Because he had no expertise in agriculture, Moran sought out a friend who came from an old farming family in southern Illinois, who was not only knowledgeable but also trustworthy and had good judgment. Moran would discuss the agriculture bills with this friend until he was comfortable that he understood what a given bill was doing and how it would affect people. The process, he recalls, was exhausting but a great deal of fun. "There you were participating in government in a very meaningful way. I can remember me recommending a veto of essentially a flag salute bill. I wrote a veto message and [the governor] signed it, and the *Daily News* published it as their editorial the next day."[18] He could remember only two bills where Governor Kerner did not follow the recommendations of the group assembled by Dawn, one on a relatively minor matter and the other a politically hot issue for the Teamsters Union.

Kerner did not usually knuckle under to the Teamsters, though. Otis reviewed one bill that would essentially have exempted truck transportation in Cook County from regulation by the Illinois Commerce Commission and allowed truckers to charge whatever they wanted in that area. Familiar with the statutory background from his prior service on the Illinois Commerce Commission under Stevenson, Otis drafted a veto message; and the governor vetoed the bill even though the Teamsters threatened to withhold their support from him in the following election as a result.[19] Otis also recommended vetoes on state funding for a number of projects dear to the heart of the powerful downstate Democrat Paul Powell, and the governor went along.

Sometimes it required a good deal of work to discover what interests were at stake in a bill. A particularly interesting example was a bill to amend a slum clearance law that made municipalities liable for injuries inflicted in the course of destroying unsafe buildings rather than holding the contractor liable personally. The bill introduced in 1963 amended the earlier statute to insert the word *not,* thus turning municipal liability into municipal immunity. None of this was apparent from the face of the bill. Dawn assigned the bill to Otis, saying that it seemed strange. Otis spent a whole weekend researching the legislative history of the bill in the Illinois legislative archives, looking through reports until he found a committee report from the late 1940s that made clear that the new amendment diametrically opposed the purpose of the original legislation. He called the bill's sponsor to ask what it was about, only to be told that a constituent had asked him to introduce it and it had passed on the so-called consent calendar. The consent calendar is an omnibus package of presumably noncontroversial bills at the end of a legislative session, and everyone had voted for it without realizing what they were doing. After drafting a veto message, Otis called up his old CIG friend Abner Mikva, who was then in the legislature, and told him, "Some public watchdog you are!"[20] In short, without the careful review by Dawn's team of lawyers, bills benefiting special interests would have passed without anyone being the wiser. With their help, the governor could be sure that not only Dawn but also another highly competent lawyer had reviewed every bill, and all at very little expense to the state.

If the governor vetoed a bill, it was dead for almost two years because the legislature was not in regular session and was unlikely to put together the votes to pass it over the governor's veto in the fall. This presented problems for the governor and his staff as well. If there was an error in or last-minute amendment to a bill they supported, there was nothing to do but to veto it and wait until the next regular session of the legislature almost two years later to reintroduce a corrected version. For example, a bill to shorten the period of state residence necessary to vote, which the governor supported, came to him with a last-minute amendment that required three different periods for different types of elections, which would have made the process unworkable. Although he was very much in support of the bill, the governor was forced to veto it and wait two years to remedy the situation because it was not possible to strike out the portion unrelated to the intent of the bill. This experience led Dawn to begin research on the possibility of an amendatory veto, which was later included in the Illinois Constitution in 1970.[21]

Review of Agency Proposals, Appointments, and Review of Pardons and Paroles

The bill review and veto process took several months, well into September. In the fall, legislative proposals would come in from the various administrative agencies. Every agency was invited to make whatever proposals they thought important in their area, and their responses occasioned the next step in Dawn's duties related to legislation. Dawn read all the legislative proposals coming in from the agencies and selected those that seemed worthy of inclusion in the governor's legislative program during the next session. If substantive issues were involved, she would often seek input on them from people in the agency or others affected before presenting her findings to the governor to consider when putting together the legislative package to submit to the leaders of the General Assembly.

In the time left over from her work on legislation, Dawn worked on coming up with names of people for appointment to various boards and commissions. She also began, after a year or two, to review recommendations from the board that heard petitions for pardons and paroles. This process was both time-consuming and emotionally draining, as she sat up on the nights when people for whom either pardon or commutation was denied were executed. On the night Vincent Ciucci was electrocuted in March 1962, Dawn was left behind in the governor's office at the capitol to handle phone calls from death-penalty opponents, despite her personal opposition to the death penalty.[22] She told callers that the governor also opposed the death penalty but that it was the law of the state and they needed to try to abolish it. Dawn also wrote the statement for the governor commuting Paul Crump's death sentence later that same year.[23] Crump had become a cause célèbre for liberals after he wrote an autobiographical novel from prison.

Kerner's Second Term

In 1964 Otto Kerner was easily reelected governor of Illinois. At the same time, an unusually large number of liberal Democrats made it into the state legislature, including many of Dawn's friends. The circumstances were unusual. After the decennial census, the Illinois legislature did not manage to draw new legislative districts to reflect population changes in time for the 1964 election. (Kerner had vetoed the map the Republicans passed in the summer of 1963, and the legislators failed to put a new map together in time.) As a result, the election took place on what has been called the bedsheet ballot, for its size: all the candidates for all the legislative districts in the state were listed and elected at large. Each party slated candidates for two-thirds of the total number of seats, so that neither would fail to have at least one-third of the seats. Because the candidates needed to be elected by voters throughout the state rather than just in their own district, each party slated not only incumbents but also people with name recognition or ones who would be attractive for newspaper editors to endorse. Adlai Stevenson III headed the Democratic ballot, and Eisenhower's brother headed the Republican ballot. Stevenson and Jim Moran were both elected to the legislature, along with other progressives like Harold Katz and Harold Washington, the future mayor of Chicago. Democrats heavily dominated the new legislature, and many of the Republicans elected had attracted newspaper endorsements, so that the body that convened in January 1965 was of unusually high quality. Conditions were optimal for passing much of the legislative program that CIG had advocated for so long.

Given this opportunity, Dawn again called on her CIG friend Jim Otis and asked whether he could come down to Springfield and help her put together a program to submit to the new legislature. Otis obliged once again, going to Springfield right after Thanksgiving and staying almost three weeks. Dawn and Otis spent most of this period talking about matters of substance and trying to put together a comprehensive program for the governor to deliver in his State of the State address in the beginning of 1965. Otis did a first draft, and he and Dawn met for hours each day to discuss every issue covered in it. When Otis left on December 18 to drive his family east for Christmas, he left Dawn with a pile of paper several inches high, full of ideas; and she labored on through the holidays to get it in shape. Much of what they put together made it into Governor Kerner's 1965 State of the State address. "I can't recall anything that CIG had thought about that wasn't in there. If anything was left out, it was by accident," says Otis. "When he delivered the message, the *Tribune* went into a fit."[24]

Despite the auspicious circumstances created by the at-large election and the presence of her friends in the legislature, toward the beginning of Kerner's second term Dawn began to think about leaving her post. One reason was the continuing and pervasive influence of Ted Isaacs on the governor. He remained the governor's closest confidant and had constant one-on-one discussions of policy with him without including Kerner's top policy advisers. Isaacs came and went to the governor's office through a back door rather than entering through the formal reception area off the rotunda. "It was frustrating," Dawn says, "fighting this presence we could never quite reach out and touch. When we worked on the bills, we would just deal directly with the governor, but a couple of times we realized that Ted had gone in to see him behind our backs and not told us, but had had an influence on how some piece of legislation was treated."

Although the governor was receptive to the reform program Dawn was proposing for the new session, Isaacs determined that she should have nothing to do with Kerner's legislative program in the future. Dawn ultimately confronted Isaacs directly about this, telling him, "If I'm not going to have anything to do with the legislative program, I'm out of here."[25] And so, in the face of increasing isolation from the governor's inner circle, she resigned early in 1965.

The Downfall of Otto Kerner

Ted Isaacs drove Dawn away from her job, but his influence and ultimate impact on Otto Kerner had much more serious repercussions. Kerner resigned the governorship in 1969 to accept an appointment as a judge on the U.S. Court of Appeals for the Seventh Circuit, where his father had served from 1938 to 1952. In July 1970, however, two special agents from the Internal Revenue Service visited Judge Kerner in his chambers in the federal building and told him that he was under investigation for income tax violations. The transactions involved the purchase and sale of certain racetrack stock during his period as governor.

Marjorie Lindheimer Everett, owner of several racetracks, was a big contributor to Kerner's 1960 campaign for governor. After he was elected, Everett exercised a great deal of influence over appointments to the Illinois Racing Board.[26] She also distributed shares of racing stock to people who might help her company, including to Ted Isaacs and Otto Kerner. Isaacs and Kerner had been told that they were the beneficial owners of certain shares in late 1962, at a price of $1,000 a share, when the stock was worth $2,000 a share. Through an elaborate financing scheme using loans, the purchase price was never paid until the stock was sold in 1967, at a profit of $159,000 each to Isaacs and Kerner.

After coming into beneficial ownership of these shares, Governor Kerner was involved in allocating racing dates among Illinois racetracks and could have exercised his influence in a way that benefited the tracks in which he then had an interest. He was also involved in revising legislation in 1965 concerning the amount the state was owed from the receipts from horse racing. Moreover, applications for racing dates filed by the company in which Kerner and Isaacs held stock failed to reveal their beneficial ownership, despite a clear legal requirement to do so.

Information about these arrangements came to the attention of the IRS after Marj Everett reported the transaction as a long-term capital loss on her 1966 tax return; when the agency investigated, she described the arrangements with Kerner and Isaacs. Kerner had reported the sale on his 1967 return as a capital gain, but the IRS ultimately claimed that it was the proceeds of a bribe and thus ordinary income, which is taxed at a higher rate. When the IRS agents came to Judge Kerner's chambers, he compounded the problem by presenting an explanation that was demonstrably false and continued to do so to the grand jury investigating the matter in 1971.

Kerner and Isaacs were indicted for conspiracy and use of interstate facilities in furtherance of bribery, mail fraud, and tax evasion, and Marj Everett was the government's chief witness. Kerner was also charged with perjury for his false statements to the grand jury and with making false statements to IRS agents. The two were convicted after a six-week jury trial in early 1973. The Seventh Circuit affirmed their conviction on these counts in 1974, with all of the judges having disqualified themselves because they were Kerner's colleagues; judges from other circuits replaced them. Kerner always maintained his innocence, representing the stock transaction as a simple investment and arguing that the State of Illinois had never suffered from it. He was sentenced to three years in prison but was paroled in 1975 when he developed cancer. He died on May 9, 1976.

Dawn knew nothing about Kerner's and Isaacs' stock transaction when she worked for Kerner. After Kerner's indictment, Dawn and many others close to Kerner persisted in believing that Isaacs had misled him. She still believes that:

> It was Isaacs who got the governor in trouble. Race track stock was handed out all over the place in Springfield and they were given an opportunity to buy it. Marj Everett was offering this stock as a way of ingratiating, not necessarily as a bribe. Ted [probably] went in and said, "There's nothing wrong; it's a great opportunity; go ahead," to the governor. Kerner was so trusting of Isaacs and may not have thought it through clearly. There was never any real evidence that he fixed any of the racing dates, though he was not truthful to [government agents] when they first started talking to him and that easily made it seem scandalous.[27]

She contributed to efforts initiated by Kerner's children to get President Clinton to pardon Kerner posthumously before leaving office in 2000, contributing an affidavit to the following effect:

> I had the opportunity to observe and know Otto Kerner under a wide range of circumstances that confront a governor. And what I saw was a man of honor, caring and compassionate, willing to take courageous stands, politically and on sensitive issues, and a Governor committed to the highest standards of integrity. Everything that I observed was completely incongruous with his later conviction.[28]

—— *Chapter 9* ——

Walter Netsch

In early 1965, Dawn had other reasons for concluding that it was time to leave Springfield. In October 1963, she had married Walter Netsch, and her husband lived in Chicago. After their first meeting in connection with the Schiller-Banks Democratic Club in the late 1950s, Dawn and Walter had been spending more and more time together. Dawn was attracted to Walter because he was exceptionally bright and creative, with an impulsive enthusiasm. The two gradually grew close. Dawn took Walter to meet her dear friends Jim and Kay Clement in Hyde Park, and Walter took Dawn to Evanston to meet his sister and her husband. Nancy Stevenson says, "We were delighted when we began to see signs of this romance. We didn't sense she was looking for a husband. Dawn was a friend, and suddenly there were two of them—which was very nice."[1]

Walter was the grandson of German immigrants.[2] His father had won a scholarship to Dartmouth and ultimately became vice president of the Armour meatpacking company in Chicago. His mother came from a wealthy family and was a devout practitioner of Christian Science. Walter, born in 1920, grew up in comfortable circumstances in the South Shore area of Chicago and studied architecture at Massachusetts Institute of Technology. By the time he was twenty-seven, he was associated with the preeminent architecture firm Skidmore, Owings, and Merrill, where he remained for more than thirty years, most of them as one of the top equity partners.

Netsch's most famous work was the Air Force Academy in Colorado Springs, Colorado, and especially its chapel, a soaring building that has become one of Colorado's top tourist attractions and has been designated a National Historic Landmark. It has been described as "massed like a phalanx of fighter jets shooting up into the sky."[3] Many of the buildings Walter designed were for educational institutions, especially libraries, including the libraries at Northwestern and the University of Chicago, Wells College, and Sophia University in Tokyo. He created the master plan and designed all the original buildings for the new University of Illinois campus built at Chicago in the 1960s. He also did extensive design work for Massachusetts Institute of Technology, the University of Iowa, Grinnell College, and Miami University of Ohio, where he designed an art museum. As his fame grew, Netsch was in demand internationally and designed buildings in Saudi Arabia (a zoo that was never built), Algeria, Australia, Japan, and Iran. Netsch's unique contribution to architecture is known as field theory, a theory of design based on rotating geometric shapes sometimes radiating from a core and thus defining open spaces on multiple levels where light and space meet.[4]

When Dawn met Walter in the late 1950s, he was already a partner at Skidmore and had become quite well known for his designs both of the Inland Steel Building and the Air Force Academy Chapel. He had also begun collecting modern art. Beginning with trips to galleries, primarily in New York, in the 1950s, and acquiring works of artists before they became well known, he amassed an extraordinary collection of paintings and sculpture. He focused especially on abstract expressionist works, by painters such as Hans Hoffmann, Robert Motherwell, Gene Davis, and Roy Lichtenstein, though he also collected hard-edge painters like Ellsworth Kelly and Jack Youngerman, along with pop art pieces by Robert Indiana and sculptures by Richard Hunt and George Rickey.

When they began dating, Walter undertook to initiate Dawn into the world of art. He loaned her a huge modern painting to decorate her high-ceilinged office in the governor's suite at the state capitol. The reactions of those who saw it amused her. "I had this large abstract expressionist [painting], with reds flowing down. You can't imagine the comments, especially from downstate legislators," she says. "One said, 'Looks like somebody had a horrible automobile accident and there's blood all over the street.'"[5] The more Dawn saw and understood the work Walter collected, the more she liked it.

Dawn taught Walter in return about her own world of politics, and he responded with characteristic enthusiasm. He became very involved in Frank Fisher's campaign for alderman and loaned his apartment for Schiller-Banks functions often, including for viewing the 1960 Kennedy-Nixon debates. Dawn especially appreciated Walter's sense of fun. She remembers one escapade with particular pleasure. The two decided, on an impulse, to walk over to Paddy Bauler's office to pick up some election literature, which Bauler rarely bothered to distribute in the lakeshore precincts. She remembers it this way: "We walked in. He always held court in the room in the back of the bar, which was his ward headquarters. Someone led us back there, and we tried to introduce ourselves. He said, 'I know who youse are; youse are the ones who got that vote against me in that aldermanic.'"[6] He did give them some literature, though, but did not have everything they needed because he was not very interested in candidates for Congress.

Dawn and Walter also both loved baseball and in particular the Chicago White Sox. When Dawn went to work for Governor Kerner in early 1961, she rented an apartment in Springfield but kept her place in Chicago and would fly or take the train to Chicago on a regular basis on business and for weekends as often as she could. Walter would meet Dawn's plane and take her to Comiskey Park to see the White Sox play. "I would pick her up at the airport and take her to the ball game," he recalls. "She would have two hotdogs with onions and a beer and watch the ball game. Cheer—she cheers loudly. So it surprises me how she sort of forgets herself. I'm clapping and she's jumping. She really loves the game."[7]

Both Dawn and Walter were workaholics, with Walter working on commissions to design buildings all over the United States and the world. Yet somehow they carved out the time for a trip of several weeks to Turkey and Greece together in 1962, visiting Istanbul, Troy, and other ancient ruins along the coast—Dawn's first visit to the area of the world that had fascinated her since college. Along with art, travel was something that Walter offered Dawn in their life together.

Dawn's long reluctance about getting married, however, continued. She made it clear to Walter that she intended to work until the day she died. That was fine with him because he didn't intend that marriage should interfere with his career either.[8] Contemplating such a move, Walter gave up his penthouse on Lake Shore Drive and moved into a larger apartment at 20 East Cedar Street, near the lakefront, and began to fix it up. The apartments in this 1920s building had high ceilings, and the one he selected had a two-story living room, a separate dining room, two large bedrooms, a spacious entrance hall, and a small maid's room that became Dawn's office. The modern art Walter had been collecting adorned the walls. Dawn had no role in picking out or decorating the apartment. "When you're married to an architect," she says, "you get used to that."[9]

Still Dawn continued to waver on the question of marriage. Although they set a date in the fall of 1963, she was convinced that she would back out at the last minute and was rather embarrassed about taking the step at all. As a result, Dawn and Walter got married without telling anyone. Neither of their mothers was informed in advance, which took some appeasement later on. Dawn did tell Governor Kerner, to explain her absence, but none of their many friends. Among their closest friends were Jim Clement and his wife Kay. Kay was startled by this sudden turn of events:

> Dawn would come up from Springfield, and we'd get together often, for dinner or something. One week she said, "I'm not coming up; I'm staying in Springfield." Later I pulled onto Lake Shore Drive at Division and saw her walking down the street in a suit and hat! I thought, "That's strange; something must've come up. She would have no reason to lie to me." This was on Friday, and on Saturday the phone rang when Jim was in the shower. Dawn said, "Walter and I just got married."[10]

The wedding ceremony took place on Saturday, October 19, 1963, shortly after noon. Walter was forty-three, and Dawn, thirty-seven. Dawn's old employer, Judge Hoffman, performed the formalities in his chambers at the old Federal Building. Flowers filled the room, and the judge had written a nice, personal ceremony that was also brief. Walter's sister and her husband were the only witnesses, and they went back with the couple to 20 East Cedar Street for champagne after the ceremony was over. Walter and Dawn then caught a plane to Martha's Vineyard, where they spent a week walking on the beach and rowing in the autumn sun.

When the couple returned to Chicago, their friends took revenge. Soon after, when Dawn and Walter went to a football game at Northwestern with his sister and brother-in-law, they came back to his sister's Evanston home expecting to have a meal together. Instead, they encountered a surprise wedding reception, with law school classmates, friends from CIG, and Walter's architecture friends in attendance. Jim Otis remembers attending the surprise reception, but could not remember why he and Peg did not go to a wedding first.[11] Yet no one was surprised that Dawn and Walter had gotten married because everyone had become accustomed to them being together over such a long period.

Soon after the wedding, Dawn returned to Springfield, where she continued her job with Governor Kerner for the first year and a half of their marriage—an early commuting marriage. When she finally decided to leave Springfield and government service, she had no job lined up to go to. She had not decided what to do next. For the first time, however, she no longer had to depend just on her own salary for support. A period between jobs was unique in her life, so she and Walter decided to take advantage of it by indulging in another of their shared passions: they embarked on a two-month-long around-the-world trip.

At long last Dawn reached Egypt, and in style. They flew to Luxor and visited the ancient monuments she had longed for so long to see. They went to Abu Simbel, Luxor, Karnak, the Valley of the Kings, all before the Aswan Dam was completed and the monuments moved. Both Walter and Dawn were fascinated by ancient things but for somewhat different reasons. Walter was interested in them as evidence of how people construct their environment, the built world. Dawn's interest was not so much in the buildings themselves as in what archaeology reveals about ancient civilizations, with the monuments as clues to how they operated. (When asked what she would like to have done with her life if she had not gone into government and politics, being an archaeologist comes in a close second to having the talent to sing opera.)[12]

After several weeks in Egypt, Dawn and Walter flew to Iran to see Persepolis, capital of the ancient Persian Empire. From there they flew to Kabul, Afghanistan. Just after unpacking at the grand old hotel where they were staying, they went out to walk around. When they reached a large plaza, a car came screeching to a halt. Its door opened, and to their astonishment, Walter Schaefer (from Northwestern Law School and the Stevenson administration) greeted them. He was in town to work on modernizing the law for the king of Afghanistan. Dawn's legal and political career seemed to follow them wherever they went.

Most of the time, however, their trip focused on Walter's interests, as they met with famous architects he knew throughout the subcontinent. They had arranged to meet one young man who had worked for Walter and was now with the Peace Corps in Lahore, Pakistan. When fog made air travel out of Afghanistan impossible, they hired a car and driver with another couple and drove through the Khyber Pass, the thirty-three-mile passage through the Hindu Kush mountain range connecting the northern frontier of Pakistan with Afghanistan. The scenery was varied but invariably spectacular.

When they finally got to India, they spent their trip with some of the world's famous architects. They flew to Bombay, then took a train to Ahmedabad, the capital at that time of Gujarat state. Ahmedabad was their destination because it was the home and workplace of Balkrishna Doshi, one of India's most famous architects, with whom they stayed. Doshi, a student of Le Corbusier, supervised Le Corbusier's work in Ahmedabad and developed his own style, applying modern architecture in the Indian setting. He had founded a prestigious school of architecture and planning in Ahmedabad and a research institute that did pioneering work in low-cost housing and city planning. By 1965 he had visited the United States a number of times and had been a visiting professor in several American universities. Walter had known him for some time and had helped him get a grant from a Chicago foundation.

When Walter and Dawn arrived in Ahmedabad, Louis Kahn, the well-known American architect who collaborated with Doshi, was also there. The three architects spent a great deal of time talking architecture and Dawn accompanied them to visit buildings; Doshi also took them shopping for fabrics. When they went to New Delhi, Walter was involved in an international conference on architecture and planning, but they did manage to do some sightseeing together as well—to see the Red Fort and the Taj Mahal, for example. From Delhi they drove to Chandigarh, the city completely designed by Le Corbusier as a new capital for the Punjab, to replace Lahore, which had been lost to Pakistan in 1947. Dawn found the government buildings to be quite marvelous but their sad state of repair disappointed her, given that the planned city was only about a decade old.

After a month in India, Dawn and Walter went to Bangkok, Angkor Wat, and Tahiti before returning home to rest up before she started her new job, as a law professor at Northwestern.

—— *Chapter 10* ——

Teaching Law

WHEN SHE LEFT SPRINGFIELD, Dawn did not want to return to the practice of law. Working for a law firm was not what she wanted to do with her life; politics still beckoned. She had never thought about teaching law, although some of the members of the Northwestern faculty had raised the possibility with her. When frustration led Dawn to quit Governor Kerner's staff in early 1965, the idea of teaching began to interest her, and she discussed the possibility with Northwestern faculty member James Rahl. Rahl had been her antitrust professor and was of counsel to Snyder, Chadwell, where she had spent four years. He encouraged her to join the law faculty at Northwestern.

Dawn sat with Rahl in his living room, toting up the pros and cons of a teaching career. On the positive side, it would be an intellectually stimulating way of life, requiring her constantly to think and study and to spend time with bright young students. It also offered a flexible timetable, with freedom, within limits, to schedule her own days. On the down side, teaching was something entirely new to Dawn, and she would have to work hard to learn the craft and keep up with the subjects she taught. The ivory tower atmosphere of academe also seemed removed from the active world she enjoyed.

A professor's pay was comparatively low for an experienced lawyer like Dawn, but this was not a major factor now that she was not dependent solely on her own income. She could choose to do whatever she wanted. So when Willard Pedrick, chair of the appointments committee at Northwestern Law School, offered her an entry-level job, Dawn accepted, to begin in September 1965. She warned her new employer that she would continue to be involved in politics and government as well.

In 1965 there were few women law professors in the United States. Dawn was among six women hired into tenure-track positions that year, which marked a substantial breakthrough nationally. Only thirteen women had ever been law professors in the United States before the 1960s, and law schools hired a total of forty during that decade. It was only during the 1970s that women began to enter law teaching in significant numbers.[1] Dawn was the first woman hired at Northwestern Law School.

The faculty Dawn joined after returning from her around-the-world trip was more like the one she had known as a student than the one that exists today. Faculty members regularly lunched together in a well-appointed dining room in Abbott Hall, across Superior Street from the law school building, ordering off a menu and served by waiters. Jack Heinz, who also joined the faculty in 1965, describes Northwestern as having been a very collegial place.[2] The faculty was small—all but Dawn, white males—and its members interacted frequently. They socialized on a daily basis at lunch and at the law school, as well as carpooling back and forth to work and going to dinner at one another's houses often. Unlike today, when faculty often work at home, connected to the law school by computer, faculty members came to the school and worked there all day long every day.

Dawn found her new work environment pleasant after the hectic pace in Springfield and the tensions that had developed from the hovering presence of Ted Isaacs. Although she had enjoyed her work there, a quiet, nonconfrontational atmosphere made a nice change of scene. But Dawn was learning how to teach for the first time and striving to keep up with some subjects with which she was not familiar. New law professors taught four courses a year, two each semester, and could be assigned to any course the school needed taught, even if it was far removed from their area of expertise. Dawn came in with the understanding that she would teach antitrust law because she had so much background in that area, but she was also assigned to teach real estate transactions, about which she knew very little. She arranged to team-teach the real estate course with Jack Coons, her friend from law school, who had joined the faculty in 1955. Jack remembers this as a strange reversal of roles. While he had been so awed by Dawn when he arrived at Northwestern as a student, Dawn was now asking for his help.

The real estate course was divided into two sections, taught at different times, but Dawn would sit in on Jack's section to observe the approach of someone with more experience teaching the subject. She recalls preparing for class at home each night with "about seven different texts and treatises spread out around me in addition to the casebook. I worked ten times harder than the students to make sure I was getting it."[3] She would ply the experienced older professors with questions at lunch in Abbott Hall.

Dawn and Coons enjoyed collaborating on the real estate transactions course. On the last day of class, he made up a hilarious song, and they did a little soft-shoe dance for the students, about incorporeal hereditaments (a form of property consisting of hereditary titles). The hilarity one day was entirely unplanned, though. As Dawn was sitting in on Coons's class, he was discussing the concept of a bona fide purchaser, or good-faith purchaser, often referred to in law school as a BFP. Earnestly and vehemently, Coons loudly proclaimed to the class at the end of the session that they needed to "focus on the party's BFP-ness." The class sat in stunned silence as Dawn quickly left the room and returned to her office. Jack walked down the hall to see her and found her laughing so hard that she was crying.[4]

Dawn also team-taught antitrust law with Rahl as she started out, not by splitting up the section but by keeping the students together and splitting up the topics to be covered, the first time this had ever been done at the law school. Rahl was a respected authority in the antitrust field, and he was a tall, imposing—often described as Lincolnesque—character. Dawn would always attend Rahl's sessions although he did not need to attend hers. She enjoyed watching him teach. He was very scholarly, slow and methodical, and he took a long time to get through what he was trying to convey. Dawn's approach, by contrast, was more pragmatic, and her teaching style quite different. The combination seemed to work for the students, who gave the professors many compliments on the course. After a few years, the scheduling became too difficult, however, and each professor taught a separate section of the antitrust course.

From the very beginning, Dawn also taught two seminars—one on advanced antitrust law and one on state and local government. What began as a seminar in state and local government ultimately became a three-hour class. This, of course, was an area in which Dawn had a great deal of practical experience from her years in Springfield. She adopted a text called *Managing Our Urban Environment* by Daniel R. Mandelker, a law professor at Washington University in St. Louis. Eventually Mandelker called Dawn and asked whether she would like to coauthor a casebook with him. The result of their efforts was a 1,163-page tome, *State and Local Government in a Federal System,* published in 1977. The book has been through multiple editions by now and has six authors instead of just Mandelker and Netsch.[5] In the edition published in 2006, Dawn remained responsible for revisions to chapter 10, "The Role of the Judiciary," which covers occupational and professional licensing, reapportionment and voting rights, and school finance.

As soon as a more junior faculty member was assigned to teach real estate transactions, Dawn gladly dropped that course and designed the first course at Northwestern Law in race relations, which had, of course, been a particular interest of her own since college. The time was ripe for adding such a course. The civil rights acts had just passed in 1963, and the era of movements was on the country—the civil rights movement, the black power movement, the antiwar movement, and numerous offshoots. Inner-city riots and other political and social disturbances dominated the late 1960s. Dawn constructed a course that relied on Fourteenth Amendment equal protection law, which the basic constitutional law course at that time barely covered, and focused on the many issues growing out of the civil rights movement. She invited radical speakers to give guest lectures in the class from time to time. The students found the course fascinating because it involved law that was being developed at the very time they were studying it.

After she had been teaching for about six years, Dawn received tenure. The process at that time, as both she and Coons report, was not very elaborate. Coons received a visit from the dean, who told him that they wished he would write something so they could give him tenure. So he did write an article, and they gave him tenure. Dawn had only written a few pieces about state constitutional law by the time she was considered for tenure, for the most part background papers for the Illinois Constitutional Convention rather than the more traditional, heavily footnoted law review articles required in later years. If the requirements had been as onerous back then as they are now, Dawn is not sure she would have wanted to go through the tenure process. Although she writes easily and very well, the extensive research and writing required would have taken away from her time for politics and the public sector. In the early 1970s, however, tenure standards were different, and the faculty seemed to appreciate that Dawn was contributing to public life and bringing her experience back to the law school. When she was a student herself, she had wished that her teachers knew more about what went on in the real world, and that was something she was able to offer her own students.

After giving tenure to Dawn, the law school decided that it needed to recruit a second woman to join the faculty. The 1970s was the period during which law schools and law firms were successfully sued, under the new civil rights laws, for failing to admit and to hire women, and women were flooding into the profession. So the dean approached Dawn about helping him find some women candidates for the Northwestern Law faculty. Dawn began to compile a list of possible recruits by calling people she knew at other law schools to inquire about women who were either teaching already or who might be interested in teaching. After putting together a list of names, she tried to find out what she could about each one of them—not an easy task because many were not very well known. She recalls that some of the people she called at other law schools to ask whether they knew of any women looking to go into law teaching were surprised by the question and that "it was sort of fun to stir that pot up a little bit."[6]

The result of Dawn's recruiting efforts was the hiring of Joyce Hughes in 1975 as the second woman law professor at Northwestern. Hughes, who is African American, had previously been teaching at the University of Minnesota but was attracted to Northwestern in part by Dawn's political activism and the fact that the law school seemed to approve of it. (Hughes herself went on to be appointed to the Chicago School Board and ultimately to serve as general counsel of the Chicago Transit Authority under Mayor Harold Washington.) She describes Dawn as having been a beacon for her in many ways, not only intellectually and politically but also in the realm of style. "As we pass one another in the halls en route to teach our respective classes, I delight in the brilliance of her wardrobe and her flair with scarves and jewelry," Hughes reports.[7] Dawn had always been a stylish dresser, but marriage to Walter meant that she had more money to indulge her taste. She is invariably smartly dressed, wearing brightly colored suits adorned with large necklaces and colorful scarves.

True to her warning when she was hired, Dawn did not abandon her political involvements when she entered law teaching. Now that she was back in Chicago, she continued to work with the Committee on Illinois Government. Many of the original members made special attempts to revive its activities after they were shocked by the events at the 1968 Democratic convention, when the mayor ordered Chicago police officers to attack the demonstrators in the park. The group produced a number of documents and materials in the late 1960s, including the twenty-eight-page *Financing Public Education in Illinois: A Public Policy Analysis* in April 1969.[8] In 1970, CIG issued a thorough, detailed, and helpful campaign manual, with step-by-step instructions, seventy-two pages of them, on how to set up and run a political campaign, including models for petitions, press releases, and the like. Following these instructions, an independent candidate would have all the information he or she needed to take on the machine, as long as he or she could recruit workers and raise some money. In 1970 an organization of precinct workers was still the key to winning local elections in Chicago.

Dawn also undertook new political commitments in the latter part of the 1960s. In 1967 she became a member of the board of the American Civil Liberties Union of Illinois. Organized in the 1920s by luminaries such as Jane Addams and Clarence Darrow, the Illinois group had become one of the strongest chapters in the national organization with which it affiliated. It had been active in civil liberties and free speech issues throughout the 1930s and 1940s and had focused on opposing McCarthyism in the 1950s. After a radical period during World War II that had resulted in its ejection from the national group, the Illinois ACLU became more conservative in the postwar period, wedded to a narrow concept of civil liberties and to a strategy of filing friend-of-the-court briefs rather directly undertaking litigation by itself. By the time Dawn joined the board, the group was heavily involved in debates over this vision and this strategy.

The ACLU board met twice a month and was an active policy-setting board, deciding both what issues the group would undertake and how to implement the decisions—to push for legislation in Springfield, for example, to intervene in cases, or to initiate litigation on its own. Dawn was a very active member from the late 1960s to the early 1990s, even after she began to spend much of her time in Springfield. She was instrumental in helping to set up the ACLU's office in the state capital, and a staff attorney was hired to lobby there. According to Jay Miller, former executive director of the ACLU of Illinois, Dawn's advice with respect to the group's lobbying work was invaluable.[9]

Jay Miller remembers Dawn as perhaps the second woman on a board that consisted of sixty members. She was "very smart, quite intellectual, very together, a very impressive person," whose "voice and ideas carried a lot of weight" with the board. Dawn immediately began to have an impact on the group's internal debate over whether to embrace a broad or a narrow construction of civil liberties. One issue over which the ACLU board members were struggling was whether the right to abortion was properly within their purview as a civil liberties organization. Dawn played a role in convincing the board that it was, and she pushed the organization to become involved in the issue. She reports always having been clear in her own mind that a woman's right to choose fit within the ACLU's civil liberties perspective, although others on the board had to struggle their way through to reach that conclusion.[10] Serving on the legislative committee of the ACLU in the late 1960s, she helped draft legislation to decriminalize abortion in Illinois before the 1973 decision in *Roe v. Wade*.

In the late 1960s, the ACLU also began to play a major and direct role in the litigation of a variety of issues—not just defending persons whose civil liberties had been violated or filing amicus briefs but also initiating large class actions. One of these was *Doe v. Scott*, filed in the federal district court in Chicago to challenge the Illinois abortion law on a number of grounds—inequality of access to abortion based on class, the right of women to make the decision on their own as an inherent aspect of personal integrity and liberty, and the right of privacy. Members of the ACLU board favored arguing the case on privacy grounds alone, but the two feminist lawyers briefing and arguing *Doe* insisted on including the alternative arguments as well.[11] The plaintiffs included not only women but also physicians, on behalf of whom the ACLU attorneys argued that the criminal law against abortion was void for vagueness and thus violated the due process clause, because its language left doctors wondering what was and was not legally permissible.

The 1971 federal district court decision in *Doe v. Scott* found the Illinois abortion law unconstitutional both for vagueness and as a violation of "women's rights to life, to control over their own bodies, and to freedom and privacy in matters relating to sex and procreation," at least during the first trimester of pregnancy.[12] A physician on the ACLU board immediately performed an abortion after this decision, but the Cook County state's attorney quickly appealed and obtained a stay of the judgment until the higher court could rule. In January 1973, the U.S. Supreme Court reached a similar conclusion in *Roe v. Wade*, although on the narrow ground of privacy. Thereafter the Illinois ACLU became involved in case after case challenging antichoice legislation passed in the backlash to the Supreme Court decision. Indeed, the Reproductive Rights Project established by the ACLU in Chicago carried the largest docket of such cases in the nation. Thus, the issue Dawn had helped to persuade the group to take on became a central focus of its work, and the direct litigation strategy that she also supported became its main tactic. When she became a state legislator, however, the best she could do under the circumstances was to argue against the antichoice bills introduced on a yearly basis in Illinois, telling her fellow senators that it was a waste of time to pass laws they knew would be found unconstitutional.

Another major case initiated by ACLU lawyers in the late 1960s was *Gautreaux v. Chicago Housing Authority*. This lawsuit joined interests that had been close to Dawn's heart at least since her involvement in the campaign to integrate campus housing as an undergraduate at Northwestern: race discrimination and affordable housing. Public housing that had been constructed in Chicago since the late 1930s conformed to a federal policy requiring the tenants of a housing development to be of the same race as the people of the neighborhood in which the housing was situated. Postwar public housing, particularly that built by the housing authority between 1957 and 1961, consisted of clusters of high-rise buildings constructed in African American neighborhoods on the South Side of Chicago. The *Gautreaux* suit accused the Chicago Housing Authority of deliberately segregating black families in its selection of both tenants and sites. The federal court ruled in 1969 that the agency was guilty of race discrimination and segregation and enjoined the CHA from building additional family housing in black residential areas. The agency was ordered to build scattered-site housing elsewhere in the city instead.[13]

Gautreaux and a case to desegregate the schools in Waukegan were the major cases the ACLU initiated in the late 1960s in the area of race. The Illinois chapter also kept busy through that period and the 1970s with numerous free speech cases arising out of opposition to the war in Vietnam—flag burning, police surveillance of groups, and the like. Dawn remembers that the board discussed whether the ACLU should come out in opposition to the war. It decided that this issue went beyond its institutional mission, and the organization focused on civil liberties issues arising out of the war instead.

In 1976 the group faced its most controversial free speech case—the decision to defend the right of the National Socialist Party of America to demonstrate in Skokie, a suburb of Chicago that was home to five thousand to six thousand survivors of the Holocaust. The town obtained an injunction against the march, on the grounds that it would impose psychological harm on the residents of the community and spark violence. The ACLU represented the Nazis in asserting their First Amendment right to demonstrate and won the case, at the cost of thirty thousand members leaving the organization. Dawn remembers this as a tense and trying time not only for the institution but also for individual members of the board. Although many people did not think the ACLU should take the case, Dawn totally supported the principled position adopted by the board, that is, to defend the free speech rights of even the most despicable organization.[14] (Ultimately the Nazis never did march in Skokie, deterred by the huge numbers of counterdemonstrators.)[15]

Although the ACLU board required a very heavy commitment of time, participation in it and in CIG were not the only extracurricular political activities Dawn undertook during the early years she was a law professor. She also became involved in the Leadership Council for Metropolitan Communities in the late 1960s, and was still involved in it when the organization shut down four decades later. The council was a response to Martin Luther King's open housing marches in Chicago in the summer of 1966. King came to Chicago to publicize and confront racism in its de facto forms in the North. Together with Chicago civil rights leaders, he led marches into all-white neighborhoods, provoking enormous hostility on the part of the residents. When the group marched through Marquette Park, a white working-class area on the Southwest Side, violence broke out and King was injured by a rock counterdemonstrators threw at him. This situation put Mayor Richard J. Daley in a very difficult position, because the white ethnics opposing the marches were a major part of his base of support; yet with the confrontations attracting national media attention, he had to employ the Chicago police to protect the marchers. He was determined to put an end to the crisis. In August 1966, city leaders, religious and civil rights activists, and representatives of the Chicago Real Estate Board entered into negotiations that culminated in a summit agreement pledging to open up housing opportunities in metropolitan Chicago. The council was an offshoot of that agreement.

Formed in 1966, the council was chaired by Thomas Ayers, head of Commonwealth Edison, and included on its board other captains of industry such as Ben Heineman, and civic and religious leaders like Rabbi Robert Marx and the Roman Catholic Cardinal John Cody. The new organization was charged with establishing and administering whatever programs were necessary to achieve fair housing in Chicago. Not long after the council's formation, Dawn's law school colleague Dan Walker persuaded her to join its board of directors.

The council raised money and set up an office with a legal staff that undertook litigation, advocacy, and education about open housing. It filed individual lawsuits using testers (minorities and whites with similar financial qualifications who applied for housing to find out whether the two groups were treated differently) against real estate firms and boards to force them to change their tactic of steering minorities into certain areas. The council undertook many educational and counseling activities as well.

It convened meetings of real estate professionals, local officials, and religious and community leaders to teach about and encourage fair housing throughout Chicago. It also counseled minority families about their rights and opportunities with respect to housing and how to take advantage of them.[16]

The board on which Dawn served met about every other month, and its members were often asked to make decisions about filing major lawsuits, such as the Arlington Heights zoning case, or other actions, such as protesting the redevelopment proposal that would have wiped out the Hispanic community in Addison with support from the public.[17] In the 1970s, the council's programs also intersected with the ACLU-initiated *Gautreaux* litigation. After the federal court decision directing the construction of scatter-site housing, the CHA effectively ceased building in the city of Chicago. A separate suit that the ACLU filed against the federal Department of Housing and Urban Development sought metropolitan area–wide relief as a remedy. When the Supreme Court affirmed this broader remedy in 1976, the council was appointed to administer the program. Under this *Gautreaux* program administered by the council, minority CHA tenants—both those in CHA housing and those seeking public housing—were screened, selected, and assisted in finding housing in white areas of the city and suburbs, and they received supportive services designed to make their moves successful.

When serving as Governor Kerner's assistant, Dawn had attempted to push fair housing legislation through the Illinois legislature, but the efforts had failed. Service on the board of the council allowed her to pursue these goals by other means. Her interest went beyond simply opening the housing market on a nondiscriminatory basis, however. She repeatedly pushed the council's board to address the lack of affordable housing as well. She says, "One thing I kept bugging everyone about was affordable housing. 'Fine, we'll break down the legal barriers . . . but if no affordable housing, what then?'"[18] Dawn attended a conference at Wingspread (the Frank Lloyd Wright–designed conference center in Wisconsin) about affordable housing in the late 1960s, where the New York Urban Housing Corporation was discussed. She returned to advocate both in the council and in the legislature that something similar be established to provide more affordable housing in Illinois.

The latter part of the 1960s was a period of immense turmoil— urban riots, the assassinations of Dr. Martin Luther King and Senator Robert F. Kennedy, student protests, building takeovers and strikes, huge

demonstrations in opposition to the war in Vietnam, and the establishment of increasingly radical organizations to support those efforts. On
the political spectrum at that time, Dawn was very much a liberal, not a
radical. She was neither inside nor outside the 1968 Democratic National
Convention, with neither the delegates nor the demonstrators, but instead
she got together with her liberal friends from the 1950s to think of ways
to address these crises—how to open up the Democratic Party, both in
Chicago and nationally, to more diverse interests; how to protect the civil
liberties of antiwar protesters in a time of increased government surveillance and repression; how to address the problems of urban poverty and
ghettoization by passing antidiscrimination laws and constructing the
affordable housing that is critical to desegregation of both schools and
neighborhoods. Her way of pursuing social change has always been an
incremental one and from within the system. Her decades-long persistence about many of these issues, such as education, housing, and racial
equality, is remarkable.

Interestingly, although Dawn was herself a trailblazer as a woman,
she was not quick to identify with the women's movement. In a 1970
interview, she specifically denied any interest in the movement, saying,
"Mine is not a woman's angle."[19] Dawn had succeeded brilliantly in both
her educational career and her professional career and simply assumed that
people would listen to and respect her. Sex-discriminatory practices such
as exclusive clubs did not particularly disturb her, unless they interfered
with something important to her, and she assumed that other women
would be able to succeed just as she had. By contrast, Dawn more easily
identified with African Americans and with people unable to compete
educationally and economically in America than she did with women as a
group. Thinking back, she mused:

> Sometimes I think that I was not as sensitive about the problems
> for women in the professional world as I should have been. I
> remember getting a real wake-up call after I had been here
> teaching for a few years. It was still in the early '70s, I think.
> One of our students who was one of the editors for the law
> review—she was poised and a perfectly pleasant person and
> obviously had a very good record—came to talk to me one day.
> She had been through the interviewing process and had one offer
> to be a librarian at a large law firm in Philadelphia. I couldn't
> believe it. I was so stunned. As I remember with the span of time,

that more than anything alerted me to the fact that women faced discrimination. . . . I never had a big problem. I was relatively unselfconscious about being a female and so I just didn't spend a lot of time thinking about it. But that really alerted me to the fact that things were different towards women. I think I became a lot more sensitive and tried a lot more to be useful as much as I could from that point on, both for women law students and for women generally. . . . I came to realize that things weren't the same for men and women.[20]

Although Dawn was not caught up in the movements of the 1960s, she was nonetheless very much involved in the issues of that period. From time to time her former employer, Otto Kerner, would draw her back into public service. When Kerner was appointed to chair the National Advisory Commission on Civil Disorders, set up to investigate the causes of the 1967 race riots, Dawn was on his staff during the first summer of its work. And when the Illinois legislature created a commission in 1967 to consider whether, when, and how to hold a convention to write a new constitution for the state, Kerner appointed her to that commission as well. This commission began to annotate the 1870 constitution, to carry out comparative analyses, and to break down the issues involved for research and recommendations. This involvement led to Dawn's intensive participation in the process of drawing up the Illinois Constitution of 1970.

Chapter 11

Con Con

IN THE 1960s, ILLINOIS government was operating under a state constitution that had been passed in 1870. Referred to at times as a horse-and-
buggy constitution, the document reflected deep distrust of the power of
government in general and placed severe limitations on it that obstructed
the activities of post–New Deal state governments in the twentieth
century. There were explicit limits on the amount of debt the state could
incur, and those limits were woefully out of date. Taxation was required to
be uniform, and until a 1969 decision by the Illinois Supreme Court, the
requirement was interpreted to prohibit a tax on income. Passed in a time
when the state was still largely rural, the 1870 charter did not provide for
home rule for any municipalities or counties. All of their powers had to be
derived from specific grants from the state and were, under the so-called
Dillon's rule (after the author of an early law treatise on municipal government), narrowly defined.[1] Quaint electoral structures such as cumulative
voting in multimember districts were designed to ensure a balance of the
political parties dominating downstate and the growing Chicago metropolis. The executive power of state government was distributed among a
large number of elective officers. Moreover, the provisions for amending
the constitution were unwieldy, requiring a majority vote of all those
voting in the general election rather than a percentage of those voting on
the amendment itself—and with such a long ballot, many voters ignored
the amendments that were tacked onto its end.

Background to the 1970 Con Con

There had been numerous attempts to address the constitutional problems over the course of the early twentieth century, but they had all failed.

The farthest the process had gotten was a constitutional convention held from 1920 to 1922 that drafted a constitution, but the proposed draft was decisively defeated when it was submitted to the voters. Because of the cumbersome amendment procedure, attempts at piecemeal reform failed as well. One breakthrough occurred in 1950 with the passage of the Gateway Amendment, which eased the requirements for amending the constitution, requiring only a two-thirds vote of those voting on the amendment itself rather than a majority of all those who voted in the election. Most subsequent attempts at reform by amendment nonetheless either had failed to pass or were simply inadequate to the overall task.

There had been a major movement for constitutional revision in Illinois since 1945, under the aegis of a Chicago Bar Association committee headed by Samuel Witwer. The committee members began to study the issues involved and to publish articles detailing the shortcomings of the 1870 constitution; they urged the Illinois legislature to place a call for a constitutional convention on the ballot. The state bar association, the Union League, and public interest groups such as the League of Women Voters supported the committee's efforts, but they did not come to fruition until the late 1960s. After the 1965 at-large election, with its bedsheet ballot, brought many reform-minded voices of both parties to the legislature, Governor Kerner and the General Assembly jointly appointed a Constitution Study Commission. The commission's report, published in February 1967, strongly recommended that a constitutional convention be held to redraft the entire document; its authors argued that this path would stimulate public discussion of the issues and produce high quality research about them.[2] The General Assembly passed a call for a constitutional convention in 1967, to be placed before the voters on the ballot in November 1968. Its success was uncertain, given the electorate's repeatedly demonstrated reluctance to tinker with the nineteenth-century document.

After the legislature acted in 1967, the second Constitution Study Commission was established to do the background work necessary to prepare for a convention, including figuring out the logistics for how it would happen. Governor Kerner appointed Dawn Clark Netsch to the commission. The commission received extensive support from staff at the Institute of Government and Public Affairs at the University of Illinois. The staff updated a basic bibliography for study of the Illinois Constitution that had been produced in 1966 for the first commission and published a more definitive bibliography in November 1968.[3] Two lawyers—George Braden of New York, who had been involved in a similar, though unsuccessful, attempt to revise the New York Constitution, and Rubin Cohn, a law professor at the University of Illinois—put together an impressive annotated version of the 1870 constitution, tracing the history of each section, explaining how it had been interpreted by the courts, and comparing each provision with similar provisions in other states' constitutions.[4] A hardbound copy engraved with each delegate's name was presented to every person elected to the convention, and they referred to it as their bible.

Despite these preparations, it was still not a foregone conclusion that the constitutional convention would take place. First, it was necessary to get the attention of the electorate on an issue that seemed esoteric to many, especially in contrast to the hotly contested presidential election (Richard Nixon versus Hubert Humphrey) taking place on the same ballot in November 1968. An informal citizens group formed to undertake this task and received semiofficial status by asking Governor Kerner to appoint its cochairs. The Illinois Committee for Constitutional Convention convened in March 1968. With financial support from civic groups such as the Union League, the ICCC commissioned a number of surveys on which to base its campaign strategy. The key decisions supported by the polls were to focus on voter turnout and to keep the issue both nonpartisan and very general—a question of updating an outdated constitution rather than addressing any specific issue that could evoke opposition.[5]

Notes for speeches Dawn gave to interested groups during this period show that she followed this strategy. She emphasized the need for flexibility and simplification; pointed out the need to unshackle the cities and for a realistic limit, if any, on debt; and often described various obviously outdated provisions of the 1870 constitution (e.g., women could not vote, senate districts were based on area rather than population, all county officers had to be paid out of the fees they collected). She would conclude by proclaiming, "So we have an antique that is difficult to modernize. And that is why we need a constitutional convention."[6] The strategy of focusing on the need to update an outdated constitution appears to have worked: 4.7 million voters considered the call for a convention, and 2.9 million approved it, significantly more than the majority of all those voting that was required to pass it. The convention called as a result of this vote was popularly known as Con Con.

Election as a Delegate to Con Con

The Constitution Study Commission on which Dawn served was required to decide exactly how the election of delegates to the convention should be carried out. The 1870 constitution provided that there should be two delegates from each senate district throughout the state, for a total of 116 delegates. The enabling act that the Constitution Study Commission drafted and recommended and the legislature passed provided that there would be both a primary and a general election, both carried out on a nonpartisan basis.

In addition to serving on the Constitution Study Commission, Dawn was appointed in February 1969 to serve on the blue-ribbon Constitutional Research Group established by the new Republican Governor Richard Ogilvie. The group primarily included political science and law professors recruited to prepare scholarly background papers on the main issues for consideration by the convention. The authors worked independently. Dawn was responsible for the chapter on the executive, a subject with which she was very familiar from her years as assistant to the governor. The background papers covered a great deal of ground—the Bill of Rights, the legislature, suffrage, the judiciary, local government, public finance, business regulation, education, and the amending process, among others; they were given to each of the delegates to the convention and later published in an edited hardbound volume.[7]

Dawn's chapter on the executive is clear, interesting, and forceful, and it displays great erudition about the history and workings of state government, as one might expect from a law professor teaching state and local government. She began from a liberal premise—the assumption that a strong executive with adequate powers is essential to effective state government, as important as a system of checks and balances is. Such a system of limitations on government may be necessary to prevent concentrations of power, but it may also result in an inability to take action, preventing government from moving in new directions.[8] In the chapter, Dawn discussed the mistrust in the American colonies of strong governors and the problems created for efficient and accountable administration by the proliferation of elective state offices in the Jacksonian era. While the governor of Illinois has a four-year term and can be reelected, the 1870 constitution obstructed his power by providing a total of six other independently elected state officers—lieutenant governor, secretary of state, auditor of public accounts, treasurer, superintendent of public instruction, and attorney general. Dawn made a detailed and well-reasoned argument why this arrangement, while seeming ultrademocratic, cut down on the chief executive's control over his administration and thus interfered both with the ability to carry out his or her responsibilities and thus with accountability to the electorate.[9] In the Hodge scandal, for example, the governor had no power to dismiss the corrupt auditor general because he had been elected, not appointed; thus the governor had to persuade him to resign.

Dawn recommended in her chapter that a short ballot replace the long ballot, and that officers such as the attorney general, the comptroller, and others be appointed by and responsible to the governor, as they are in the federal government. She also recommended giving the governor explicit authority to reorganize executive agencies and their functions, to counter the proliferation of independent state boards and agencies that were diluting the governor's power.

Although the 1970 convention did not adopt a short ballot, there was some improvement with respect to the reforms she recommended. The new constitution provided that the lieutenant governor and the governor would run as a team in the general election, and the State Board of Education replaced the formerly elected superintendent of public instruction. The 1970 constitution also authorized agency reorganization by executive order, allowing the governor to reassign functions or reorganize agencies responsible to him.

The most radical suggestion introduced in Dawn's chapter on the executive was her proposal to broaden the governor's veto power to include an amendatory veto and the power to reduce legislative appropriations. The amendatory veto idea arose out of Dawn's research on procedures in a few other states, as well as her frustrating experience with the veto process while working for Governor Kerner. With all legislation submitted at the end of a session, and a two-thirds vote necessary to override a veto almost impossible to obtain (in part because cumulative voting ensured a legislature that was closely divided along party lines), the governor's veto was virtually absolute, even with respect to bills that had merit but needed some small revision. In the biennial legislature, these bills might not be revised and passed for almost two years. Dawn suggested the amendatory veto as an alternative, "which permits the governor instead of disapproving an entire bill, to return it to the legislature with his recommendations for change."[10] If the legislature approved those changes, the bill would pass; if not, it would either be overridden or die. In addition to her scholarly work on these issues, Dawn did a good deal of writing for bar journals and speaking to community groups about the need for a new constitution in Illinois.[11]

The primary election to reduce the number of candidates for the 116 slots as delegates to the constitutional convention was scheduled for September 23, 1969, and the general election for November 18. From the beginning of her involvement with the Constitution Study Commission, Dawn had been interested in running for election as a delegate. Her interest in the issue was of long standing. Governor Stevenson had attempted, unsuccessfully, to get a call for a convention on the ballot, and constitutional reform was dear to the heart of those involved in CIG. Later, as Governor Kerner's assistant, Dawn had also participated in a conference about the Illinois Constitution held at the University of Illinois conference center in January 1962. After considering background papers arguing the case for and against holding a constitutional convention, the group recommended in its final report that a constitutional convention be held at the earliest possible date.[12] In short, it did not take much thought for Dawn to decide to run for election as a delegate to the convention. "It was a no-brainer to run for Con Con," she says. "I had wanted to be actively involved in public life. Con Con was a one time thing. . . . It involved state government, which was what I knew and had a lot of background in, and cared about a lot. It seemed such a logical thing to do."[13]

In early June 1969, Dawn started to meet with various groups and seek their support, emphasizing not only her qualifications but also her determination to negotiate a constitutional framework that could be sold to the voters. She began to assemble a staff, with John McGuire as her campaign manager. She put together an impressive Citizens Committee to support her candidacy even before she announced it, and she began to get commitments of funds to staff an office and distribute literature.

In a letter of June 13, 1969, to George W. Dunne, Democratic committeeman of the Forty-second Ward, Dawn requested endorsement from the Regular Democratic Organization of Cook County, or the machine.[14] Dunne summoned her by letter to the Forty-second Ward office on the evening of June 19, 1969, for an interview.[15] Dawn appeared as summoned and told the organization that it should support her because of her activity in many campaigns on behalf of Democratic candidates, her practical experience in state government from her four years as assistant to Governor Kerner, and her position teaching state and local government at Northwestern Law School.[16] She said that she was committed to keeping an open and flexible position so as to be able to negotiate solutions to many of the constitutional issues facing the state of Illinois and to be able to write a constitution that voters would approve. Asked specifically about some of her positions, she confessed to being a passionate advocate of home rule, which was dear to the heart of Chicago's mayor. She subsequently received a brief phone call from Dunne, in which he asked for her position on "the religion issue" (in essence, about aid to parochial schools), and she replied that she thought the constitution should remain pretty much the way it was on this issue, which seemed to reassure him.[17]

Dawn did not expect endorsement, because she had been told they had already decided on two candidates for her district; but to her surprise, she received the endorsement of the Chicago Democratic Party. She proceeded, with their support, to organize her first campaign for elective office and to announce her candidacy publicly at the end of June. Dawn and more than five hundred other people filed petitions to run by the July deadline. An initial dispute arose over placement of names on the ballot, which the Seventh Circuit Court of Appeals had to resolve. The court held that the system followed by Secretary of State Paul Powell was discriminatory (in favor of machine Democrats) and mandated a modified lottery system for ballot position.[18] Dawn was one of seven people running in the primary in the Twelfth Senatorial District, where she lived; four people were to be selected in the primary, and her name was second on the ballot. Although the election was formally nonpartisan, the Chicago Democratic Party did endorse and work for its own candidates, and this turned out to be more important than position on the ballot in most cases.

Dawn campaigned throughout the district, including in the Cabrini Green public housing project, where white candidates typically did not go. With the help of John Stevens, an African American community activist, she set up several meetings over there, one of which did not go well. A respectable number of people gathered at one of the churches, and the meeting was going fairly well at first, apart from some hostility toward white liberals. Dawn's husband Walter then stood up and asked a very difficult, go-for-the-jugular question, and things went badly from then on. After this experience, Dawn asked Walter not to come to her political meetings or, if he did come, not to ask questions.[19]

By the middle of August, Dawn was regularly attending two coffees to meet voters in the homes of supporters every night of the week or addressing meetings at churches and civic groups, typically at 7:30 and 8:30, and she continued to do so on a daily basis after she returned to teaching in the fall. Several civic organizations and both the *Chicago Sun-Times* and the *Chicago Daily News* newspapers endorsed her. At the primary on September 23, 1969, Dawn won the most votes of the seven candidates in her district, receiving 33.5 percent of the vote and thus continuing with three others to the general election in November.[20]

Dawn redoubled her campaign efforts during October and early November, sometimes addressing as many as three groups a night and more on the weekends. She repeatedly emphasized the need for constitutional reform to resolve critical questions such as how the state was going to raise the money to pay for services in a way that was fair, how local governments could receive the powers they needed to solve the problems of modern life, how to make the legislature more efficient and responsive, and how to give the executive branch the powers it needed to do its job and be accountable to the voters.

It was difficult to attract voters' attention to these seemingly esoteric issues, and voter turnout at both the primary and general elections was very low, ranging from 10 to 25 percent of eligible voters.[21] Nonetheless, on November 18, 1969, 101 men and 15 women were elected delegates to the Sixth Illinois Constitutional Convention. In the Twelfth District, Dawn Clark Netsch won the most votes, with 38.3 percent of the total vote; Malcolm Kamin was also elected, with 30.2 percent of the vote.[22]

Because the convention was scheduled to begin on December 8, Dawn arranged to teach only one seminar during the spring semester and booked accommodation in a hotel just down the street from the state capitol. Walter Netsch was working frequently on commissions abroad at that time and was rarely at home. Dawn returned to Chicago every weekend during the convention, at least until her mother had a stroke; until she recovered, Dawn flew to Cincinnati at least every other weekend.

Con Con Begins

After several days of orientation programs for the delegates, the convention officially opened on December 8, 1969, to much pomp, in the Illinois House of Representatives chamber. Delegates were seated alphabetically, to underscore the formally nonpartisan nature of the body. After several months, the convention moved to the old state capitol, which had been restored as a museum. They met in the historic chamber where Abraham

Lincoln had delivered his "A Nation Divided Cannot Stand" speech in 1858. The room, if a bit small for the purpose, impressed everyone with a sense of the history involved in their undertaking. The colonial-style room is all white and features classic columns and square windows with old-fashioned glass that nonetheless admits plenty of light. The chamber is usually furnished with period furniture, quill pens, and candles, and there is a woodstove; but new small desks and other supplies were installed for the convention delegates. There is a dais at the front of the room, and a large portrait of George Washington presides over the speaker's desk in the center. The setting is small and intimate.

The modern historical context for the convention was one of great civic unrest in the United States—large antiwar demonstrations, the bombing of Cambodia, sit-ins, and the National Guard troops' killing of student protesters at Kent State and Jackson State universities. The state political context was not an easy one, either. The Con Con delegates represented a cross-section of Illinois—Chicago versus downstate versus the suburbs, and Republican versus Democrat versus independent—and there was a great deal of suspicion that the mayor of Chicago and his political machine would attempt to call the shots. At the same time, the need for compromise was obvious. If the Chicago Democratic Party did not support the document that emerged, it had no hope of passage.

The convention's first business was that of organizing itself. Sam Witwer, in recognition of his long efforts for constitutional reform, was elected president and given the power to appoint committees and their chairs. He worked on this task over the Christmas recess, during which Dawn and Walter were vacationing in Jamaica. Dawn expected that her prominence and experience in the field of state and local government would be rewarded with a committee chair, and she very much wanted to chair the committee on local government. When asked for their preferences, nearly half of the delegates listed the Local Government or Revenue and Finance committees first on their list.[23]

Witwer, a Republican, was a somewhat stiff person who did not have a warm relationship with most of the delegates.[24] The one force driving him appears to have been his strong desire to produce a constitution that was both substantively and politically acceptable—an improvement over the nineteenth-century constitution and one that both the delegates and the electorate would approve. Witwer was determined that the appointments of committee chairs and vice chairs should be balanced both geographically and by party. He also wanted to appoint chairs without preestablished positions on the issues that would come before their committees.[25] This could mean that the person who knew the most about a certain area would *not* chair the committee covering that subject.

Dawn felt that she was entitled to a chair and was furious when informed that she had not been appointed to head any committee, contacting Witwer from Jamaica to ask for an appointment. He described his reasons for not doing so in his memoirs of the convention:

> Mrs. Netsch was in Jamaica; a telephone call earlier in the week indicated that she was greatly displeased by the fact that I would not name her a chairman. My failure to name Mrs. Netsch a chairman was in large measure due to the fact that she is unacceptable to her own political organization. I found to my surprise when I discussed her name with an aide of Governor Ogilvie that she is also somewhat less than popular with the Republican organization. It seems that some feel that she is too doctrinaire to be a good leader of a committee.[26]

Although they had endorsed her election, apparently the Democratic organization was not comfortable with Dawn, known for her independence, as a committee chair, and neither were the Republicans. Witwer did name her vice chair of the prestigious Revenue and Finance Committee; she was the only one of the fifteen women delegates who was appointed to a leadership role on a committee.[27] Nonetheless, Dawn felt cheated out of a leadership position she thought she deserved. The *Chicago Tribune* also criticized the surprising appointment of John Karns as chair of Revenue and Finance because he had no knowledge of revenue and "will need a great deal of help from delegates who know something about how to improve the state's tax system."[28]

Witwer wrote in his memoir of the convention that he attempted to explain to Dawn his failure to name her to a chair position at a meeting a few months later:

> I told her that during the period I considered my appointments, I had tried to advance her name for over a week, and that every time I made the effort, she was "axed" by her own party leadership consisting of Lyons and Elward; that even in terms of making her a vice chairman, I had to fight her cause because their desire was

to make sure she wasn't in any capacity as a leader. This seemed to shock her and I suspect I opened her eyes to some of the political problems I faced.[29]

Even without a chair, Dawn played an extremely influential role on the Revenue and Finance Committee—largely because she knew so much more about the subject than Karns did and was an indefatigably hard worker.

Revenue and Finance Committee

During the early months of the convention, most work occurred in the newly established committees. Although neither Dawn nor Karns had really wanted to focus on revenue and finance, they quickly got down to the tasks of setting up a place to work, organizing staff, and holding hearings. Dawn describes the day-to-day work:

> We heard from witnesses, had hearings, and a lot of people had a lot to say, especially business and real estate groups, some civic groups, some individuals. We would hear from the delegates who had proposals that were within our jurisdiction; they would come in and testify about proposals. I testified before my own committee about a simplified revenue article. We would have deliberations, fairly extensive discussion before drafting. Then staff, primarily Glenn Fisher and Joyce Fishbane, the assistant, would begin to draft up language. In some cases we did some of our own drafting but the staff was the primary source. Then we'd discuss drafts they presented to us, to see if they reflected what we were thinking. Listening, discussing, deliberating.[30]

The first witnesses to testify before the committee were a series of academic experts who discussed the current state of revenue and finance in Illinois and its inadequacy and made recommendations for change.[31] The need for reform had been obvious for some time. The state had been relying on personal property taxes, sales taxes, and real estate taxes to fund the activities of government, and the sources were clearly inadequate. Although the 1870 constitution provided that all taxes must be uniform, Cook County had been classifying residential and business real estate differently for purposes of taxation for some time, so as to reward homeownership without sacrificing necessary revenue. The county feared that a lawsuit could result in a holding that this practice was unconstitutional. Moreover, farmers in downstate Illinois were strongly opposed to the personal property tax, which increased the cost of expensive farm machinery, and so were businesses. But the City of Chicago could not fund all its necessary services if that tax were eliminated without a substitute source of revenue.

When Governor Kerner came into office in 1961, he had declared the state almost bankrupt. Various efforts at reform were attempted, but all failed until 1969, when the Supreme Court held that a bill introduced by Governor Ogilvie to establish an income tax was in fact constitutional.[32] The bill provided only for a flat tax, that is, one based on a certain (rather low) percentage of income across the board rather than a graduated income tax as in the federal system.

The Revenue and Finance Committee at Con Con thus entered a situation that was extremely contentious and already in flux. The interests of city and rural areas were opposed to one another, as were those of business and labor, as well as the ideologies of the Democratic and Republican parties. The eighteen members of the Revenue and Finance Committee reflected all these conflicting interests.

The finance experts who testified before the committee argued that the revenue and finance article should be very minimal, declaring that the legislature had the right to tax and not going into much detail. This was Dawn's position, designed to give maximum flexibility to future legislatures. But the academic expert testimony was followed by that of a variety of interest groups, and it was soon clear that most people were unwilling to entrust that much discretion to the legislature. So it would be necessary to include some limits on the amounts and types of taxation allowed in the constitution. Dawn made a last-ditch speech to the committee in which she argued against writing details on these issues into the new constitution; she drew rare applause for the quality of her presentation but changed few minds.[33] Yet it was clear that the limits set by the 1870 constitution were unworkable in the modern world.

The committee decided to divide the issues referred to it into two articles, one on finance and one on revenue, and to move forward on the first, which was relatively uncontroversial. An article providing that the governor would draw up a budget for each fiscal year and submit it to the legislature for passage was quickly drafted; it required that the budget be balanced both as submitted and as passed. The finance article also included Dawn's suggestion in her background paper that the governor be given a reduction veto with respect to any appropriations item. As finally adopted on the floor, however, a simple majority could override this veto. A new office of auditor general was created, to be appointed by the General Assembly for a ten-year term, charged with conducting an audit of public funds and reporting the findings to both the legislature and the governor. The finance article, separated off as it was, quickly went to the floor for a first reading and easily passed both that stage and the second reading, encouraging the committee members that they could in fact work together to produce results.

The remaining issues were more troublesome. In April, Dawn prepared the outline for a revenue article designed to retain maximum flexibility by first setting forth a provision that declared the general authority of the state to tax and then including sections limiting the taxes that could be passed, thus framing the question as one of a general power on which some limitations were placed. The outline was noncontroversial but very influential. Commentators have said that "Netsch's sensitivity to the impact of such little-debated decisions as this one, coupled with her constant adherence to the theory of constitutional flexibility, was significant in producing a revenue article consistent with the legal philosophy that sovereign states have inherent tax powers subject only to specific limitations imposed by the constitution."[34] In other words, in contrast to the 1870 constitution, inherent power was to be the rule and limitations on that power the exception, not the other way around. The committee also agreed to eliminate various clearly outdated sections of the earlier constitution and then settled down to debate, and to negotiate, the tougher issues that remained—real estate classification, restrictions on the income tax, and elimination of the personal property tax.

The question of real estate classification pitted Chicago against downstate. It was estimated that abandoning the classification system in use in Cook County would mean tax increases of 30 to 40 percent for homeowners there, clearly a political disaster.[35] From the very beginning, every member of the committee realized that the Chicago delegates would not support any constitution that did not allow classification, and that this would doom any hope of passing the new charter; the committee therefore voted relatively early (in mid-March) not to retain the uniformity clause with respect to real estate taxation.[36]

The newly introduced Illinois income tax was assessed at a flat 2.5 percent rate. It was Dawn's position that the new constitution should include no specific limit on income tax rates. This was a minority position. If a limit were to be included, there was also an issue about what the ratio between the rate of tax on individuals and that on corporations should be. The personal property tax presented even stickier issues, and they were intertwined with the provisions on other types of taxes. Personal property taxes, primarily on corporate property such as inventory and equipment (the personal property tax had not been collected from individuals in Cook County for some time), accounted for 20 percent of the amounts that local governments collected in property tax.[37] If the tax were to be abolished, the delegates from areas heavily dependent on this revenue wanted to know exactly what would replace it. Because the issues were so divisive and the issues themselves so intertwined, it proved impossible to reach consensus in the committee after debating the issues for all of April and May.

Fearful that it would be unable to submit any report on the revenue article to the floor, the committee decided to submit a package containing dissents and minority proposals instead. Dawn signed on to the minority proposal to eliminate any form of limitation on the income tax, as did four other committee members, including Karns, the chair. The final report consisted of 144 pages, with dissents by eight members to the income tax section, nine to the real estate classification section, and ten to the personal property tax section.[38] Decisions on all the issues would be left to the convention as a whole. The report that the Revenue and Finance Committee submitted to the convention on June 16, 1970, stated the following:

> The Committee spent many months deliberating the important and controversial revenue questions. We resolved many important issues and present several of the proposed Sections with only a few dissents. On the other hand, there were several policy areas in which sustained efforts to reach agreement failed.
>
> In spite of the failures, the Committee is united on one thing: we were determined to present a report that will provide the Convention with the maximum possible assistance in arriving at reasonable decisions concerning a Revenue Article. We believe that this can best be accomplished by presenting to the Convention a complete Revenue Article even though some sections represent the first choice of only a few members of the Committee.[39]

The compromises contained in the committee's proposed revenue article included a flat-rate income tax of no specific percentage, with a proviso that the rate imposed on corporations should not exceed that imposed on individuals by more than a ratio of eight to five; authority for any county with a population of more than two hundred thousand to classify real property for tax purposes; and a provision that the legislature could abolish the personal property tax if it desired and authorize other taxes in lieu of it.

Apart from signing the minority proposal that would have deleted any section imposing limits on the income tax, Dawn also filed a brief dissent to the county option and population limit used to determine the availability of local classification of real property for purposes of the real estate tax.[40] The ground for her objection was her belief that every locality should be able to classify; the right should not be limited in any way.

The New Constitution on the Floor of the Convention

When the revenue report was submitted on June 16, there were only seven weeks budgeted until the Con Con was to adjourn, which created a great deal of pressure to complete the first reading of all the committees' proposals. It was quickly decided that the various revenue provisions were so intertwined that they could not be subject to a final vote individually but needed to be considered as a package. Disagreement over what should be in that package, trade-offs, and compromises took up several weeks on first reading, and the article that emerged was still not acceptable to all the factions whose approval would be necessary to an affirmative vote on the constitution as a whole. As for the income tax, questions remained as to whether a graduated tax would be permitted, whether there would be a required ratio between corporate and individual rates, and whether specific, or maximum, rates would be included in the constitution. Dawn emerged as the spokesperson for the minority proposal that no restrictions should be placed on the income tax, so that the legislature would remain free to determine the state's tax structure. That proposal failed by a roll call vote of thirty-two to sixty-nine.[41] Although a compromise on the question of classification was reached fairly quickly, sharp divisions persisted over the retention or abolition of the personal property tax; and this issue became linked to the percentage limit on the income tax and the eight-to-five ratio between corporate and individual tax rates.

Hostility between downstate delegates and the Chicago Democratic bloc began to worsen, especially as the Chicago group issued ultimatums that there would be no constitution without classification and a personal property tax. There was no question that the personal property article as reported out of committee, leaving the legislature the authority to decide whether to keep or abolish the tax, was a nonstarter with the Chicago Democrats, who feared the loss of income necessary to run the Chicago school system and, indeed, the city itself. This was not the only issue dividing the blocs, however, and intense disagreements over other issues to be debated, such as merit selection of judges, home rule, and whether cumulative voting should be abolished, exacerbated tensions among them. Hostility between the groups made it difficult to negotiate a compromise, and the version reported out after the first reading, which abolished the personal property tax as of January 1, 1979, and directed the General Assembly to replace the revenue lost by other taxes, was unacceptable to the Chicago group.

To the surprise of many, after spending three months on first reading, the convention wrapped up the second reading phase in eleven days. Debate on the revenue article began August 7, 1970, and multiple roll-call votes were taken on all the contending issues. A breakthrough occurred when a compromise was reached on the personal property tax, requiring that the taxes to be passed to replace it in 1979 must fall solely on the classes relieved of the burden of the personal property tax. For Chicago, the addition of this requirement meant that the burden of replacing the revenue would fall on corporations; it could not be shifted to the individual income tax. Although this compromise basically left a final solution to the personal property tax controversy—that is, what source of revenue would replace it—to the legislature in the future, the Chicago Democrats decided to give in on the issue and voted for the revenue article as a whole, which thus survived its second reading. (In 1979, the Illinois Supreme Court ruled that the personal property tax could no longer be collected even though the legislature had not yet been able to agree on an alternate source of revenue.)[42]

Although a compromise had thus been reached on the revenue article, other major issues needed to be decided before the convention could adjourn. It had been clear since quite early in the process that there were several issues on which agreement simply could not be reached: whether to lower the voting age to eighteen, whether to abolish the death penalty, whether judges should continue to be elected or be appointed based on merit, and whether to abolish the system of cumulative voting and multi-member districts and replace it with single-member districts. Dawn and the group of independent Democrats with whom she was allied played an active role in these disputes. An early, and tactically brilliant, decision was made to place certain issues outside the main document, to be voted on separately by the electorate, so that a defeat on one of them would not bring down the whole constitution. The voting age and death penalty issues were quickly placed in this category, but by the time of first reading it remained an open question what to do with the issues of cumulative voting and judicial selection. The Chicago Democrats wanted to keep the current system of an elective judiciary as well as the multimember district electoral system. And there was a strategic advantage to having the issue formulated in their favor inserted within the document, with an alternate version available separately on the ballot. It also made it much easier for precinct captains to instruct voters how to vote on the issues on which they must vote separately.

Quite apart from her work on the Revenue and Finance Committee, Dawn had emerged as an important leader at the convention as a whole. From the beginning, she was regarded as exceptionally knowledgeable about the issues the group was to address. A preconvention Brown University survey of the delegates put her among the top ten delegates "perceived as one from whom advice would be sought by other delegates."[43] Retrospective evaluations were similar. When asked who the top-level leaders of the convention had been, representatives of the delegates, staff, press, and others came up with a list of thirteen; Dawn's name appeared as No. 8.[44] She was described (and obviously perceived) in a variety of ways—as "complex, hard-working, unyielding, tough, informed, and bright" by Elmer Gertz and Joseph Pisciotte in their 1980 book, and by Sam Witwer as "a very cool, intelligent woman [with] a certain degree of brilliance" but "doctrinaire."[45] Witwer complained that Dawn talked too much on the floor.[46] Ann Lousin, a staff member, agreed that she talked a great deal but characterized Dawn's behavior differently: "She could be quite voluble. She would talk a lot. She had an opinion on everything and usually expressed it. But again, to be perfectly fair, she usually had more experience and more knowledge than a lot of these guys did."[47] Dawn's persistence was, and remains, a noted characteristic. Peter Tomei, one of the other independent Democratic delegates to the convention, told her after the convention was over, "Dawn, you just would never give up. You just never knew how to throw in the towel."[48] She took this as a great compliment.

The group of independent Democrats to which Dawn belonged, including Tomei, Ron Smith, Frank Cicero, Al Raby, Bernard Weisberg, Wayne Whalen, Elmer Gertz, Mary Lee Leahy, and others, emerged as a powerful "third force" toward the end of the convention. Sam Witwer, the convention president, went back and forth in his diary as to whether this bloc would prove decisive to the outcome.[49] The independents and some Republicans strongly favored the so-called merit selection of judges, under which the governor would appoint judges from nominees that bipartisan judicial selection commissions submitted. This would take a vast source of patronage away from the Chicago machine, whose endorsement was tantamount to election in Chicago under the system then. The issue of legislative representation was more complicated. At the first reading stage of the legislative article, most Republicans voted to change the electoral system to single-member districts and abolish cumulative voting; Chicago Democrats wanted three-member districts with cumulative voting in the general election but not the primary; and most independents wanted cumulative voting in both the primary and the general elections because the system ensured minority representation through bullet voting (casting all three votes for the same person). Dawn appears to have been a maverick on this issue, voting with the Republicans:

> I changed my mind on this one. I spent a lot of time looking at the history of what had happened and what I thought were the results, and I kept thinking, "You know, if we were really starting from scratch, would we really do this, or would we have single member districts?" I came to the conclusion . . . that I would not have done it that way . . . because it froze patterns and really kept in a lot of nonperforming legislators.[50]

Dawn is not sure that she was right on this issue and admits that she has been on both sides over a period of time. After later serving in the General Assembly and observing the difference between the state senate, which never had cumulative voting, and the Illinois House of Representatives, which did, she became a supporter of the cumulative voting system used in the House.

The story of the coup by which both the judicial selection and legislative representation issues ended up outside the document, with voters invited to choose between the two alternatives, is an interesting one. By the relatively brief third reading stage at the end of the convention, the

Chicago Democrats had succeeded in getting both cumulative voting and judicial elections into the main body of the document to be submitted to voters, with the alternatives to be voted on separately. On August 28, the convention adjourned early for a reception given by the Witwers, and the Chicago delegates neglected to have the entire legislative article forwarded for final enrollment in the proposed constitution, usually a formality. At the party, Dawn said to Ethyl Witwer "something that was rather cryptic, to the effect that it wasn't all over and that things were likely to start again the next morning."[51]

The Chicago Democratic Organization group partied late that night and slept late the next day. Early the next morning, a group of independent Democrats, including Dawn, and some Republicans greeted Witwer with the news that they had put together a coalition to support putting both the remaining issues outside of the main package if he would entertain their proposal.[52] When the convention came to order at 9:30 A.M., seven Chicago Democrats were still absent. Thus when the motion to approve the legislative article on third reading was made, it failed, leaving it subject to further action. The informal coalition then put forward a motion to suspend the rules to consider an amendment to place both judicial selection and multimember districts outside the main body of the constitution. The Chicago Democrats had by now appeared, and the convention exploded into turmoil. But after a day spent wrangling over the issue, the amendment passed. Thus, Illinois voters faced a five-part vote on the constitution the following December:

1. Whether they approved the main text
2. Whether they favored single-member districts or multimember districts with cumulative voting
3. Whether judges should be elected or appointed
4. Whether the death penalty should be abolished
5. Whether the voting age should be lowered to eighteen

The decision to submit the second through fifth questions separately removed the last issues preventing agreement on the whole document, and the convention soon adopted the new constitution and formally adjourned on September 3, 1970. At the closing ceremony, Governor Ogilvie characterized the political necessity of separate submission as an "affirmative demonstration of faith in the democratic ideal." He continued, "In an age when growing numbers of our citizens feel excluded from the business of self-government, your perceptive decision to doubt your own infallibility makes supreme good sense." In his address to the assembly, Sam Witwer praised the delegates for their work:

> To your credit, my fellow delegates of this Convention, you have come into this arena to openly debate the issues of our day. You have dared greatly, and I am so proud of you.
>
> Whether the product of our debate results in victory or defeat, only the good citizens of Illinois whose mandate sent us here will determine.[53]

The group of 116 delegates who had worked together so intensely for nine months then disbanded and returned home. Their collective experience was so memorable, however, that there have been repeated reunions of the Con Con delegates over the years.

As the convention ended, a twenty-four-page, newspaper-style document, *Address to the People,* was prepared, which set forth and then explained, in blue typescript, each section of the new constitution and how it did or did not change the previous charter. Funded by the Con Con itself, 12 million copies were printed and mailed out to every voter and also inserted into newspapers.[54]

Submission of the New Constitution to the Voters

In December 1970, Illinois citizens were to be given the chance to adopt a new constitution, one with a more flexible revenue article, a very progressive Bill of Rights, home rule for municipalities with more than twenty-five thousand people and any county with an elected county executive (in essence, Cook County), and other reforms. The task that remained was to convince the electorate to adopt it. The Illinois Citizens for the New Constitution presided over the overall effort, but there were also four minicampaigns by groups concerned with the four separate issues on the ballot. The ICNC was underfunded, however, and not as active as might have been expected, leaving much of the lobbying for passage of the new constitution to delegates who chose to be active in this respect.

Dawn returned to Chicago and to full-time teaching that September, but she also devoted a great deal of time to the campaign to pass the new constitution. By September 9, she had drafted a detailed document called

"Notes for Explanatory Talk on 1970 Constitution," which explained the major changes, section by section, without taking a position on the issues for separate decision.[55] In November, however, she sent out a three-page, single-spaced "Dear Friend" letter to a variety of groups and a large number of individuals, urging support for the constitution as a whole and outlining her recommendations as to two of the separate submissions:

> The proposed Constitution deserves your support because it is a far better charter for Illinois in 1970 than the one it will replace. It is a sound document. It is progressive, in some areas significantly so, but in no sense radical. At a time when many people were deeply concerned that a constitutional convention might be reactionary, we can be proud that Illinois has moved forward, not backwards. . . .
>
> * * *
>
> I have concluded that Illinois will be better off with single member districts because it provides greater opportunity to elect more responsive legislators, to compel our two major parties to be more responsible in their support of candidates, and to strengthen the role of independents. . . .
>
> * * *
>
> I strongly support this merit-appointment system. The elective system has failed, with all too rare exceptions, to give us the quality judges we must have.[56]

Dawn addressed civic group after civic group about the new constitution, as she had also done throughout her entire period of service in Springfield. Folders of these speeches show that each one was handcrafted to the group and the issues they particularly wanted addressed. Dawn prepared each talk on yellow legal paper in her attractive and eminently legible script; often she made a set of note cards to use as well. These talks were invariably well organized and often rather scholarly in tone, but only the most formal ones, such as that to the Legal Club of Chicago, were written out word for word and typed.[57] A well-worn brown plastic folder that Dawn carried with her and used to prepare the many presentations she made contains the "Notes" document and a variety of campaign brochures and other literature.

She held yet another meeting in the Cabrini Green public housing complex, on the ground floor of one of the high-rise buildings. A good number of people attended. They seemed interested and asked good questions. As the meeting went on, however, there was a sound of shouting outside, of bottles being thrown, and riot police arriving. The commotion did not seem to bother the people attending the meeting; and they kept right on going, although Dawn had to raise her voice to be heard over the chaos outside. She remembers, "I was so impressed. I'd tell my middle class friends who weren't paying attention to the constitution that if folks with their burdens could come listen, you should too."[58]

Some seventy organizations endorsed the new constitution, but notably missing were the major trade unions and, up until the last two weeks, the Chicago Democratic Party. The absence of a progressive income tax and the potential implications of the abolition of the personal property tax and lack of effective tax limits on individuals upset the unions. The Daley organization was concerned not only about revenue implications but also about the addition of a state board of elections and the gamble involved in submitting cumulative voting and an elective judiciary to a separate vote.

When it was getting close to the election and the mayor had still not taken a position, Dawn telephoned her organization "sponsor," George Dunne, and said, "Look, it's getting close and if he doesn't support it, you know it's not going to happen. Doesn't he understand what there is in that constitution that's support for the city. . . one of the strongest home rule provisions in the whole country?"[59] David Stahl, one of Daley's chief aides, arranged for Dawn to meet with the mayor soon before Election Day. She emphasized to Mayor Daley that home rule represented an enormous breakthrough for the city. Ultimately, the organization did send its precinct workers out to campaign for passage of the constitution, though their instructions focused first on all the reasons not to vote for single-member districts or merit selection of judges and only later on instructing the voter to vote yes on the main document.[60] Stahl later told Dawn that her meeting with the mayor was crucial to his support of the constitution.

On December 15, 1970, the voters of Illinois went to the polls, and 55.5 percent approved the new constitution. Its passage heavily depended on the vote in Chicago and Cook County, which outbalanced negative votes downstate.[61] None of the reforms placed separately on the ballot succeeded. Voters rejected both the abolition of the death penalty and the lowering of the voting age to eighteen (but the latter was brought about by an amendment to the federal constitution a few months later).[62] Although voters did not abolish the multimember-district, cumulative voting system in 1970, they did do so in a subsequent referendum in 1980.[63] The most hotly contested issue on the 1970 ballot turned out to be judicial elections. Independent Democrats campaigned so fiercely for merit selection that they were able to neutralize the machine vote in Cook County, but downstate opposition to the appointment of judges based on merit doomed the proposal. Nonetheless, fully 46 percent of the voters did vote for an appointive judiciary.[64] Dawn strongly supported merit selection and has persisted in raising this issue in every possible forum since that time.

Among the proposals submitted by Dawn to the convention, one that has proved very controversial did succeed in passing. The new constitution included both the reduction veto and the amendatory veto for which she had argued in her article on the executive. Since the amendatory veto was first used in 1971, it has proved a source of friction between the governor and the General Assembly.[65] Republican Governor James R. Thompson began to use the power repeatedly, often in ways that appeared to rewrite the very purpose of a bill. Legislators began to claim that the veto could be used only to correct technical errors, an interpretation that was belied in the legislative history by a colloquy Dawn had with another delegate on the convention floor. The issue has been the subject of repeated litigation reaching the Illinois Supreme Court, but the only guidance resulting from the court is a decision that the veto's purpose is somewhere in between— that is, it allows more than technical changes but less than a total rewrite of a bill. The legislature has set up repeated task forces to study this issue and to make recommendations. Dawn herself served on Speaker Michael Madigan's 1984 Task Force on the Governor's Amendatory Veto Power. The controversy continues to this day, but the only attempt to amend the constitution to restrict the amendatory veto failed in a 1974 referendum.[66]

Indeed, the people of Illinois appear to be reluctant to tinker with the constitution that succeeded in 1970. Article 14 of the constitution provides that the question of whether to call a constitutional convention be submitted to the voters every twenty years, but they have thus far rejected the call to do so.

—— *Chapter 12* ——

Taking On the Machine, Act 2

IT MUST HAVE SEEMED rather tame for Dawn to return to her life as a law professor and wife of a prominent architect after the excitement of Con Con and the campaign to pass the new constitution. Politics and government were in Dawn's blood. So when Jim Houlihan approached her about the possibility of running together for the legislature on a joint ticket, the idea was appealing. There was still so much to be done, not only to implement the new charter but also to attack the many problems of the state. The nation as a whole, moreover, was still involved in an unpopular war and experiencing both an economic recession and an energy crisis leading to long lines at the gas pump.

The Campaign for the Illinois Senate in 1972

In 1971 Jim Houlihan, who later became Cook County assessor, was a relative unknown—a young man who had given up his studies in a Catholic seminary in 1969 to pursue a more secular mission. He had worked for a number of political organizations, including the Committee on Illinois Government, had tried and dropped an MBA program at the University of Chicago, and considered becoming a community organizer. He had also worked in a number of political campaigns for independent Democratic candidates, including Bill Singer's 1969 aldermanic campaign, Dawn's campaign to be elected as delegate to Con Con, and for other independent candidates up and down the lakeshore. (The independent Democratic vote in Chicago tended to cluster along the shores of Lake Michigan, in high-rent and academic areas from Hyde Park in the south to Evanston in the north, giving rise to the somewhat-pejorative term *lakefront liberals*). In 1971 Houlihan decided to run for office himself.

Sometime in September 1971, Houlihan approached Dawn to see whether he would be stepping on her toes if he ran in the Democratic primary for the Illinois House of Representatives from the Thirteenth District. If she were planning to run herself, he intended to support her; but, if not, he wanted to ask for her support of his candidacy. Dawn told Houlihan that she would be glad to support him, and they began to hold grassroots meetings in the neighborhood—"direct democracy in action," as Dawn describes it—during which she would speak on his behalf.[1] As she campaigned for Houlihan, Dawn's own interest grew.

In 1971 the Chicago Democratic Organization was facing opposition on a number of fronts. CIG's Dan Walker challenged Lieutenant Governor Paul Simon for the Democratic nomination for governor. Walker, whom Dawn knew from law school, had served as an aide to Governor Stevenson and rose to national prominence through his chairmanship of the Walker Commission, which issued the famous report about police violence during the 1968 Democratic National Convention.[2] Although she regrets it to this day, Dawn supported Walker over Paul Simon, who later became one of her closest political friends. In 1971, however, she and many of her independent Democratic allies in Chicago did not think that Paul Simon would be willing to take on the machine, while Walker openly attacked it in a dramatic campaign that included walking from one end of the state to the other.

Walker had spoken to Dawn about being his candidate for attorney general, but "something told me that I didn't want to do that," she says.[3] Although Walker went on to defeat the incumbent Republican Governor Ogilvie at the general election, a deep personal enmity toward Mayor Daley characterized his administration, and Daley reciprocated. Walker's rigid opposition to the machine led him into constant battles with the legislature while he was governor, and he was defeated by the machine's candidate in the 1976 primary. Dawn, who knew Walker well, tried to counsel him to work with other groups and to be willing to compromise rather than to maintain his constant battle stance.

> I said that one thing they needed to be careful about was not just closing everyone else out, circling the wagons and assuming everyone else was hostile, an enemy. . . . I told him, "Don't distrust everybody who is not part of your circle or who disagrees with you." I think that is largely what happened and a good part

of their downfall. . . . They did circle the wagons and took every opportunity to pick a fight with the mayor.[4]

It was just as well that Dawn steered clear of involvement in the short-lived Walker administration.

But when Jim Houlihan and those in his campaign organization began to ask Dawn to run for the Illinois Senate on a joint ticket, her reaction was quite different. Her name recognition from Con Con would add a great deal to the ticket. She remembers it this way:

> We had lots of little cell groups or neighborhood groups . . . and I sat around in people's living rooms and helped persuade people that Jim would be very good. Everyone kept saying we should take on the senate race also and would turn and look at me, because I had already run in that district for Con Con. So I finally decided "Why not?" That's what I had wanted to do but assumed I could not because of other obligations—teaching and marriage—but Walter was gone a good deal of the time then.[5]

The race for senator was much more difficult than that for representative, because Houlihan could take advantage of the bullet voting still made possible by the cumulative voting system. And Dawn's opponent was an incumbent, Senator Daniel O'Brien, the Forty-third Ward Democratic committeeman and senator from the Twelfth District, who was running in the Thirteenth District as a result of redistricting. The Chicago Democratic Organization had endorsed O'Brien. Dawn did not believe that she could defeat O'Brien but realized it would help Houlihan's chances if they ran a joint campaign, both saving money and taking advantage of her name recognition.

The Thirteenth District, which Dawn and Jim Houlihan sought to represent, was made up primarily of the Forty-second and Forty-third wards, and ran from the lakeshore in the east to the Chicago River on the south and west (the North Branch of the river) and to Belmont Avenue on the north (plus a segment that jogged out up to Addison Street between Sheffield and Ravenswood Avenues). It took in a number of diverse areas—the wealthy Michigan Avenue and Gold Coast areas north of the Loop, for example, and the vast Cabrini-Green public housing project, occupied almost entirely by low-income African Americans and known

as a very tough, high-crime area. The district also included several neighborhoods—Old Town, Lincoln Park, Lakeview, and the DePaul area,
for example—that white working-class groups loyal to the machine had
populated; but those neighborhoods were beginning to be redeveloped
and to change, as professionals, artists, and the first of many gays and
lesbians moved in. In short, the areas were beginning to be gentrified.

After deciding to run, Dawn called into her office two of her students
who were most interested in state and local politics and to whom she felt
closest—Michael Holland and Bill Luking. She told them that she was
going to run for a state senate seat to help Jim Houlihan get elected and
thus more independent Democrats into the legislature. She asked them to
help with her campaign, and they instantly agreed, resigning from their
work on the McGovern presidential campaign to do so. They helped get
petitions signed to get Dawn on the ballot in December 1971, and then
both became developers for working-class precincts on the western side
of her district, which included a major public housing project.[6] The two
young men came from Catholic working-class (Holland) or farm (Luking)
backgrounds themselves and had been caught up in the radicalism and
counterculture of the antiwar movement while in law school. Holland, for
example, wore his hair down to his shoulders, but he cut it to work in the
campaign.

Houlihan remembers the 1972 primary campaign as one of the most
exciting times in his political life. Their joint campaign staff included
people he describes as "incredibly dedicated and talented." They copied
the machine's tactics, organizing by precincts; sending out workers to
canvass the community; posting signs all over, including on the pedes-
trian bridge over Lake Shore Drive; and filling the streets on Election
Day with volunteers and visibility. "It was a time of incredible energy and
enthusiasm for changing a system that was closed and for trying to find a
way to make an impact," Houlihan says. "It was a crusade to change the
way things were."[7]

Houlihan and Dawn campaigned both together and separately,
but always for both of them. In the morning, they would each go to a
different bus or el stop to pass out literature and introduce themselves.
Dawn would then go to the law school while Houlihan worked full-time
on the campaign and could walk the precincts. She also did door-to-door
campaigning later in the day. Dawn began to sense that, when a woman
opened the door, there was a more positive response to a woman running
for office.

Between the two of them, Jim and Dawn could manage as many as five coffees in an evening—set up by their staff so that a chair would greet the guests and describe the campaign before one of the two candidates would arrive and deliver their pitch. Later in the evening they would go together to bars. Houlihan recalls that they would "walk into a bar at 9:30 or 10. Dawn might be reticent at first but then she would warm up and make a great connection with people."[8] Former student Mike Holland remembers that they would work the bars on the western side of the senate district every Friday and Saturday night with Richard Walsh, who was also working in the campaign, and that Dawn was great at it:

> One of us would go in and ask the bartender, "Do you mind? This is Dawn Clark Netsch; can she come in and say 'hi' to people?" She'd wait at the door, not come in; we'd play by the rules of the house. In Chicago you had to go through your alderman to get a liquor license, you had to be part of the Organization. . . . She'd go from table to table and one of us would advance her. "This is Dawn Netsch who is running for senate from this district." . . . We'd steer her away from anyone pie-eyed and would never go so late that the house was in their cups. She would shake just about every hand in the place, no matter what they looked like—tattoo on arms, big hair, whatever. . . . And she would work to answer almost every question. . . . Anyone who wanted to talk, she'd talk to. It was hard to get her out of there. And she remembered people. She had a politician's eye for a face, a voice. Twenty minutes and we'd have to drag her out. She grew to really like it and be very, very good at it.[9]

Dawn often felt exhausted by the constant campaigning but came to appreciate how important it was, both for the voters and for the candidate:

> You say, "How do you do, my name is Dawn Clark Netsch, I'm running for state senator. I hope you'll vote for me" over and over. It's mentally exhausting. I felt that it was so superficial. . . . but I came to realize what a difference it makes to people. Some of the workers who were going door to door doing the pluses and minuses would come back and tell me the number of times someone would say, "Oh, I know Mrs. Netsch, I met her at the bus stop the other day."

In short, what is now called retail campaigning has a real function for voters that is lacking in the electronic campaigning of today. "It gives people a sense of belonging, that it really is their elected representative, that someone out there cares enough about them to come out and shake their hand."[10] For the candidate, this type of face-to-face contact serves an educational purpose; Dawn also found it enjoyable much of the time. "You meet a lot of people from a lot of different backgrounds, and that is kind of fun even though you don't get to know them well. You develop a feeling that you have a better sense of what's out there, what people are thinking and feeling." As for the constant and repetitive public speaking, she says that she "grew into it."

Dawn and Jim Houlihan kept up this grueling pace from late September 1971, through the filing deadline in December, until the March 1972 primary and beyond, although the pace was not quite as harried after they had won the Democratic primary. They raised money through a finance committee—an incredible amount of money for that time, more than $70,000, much of it from coffees and fund-raisers, an art auction, and ice cream parties.

The campaign for the nomination took on the character of a mission. The Netsch-Houlihan team had 2,000 to 2,500 volunteers determined to take on Mayor Daley's political machine, which was in very bad odor after the 1968 Democratic National Convention, when television audiences had seen Daley's anger at the demonstrators and his unleashing of the Chicago police against them. (Indeed, at the 1972 Democratic National Convention in Miami, a delegation of independent Democrats led by Alderman Bill Singer and Rev. Jesse Jackson succeeded in unseating the delegates iden-tified with the Chicago Democratic Organization because they had been slated in closed party sessions and did not represent the party's racial, ethnic, and gender diversity.) So troops were available for the campaign in the Thirteenth District. "There was a mission—anti-Machine, open up the party. In the minds of some, the mission was to destroy the Machine, but for a lot of us it was to force it to recognize that the Democratic Party was more than the small elite clique who had been running it so long," says Dawn.[11] Governor Stevenson's son Adlai Stevenson III, who was by then the U.S. senator from Illinois, endorsed Netsch and Houlihan, as did the group Independent Voters of Illinois.

Dawn's individual campaign literature for the March primary was rather staid, featuring a photo of her underneath her name, with a rising sun drawn over the *w*, accompanied by a list of her numerous accomplishments, and the proposition "If we are to have responsible, responsive state government[,] private citizens must be willing to challenge the idea that elected officials are in Springfield to service the special interests."[12] The biographical sketch highlighted Dawn's connection to independent Democratic politics. Most of the joint campaign literature, however, featured the Netsch-Houlihan team and their joint program, emphasizing ethics in politics and government, judicial reform, and a variety of local issues such as the sale of meat after 6 P.M. and the teardown of older buildings that cheaply built, ugly modern developments (four-plus-ones, as they are known in Chicago) were replacing. The two candidates made public disclosure of their assets and income, which was not a problem for Houlihan, who was unemployed, but raised concerns about Walter Netsch's privacy interests. Ultimately, only the sources of Walter's income were disclosed and not the amount. Netsch and Houlihan established a precedent by making public all contributions their campaigns received.

The following anecdote underlines Dawn's uniqueness as a political candidate: Key members of the joint Netsch-Houlihan campaign staff would come together in both the 1972 and 1974 campaigns for Sunday-morning meetings to plot strategy. As was typical of political campaigns, the frequent use of foul language marked the discussion. One day Dawn visibly became more and more tense, until she suddenly banged her fist on the table and declared, "There will be no more swearing in this campaign!"[13] There was a long, startled silence before everyone started to laugh. But the staffers did try to curb their use of obscenity after that for Dawn's sake. Whenever veterans of the Netsch-Houlihan campaigns get together for a reunion, everyone reminds her of how she told them to clean up their language.

On March 21, 1972, the voters went to the polls. Dawn was quite certain that she would not win:

> I remember on election night, which was of course primary night, being over by myself in Streeterville shaking hands and reminding people to vote before seven o'clock. It was dark by then and felt gloomy and depressing. I went back to our apartment on East Cedar . . . , went in the dining room and sat down and started writing my concession speech because I was positive I'd lost. As the evening wore on, it wasn't so clear . . . and at some point it was clear enough that I was going to make it. I remember walking into this hall and going up these stairs, and this huge

cheer went up. It was like winning an Olympic gold medal or something because no one thought we could do this. Nancy and Adlai showed up. I don't remember what speech I could have given because I'd only written a concession speech.[14]

As it turns out, she had defeated O'Brien by a five-to-four margin. The Chicago newspapers described her victory as posing serious problems for Mayor Daley and the Chicago Democrats, perhaps preventing them from controlling the organization of the Illinois Senate. Journalists also spoke of the possibility of a developing "third force" of independents, who would hold the balance of power in the General Assembly.[15] The machine was furious and vowed to get revenge in the next election, scheduled for 1974. (Illinois Senate terms are typically four years, but the districts are redrawn after each decennial census; thus, each senator serves two four-year and one two-year term during every ten-year period.)

Although Houlihan and Netsch continued to campaign after the March primary, the winner of the Democratic nomination in Chicago was virtually guaranteed victory. Moreover, in late September, Dawn's Republican opponent, Richard K. Means, withdrew from the race, saying that his views were very similar to those of his opponent.[16] A little more than a month before the election, the Republicans replaced him with another candidate for the senate from that district, but Dawn won the election with ease.

In January 1973, Dawn Clark Netsch was sworn in as the new state senator from the Thirteenth District. She returned to a life of constant movement between Chicago, where she continued to teach a course each semester, and Springfield, where she maintained an apartment near the capitol. She also set up a legislative office in her district in Chicago and hired Rita McLennon as her legislative assistant. Dawn wanted very much to be accessible to her constituents. Her first office was not far from Cabrini-Green, but Dawn reluctantly agreed to move it to a storefront on Armitage Avenue when McLennon expressed concerns for her personal safety.

McLennon kept Dawn's calendar, attended a lot of community meetings, and briefed Dawn on what was going on in her district. Although Dawn initially struck Rita as "patrician" and a bit intimidating, she soon saw how interested Dawn was in other people and her comfort with the diversity of people she represented. With amusement, McLennon remembers Dawn going to a community meeting at the Cabrini-Green public housing project on a cold day wearing her full-length fur coat:

She walks into this basement in Cabrini Green and sits down on the floor in her full-length fur coat with all these people. They all talked to her as though she were their best friend and supporter and talked openly to her. . . . She was their vehicle. They came to hear and taught her about the issues, and she used her expertise in government and law to turn it into a solution. She would constantly advise them about the best way to move forward, to get what you want, to move incrementally. One reason she was so effective getting things done and convincing people in the community she was on their side was that she never lied to them. She said, "This is going to be hard."[17]

As the newspapers had predicted, Dawn lost no time entering into alliances with other independent legislators in Springfield. In particular, she joined a small study group of Democratic senators from districts outside Chicago—Terry Bruce, from Olney; Ken Buzbee, from Carbondale; Betty Keegan, a former Con Con delegate from Rockford; and Don Wooten, from Rock Island. The five got together on a regular basis to discuss issues, although they did not yet have the strength to make their mark as a caucus on the floor of the senate.

In her first year and a half in office, Dawn sponsored a number of consumer and tenants' rights bills for, among other things, the sale of meat after 6 P.M., unit pricing of groceries, simplification of food-dating codes on groceries, the posting of drug prices, and landlords' disclosure of the portion of rent used to pay property taxes and an income tax deduction for renters on that portion. Although she succeeded in raising all these issues, none of her bills passed the legislature. She did manage to obtain more state funds for subsidized day-care programs, however, and assumed major responsibility for passage of the Equal Rights Amendment. She also worked for the passage of a bill to establish a Regional Transportation Authority to build a transportation network for the Chicago metropolitan area, which was submitted to a referendum in March 1974. One of her main themes, repeatedly emphasized, was the necessity for greater state funding of local school systems.

Dawn spoke up often on the floor, embracing causes that were not dear to the Chicago Regular Democrats, including issues on which she had differed with the organization's delegates at Con Con, such as merit selection of judges. She also fought for a law requiring campaign finance reform, specifically for requiring campaign-fund disclosure and stricter accounting of elected officials' financial interests. On many of these issues, she did not endear herself to the political forces she had defeated in the 1972 election, and she clearly showed her independence of them.

The 1974 Election

In November 1973, Dawn announced that she would seek reelection to the Illinois Senate, pledging to "continue to press for consumer bills, for reform of the landlord-tenant relationship, for a more equitable tax structure, and for the passage of the Equal Rights Amendment."[18] The Chicago machine determined to defeat her in the 1974 primary and reclaim the Thirteenth District as its own. Danny O'Brien and George Dunne decided to try a new approach, however. To oppose Dawn in the primary, they chose a young (thirty-two years old) political science instructor, Arnold Levy, an urban planner who had worked in the Model Cities program and who had not been historically connected with the machine. On the theory that old-style, ethnic-based politics could still reclaim the lakefront, Levy's primary advantage in the eyes of the organization was that he was Jewish. Counting on the Jewish population along the lakefront to vote on the basis of ethnic identification rather than reform, the organization threw its support behind Levy.[19]

Dawn quickly acquired endorsements from Senator Adlai Stevenson III, Congressman Sid Yates, Abner Mikva, the Independent Voters of Illinois, the United Auto Workers, and many other groups, as well as from each of the local newspapers. Nancy Stevenson set up the Women's Task Force for Netsch, a group of more than one hundred women who did precinct work throughout the district and were known as "Dawn's patrol," wearing buttons with that name.

The media widely depicted the March 1974 primary in the Thirteenth District, taking place amid the political cynicism of the Watergate crisis, as a major battle between Mayor Daley and Governor Dan Walker, on the state level, and between Mayor Daley and Alderman Bill Singer, in the city. Singer planned to run for mayor of Chicago in 1975, but if his independent allies could not hold onto the lakefront district that was their original base of support, his plan would seem unrealistic. Governor Walker endorsed a complete slate of candidates, billing it as antimachine, but he was so unpopular by that time that Dawn and Jim Houlihan, again running a joint campaign, did not ask him to campaign in their district.

As it was, Arnold Levy tried to paint Dawn as a puppet of Dan Walker. Dawn herself was quoted as saying that the overriding issue at stake in the election was "machine domination versus nonmachine domination. Everything that we've been trying to do to open up the political process—getting away from the old way of having party bosses handpick candidates—is at stake."[20] Levy shot back that Dawn was part of the "independent" machine and closely tied to Governor Walker.

As one might expect in a campaign thus turned into an Armageddon-like battle, the March 1974 primary became bitter and was characterized by "dirty" tactics. When Dawn or her supporters attacked Levy, they were made to seem anti-Semitic. In response, Dawn's campaign literature featured the names of her prominent Jewish supporters. A journalist followed Dawn into the grocery store and reported that she selected "a nice can of matzo ball soup for Walter."[21] Dawn tried not to get caught up in this "sideshow," she says, but to stick to the issues.

Dawn charged that Levy was misrepresenting her legislative record by accusing her of voting against subsidies for the Chicago Transit Authority, against funding for the public library system and to improve the lagoons in Chicago's parks, and either failing to vote for or voting against a number of other causes dear to liberal voters. Indeed, he seemed to claim that a recent fire in her district would not have occurred if she had voted differently on one bill. Dawn's campaign issued a brochure called "Have They Lied Enough to Steal the Election from Senator Dawn Clark Netsch?" that addressed and refuted each accusation. The campaign literature concluded, "The boys in the back room . . . are insulting your intelligence and assaulting your sensibilities with lies . . . half truths . . . distortions. They are out to get Senator Dawn Clark Netsch with every trick known to machine politicians."[22]

Netsch and Levy met in a series of debates. The two, both liberal Democrats, did not appear to differ in any significant respect on substantive policy issues, both opposing the death penalty and favoring gun control, adequate funding of social services, the Regional Transportation Authority, the Equal Rights Amendment, and public disclosure of campaign contributions, for example.[23] Dawn was taken aback by Levy's vigorous attacks on her legislative record at the first of their confrontations. According to the *Chicago Sun-Times*, "It started getting harder for the senator to smile. . . . Dawn Netsch's angular face had tightened into the stiff, uneasy grin that comes when someone tries too hard to look comfortable."[24] By their second encounter, however, Dawn was prepared for Levy's tactic and turned the focus instead to her experience in the legislative process, pointing out Levy's lack of knowledge when he made an erroneous statement about potential sources of funding for the RTA.[25] By the time of their final debate on March 10, Netsch and Levy hurled angry comments at each other, with Levy opening by saying, "My opponent has made it a point to attack my integrity, my honesty, and my independence."[26]

In an unusual move, a group of six state senators, three Democrats and three Republicans, issued a statement defending Dawn's voting record on the various points put at issue, holding a press conference just before the election to say, "We must universally deplore a campaign tactic that is unfair, deceptive, and could be used against any of us by an unethical opponent. The blatant misrepresentations and half truths [used against Senator Netsch] have no place in American politics."[27] Levy quickly called a press conference to accuse Netsch of "blatant demagoguery and libelous insults."[28] Indeed, tensions ran so high in this primary that massive security was deployed to prevent vote fraud or other irregularities. The U.S. attorney, James R. Thompson, set up "special surveillance . . . of polls in the west section of the . . . Senate District where Arnold Levy, a Regular Democrat, is challenging incumbent independent Sen. Dawn Clark Netsch."[29]

The battle between Netsch and Levy went down to the wire, but when the votes were counted on March 19, she had defeated him by between two thousand and three thousand votes. Admitting that her reelection had "looked very, very squeaky" up to the last minute, Dawn asserted that her victory showed that "the people want a more open process. That's what the independent movement is about."[30] After 11 on the night of the election, at a jubilant Netsch-Houlihan victory party attended by Singer, Stevenson, and Mikva, Dawn told the crowd, "We can say the whole city of Chicago will never be the same again. . . . We have opened the political process and made it available to all."[31]

Reflecting on the vote a day later, Dawn exulted in beating the machine. "We took their full power, their full thrust, and we beat 'em anyway. . . . They could hardly have thrown more power than they threw against us."[32] Analysis of the election results showed that Levy had in fact cut into her margin in the Jewish community, but that she had cut into the machine's traditional vote in the working-class areas on the western side of her district. She and her campaign workers had gone from house to house to persuade what they called "the ethnic precincts" and had succeeded in making gains in the machine's own stronghold. By repeatedly attending community meetings and spaghetti suppers at St. Alphonsus Church, for example, Dawn had gotten to know people one on one and had demonstrated that she was not an ogre.

Apart from Dawn's narrow win and a few other races, Mayor Daley, though not himself a candidate, was generally agreed to be the victor in the 1974 primary election, with his endorsed candidates defeating most of those endorsed by Governor Walker. The RTA was also approved in a six-county vote. But the Chicago Democratic Organization never mounted a primary challenge to Dawn again for the sixteen more years she remained in the Illinois Senate.

"The Crazy Eight"

After the 1974 election, the Democratic study group Dawn belonged to in the Illinois Senate was joined by newly elected Vince Demuzio, of Carlinville; Jerry Joyce, of Reddick; and Bill Morris, of Waukegan. Vivian Hickey, of Rockford, replaced Betty Keegan, who had died. Along with Dawn, Terry Bruce, Ken Buzbee, and Don Wooten, the group now totaled eight. Terry Bruce later named them, jokingly, the Crazy Eight. Their meetings to share information and discuss issues grew more frequent. At times—during the third reading of bills, for example, they met nearly every day, early in the morning.[33] The meetings usually took place at the capitol building but occasionally at Dawn's apartment in the Lincoln Towers near the capitol. Members of the group represented diverse geographical perspectives and differed on many issues, but they strove to educate one another. Jerry Joyce contributed the viewpoint of the agricultural community—for example, farmers' opposition to inheritance taxes. Coming from the city of Chicago, Dawn was a big RTA booster, but Bill Morris, from Lake County, was an opponent.[34] Dawn brought to the group her insider's knowledge of state government going back to Governor Kerner and before, as well as a profound understanding of the state constitution and rules. All of them were serious about researching and debating the issues, but they did not expect to vote as a bloc.

The one thing on which the eight did agree, however, was their determination to open up the organization of the state senate; the Chicago Democratic leadership had long controlled all the leadership posts and committee assignments. In this respect, Dawn's knowledge of the legislature and its rules was helpful. She eventually put together a list of the procedural changes needed to approach the vision of a more participatory democracy the group shared. Terry Bruce suggested that the group hold out on the vote to elect the senate president at the beginning of the legislative session as a strategy to force some of the reforms Dawn had designed. The Crazy Eight's first major rebellion took place in late 1974 and early 1975.

Cecil Partee, an African American senator from Chicago identified with the Daley machine, called together the senate Democratic caucus to select leaders for the 1975–76 session. Partee, who had presided over an evenly divided senate in 1971–72, assumed that he would easily be elected to the same role now that the Democrats had taken control of the chamber, and then he would name the other leaders of the senate. He had not counted on the independent Democratic senators' determination to open up the senate leadership to individuals and groups other than those controlled by the Daley machine. In December 1974, the Crazy Eight signed a telegram of protest to Partee, objecting to his "secret and high-handed methods" of setting the vote for majority leader of the senate. Terry Bruce told the press, "The issue is whether Partee will conduct an open leadership and consult his members on meeting dates, committee assignments, and the naming of committee chairmen." Dawn added that, if individual senators were not consulted on organizing the new senate, "we might as well not be there."[35]

When the day arrived to elect the new president of the senate, the independents nominated Bruce to oppose Partee, making it impossible to reach a majority with the Democratic vote thus split. Given the disciplined voting by most Democratic senators in the past, this was unthinkable. But at the end of the first roll call in January, Partee did not have the thirty votes required for election as president of the senate. A recess was called.

The Crazy Eight had a list of demands drawn up by Dawn—for inclusion of independents on each committee, for committee staff, and to allow African American members to choose their own leader, for example. During the tense discussion that followed the recess, they presented these demands to Partee and the Chicago Democrats. After caucusing for several hours, a compromise was reached: Partee had enough votes to be elected president, but Bruce became one of his assistant majority leaders, and members of the Crazy Eight were represented on all of the major committees. This successful rebellion lasted just one day, but it was only the first round.

During the two years that followed, the Crazy Eight became good friends, and the group began to expand. Morris recalls that they had dinner together once a week and got to know one another as people rather than just as members of a coalition, building a personal relationship that has persisted to this day.[36] George Sangmeister, from Joliet, joined them, and by 1976, the now nine members of the study group began to meet with members of the Black Caucus as well—Kenneth Hall, from East St. Louis; Harold Washington; Richard Newhouse; and Earlean Collins, from Chicago. This meant that they commanded thirteen votes and could demand more reforms.

When it came time to elect the president of the senate on the second Wednesday in January 1977, Terry Bruce opposed Thomas Hynes, the machine's candidate for the position. The Chicago group, citing Hamilton and Jefferson, insisted on the prerogative of the majority to pick their leader and the constitutional authority of that presiding officer to select the assistant leaders and committee chairs. Phil Rock, one of the Chicago Democratic Organization's members from Chicago and later president of the senate himself, remembers that the Crazy Eight "had almost a manifesto of what they wanted to see. First was participatory democracy, and the spokesperson for that was Dawn Netsch, who tried to explain that the decision making and general operation of the process ought to be more diffuse, with power not centered in one or two persons."[37] A particularly strong demand that the now-thirteen members pushed was the right of the black senators to choose their own representative in senate leadership. As they put it in a February 3, 1977, press release, "It is central to our position that no one can tell any group who will press their cause, who will express their ambitions, or who will develop their issues."[38]

The senate ground to a halt over the impasse between the two groups of Democrats. This stalemate persisted for five weeks and 186 ballots, the most ever cast in the General Assembly on any single issue. As people throughout the state became concerned that the senate was at a standstill, with then governor James R. Thompson forced to preside over roll call after roll call, Dawn wrote to the *Chicago Tribune:*

> The vote to organize is the single most important vote we will cast this session. It will determine whether everyone in the state will be fairly and evenly represented or whether decisions will continue to be made by a few individuals. . . .

This is a fight over a basic principle, not over personalities or positions. We want permanent rules put together by a cross-section of senators from both sides of the aisle. We want a fair hearing for our proposals to expedite Senate business, made more than two years ago.[39]

A famous soup-throwing incident was perhaps a sign of the level of tension in the senate at this time. During the day when a compromise was being worked out to end the crisis, Dawn was standing near the press box talking to reporters while the senate was in recess. Senator John Knuppel, an eccentric character who was generally hostile to the Crazy Eight, told them to get out of the aisle. When Dawn told him that they had every right to be there and meant to stay, Knuppel rushed to his seat, picked up a cup of hot vegetable soup, then came back down the aisle and threw its contents all over Dawn and the two others with whom she was speaking, including Charlie Wheeler, the Springfield correspondent for the *Chicago Sun-Times*. Knuppel told the press, "I was in a rage."[40] A picture of the incident appeared on the front page of the next day's *Sun-Times*. Dawn sent Knuppel the cleaning bill for her suit, but he never paid it. (He later gave her an autographed can of Campbell's soup.)[41]

At long last, Phil Rock negotiated a compromise that included a substantial number of concessions to the list of the Crazy Eight's demands. After seventeen hours of continuous negotiations, at around 5 A.M. on February 16, 1977, Hynes was elected the new senate president. Both Kenny Hall, the choice of the Black Caucus, and Terry Bruce became assistant majority leaders. Richard Newhouse was appointed chair of the Advisory Committee on Public Aid, and each member of the expanded Crazy Eight got a major committee assignment. The powerful Senate Judiciary Committee, headed by Mayor Daley's son Richard M. "Richie" Daley, was split into civil and criminal committees, and Dawn was named chair of the second. The *Chicago Tribune* described Senator Daley as forced to "give a chairmanship to his most severe critic—Sen. Dawn Clark Netsch."[42] The irony was that Dawn did not want to chair the criminal committee, especially at a time when all its members except for her were obsessed with law and order and repeatedly outvoted her. What she wanted instead was to chair the Revenue Committee.

The 1977 Crazy Eight rebellion is one of the things of which Dawn is most proud from her period in the legislature:

We did begin to get them to understand that how the senate conducted its business has a lot to do with the work product that came out of it. . . . This was the beginning of breaking the stranglehold [of the Cook County Democratic Organization on the process]. . . . It came about through the cohesion of the Crazy Eight.[43]

Dawn subsequently introduced seventeen amendments to the rules, the procedural reforms from the 1977 list that they had not succeeded in obtaining. Almost all of her proposed amendments were defeated at that time, but a few were eventually adopted, such as doing away with proxy voting, allowing the principal sponsor of a bill to decide who would sponsor it in the Illinois House, and giving legislators some limited freedom in selecting their own staff, who had previously been assigned by (and were loyal to) the leadership.

The Crazy Eight remained intensely loyal to one another and supportive of one another's political careers. When Vince Demuzio, the first of them to die, planned his funeral in 2004, he insisted that the Crazy Eight be honorary pallbearers, and they were all in Carlinville for the well-attended Catholic service. Richie, the boss's son, was himself mayor of Chicago by that time. When he arrived, the Crazy Eight were lining up for the procession. Phil Rock said to Rich Daley, "Here's the crazies." Rich Daley said jokingly, "I can confess now; I was the ninth member of the Crazy Eight."[44]

The Other Richard Daley

Richard M. Daley was Mayor Richard J. Daley's oldest son, born in 1942. After an undistinguished law school career, he began his professional life in city hall as an attorney in the Corporation Counsel's office. He soon left for private practice, in a family law firm that clearly benefited from its political connections. His first involvement in politics was Con Con. He easily won election as a delegate with the backing of his father's political organization and the strength of his name; in fact, he won more votes than any other candidate did. Only twenty-seven years old at the time, Rich did not play much of a role at the convention. In 1972, Mayor Daley asked an aging state senator from Bridgeport, the Irish neighborhood where the Daleys lived, to step aside so that his son could run for the position. Again, Rich won in a landslide, and his father also gave him day-to-day responsibility for managing the Eleventh Ward Democratic Organization (Bridgeport), the largest and most patronage rich in the city.[45]

The young Daley thus arrived in the Illinois Senate at the same time as Dawn Clark Netsch, after she defeated the machine candidate for her district. They were natural enemies. Their interactions were not good from the beginning. New senators choose their seats on the senate floor after the incumbents have taken those they want. The new senators in 1972 drew straws to determine who would be the first to select a seat, and Dawn got the first pick. Surveying a map of seats on the floor, she chose one that seemed good, not in the front or the back, in a place where she could look at both sides of the chamber. After indicating her choice, she heard a gasp. One of the Daley regulars, Charlie Chew, immediately took her aside and told her, "You've got to give up that seat; it's the kid's seat. It's the [Eleventh Ward] seat. It's where the old man sat." Fresh from an electoral confrontation with the machine, Dawn wanted to establish that they could not push her around. She replied, "If someone had told me that beforehand, I would have been happy to let him have his traditional seat; but if you do not take me into things, I won't go back on a decision."[46] She kept the seat for her eighteen years in the Illinois Senate.

During her first years in the senate, Dawn focused to a large extent on consumer bills—ones concerning open dating of groceries and their shelf life, for example. The machine repeatedly killed her bills, so that she would not get credit for statewide reforms identical to those they were proposing in Chicago as city ordinances. Dawn was given no position of leadership. By contrast, the young and inexperienced Rich Daley was made chair of the Senate Judiciary Committee within two years, and he used that position to kill bill after bill that Dawn proposed. Speaking to reporters after one of her bills had just been killed, Dawn spoke angrily about "little Richie" and his dirty tricks. This was translated by the press into "a fuming Mrs. Netsch told reporters that 'dirty, little Richie' has fouled up her bills again."[47] Although Dawn denies she ever used that phrase, the myth took on a reality of its own.

Rich Daley was at odds with the Crazy Eight on almost everything; and when it was suggested in 1975 that he might become president of the senate, Dawn was quoted as saying, "As long as it takes a majority of the Senate to be elected, Richie Daley will never be president."[48] Interviewed in 1982, she said, "I don't make any bones about the fact that he was pretty awful back then. . . . It was hard for someone like me to get anything through his committee or others he was on. It got very petty and very mean."[49] The *Chicago Tribune* reported that "Netsch was particularly enraged when Daley publicly denounced her bill to allow meat sales after 6 P.M. as a 'cheap publicity stunt,' and when he blocked a series of minor technical revisions in state statutes because they bore her name."[50]

Just before Christmas in 1976, Mayor Richard J. Daley, who had survived a primary challenge by Bill Singer in 1975, died of a heart attack. Bridgeport resident Michael Bilandic was appointed mayor by the city council, but it was unclear who was really in control of the organization. Young Daley was soon advised that he needed to make his mark by taking on some substantive legislation, and he chose to focus on reform of the state's mental health code, which was before his committee.

A special commission appointed by Governor Dan Walker had been working on revisions to the mental health code for several years and had come up with an extensive package of bills covering a number of areas— the mental health code, the insanity defense, creation of a guardianship and advocacy commission, and so on. Dawn was in charge of shepherding the package through the senate. When it was clear that problems needed to be worked out between the senate and the house of representatives, she proposed establishing a joint bipartisan committee to work on them. Normally she would automatically have been made chair of this committee because she had sponsored the bill to create it. But Dawn was repeatedly told by the powers-that-were that Rich wanted to chair the joint committee instead. Realizing that she would be outvoted on this, she chose to meet directly with Daley. She told him that the committee was going to be a lot of work and would take a great deal of time. He seemed hesitant at first, then came back to her after thinking about it and said that he wanted to be chair. So she told him that she would even second the motion so long as he was willing to put in the necessary time, because the commission had done so much good work and she did not want the important reforms to fail.[51]

Dawn realized that the inexperienced Daley would clearly need staff with expertise in the area and recommended that he approach a young University of Chicago doctoral candidate who had been on the staff of the governor's commission to study the code, Frank Kruesi. Daley eventually did get in touch with and hired the scholarly Kruesi, who served as his intellectual alter ego through much of his public life thereafter. This odd couple somehow made an effective team.

Dawn was on the joint bipartisan committee herself and cared deeply about reform of mental health laws in Illinois, a subject that had been of interest to her since her early newspaper clipping days in the Committee on Illinois Government, so she and Daley spent a huge amount of time working together on this bill. To her pleasant surprise, young Daley really got interested in the subject and spent a great deal of time on it. Dawn thinks it was probably the first time in his life he had been involved in an issue of substance, with no political agenda. Toward the end of the work on passage of the mental health code, however, Daley and his wife Maggie's son Kevin was born with spina bifida and required full-time medical attention. His parents took turns staying with him in the hospital. With Daley spending so much time in Chicago, Dawn did a good deal of the work on the senate floor to get the bill passed, communicating with him by phone.

The Illinois Mental Health and Developmental Disabilities Code was finally approved on September 5, 1978, to go into effect the following January.[52] After all of Dawn's work on it, Daley was the person who got credit for passage of the new code. Dawn says, "I didn't mind. This is one of the things you have to learn, particularly when you go into the game as an outsider. They'd take our good legislation away from us and not give us credit."[53] And her improved relationship with Daley yielded benefits when Dawn needed the Chicago Democratic Organization's support thereafter, such as on the generic drug substitution bill, which needed unified Democratic support to pass because almost every Republican opposed it.

During this period of gradual rapprochement between Daley and Dawn, Dawn held her annual softball game event in her Chicago district, where the "politicians" would play against the "people," and Dawn would coach the latter. On a whim, she invited Daley in 1977, although she did not expect that he would come. Players and spectators alike were astonished when he showed up. Daley stayed for the entire game, although he simply watched and cheered rather than playing. After the game, regulars who played in it each year would retire to Dawn's house. "Rich came along and stayed for a long, long time," Dawn says. "Our joke was that it was the first time he'd been north of the river in his life. . . . It was funny to see people who'd spent their lives fighting the Daley machine standing around talking to him, in awe of being that close to a Daley."[54] Apparently he impressed them as a regular guy. The event made headlines.[55] And overcoming their mutual hostility proved very important to the careers of both Daley and Dawn in the future.

—— *Chapter 13* ——

Legislative Losses and Gains

AFTER DAWN NETSCH AND Rich Daley buried the hatchet, Dawn's legislative initiatives had more chance of passing. It is impossible to cover her activities over eighteen years in the legislature in any detail. This chapter instead focuses on a number of areas and issues about which Dawn cared intensely: consumer legislation; ethics and campaign reform; continuing struggles to expand the leadership of the senate; revenue and finance; and a variety of gender-related issues important to women, such as the Equal Rights Amendment, reform of Illinois' rape laws, and family leave.

The Generic Drug Bill and Other Consumer Legislation

In the late 1970s, some of the consumer legislation Dawn had sponsored began to bear fruit. One issue in which she was particularly interested was lowering the price of prescription medicine, which was becoming unaffordable for many citizens. As early as 1975, a bill she sponsored to allow prescription drug advertising passed the senate, the first drug-related consumer legislation to do so. Dawn's perspective derived from her background in antitrust law: "Any restriction on price information is a restriction on competition," she declared, arguing that advertising would stimulate competition among pharmacists and result in lower prices.[1]

The consumer legislation about which Dawn is most proud is the generic drug bill, which she introduced soon after becoming a senator and continued to fight for until its passage in 1977. Generic drugs are nontrademarked and cheaper but chemically identical versions of prescription drugs. Before this legislation, generics could not be used under any government-paid programs in Illinois, such as Medicaid and Medicare, and this cost the state a great deal of extra money. Pharmaceutical companies opposed the generic drug bill because they made a much higher profit on labeled drugs. Dawn had presented several well-known doctors as witnesses before the Senate Committee on Public Health and Welfare, of which she was a member, to allay people's concerns that generic drugs were inferior. Because of opposition by most of the Republican senators, however, the bill did not make it out of committee. These were the years during which Dawn's identification with a bill or issue tended to prevent machine Democratic senators from supporting it. Fred Smith, a black senator from the South Side, for example, would ask of every piece of legislation whether Dawn was supporting it: "If it's her bill, don't bother me."[2]

Dawn was committed to passage of the generic drug bill and continued to work on it, meeting with people in the pharmaceutical community and gaining the cooperation and advice of John O'Connell, then the lobbyist for Walgreen drugstores. After the bill passed the state house of representatives, she spent many hours with Paul Peterson, Governor Thompson's director of public health, making adjustments to the bill so that it would not be vetoed if it passed the senate. Dawn's version of the bill provided that a pharmacy could substitute any generic drug unless it was on a list of nonsuitable substitutes. Peterson wanted a positive rather than a negative formula—that is, acceptable generic drugs would be listed in a state formula. Although his version was more restrictive, the bill was revised to avoid the governor's opposition.

Although it seemed likely that the generic drug bill would pass on the senate floor, it was still necessary to get it out of the Committee on Public Health and Welfare. This required Dawn to engage in intensive lobbying of several Democratic senators on that committee. One of them was Charlie Chew, who was not averse to supporting the bill as part of a favor-swapping deal. At that time, Dawn also had legislation pending that involved requiring a commitment by banks to the community in which they were located. The bill had very little hope of passage. Chew, an African American, did not want to be forced to vote against the bill on the floor, although he intended to do so because of his commitments to various banks. So Dawn made a deal. She would not call the banking bill to the floor, where it would not pass in any event but would embarrass Chew in front of his constituents, if he would vote for the generic drug bill. When Chew appeared to be wavering on the committee vote, Dawn leaned over and whispered in his ear, "Charlie, you promised."[3] He voted yes; the bill left committee and passed the senate, and the governor did not oppose it.

Dawn attributes her ability to get the generic drug bill through in 1977 at least in part to her new and improved relationship with Daley.

Dawn later helped Daley out by agreeing to support him in his 1980 race for state's attorney of Cook County. But, she insists, she did not promise her support until she had assured herself that he would be strong both on ethics violations and on election law. Daley was opposed in the primary by Ed Burke, a machine regular, and Dawn was able to persuade some of her independent Democratic allies to support Daley in the race. "Most of them didn't want to touch him with a ten-foot pole," she says. "He was a good state's attorney, and he kept his word on the things we had talked about."[4]

A 1980 study by the University of Illinois College of Pharmacy about the impact of the generic drug bill showed that the new law had saved consumers money but was not used as often as possible because the prescription forms were confusing to doctors. There were two possible signature lines, each accompanied by a box to check, one indicating that a generic drug was acceptable and the other directing pharmacists to fill the prescription as written. To remedy this problem, Dawn introduced another bill in March 1981 to amend the 1977 act by eliminating the sign-and-check system on prescription forms. Unless a doctor affirmatively stated that the generic form of a drug was unacceptable, the pharmacist could offer a generic substitute. The amended version passed both houses of the legislature, and the governor signed it.

Bob Creamer, who founded the Illinois Public Action Council, a public interest lobbying group, often worked with Dawn to pass consumer-oriented legislation, and her ability as a negotiator impressed him. "Dawn was always pretty good at negotiating deals with people in the legislature to pick up votes. She's a good negotiator. Being a good negotiator requires that you understand the other person's self-interest. . . . You put yourself in their place and understand how to 'get to yes.' She's good at that."[5] Like Creamer, Jan Schakowsky also worked closely with Dawn as a lobbyist for IPAC. Dawn was very supportive of their work and would give them sound advice about how to proceed, often sponsoring their bills, moving them through committee, arguing for them on the floor, and lining up the votes needed for passage. She would also act as a major spokesperson for bills to which she was committed, setting up public events, press conferences, and going on television talk shows to line up popular support.

In the mid-1980s, Dawn worked intensively with IPAC and others on the rewrite of the public utility act—the first revision of the Illinois utilities law since it had been passed in 1913, the era of utility baron Samuel Insull; the earlier version was predictably slanted toward the utilities. The bill that passed in 1985 included a number of consumer-oriented provisions, including establishing a public counsel to represent consumers before the Illinois Commerce Commission, making it easier for courts to overturn ICC rate case decisions, allowing the ICC to require audits of power plant management, and requiring utilities to submit long-range energy plans.[6] However, the basic bill passed in 1985 did not deal with the issue of so-called excess capacity. The issue there was whether the big electric utilities had overbuilt substantially and incurred huge cost overruns in the construction of nuclear power plants and, if so, whether they could charge consumers for their bad judgments. Dawn introduced, and reintroduced, legislation to place a 25 percent limit on unused capacity over peak demand; utilities would have to eliminate any generating capacity beyond that from the rates charged to consumers.[7] Although she did succeed in getting this bill through the senate, it failed in the house of representatives. She is philosophical about this failure: "Although we didn't get that bill passed, we did get some things that helped into the main bill; we got Com Ed focusing almost 100 percent on excess capacity, so they beat us on that, but the other things got through."[8]

Ethics and Campaign Reform Legislation

Dawn worked tirelessly throughout her senate career on legislation to improve governmental ethics and to reform campaign finance, with some small success along the way. In her first term, a campaign-finance disclosure bill had passed the house but was bottled up in a senate committee. Dawn stood up on the floor and demanded action on the bill, thus forcing the senators to take a stand they might have preferred to avoid. They voted thirty-five to twenty against bringing the bill to the floor, but Dawn won praise in the Chicago press for her courage.[9] She and her staff later drafted a major rewrite of the Illinois Governmental Ethics Act in an attempt to construct a coherent code of ethics for the executive branch, covering topics like conflicts of interest, revolving door appointments, and the like. After working on the draft for a year and a half, Dawn introduced the bill in the mid-1980s but could never get it through the senate.

In 1981 Dawn sponsored a bill to establish public financing of gubernatorial elections, to be funded by a $1 check-off on state income tax forms; the senate rejected it by a vote of thirty-two to twenty-four.[10] With assistance from Harriet McCullough, the lobbyist for Common Cause, Dawn also drafted the first campaign finance reform bill, which would have limited campaign contributions in gubernatorial elections to $1,000 per individual and $5,000 for corporations and political action committees. This bill did get through the legislature, but Governor Thompson vetoed it.[11]

Dawn's one outright success with legislation in this area was a Code of Fair Campaign Practices, which she drafted by taking bits from similar codes in other states. The code was voluntary but intended to be signed by all who ran for state office, who thereby promised, among other things, not to engage in the misrepresentation of facts or unfounded accusations or to appeal to prejudice based on race, sex, sexual orientation, religion, or national origin. The only sanction was exposure by their opponents if they violated it. Dawn's bill did become law in 1987, but it was buried in a larger piece of legislation so that she was not given credit for it.[12]

Merit Selection of Judges

Perhaps Dawn's most relentless campaign was for a constitutional amendment to establish merit selection of judges, an issue the independent Democrats had supported but had lost in the referendum on the 1970 constitution. Judges in Illinois—trial, appellate, and supreme court—are all elected and then required to stand for retention in a yes-no election. Candidates for the judiciary in Cook County were virtually required to seek the support of the Democratic organization if they wanted to succeed and were often required to have given substantial service or money to its precinct organizations to be slated. They must raise funds for their campaigns, often from the very people and groups who appear before them. And the voters are faced at the polls with long lists of names of judges for election or retention—names most voters do not recognize. The vote on this section of the ballot drops off substantially and tends to mirror the recommendations handed to voters by the organization's precinct workers outside the polling places. Even when elections were contested, which under the first Mayor Daley was rare, voters had so little information about judicial candidates (and many voters simply did not care) that unqualified candidates could be elected just because they had an Irish name. The system poses obvious problems in terms of judicial quality and independence. Arguments raised in favor of the elective system emphasize its democratic nature and the virtues of mirroring the diversity of the electorate on the bench, as well as the ability to hold judges accountable at the polls. The other side of this, of course, is that judges can be defeated at the next election for rendering decisions that become unpopular for any reason, with obvious consequences for the independence of the judiciary. Moreover, studies show that racial minorities and women in fact do better under judicial systems basing selection on merit.[13]

Ever since merit selection failed to pass at the 1970 referendum on the new constitution, bills were introduced into the Illinois legislature virtually every year proposing to pass a constitutional amendment requiring merit selection. Dawn Clark Netsch was the principal sponsor of these bills and played a major role in this advocacy during her entire period in the legislature. Varying merit selection plans competed—not only those introduced by legislators but also others proposed by the Illinois State Bar Association, the Chicago Bar Association, and various task forces that the governor or the Cook County court system set up. All included nominating commissions for each judicial circuit as a central feature, but they varied both as to how the commissions would be created and composed and as to who the appointing authority would be. All provided for judicial nominating commissions of an odd number of people, including both laypeople and lawyers, usually with laypeople in the majority. To ensure bipartisanship, the attorney general was to choose half of the lay members and the next highest state officer of a different party was to choose the other half. Some plans provided that other lawyers would elect the lawyers, and some provided that the Supreme Court appoint them. Typically the governor was the person designated to choose among a small number of candidates (usually three) presented to him by the commissions after they had investigated and evaluated those who had applied. Under one proposal, if he turned down the first candidate, the winner would be chosen by lot from the remaining candidates on the list presented by the commission.[14] Another plan provided that the supreme court choose among the names nominated by the commission.[15] The varying plans were widely debated both in the legislature and in the legal community at large.

The bills proposed by Dawn, always with bipartisan sponsorship, stayed fairly close in structure (though not in breadth of application) to the original plan reported out by the constitutional convention for a separate vote in 1970.[16] The governor was the appointing authority; other lawyers in the same district elected the lawyer members of the judicial nominating commissions; and the attorney general and the next highest-ranked state officer of a different party each selected half of the laypeople. Although Dawn believed in merit selection at all levels of the judiciary, her proposal provided only for requiring it at the supreme and appellate court level, while leaving a local option as to the circuit court judges. This was a strategic choice, made to recognize the different contexts in which the issue arose in downstate Illinois versus in Cook County. Downstate voters tended to be well informed about and to know the candidates, whom they had in fact closely observed over some time. Not suffering from the problems encountered by judicial election in Cook County, they preferred to continue electing their judges. Political realism, Dawn thought, necessitated incorporating a local option so that the constitutional amendment might pass. By contrast, although the Cook County Democratic Organization was vehemently opposed to it, the voters in Cook County had given the merit selection proposal a majority of their votes in the 1970 referendum on the constitution.

Dawn's first merit selection bill, Senate Joint Resolution 37, cosponsored with Republican Bradley Glass, was introduced into the senate in 1977 and applauded by the media.[17] In 1980 it actually reached the floor of the senate for what was the first debate and recorded vote on merit selection in that chamber. Opposed by the Regular Democrats, it failed to pass. During the Greylord scandal in the 1980s, during which an investigation into various forms of bribery and corruption in the Cook County judiciary resulted in the indictment of seventeen judges and the conviction of most of them, the arguments for merit selection appeared even stronger and garnered more support. Nonetheless, the legislature rejected proposal after proposal, and to date, Illinois still elects its circuit, appellate, and supreme court judges (except for associate judges, whom circuit judges select). The only change in the system has been to divide the Cook County circuit into a number of smaller subcircuits, on the theory that voters would be more likely to know the candidates.

Continuing Struggles with the Senate Leadership

Needless to say, many of the positions or policies for which Dawn fought were not popular with the Regular Democratic leaders, and she continued to struggle with them in the senate over both substantive issues and leadership within the party and the senate. In hopes of ridding themselves of her, when the 1980 census required redrawing the legislative map, the organization sponsored a map that would have consolidated two districts and pitted Dawn against another liberal Democrat for reelection. Phil Rock, whose leadership of the senate Dawn had repeatedly challenged, supported the map.[18] Later that same year, Michael Madigan, minority leader of the house, joined the attempt to redraw Dawn's senate district, causing the *Chicago Tribune* to comment, "As minority leader of the Illinois House he should have plenty to occupy him, but Mr. Madigan seems to be making a singleminded crusade out of his efforts to rid the Senate of one Independent Democrat."[19] Ultimately, the district was redrawn in a way that preserved the districts both of Dawn Netsch and Bill Marovitz. Dawn's district, thenceforth known as the Fourth, emerged from the redistricting with only minor changes from its previous boundaries.[20]

Dawn continued to challenge Rock in the senate. In January 1981, she threatened that her bloc within the senate Democrats, now commanding fourteen votes, would vote against Rock for senate president if he did not reduce the influence of Chicago Mayor Jane Byrne on legislative affairs and further democratize the senate. The dissidents also urged putting Dawn, who had declined reappointment as chair of the Criminal Judiciary Committee, into a leadership position; but they did not try to block the election of Rock that year.[21]

In January 1985, Dawn, the Crazy Eight, and members of the Black Caucus challenged Rock once again, demanding more input into the leadership of the senate in return for their votes. Although Rock narrowly won reelection, he did yield to the desire of this coalition and of then mayor of Chicago Harold Washington, the first African American to hold that office, to add a sixth leader to his senate team.[22]

The final showdown occurred in January 1987, when Dawn and others succeeded in holding up Rock's election as senate president for a day, until he agreed to increase the role of women in the senate. By then, women were a part of every leadership team in the General Assembly except for the senate Democrats. The dissidents' goal was to put Dawn in a position of leadership, but Rock again refused to do so. He reports that he told her:

> There is no way that I can accommodate you in a position of leadership. You ran as an independent against the Organization. You have consistently stood up against things that the Organization wanted. People recognize the fact that you are by self-definition an independent, [that] you are not relying upon the Organization.

Now that you've judged the Organization, to promote you for an assistant leadership spot is simply not going to happen.[23]

However, as the price of the dissidents' votes, Rock did finally promise to name a woman to the next vacancy among his assistant majority leaders and also to the powerful Senate Rules Committee. Dawn told the press that what was important was that the role of women in the senate and in the Democratic Party was being addressed for the first time.[24] Despite their power struggle, Rock seems to have respected Dawn, and the two in fact cosponsored many bills.

Revenue and Finance

Rock had, however, finally appointed Dawn to chair the committee she had long wanted, Revenue. For most of the 1980s, in fact, she both chaired the Senate Revenue Committee and chaired or cochaired the Economic and Fiscal Commission of Illinois. She thus was in the thick of the repeated fiscal crises of the state and the search for new sources of revenue. Changes in the federal tax laws under the Reagan administration diminished revenue to the states. Recession in the early 1980s also led to shrinkage in the revenue collected in taxes, producing repeated cash-flow crises and potential deficits. As chair of the Economic and Fiscal Commission, Dawn was particularly knowledgeable about these grim problems. The bipartisan commission, made up of members from both the house and the senate and supported by a highly skilled staff, was charged with, among other things, producing the official revenue estimates for the General Assembly. This task was necessary to ensure that the legislature did not violate the constitutional mandate to balance the budget by appropriating more funds than were expected to be available. The estimates of revenue were repeatedly revised downward in 1982 and 1983, forcing both the governor and the legislators to propose new sources of income to support state government. While Governor Thompson regularly assured voters that state finances were in good shape whenever he was running for reelection, soon after the election he would say that an income tax increase was required. In 1983 Thompson made a personal pitch to the senate as a whole for substantial and permanent increases in both income and corporate taxes. He outlined the drastic cuts in state services that would be required otherwise in what became known as the "doomsday budget."[25] Dawn chaired the special senate session, which did succeed in moving the income tax increase out of committee. But it took until almost 11 P.M. on June 30, an hour or so before the fiscal year expired, for the senate to approve a huge package of tax increases, some of them temporary, by a vote of thirty to twenty-nine. The income tax was raised from 2.5 percent to 3 percent and the sales tax from 4 percent to 5 percent until June 30, 1984, along with hikes in the gasoline tax and driver's license fees, as part of an almost $1 billion increase that rescued the state budget, at least temporarily.[26]

In 1987 Governor Thompson appointed Dawn to the Whitley Commission, which he had established to consider the urgent revenue issues facing Illinois. The commission focused on restructuring the collection of sales tax in the state. Local governments levied the sales tax pursuant to their home rule powers, so that different rates applied in different areas of the state, making it hard for businesses selling in all of them. Dawn spent a great deal of time working with the commission, which ultimately proposed that the state collect a single sales tax and then distribute what was due to local governments. A provision to that effect did pass the legislature. The commission also began to discuss extension of the sales tax to a tax on services and goods. Before moving in this direction, however, the commission concluded that research needed to be done to ascertain whether such a change would make the sales tax more or less regressive in its effect.[27]

As the decade drew to its close, one after another revenue source was urged on the legislators. In 1989 Thompson and the Republicans proposed a sharp increase in the state excise tax on cigarettes and liquor; the senate rejected the proposal, though Dawn was one of three Chicago Democrats to support the measure. The Republicans also proposed to raise the income tax rate and expand real estate tax relief. The house leader Mike Madigan proposed instead that income taxes be raised for two years only, a surtax that might be unnecessary when the state's economy recovered.[28] The 20 percent income tax surcharge, which passed, was to expire June 30, 1991, leaving many questions about how schools and local governments would be funded after that time. (The surcharge was in fact made permanent after Dawn left the senate.)

As local governments were forced to rely excessively on real estate taxes to fund education and other local services in Illinois, taxpayers began to rebel, especially in Cook County. A variety of property tax relief proposals were introduced, among them one cosponsored by Dawn and Phil Rock in 1989, which would have frozen assessments for one year, provided for reassessing property every two years instead of four, and increased the homestead and senior citizens exemptions, among other things.[29] Dawn also sponsored a plan that would require a three-fifths vote by taxing bodies to increase property tax revenues by 5 percent and submission to a referendum for increases of 9 percent or more.[30] The measure failed to pass in May 1990 by a vote of twenty-three to twelve in the senate.[31]

By the end of the Thompson administration, the state was deeply indebted, as the governor had financed his many building schemes—Build Illinois projects, the McCormick Place extension, and a new White Sox baseball stadium—by issuing bonds.[32] The tax rebellion grew so severe that a constitutional amendment to limit the General Assembly's ability to raise taxes was introduced and debated in the senate. Dawn was outspoken in her opposition, both for reasons consonant with her position at Con Con that the legislature should not be constitutionally restricted in its power to tax and because, as she warned, this would simply force local governments to raise property taxes instead.[33] The senate rejected the amendment, but supporters of the so-called Tax Accountability Amendment proceeded to gather enough signatures to put it on the ballot; this was prevented only by a ruling of the Illinois Supreme Court.[34]

In the newsletter mailed several times a year to her constituents, Dawn carefully laid all the complex fiscal issues before the electorate, sometimes overshadowing coverage of popular legislation she had sponsored. Her newsletter was unique among this type of publication. Four pages long and eleven by seventeen inches laid out, it looked more like a serious newspaper than a political brochure. Indeed, another politician called it the *New York Times* of newsletters. Dawn's overview and analysis of the 1988 legislative session, for example, was so extensive that the typeface was reduced on the interior to fit in all she had to say.[35] While this was probably not very astute politically, especially among older constituents who need larger type, these Fourth District newsletters show Dawn's commitment to explaining the complex issues debated in Springfield to the voters in her district. One has to wonder how many people read the newsletter from cover to cover, however.

Gender Issues: Equal Rights Amendment, Rape Reform, Family Leave, and Gay and Lesbian Rights

Dawn also took a leadership role in the Illinois Senate on a number of major issues of particular importance to women—the campaign to pass the Equal Rights Amendment, the reform of the Illinois rape laws, and proposals for family and medical leave. Only one of them—the rape law reform—was successful. She was also an early and committed champion of gay and lesbian rights.

The Campaign for the Equal Rights Amendment

The Equal Rights Amendment, passed by both houses of Congress in 1971 and 1972, provided that "equality of rights under the law shall not be denied or abridged by the United States or by any State on account of sex." Thirty states had ratified the amendment by the end of 1973, but a total of thirty-eight was required to amend the Constitution. Opposition to ratification began to build at this point, in part as a backlash to the decision of *Roe v. Wade* in 1973, guaranteeing the right to an early-stage abortion. Phyllis Schlafly, a conservative antifeminist from Alton, Illinois, coordinated much of the opposition and organized the Stop the ERA campaign. By 1977, thirty-five states had ratified the ERA, but Illinois was not among them. It was the only northern industrial state not to have done so. On June 30, 1982, the extended time limit for ratification expired, and the ERA failed, still shy of the number of states required to ratify.

Dawn was the principal supporter of the ERA in the Illinois Senate, although she always insisted that the president of the senate be listed as the principal sponsor. She was in charge of counting noses and deciding on strategy for most of the period the ERA was before the legislature. In Illinois, the opposition to the ERA came from most of the Republican senators and from conservatives across the board.

In May 1972, the year before Dawn joined the legislature, the ERA had in fact passed the Illinois Senate by a vote of thirty to twenty-one. A simple majority was adequate to pass the amendment in most states, but the Illinois Constitution required a three-fifths vote. Dawn and another female legislator filed suit in federal court challenging this requirement under the federal constitution, but a three-judge federal panel decided that a state legislature could adopt whatever rules of procedure it chose in ratifying an amendment to the federal constitution.[36] Both houses of the Illinois legislature adopted a three-fifths rule, and so the ERA required thirty-six votes to make it through the Illinois Senate.

In the early years, Dawn argued for the ERA to be brought to the floor of the senate. When refusal to discharge it from committee killed it for the session ending in 1973, she declared, "All we are asking is an opportunity to discuss this very important question. It is unthinkable to beat this resolution without the consent of the full Senate."[37] As she became a more experienced legislator, however, Dawn learned that it was not a good idea to force a vote on a bill without being assured of a sufficient number of votes to pass it. To call the ERA for a vote on the floor would put members in the position of voting against it if they had not yet made up their minds to support it, and this would rigidify their positions, making it difficult to change their minds later. Over the period from 1973 to 1980, the ERA seesawed between the two houses of the Illinois legislature, passing one house only to fail in the other. The senate approved it in 1972 (though by a simple majority), and the house rejected it. The house voted in favor of the ERA in 1973 and 1975, but the senate rejected it each time (or simply did not report it out of committee for lack of votes on the floor).

Phyllis Schlafly and her supporters were extremely active on this issue in Illinois, doing grassroots organizing and making their presence known constantly in the capitol building, where they presented pies and flowers to legislators. Arguing against the amendment initially on the grounds that it would require unisex bathrooms and lead to the drafting of women, they expanded their arguments to the even more questionable propositions that passage of the ERA would lead inexorably to gay marriage, expanded rights to abortion, and the loss of a wife's right to be supported by her husband. As Dawn commented in 1975, "There is an hysterical campaign against it. The opposition is organized and they have planted all these fears. . . . There is a kind of McCarthyism about it. The ERA is a symbol of the fact that society already has changed, and these people don't want it to change. The pressure on the legislators is enormous."[38]

Dawn's own support for the ERA was a reasoned one, and the speeches she gave on its behalf were very academic, carefully disputing the claims made or defusing the anxiety over them. In one 1973 speech (given, as she recalls, to Northwestern Law alumni), she pointed out that both spouses were responsible for each other under Illinois law, that the military draft was about to be abolished and would not require women to serve in combat positions in any event, that the right to privacy would protect single-sex bathrooms, and the like. She also traced the history of women's unequal status under the law, pointing to disparities that still existed at that time (with respect to criminal sentencing, grounds for divorce, exemptions from jury service, and the availability of credit, among other things).

Dawn was careful to distinguish herself in this speech from the women's liberation movement: "ERA is not synonymous with Women's Liberation or abortion. It is supported by many rational middle class, middle-aged women like me! . . . I support ERA but I am an advocate, not a nut. You will find that I do not bellow like Bella; I am not strident like Steinem."[39] Bella Abzug and Gloria Steinem, of course, were leaders of the National Organization for Women, or NOW, which was leading the campaign to pass the ERA. Among their tactics was the organization of giant marches—more than one hundred thousand people in Washington, D.C., in 1978 to urge extension of the deadline for ratification, and six thousand people in Springfield, Illinois, in 1976 to pressure the Illinois Senate to approve the amendment. Dawn was skeptical of such tactics, fearing that the presence of out-of-state women might link the ERA to other issues such as abortion and lesbian rights and backfire with the conservative legislators from downstate Illinois.[40] In another instance, NOW supporters picketed the home of a Republican senator from Decatur, infuriating him and angering many other members of the legislature. Other more radical ERA supporters chained themselves to posts on the second floor of the rotunda of the state capitol and spilled animal blood, tactics that got them press but not votes. Dawn thought all of these tactics hurt rather helped the cause.

The final push to pass the ERA in Illinois took place from 1980 to 1982. President Jimmy Carter invited key people from Illinois, including Dawn, to the White House for a strategy session in May 1980, during which he reviewed a list of the names of the Illinois senators whose votes were needed and asked how they could be picked off. The small Illinois delegation gave him a list of phone calls to make on their behalf, and he did so; but the amendment again failed to pass.

In the last session possible before the ERA would expire, Jim Taylor, an African American senator from the South Side of Chicago who was allied with Mayor Jane Byrne, reintroduced the ERA before anyone else did. Taylor then took over control as lead sponsor and strategist in this last session, with results that possibly determined its fate. Taylor pushed to call the measure to the floor when Dawn and Phil Rock both knew they did not yet have the votes to pass it. As Rock recalls, Taylor said to him, "The mayor wants a vote on ERA." Rock told him that this was not possible on that particular day, until another major problem had been dealt with; Rock also wanted to wait until Phyllis Schlafly and her troops left town. Taylor nonetheless called the matter to the floor, and Rock himself, always a strong ERA supporter, voted no on the motion to discharge it from committee. Dawn reports standing there with her mouth open in shock. "The whole place," she says, "was laden with tension. People were shouting at one another. I was trying to get Taylor not to call it. But if it was called, you don't vote against it!"[41] Rock reports, "All hell broke loose. The mayor got mad as hell. The Democrats were meeting in Philadelphia or Boston or somewhere for a mini-convention; they got mad as hell. I got maybe fifty or sixty phone calls from the President on down. I wish I could explain it to you, but it was a procedural matter."[42] Both Dawn and Rock credit this sequence of events with effectively killing the measure for good by exposing that they did not have enough votes. So the ERA went down to defeat, in Illinois and in the nation at large. It is particularly ironic that the state of Illinois played such a central role in defeating the ERA, given that the 1970 Illinois Constitution already included an equal rights amendment of its own.

Reform of the Illinois Law on Sexual Assault

The years of mobilization to pass the ERA had brought together networks of activist women in Illinois and taught them how to organize and to lobby for legislative change.[43] Sorely disappointed by the failure to pass the ERA, the Illinois chapter of NOW decided to focus next on reform of the rape laws in the state. In 1982, the Illinois rape statute provided that "a male person of the age 14 years and upwards who has sexual intercourse with a female, not his wife, by force and against her will, commits rape." In short, the law was gender specific, limited to heterosexual penetration, and focused attention not on the perpetrator but on the conduct of the victim, with the case law requiring that she demonstrate her nonconsent by resistance. A man could not be raped, nor could a wife be raped by her husband. The offense was a class X felony, attended by a sentence of six to thirty years in prison. Other sexual offenses, short of intercourse and/or involving children or family members, were scattered throughout the statute books and were both defined and punished inconsistently. Thus, sex crimes against children could merit lesser penalties than sex crimes against adults. Despite a national movement to reform antiquated rape laws and discussions carried out by the Rape Study Committee in the Illinois House of Representatives for almost a decade, presided over by Representative Aaron Jaffe, no comprehensive rape reform had taken place.[44]

In 1982 a group of women who had been brought together by the struggle to pass the ERA decided to do something about this failure. Polly Poskin was working in Springfield as the executive director of the Illinois Coalition of Women Against Rape (renamed in 1984 as the Illinois Coalition Against Sexual Assault), a coalition of rape crisis and advocacy centers around the state. Polly Poskin knew Julie Hamos from her work at a women's center in Springfield as well as from the battle over the ERA. Hamos was then working as legislative liaison, or lobbyist, in Springfield for the Cook County states attorney's office and as policy adviser on women's issues for the state's attorney, Rich Daley. Tina Tchen had been president of NOW in Springfield and active on the ERA there before leaving to enter law school at Northwestern in 1981. Linda Miller was president of Illinois NOW in 1981–82 and then a lobbyist for NOW; she had worked with Illinois NOW on the ERA from 1972 on, meeting Tchen, Poskin, and Hamos through that activity. Barbara Engel was the director of women's services at the YWCA in Chicago, which had started a group called Chicago Women Against Rape, a member of ICWAR, and had testified before Aaron Jaffe's House Rape Study Committee. The women had belonged to the close-knit women's community in Springfield and were friends.

After the ERA went down to final defeat in the summer of 1982, the women decided to undertake a research project on the new rape laws being passed in other states. Tchen, the law student, did much of the research and then she and Hamos began to write a draft of a new Illinois law in the fall of 1982. The group met constantly to discuss what should go into the new statute, drawing heavily on the experience of Engel and Poskin with rape victims who had come into their centers for whom the law provided no remedy (for example, wives who had been raped by their husbands or women penetrated by physical objects rather than by a penis). After four or five months of work, they produced a seventy-five-page bill, which they handed over to the Legislative Reference Bureau to put into the proper form for introduction into the legislature.

The proposed new law consolidated all sexual offenses into four grades of offense, with graduated penalties—criminal sexual assault (gender-neutral and involving penetration but also including oral and anal penetration and penetration by objects), aggravated criminal sexual assault (involving, for example, the use of a weapon or serious physical injury), criminal sexual abuse (not involving penetration), and aggravated criminal sexual abuse. It abolished the exemption for marital rape, and it redefined the crime to focus on the perpetrator's use of force or threat of force rather than the victim's lack of consent or resistance; consent was instead made into a defense that the offender must raise. The bill easily passed the house with some amendments but was expected to run into substantial difficulties in the senate. The drafters decided to approach Dawn Netsch to sponsor the bill in the senate, both because of her work on the ERA and because the bill was quite complicated and "we needed a really smart person."[45]

They knew it could take some effort to convince Dawn to sponsor the bill, because it would clearly involve a tremendous investment of time and energy. They knew that if she undertook to sponsor it, she would want to cover all the bases. Once the group sat down with her and walked her through the lengthy piece of legislation, however, Dawn was eager to sponsor it. It was clear to the five women that, as soon as Dawn read through the lengthy bill, she understood the many issues involved and wanted to work in close collaboration with the women who had drafted it. She respected their leadership on the issue and let them use her office and some of her secretary's time as well. As Hamos recalls, "This was a stunning amount of commitment for a legislator."[46]

The bill, House Bill 606, was assigned to the Criminal Judiciary Committee, then chaired by George Sangmeister, a Democrat from Will County who was a former district attorney and known as a law-and-order kind of guy. This was particularly relevant, because a major source of opposition to changing the rape law came from downstate prosecutors (with the exception of the state's attorney in Bloomington), who were satisfied with the law as it was and did not want to have to retrain under a new system. The Cook County state's attorney, Rich Daley, however, firmly supported the draft that his gender adviser Hamos submitted. If Sangmeister also supported the bill, it would be very important.

Dawn convinced Sangmeister to refer the bill to a special subcommittee, a working subcommittee that she chaired, although he sat in on the meetings. She convened the subcommittee with a commitment to discussing the issues involved in the proposed law. The women who had drafted the bill were included in the three-hour meetings and would bring in witnesses to testify—for example, experts about experience under the reformed rape statutes in other states. The women worked tirelessly outside of committee as well. Hamos drew up fact sheets to use when approaching legislators for their votes, charts demonstrating the differences between the new and old laws, and lists suggesting responses to the most common questions that might be asked about the bill. They solicited opinions from persons likely to oppose the bill, getting their feedback and attempting to address their concerns. They talked to every single senator. George Sangmeister was so thoroughly impressed by the work done in his subcommittee that he came out in support of the reform.

Dawn did the work required on the floor of the senate. She could count on her Crazy Eight allies to support her, and Rich Daley's support brought along the Chicago Democrats Jeremiah Joyce and Tim Degnan. Dawn would return from the floor and strategize with Poskin, Hamos, Tchen, Engel, and Miller, telling them the names of senators they needed to work on; and they discussed the best way to approach each individual. In short, she worked comfortably with the group of feminist activists as their partner, a member of an effective team. Hamos recalls, "Dawn was tickled to be part of this. She's very proper in many ways, but she'd get this funny little smile. I think this outside group of feisty feminists, who were not going to take no for an answer—she was proud to be head of that."[47]

At one point, the "feisty feminists" brought their outside connections to bear on the operations of the senate. Dawn came out of the chamber one day, according to Hamos, "looking really frazzled and pale, scared to tell us the bad news: the boys are not going to call the bill." In other words, Phil Rock, senate president, had decided not to call the bill to the floor. The five women were furious, and they quickly got to work by telephone. Rock was on the Democratic National Committee and was running for a committee chair. The NOW people called Elly Smeal, the national president of the organization, but got Molly Yard, the former president, on the phone. Yard, close to eighty years old but still a fiery feminist, said, "I will call the DNC." She spoke with Ann Lewis, head of the political division at the DNC. Lewis said, "Oh, no, that's not going to happen. They *will* call the bill. Let me take care of this."[48] Within half an hour, Lewis had contacted Rock's office, and his chief of staff emerged to say, "I give up; you can have your bill."[49]

House Bill 606 came to the floor of the senate in June 1983, not long before the end of the session. At its third reading on June 27, Dawn presented it and argued for passage:

> The objectives of House Bill 606 are to create one comprehensive
> law that reflects the fact that rape encompasses all types of sexual
> assault committed by both sexes against victims of both sexes

and all ages. A second purpose . . . is to increase convictions of sex offenders by creating the uniform statutory elements and by providing the flexibility in sentencing which depends on the seriousness of the sexual assault, the dangerousness of the offender and the vulnerability of the victim.[50]

Republican senators, led by Senator Prescott Bloom, attacked the bill but were convinced to vote for it on the assurance that it would then go to a conference committee; Bloom did not believe that a conference committee could get the bill in shape for final passage by the end of the session.[51] The bill passed by a vote of fifty-six to zero.

On July 1, however, the conference committee reported back to the floor of the senate, having addressed most of the issues that Senator Bloom raised. The most persuasive change, however, was one made in response to a suggestion by Rock—to delay the effective date of the bill until July 1, 1984, giving prosecutors a full year to examine its provisions and to point out any problems with it. Rock promised he would cooperate in making any changes they found might be needed.[52] The conference committee report was adopted by a vote of fifty to one, with eight members voting present.[53] The new Criminal Sexual Assault Act then went to the governor for signature.

Dawn had spent a good deal of time negotiating with Governor Thompson's assistant on criminal law matters, which she describes as "not always easy." (In fact she described him as Thompson's H. R. Haldeman, after Nixon's notorious chief of staff in the White House.) One of the most controversial sections of the proposed law was the abolition of the exemption for rape by a spouse. To protect the bill from a veto, this section had been amended to restrict spousal rape claims to situations where the parties were separated and divorcing, the accused used or threatened to use a dangerous weapon, and he caused great bodily harm to the victim, in a marriage characterized by a history of violence.[54] These restrictions did not satisfy Governor Thompson, who responded with an amendatory veto on September 23, 1983. In addition to a number of changes that were primarily technical (though nonetheless annoying to the bill's drafters), Thompson insisted that spousal rape claims should be brought only for aggravated criminal sexual assault and that such crimes must be reported to the state's attorney's office within thirty days of occurrence. The bill's sponsors decided to accept the governor's changes rather than jeopardize passage of the bill as a whole. The vote to accept the recommended changes on November 2, 1983, was forty-nine in favor, five against, and two present.[55]

The new law's drafters were very satisfied with the act, even though they had been forced to make many compromises in their original draft to obtain passage. The Illinois Coalition Against Sexual Assault received funds for education and training about the new statutory scheme throughout the state; they made a film, wrote a training manual for prosecutors and police, and carried out numerous training sessions for rape crisis centers and the police. A study by the *Chicago Tribune* a year after the law had been in effect showed that prosecutions for felony sex offenses were up by 16 percent in Chicago and that the overall conviction rate had increased to 63 percent from 36 percent under the old laws.[56]

But the group of women who had drafted the Illinois Criminal Sexual Assault Act did not give up on getting a law closer to the one they wanted. Nearly a decade later, the act was amended almost without anyone noticing, to allow spouses to be charged under all four grades of sexual offense.[57] Ten years after that, the requirement that spouses, unlike other victims, must report the offense within thirty days was also deleted.[58] As for Dawn, the passage of the Illinois Criminal Sexual Assault Act is one of the legislative achievements of which she is most proud. Although she had spent most of her life simply as one of the boys, not identifying with the women's movement per se, she became very committed to a number of women's issues as the years went by and clearly was a reliable ally for women who had devoted their lives to such issues.

Indeed, one wonders whether Dawn had trouble identifying with the new feminism precisely because it sought better treatment for a group to which she herself belonged. Whereas she instinctively saw that African Americans and, as we shall see, gays and lesbians, deserved better treatment as a group, when it came to women's issues, her support was very much an issue by issue matter—that is, she never supported a legal reform because it would benefit women but because it struck her as a particular injustice. Along the way, however, her own consciousness did expand. Discrimination against women was not an issue she embraced early in life, perhaps because she had not encountered it as an obstruction to her individual path. Indeed, it may have been instrumental to her own self-confidence and assertiveness as a law student, young lawyer, and politician that she not see it. Yet as time went on, it was hard to ignore unequal treatment of other women. The lightbulb moment occurred for her when a highly qualified, young female law student came to her at Northwestern

Law School in the late 1960s or early 1970s and told her she was having trouble finding a job. At this point—when it involved someone other than herself, someone to whom she owed a duty of care as her professor— Dawn found it impossible to avoid the conclusion that structural problems were preventing the student's success and to identify them as sex discrimination.

Gay and Lesbian Issues

Interestingly, although Dawn did not naturally or easily identify with women as an oppressed group, she was instinctively supportive of the issues that gay people faced from an early point in both her own career and in the gay and lesbian movement. For years she was an enthusiastic supporter of a bill introduced into the Illinois House of Representatives in the mid-1970s to amend the Illinois Human Rights Act to add sexual orientation as a prohibited ground for discrimination in employment, public accommodation, and housing. Once it got out of committee in the house, those who had been working on it came to her to start working on it in the senate. Given that her sponsorship at that time might not help the cause, they agreed that she should not be the lead sponsor in that chamber but should instead find someone else to play this role. Dawn talked to at least ten other legislators and was unable to find a single one willing to be the lead sponsor on the bill. As it was, however, the Human Rights Amendment never even got to the Illinois Senate until after Dawn had left it. At the request of gay and lesbian groups, she did try to lobby some representatives about it. The amendment to add sexual orientation as a protected ground under the Illinois Human Rights Act did not pass both houses and become law until 2005, effective January 1, 2006.

Dawn was the first person running for office in Chicago to openly boast of her endorsement by gay and lesbian groups in her campaign material. She regularly attended fund-raising events in the gay community, such as the annual dinners of Impact, a political group formed in the early 1980s, and of Equality Illinois, a bipartisan lobbying group, as well as events held by the AIDS Foundation of Chicago. She attended forums held by the gay community to ask legislators about their views on the gay rights issue; Dawn always responded that she saw it as a simple matter of human rights. As the AIDS epidemic hit the Midwest in 1983 to 1984, Dawn was one of the first people in political office who understood the importance of providing resources for medical care. She was a stalwart supporter of the Howard Brown Clinic, a gay men's health clinic that stepped into this role, and of Chicago House, a residence for people with AIDS. She helped to obtain funding to help with the visiting nurse program for both Chicago House and other residential facilities.

Dawn's early support of gay issues is extensively recognized in the gay and lesbian community in Chicago. She attended the annual Gay Pride parade before it became the huge event it is now, before politicians came out in numbers to attract the gay vote. She would ride in the back of a convertible that said "Dawn Clark Netsch, State Senator" on its side; it was usually the first car and occasioned immense cheers along the route. Dawn still loves the Gay Pride parade. "It's filled with good nature and good spirits all along the route. . . . It was a little more bizarre in the early days. . . . The thing that's most fascinating is how much they appreciate and love you for having been out there when it was not so easy to do."[59]

Michael Bauer, a gay activist friend, says that Dawn continues to get "an unbelievable reception along the entire parade route. I would bet a lot of the people on the parade route now don't really understand why she's an icon, but they're cheering because they know she's an icon."[60] Bauer says she always gets the loudest cheers when she is announced at gay and lesbian fund-raising events as well. Today, given the importance of the large gay vote in Chicago, elected officials flock to these events. At one, there is typically a parade of politicians, who are announced as they walk down a staircase into the reception. "No matter who else is there," Bauer says, "Dawn will get the biggest cheers and roaring." Asked to explain her early commitment to the cause of gay equality, Dawn simply replies that she has known many gay people and simply saw their issues as a matter of basic civil rights.

Family and Medical Leave

Dawn was also the sponsor of the Illinois Family and Medical Leave Act. Although she and Walter never had children, she, like many women, has had the experience of being the caretaker for family members who were ill, often at extremely inconvenient times. Dawn's father had died of illnesses related to his wartime service in North Africa while she was working at Covington & Burling in the early 1950s, and her brother lived far away, often abroad with the military, leaving her mother alone except for Dawn. So Dawn was the family member who took care of her mother as she aged. Her mother's stroke during Con Con, for example, necessitated multiple trips to Cincinnati to work out appropriate arrangements for her care. During Dawn's first, hard-fought campaign for the senate, she stepped into the caretaker role again. Her mother had hip surgery in Cincinnati but continued to experience severe pain. Dawn brought her to one of the top orthopedic surgeons at Northwestern's hospital, who performed another operation to repair the hip socket, which had slipped. It took three or four months for her mother to convalesce, so Dawn put her in an after-care nursing home on Wellington Avenue and stopped by to visit her after school every day, during a period when she was both teaching and running for office.[61] So she had some personal experience of the challenges families face without the resources she had.

In 1987 Dawn introduced the Illinois Family and Medical Leave Act into the senate and began to lobby her fellow legislators for passage. Legislators she approached about family leave in the early days would often reply by expressing sentiments like the following: "You women want it all your way—to have babies and yet not to lose your jobs or benefits." Dawn found that when she approached them instead about the necessity of taking care of elderly parents, male colleagues responded more favorably, for many of them had already experienced this. Sometimes personal experience can be critical to identification with an issue. Dawn herself, however, did not consciously identify with family leave as a women's issue but rather as something that was necessary for modern working families. Her own situation was different. The jobs she had held—at least as law professor and legislator—were more flexible (even if as consuming) in their time demands; she was not tied to a time clock. She did not see herself as facing the same challenges that working parents without her flexible schedule must meet. But as two-parent working families became a common phenomenon, family and medical leave seemed to her to have become a necessity of economic life.

The bill Dawn proposed in 1987 would have provided up to eighteen weeks of unpaid leave over twenty-four months for either parent on the birth, adoption, or illness of a child, or to care for a seriously ill parent, and up to twenty-six weeks unpaid medical leave for an employee who was unable to work. Although the leave was unpaid, the employee's health benefits would be continued during it and his or her seniority protected. It applied to companies with more than fifteen employees, or about 80 percent of Illinois businesses at the time.[62] Opposed by the chamber of commerce, the bill never made it out of committee. Dawn tried to argue with the business community by pointing out that leave could work to the benefit of a company in the long run, because they would not have to go to the expense of replacing and retraining workers. She also recruited some businesspeople to testify in favor of the legislation in the senate.

Two years later, Dawn introduced yet another bill, renamed the Family Responsibility Act and cosponsored with senate president Phil Rock. Again, business groups opposed it as too costly. Dawn described the bill as an "economic necessity" for families where both parents work outside the home and professed herself willing to bargain to get some family leave policy through the General Assembly.[63] The bill that eventually made its way through both houses of the Illinois legislature that June (1989)—endorsed by the senate by a vote of thirty to twenty-seven and narrowly passing the house—provided only for eight weeks of leave for employees in businesses with fifty or more employees. Governor Thompson nonetheless vetoed it the following September.[64] Senators Rock and Netsch introduced a new and identical bill in January of 1990.[65] The senate approved the Family Responsibility and Medical Leave Act by only thirty-one votes, and Thompson vowed again to veto it.[66]

Ultimately workers in Illinois did receive a guarantee of family and medical leave, but only after the federal Family and Medical Leave Act was signed into law in the early weeks of the Clinton administration in 1993. That act guarantees twelve weeks of unpaid leave during any twelve-month period for employees who work for companies with fifty or more employees, in addition to the maintenance of health benefits and seniority.[67] Dawn remains convinced that caretaking is a central issue for our society to face as a collectivity.

Evaluated in terms of results, Dawn's eighteen years in the Illinois Senate were a mixed bag. There is still no merit selection of judges in Illinois; education is still underfunded; and the tax structure is both inadequate and inequitable in many ways. Many things dear to her heart—campaign reform, the ERA, and family leave, for example—went down to defeat. In contrast, Illinois does have a modern sexual assault statute and a good deal of consumer-protection legislation that Dawn sponsored. What is perhaps most remarkable about her tenure in the legislature was her indefatigability and persistence on issues to which she was committed, pursuing them in session after session despite repeated defeats.

Legislators are, after all, constrained with respect to what they can accomplish while in office, especially legislators who want to change the status quo. In a speech to the Illinois Association of Graduate Programs in Public Administration on May 13, 1986, Dawn described those constraints, telling her audience that the legislative process was really not controlled by the legislators but instead by traditional power blocs and their lobbyists, along with the media.[68] Although she became adept at playing the game, many of the reforms she championed were opposed to the interests of entrenched groups, and they failed. Yet so many of the policies and programs Dawn sponsored seem so right, despite their rejection in the political process—transparency, accountability and citizen participation in government; equality without respect to race, sex, or sexual orientation; and a fiscally responsible government committed to the adequate provision of services basic to the public welfare. As many have suggested, perhaps she was just ahead of her time.

Dawn certainly did bring a number of unique qualities to the Illinois legislature, among them her intelligence and extensive knowledge of state government, her absolute integrity, and her commitment to the issues. She developed the ability to negotiate across political boundaries and to reach compromises when necessary to approach her goals, even if by incremental steps. Her sometime adversary Phil Rock sums it up like this:

> She was a wonderful legislator, exceptionally well-informed. . . . The first attribute that a [legislator] has to have . . . is that they have to give a damn; they have to care. You can sit there and watch all day; you can sit there and listen all day; but if you're going to stand on your feet and contribute, you've gotta give a damn, you've gotta get in there and fight. And I would say without any qualifications that Dawn Netsch gave a damn; she cared. . . . And she was smart enough, articulate enough, to be heard. She stood up, and people listened. I accused her of standing up too many times because she insisted on talking about everything in the world. But that got to be a friendly joke. She was well informed and did perform . . . a terrific service. She was like a short cut to knowledge other folks had not been exposed to.[69]

Chapter 14

Life Outside the Legislature

OVER THE EIGHTEEN YEARS that Dawn Clark Netsch was in the Illinois Senate, her influence within the local and national Democratic Party grew steadily. In 1980 she was surprised to be asked to cochair the Illinois delegation to the Democratic National Convention, which was held in New York City. Dawn was a delegate pledged to the reelection of President Jimmy Carter. She worked hard in his campaign, emphasizing his support of women's issues, including abortion and the Equal Rights Amendment, as well as his stands on energy policy and the environment.[1] Her special skills at negotiation and diplomacy proved important in New York that summer.

The Chicago Democratic Party in 1980 was split, not only along machine-independent lines but also between supporters and opponents of Mayor Jane Byrne. Byrne had been elected mayor of Chicago in April 1979 by something of a fluke. The previous mayor, Michael Bilandic, was a machine Democrat chosen to succeed Mayor Daley when he died in office in late 1976. Before the primary election in February 1979, in which Byrne, Daley's former commissioner of consumer affairs, opposed Bilandic, a record-breaking blizzard brought the city of Chicago to a halt. Roads were impassable, and public transportation was at a standstill for days. To make things worse, attempts to clear the el tracks resulted in damage to about half the train cars in the Chicago Transit Authority's fleet.[2] The result was chaos even after limited service resumed—huge crowds, long delays, and a lot of angry citizens out in the bitter cold. Service on the public transit lines did not get back to normal after the mid-January storm until early February. The primary election was to be held on February 27, and Byrne seized the occasion to blame Bilandic's incompetence for the disaster. The blizzard of 1979 generally receives credit for Byrne's victory in the Democratic primary, which, as usual in Chicago, was tantamount to election.

Dawn Netsch had already tangled with Byrne when she was trying to get her early consumer-protection bills through the legislature, only to have the Regular Democrats oppose them because Byrne wanted credit for passing them first in Chicago. At the 1980 Democratic National Convention, Byrne supported Ted Kennedy for president and sent her workers to New York to try to peel away Illinois delegates already committed to the reelection of President Jimmy Carter. Byrne's workers pursued the Carter delegates on and off the floor, often employing rather rough tactics. Heavy pressure was brought to bear in connection with a procedural issue that would prove decisive: whether delegates elected as supporting one candidate could in fact switch their choice on the first ballot at the convention. It was only after a floor vote, which Kennedy supporters heavily contested, that the party established that delegates were bound to vote on the first ballot for the candidate they had been elected to support. After fighting over this procedural issue ended, Byrne's pressure on the Carter delegates from Illinois let up, and Jimmy Carter was nominated once again.

This was the first Democratic National Convention Dawn had attended as an insider, but she learned fast. Because her cochairs, especially Roland Burris, were more interested in playing to the national media than dealing with the chaos in the Illinois delegation, Dawn ended up having to take charge of all the work involving credentials and meetings and seating on the floor. She decided that the delegation should have regular meetings and that the pros and cons of various issues should be presented to it and voted on. A particularly divisive issue was abortion. Although the majority of the almost two-hundred-member delegation supported a pro-choice plank, the minority felt strongly that this should not be presented as a unanimous position, so that those they represented would not think they had voted for it. Dawn stayed up late in an almost-empty auditorium to make sure the vote was recorded, giving the numbers both for and against the abortion plank of the platform.[3]

Commentators gave Dawn credit for the Promethean job she had performed at the convention. A 1981 article in *Illinois Issues* proclaimed, "Her role as a mediator of Illinois' unruly delegation at last summer's Democratic National Convention in New York City has once more proven her skills as a leader at a time Democrats in this state find themselves amok in divisive bickering."[4]

Problems with Byrne did not disappear after the convention was over. Byrne entered into some sort of bargain with Republican Governor

Thompson that would have involved giving up much of the state subsidy for the Regional Transportation Authority and the CTA, appalling the legislators who had fought hard for these subsidies. Dawn put together a bipartisan group to fight Byrne's plan. After the group had begun to meet to plan their strategy, Mayor Byrne sent word that she wanted to meet with them. The meeting appeared cordial as the legislators carefully articulated the reasons why the state subsidy of urban mass transit was so critical to Chicago. At the end of the session, however, Byrne said, "Thank you," and proceeded to outline her plan to invest the money in snowplows on the front of elevated trains instead. The delegation members walked out, looked at one another, and shared their conclusion that Byrne had not understood a word they had said about the principle of mass transit and the importance of the state's recognition of its obligation to subsidize it.[5] Although Byrne's scheme was defeated, she continued to poison relations with the independents by making her peace with Alderman Edward Vrdolyak of the post-Daley machine, making appointments to the board of education that were unacceptable to the black community, and other things. In Dawn's opinion, she was a "disaster."[6]

As Byrne's four-year term neared its end, Dawn was convinced that it was essential to elect "anyone but Jane Byrne."[7] Harold Washington, her old law school classmate and ally from the Black Caucus in Springfield, was initially reluctant to run for mayor; and all the polls purported to show that he could not win the primary. So when Rich Daley's deputation of Tom Hynes and Jeremiah Joyce tracked Dawn down one day in the library at the law school, she was more receptive than she might have been to their request that she chair Rich's campaign for mayor. At that time, she says, the only realistic choices seemed to be "Rich or Jane."[8]

Once Harold Washington did enter the race, the movement to elect him began to take off. Dawn tried to track him down to explain that her activity on behalf of Daley was not directed against him but only to defeat Jane Byrne. She then continued to honor her commitment, making many speeches for Daley, keeping an eye on his position papers, trying to keep old-line Democrats from coming to the fore, and helping him mend fences with the gay and lesbian community that favored Jane Byrne. The only time Dawn has ever been booed at a gay and lesbian event was when she attended a candidate forum on behalf of Daley in 1983.[9]

With Jane Byrne and Rich Daley splitting much of the white vote between them, Washington won the Democratic nomination for mayor with 36 percent of the vote.[10] The Daley group then used Dawn's connections with Washington to build a bridge toward party unity. Daley himself left on a postprimary vacation, but a group of Democrats put together a unity event, which seemed important because of the split primary and the race issues in the campaign. Dawn managed to get the mayor's brother William Daley to attend, though he was initially reluctant to do so. Dawn participated enthusiastically, though. While announcing her all-out support for Daley's candidacy at the event, she spoke humorously of Washington's emergence out of Chicago machine politics and told anecdotes from their common past as law students and legislators.[11]

Washington became Chicago's first African American mayor on April 29, 1983, after a racially charged general election campaign. Winning the election was only half the battle, as machine Democrats on the city council (twenty-nine of them) outnumbered Washington's supporters (sixteen black aldermen and five white liberals) and were able to hold up his appointments and programs for some time. This period, during which the so-called Vrdolyak Twenty-nine held a majority but not enough to override a mayoral veto, was characterized by noisy disagreements in the city council chamber and legislative gridlock; the comedian Aaron Freeman dubbed it "Council Wars." The wars ended only after court-ordered redistricting and special aldermanic elections three years later, which resulted in a split of twenty-five to twenty-five between Washington's and Vrdolyak's supporters in the city council, with the mayor casting the deciding vote in a tie.

The council wars had a particular impact on the Netsch family. Washington never held Dawn's support of Rich Daley in the primary against her. Indeed, he appointed her husband Walter president of the board of commissioners of the Chicago Park District in 1983. This appointment required city council approval, and it was held up for almost three years. The Democratic machine had long controlled the Chicago Park District as a great patronage haven, presided over by Park Superintendent Ed Kelly. Kelly and the Vrdolyak Twenty-nine fought hard to keep control of their fiefdom. Netsch was confirmed only after the 1986 aldermanic elections changed the balance of power in the city council, attempts to require a super-majority vote were defeated in the courts, and a bill to strip authority from the park commission failed in the General Assembly.[12] Kelly was finally ousted in June 1986, and Washington's appointees took control of the parks at last.

Walter Netsch, retired from Skidmore, Owings and Merrill, had dramatic plans to remake the Chicago parks—to restore the deteriorating buildings in Douglas, Marquette, Humboldt, Garfield, and Washington parks to their late-nineteenth-century grandeur; to decentralize park administration and tailor services to the needs of the various communities; and to return to the original vision of the parks as cultural centers offering a wide array of open spaces and services in addition to the heavy emphasis on competitive athletics that was the focus of the previous park administration. Park and recreation professionals rather than patronage workers would be hired, and the resources of the huge park system would be redistributed as required by a federal court consent decree entered into in 1983 in a suit charging neglect of the parks in minority communities.[13] These were no small plans.

Walter, ever the individualist and impatient with bureaucracy, soon clashed with other members of the park board. He stepped back from the presidency of the board in May 1987 but remained as a commissioner.[14] After Mayor Washington's death from a heart attack in November 1987, the park board was expanded from five to seven members, and Netsch was often at odds with the two commissioners appointed by Washington's successor, Mayor Eugene Sawyer. The press would cover blowups over various issues.[15] In December 1989, Netsch abruptly resigned from the board, saying that he was tired of fighting and intended to withdraw and "paint, sculpt and write in my studio, looking to the future, through my visions as expressed in nature, art and architecture."[16]

Despite Walter Netsch's frustration, he is generally credited with making substantial improvements to the Chicago parks during his tenure, including a plan to equitably distribute park facilities and program hours, decentralization and placement of decision-making powers in the hands of the parks' users, preservation of priceless documents and drawings in the Chicago Park District archives, establishing a planning department and the hiring of talented staff, construction of new safety surfaces and equipment for 560 play lots, and many other initiatives that came to fruition only later, during the administration of Mayor Richard M. Daley.[17] Netsch also began to reintroduce cultural activities in a system previously dedicated to organized sports.[18]

By the end of the 1980s, Dawn was well established as a prominent member of the Democratic Party in Chicago. She and Walter had also become prominent in the cultural life of the city. Dawn had been attending the Lyric Opera from her earliest days in the city; Walter joined her in that, giving up his regular attendance at the Chicago Symphony's Sunday-afternoon piano concerts and playing recorded concerts at home instead. The couple attended the opera in what their friend Kay Clement describes as "high style"—belonging to a club that serves dinner before the performance and dessert during the intermission.[19] Their seats were in the center of the seventh row until Walter later became disabled, when they switched to a box.

Walter Netsch's art collection grew, and they sometimes loaned portions of it to museums for exhibits or invited people to see it in their house. Dawn learned a great deal about modern art from him and grew to love it, but purchases were basically Walter's decision. He described her as having a "right of no" over purchases, but she exercised it only once because she "didn't like pink in paintings."[20] Mostly she trusted Walter's judgment, and the value of their art collection increased phenomenally. One Lichtenstein painting Walter had bought for $600 in the early 1960s, for example, was sold decades later for $2 million.

From 1974 on, the couple lived in a striking house Walter had designed in the Old Town neighborhood as an illustration of his field theory of architecture. The house, as Dawn once described it, is "a big 40-foot cube, most of which is open space, with 35-foot high ceilings."[21] The interior is divided into areas on multiple levels, formed from rotating the geometric shapes that lie at the base of field theory. Stairs of different shapes and sizes connect the many levels, with areas for different functions laid out along a kind of rotating pattern—a small kitchen, a dining area, a living room, two bedrooms each with its own bath, and studies for Dawn and Walter, a roof garden, and everywhere art—huge paintings, sculptures, rugs, baskets, and other artworks collected from the couple's many travels. It reminds one of the Guggenheim Museum in New York. The design was entirely Walter's, though he did once show the drawings to Dawn, who pointed out that there was no closet in the kitchen. He added one, but that was the only contribution she made to the layout. Walter clearly regarded their physical surrounding as his to design, saying that, with the exception of the one closet in the kitchen, Dawn "had no control over anything, materials, colors." He added, "I had no control over details of her career."[22] The house itself is a work of art.

Dawn's women friends knew that the house posed substantial difficulties for her, though.[23] It is not well designed for cooking and entertaining, with huge steps requiring carrying dishes up and down. Walter insisted that they do the cooking and serving themselves instead of employing anyone to serve them. He was proud of this, proclaiming, "We are not Lake Forest people; we do not have servants." But the burden fell on Dawn, who did all their cooking and for whom entertaining created an enormous amount of work. The giant stairs with no railings created additional problems for her because she suffered from inner-ear problems that caused dizziness. (Indeed, Dawn later broke her wrist falling on those stairs.)

Dawn's early legislative assistant, Rita McLennon, describes her as very depressed when they moved in 1974 from their classic apartment on Cedar Street into the new house. "The house was built for the art, not for the people. She was having a hard time with it. Walter called up and wanted to know what to do because Dawn was so unhappy."[24] Friends came by to cheer her up and distract her. Over the course of time, however, Dawn grew to love the house on Hudson Street and to be proud of it. The couple have loaned it to art and music groups to hold fund-raisers but only occasionally to political groups.

During the 1970s, when Walter was still at Skidmore, Owings and Merrill, the Netsches would entertain all the partners when partners' meetings were held in town. As the partnership grew, this created a great deal of work for Dawn. In addition, they always had a New Year's Eve party for their friends every year, which Kay Clement describes as having been a "great time," with the champagne flowing freely and everyone bringing a dish.[25] Occasionally, Dawn would accompany Walter when the Skidmore partners' meetings were held in more exotic places, like Japan, but usually her work in Springfield prevented that. Walter thought Dawn was something of a problem for his partners, both as the type of assertive woman she was (she once told off one of Walter's partners for how he treated his wife) and for her prominence in Democratic politics. "Office buildings are Republican," he said, and his partners feared that Dawn's politics could hurt the firm.[26] When the couple socialized with architects informally, it tended to be with younger men who worked for Walter rather than with the other partners. Walter gamely accompanied Dawn to many faculty social events at Northwestern as well.

At the time Walter retired from Skidmore in the late 1970s, he began a campaign to add dogs to their household. At first, Dawn opposed the idea, thinking it would be too difficult an addition to their already overburdened lives. Walter persisted. He argued that he needed exercise for his cardiac rehabilitation, and that walking a dog would be just the thing. He even went outside the house and walked around calling "Frosty, Frosty," as though looking for a lost dog, to emphasize his desire to have one. Ultimately, the name Frosty was attached to the first of what was to become a long line of Netsch Boston terriers. Although Dawn rolled her eyes and complained about Walter's latest folly to friends, she soon fell totally in love with the dogs herself, which numbered as many as three at a time at various points. The terriers accompanied Walter to his job at the park district and on foreign travels. Their photos adorned Dawn's offices.

Walter Netsch suffered from multiple health problems in the latter part of his life, and Dawn spent a good deal of time taking care of him.[27] He had his first coronary bypass in 1977. He had been designing a hospital building for the Mayo Clinic in Minnesota when he began to feel out of breath. On his way to another job in Ohio, his plane stopped at Chicago's O'Hare Airport, and he began to have more trouble breathing. He came directly home, and they called a doctor who said that he needed to check into the hospital immediately. His first heart surgery took place in early January 1977, on one of the coldest days in Chicago for years. Walter's sister Nan Kerr and her husband picked Dawn up before dawn on a grim and snowy day so as to arrive at the hospital by 6.

Walter's recovery from this operation was not easy. The fact that it took place in the middle of the Crazy Eight rebellion made this even more difficult for Dawn, who was in constant phone communication with her allies on the senate floor. After several weeks in the hospital, Walter went home but needed someone there with him. Things were not going well, and he would refuse to do the breathing exercises that the doctor prescribed. He would get frightened as soon as anything untoward happened, becoming convinced that the worst was about to happen, and he demanded constant attendance. Dawn went back and forth to Springfield, arranging for Walter's sister or the housekeeper to stay with him when she was not there.

Walter retired from Skidmore, Owings and Merrill fairly soon after his first heart surgery, although he did not officially withdraw from the firm until 1979. It seemed apparent that, if he continued to work at the frantic pace he had been maintaining, he would not survive. Living now in Old Town, the couple also bought a townhouse in Sandburg Village, not far to the south and east, for Walter to use as his workspace. In 1982, however, he required a second heart operation, this time a multiple bypass.

It soon became evident that Walter had serious problems with his vascular system as well. In the mid-1980s, he went alone to southern France for a vacation while Dawn was busy with her work, taking two of their Boston terriers with him for company. He sought out a doctor to look at one of the dogs, only to be told that he needed to seek medical care himself, that there was something wrong with his ankles and legs.

Luckily a friend from the art world in Ohio had stopped to visit just then, so she was available to stay with the dogs while Walter went to Avignon for further tests, which showed serious blockages in his legs. In Chicago, Dawn sought out doctors who could speak French to find out from the French doctors what was going on. The Chicago doctors determined that Walter needed immediate surgery, so his friend from Ohio and another friend from college who was living in France managed to get him and the two dogs on a plane to Paris and then to Chicago. Dawn, Walter's sister Nan, and Kay Clement met him at the airport, where he was wheeled out in a wheelchair with the two dogs in his arms. Surgery was required to bypass the obstructed veins. At another time, Walter had an embolism that required treatment but not surgery; he later had bladder cancer, which was successfully treated with freeze-dried tuberculosis bacilli. In short, Dawn spent a good deal of time taking care of Walter.

From the time of their courtship and throughout their life together, Dawn and Walter continued to share their passion for baseball and, specifically, for the Chicago White Sox. Dawn's attachment to the White Sox in fact preceded her relationship to Walter. She and her friend Kay Clement went to games together in the 1950s and early 1960s, often accompanied by Kay's children. The two women were such fans that they would go stand by the section where the players came out after the game to get their autographs, two adult women in a cluster of kids. They also went up to the North Side hotel where parties were held during the 1959 playoffs and sat in the hallway sipping drinks and watching the players. Between them, Dawn and Kay managed to obtain tickets for three games in the 1959 World Series (which the Sox lost to the Los Angeles Dodgers in six games)—Dawn by winning a lottery and Kay by activating family connections. Kay describes her friend as having known a lot about baseball from the time they first met and depicts her watching the games with intensity, yelling at the players to egg them on. Dawn always kept score (and in fact kept many of her scorecards, especially those from the 1959 series).[28]

When Dawn met Walter, their typical date was at Comiskey Park, where the White Sox played. After they married, they continued to attend games as often as possible when in town. They purchased season tickets, at first alone but later with a group of others and divided up the dates for the season. Being a Sox fan was a bit of an anomaly for a legislator whose district contained Wrigley Field, home to the Chicago Cubs. Dawn swears that she does not dislike the Cubs; they are her second-favorite team. "It's just that they didn't capture me at the moment that I was available to be captured. . . . It was the way that the White Sox played baseball that really got me going. And so once you are hooked, you tend to be hooked. It's totally irrational."[29] Like Dawn's other passions and commitments, this one has persisted for more than fifty years.

Her feelings for the White Sox created some problems for Dawn as a legislator when the Sox management threatened to move the team to Florida if the state did not subsidize construction of a new stadium. Dawn has never been a believer in the public bailing out private enterprises at the cost of funding socially useful causes like education. When it came down to the wire, however, Dawn was torn. She expressed her feelings about the injustice of the subsidy on the floor of the senate but voted for it nonetheless rather than risk losing the team. She does not much like U.S. Cellular Field, the cavernous new stadium that replaced Comiskey Park, and thinks that it is more of a hitter's park than it used to be, in a game that has become increasingly home-run happy. She bemoans these developments but doesn't stop going.

Her knowledge of baseball and intense fandom has probably helped Dawn in her male-dominated profession and eased her relationships with male legislators. She admits, "It means I can talk to them at least about one thing . . . and I guess they are often surprised that I know as much as I do about it and care as much as I do." This kind of passion and knowledge may strike many as out of character in this woman with her patrician looks and demeanor. Dawn's growing prominence in the political sphere has also fed back into her attendance at games. Everyone seems to recognize her at the ballpark and greets her with pleasure. Management personnel also know her. So when Walter required a wheelchair in his later years, Julie Taylor, in charge of guest relations for the ballpark, suggested to Dawn that they try out some of the handicapped seats that had just been added to the stadium. The seats turned out to be in a box, No. 133, right behind home plate on the concourse level, just about the best seats in the park. Taylor made sure that the Netsches always got those seats whenever they came to the games thereafter.

Michael Holland, Dawn's former student and friend accompanied Dawn and Walter to many games and helped Walter get there when he became disabled. Holland gives a detailed description of a trip to the ballpark with Dawn. Because it offers a lively sense of this complex woman that does not emerge from her public appearances, it is included here at some length:

It is a total routine. You never deviate. Dawn holds the tickets. Dawn sits in the back. She buys the hotdogs, she gets one beer, nurses it the entire game. Same person, same stand, gets the same burnt onions, same burnt dog. She is unbelievably attentive to the people that work there. It takes her sometimes a long time to get from one place to another. People come up to her, and she is so gracious. She buys the programs from the same vendor. . . .

She brings a bag, her baseball bag. It has old newsclips in it, the most recent statistics, pens, a scarf or two, maybe a hat. The bag is probably thirty or thirty-five years old and exclusively for the baseball games. . . . She always has napkins. She buys peanuts at Treasure Island and has those in the bag.

She has a variety of Sox caps, some of them have, so un-Dawn like, one of these little pins like of Minnie Minoso. She saw Minnie Minoso at the game a couple of years back. She almost fell over the wire to get over, sit next to him and say, "Hi, my name is Dawn Clark Netsch; I've been a White Sox fan for years."

She always wears a Sox hat, and often a White Sox jersey. Tennis shoes: white. And white socks. Corduroys when it's cool; chinos when it's summer. Her eye is on the pitch and follows the ball. She leans forward in the seat, chin on her fist, especially in the later innings; she's more erect in the earlier innings, watching the field. She follows the action. People still come up to her, security people, everyone who knows her. She is always very attentive; she always gives them time. But she's there to watch the game. She's intent on the game. She cheers and boos, makes gestures, yells, "Come on Freddy, get the ball over, get the ball over."

She and Walter always sing "Take Me Out to the Ball Game" very attentively. They both do the "one, two, three strikes" thing; it's a moment of closeness between them. When the Sox win, she jumps up and down, high fives, grabs, hugs; she's very excited, emotive. She's a fan.

If the Sox win, we always get the radio on to listen to the call-in's for at least some of the time coming back. If they lose, we dissect the game—what happened when; what the turning point of the game was; what would've happened if Konerko had not hit into the double play or Buehrle not given up that walk in the sixth. . . .[30]

The culminating event of Dawn's long love affair with the Chicago White Sox was their victory in the 2005 World Series. Ironically, it was not her political connections that secured seats for those games but her network of ex–law students. Howard Pizer, executive vice president of the Sox, had been one of her students. Just as Dawn was wondering how to obtain tickets for the series, his assistant called and asked what she needed. She said "four tickets in Box 133 all the way through the World Series," and that was exactly what she got. The 2005 season was Dawn's favorite in a whole lifetime of watching baseball. "Everything just came together. There was a sense of drama, of baseball being played just for the most part quite beautifully."

—— *Chapter 15* ——

Comptroller

In 1990, Dawn Clark Netsch was elected comptroller, the first woman to win a statewide constitutional executive office in Illinois. This was her second try for higher office. Since the mid-1980s, Dawn had become increasingly frustrated with her inability to influence public policy as a rank-and-file member of the senate and began to focus her sights on running for a position in the executive branch of government instead. In the complicated dance of Illinois Democratic electoral politics, slating by the state party is key. Being slated to run for an executive position, however, depends to a large extent on the decisions of incumbents to run for other offices, thus opening up posts for which other candidates can contend. There can be a long lead time as people toward the top of the ticket test the waters and decide whether to try to move up, thereby making room for others.

The 1985 Campaign

Such a lengthy period of jockeying occurred in the latter part of 1984, leading up to the 1985 elections. First, Illinois Attorney General Neil Hartigan prepared to take on Republican Jim Thompson in the race for governor, thus opening up a contest for Hartigan's job as attorney general. A number of people jumped in to explore the waters, including the current comptroller, Roland Burris, Phil Rock, Marty Oberman, Pat Quinn, and Dawn Clark Netsch.[1] A primary fight between Burris and Netsch would pit the first African American to hold statewide office against a candidate attempting to be the first woman to do so. For this reason, by April 1985, Dawn had decided to explore a run for the comptroller spot instead, which Burris would vacate if he became attorney general.[2]

As word spread that Dawn was interested in this post, she attracted a good deal of support. Congressman Dick Durbin wrote to offer help.[3] Harold Washington, Rich Daley, and Eddie Vrdolyak, representing contending factions within the party, all attended a fund-raiser in her honor, causing one local newspaper to comment, "Netsch has done what almost no other local politician has pulled off: successfully make the transition from independent iconoclast to mainstream Democratic Party politician."[4] Of course, the mainstream of the Democratic Party had changed quite a bit over time, as had Dawn herself. She commented that she was "less confrontational than I was, though I never was as confrontational as they thought. But I'm still considered controversial in Springfield, and I wouldn't have it any other way. I've learned to pick the things that are important with more selectivity. You don't fight everything. If you do, after a while nobody listens."[5]

By the summer of 1985, Dawn had put together a campaign committee and hired staff to explore the issues, plan fund-raising, and analyze what was necessary to do to win slating by the Democratic Party.[6] By early October, she was visiting downstate newspapers, radio stations, and local Democratic Party committees to seek their support and receive briefings about these areas of the state. Finally, on November 4, 1985, Dawn formally announced her candidacy for comptroller, touting her experience with state finance.

A series of surprise events in early November put an end to her campaign. Adlai Stevenson III, who had narrowly lost the race for governor to Thompson in 1982, suddenly decided to run again. His decision to do so set off a chain reaction. Neil Hartigan dropped out of the gubernatorial race and ran for reelection as attorney general, causing Burris to switch his sights to reelection as comptroller and the candidates for that position, including Dawn, to drop out. The new slate was hailed as a "unity ticket," although Democratic women were upset about their exclusion from it.[7] Dawn made a brief attempt to get the Democratic Party State Central Committee to slate her for treasurer, which would have required dumping James Donnewald, the Democratic incumbent, on the grounds that she not only was qualified but also—like 53 percent of the Illinois electorate—was a woman. This would certainly not constitute tokenism, she said: "With my qualifications, I am nobody's token."[8] Her appeal to the slate makers failed, however, and Dawn returned to the senate for five more years.

The 1989 Primary Election

In 1989 Dawn Clark Netsch decided to try once again to win a statewide executive office, specifically, to run for attorney general. This time around, Neil Hartigan did in fact run for governor, Stevenson having lost in 1985. Roland Burris wanted to run for governor as well, clearing the field for Dawn.[9] By the first week of April 1989, buttons reading DAWN NETSCH A.G. '90 had been spotted on many people attending the state Democratic dinner.[10] And by June 1, invitations to a preview performance of *Bleacher Bums* at the Organic Theater said that it was "a fund-raiser to start Sen. Netsch's campaign for Illinois attorney general."[11]

Encouraged by the support of both Phil Rock and Rich Daley, now mayor of Chicago, Dawn announced her candidacy for attorney general at a press conference at Northwestern Law School on July 27, 1989. She was the first candidate to announce for the office, and began a fly-around of the state immediately.[12] By the following week, however, Burris had ceded the gubernatorial slot to Hartigan and announced his candidacy for attorney general as well. Dawn received a midnight phone call from Tom Hynes telling her about the switch.[13] Michael Howlett Jr. and Jim Burns were also running, in what was shaping up to be a four-way race. Although Democratic Party leaders would have liked Dawn to change her plans and run for comptroller, she vowed, "I'm not dropping out of the race. Everyone tells me that I'm running for something else, but nobody's bothered to ask me about it."[14]

By late October, however, Dawn became convinced that she should not oppose the first and only African American statewide elected official, a decision that delighted other Democrats, including her old friend Vince Demuzio, who was now state party chair. On October 30, she held a press conference to announce that she was dropping out of the race for attorney general and would instead run for comptroller, saying that the diverse coalitions in the Democratic Party were better served by avoiding a primary pitting a black against a woman.[15] Even though she would have preferred to run for attorney general, fiscal matters had also been of particular interest to her over the years. "I consider myself a fiscal groupie," she says, "and have spent a lot of my time in the legislature and, of course, in the constitutional convention on matters of revenue and finance. . . . Although that was not my first choice, at least it was in an area that was of enormous interest to me."[16]

This switch placed Dawn in the midst of another four-way race, and the candidate who had been running for comptroller much longer than she was her political ally Woods Bowman. By the end of November, however, Dawn had been slated by the state party as part of a ticket that included Paul Simon for U.S. senator, Neil Hartigan for governor, Jim Burns for lieutenant governor, Roland Burris for attorney general, Jerry Cosentino for secretary of state, and not one but two women—Dawn for comptroller, and Peg Breslin for treasurer.[17] The Republicans responded by running a woman against Dawn—Sue Suter, the former director of the Illinois Department of Public Aid and of the Illinois Department of Rehabilitation Services, whose appeal was possibly enhanced by the fact that she was disabled as a result of childhood polio.[18]

The four-way Democratic primary race required a sudden reorientation and a great deal of work between early November and the March primary. Dawn engaged Chris Meister to manage her campaign; Meister had previously worked for Vince Demuzio in his capacity as state party chair.[19] A key problem was how to stir up interest in such a low-profile race. Most people do not even know what the comptroller does, and what the comptroller does is not very exciting to the ordinary citizen. Essentially, the comptroller keeps the state's "checkbook" and pays its bills. The office stores records, keeps accounts, and makes monthly fiscal reports on the financial condition of the state. It also audits the financial statements of all local government bodies and oversees the operations of cemeteries and burial trust funds for the care of graves.

Dawn saw the position as having potential to inject improved financial planning into state and local government and also as a stepping-stone to higher office, even though she was now sixty-two years old. But the nature of the office of comptroller does not lend itself to easy sound bites about issues the electorate cares a great deal about, like abortion, or the death penalty, or crime. A potential drawback for Dawn was her well-known position at Con Con, when the office of comptroller was created, that it should be an appointive rather than elected office, and her statement that the job consisted essentially of "check-writing" that computers could do.[20] Each of the four candidates for the post basically had to convince the voters that he or she could do the apparently mundane job better than the other three. Dawn touted her experience as vice chair of the Revenue and Finance Committee at Con Con and as chair both of the Revenue Committee and of the Economic and Fiscal Commission while in the senate. Bowman boasted of his doctorate in economics, master's degree in public administration, three years as a research economist for the Federal Reserve, and seven years as chair of the Illinois House Appropriations Committee. William Sarto argued that he was best qualified because he had worked at the comptroller's office as an auditor for twelve years, and Shawn Collins, a commissioner of the Joliet Housing Authority, made no-bid contracts the theme of his campaign.[21] Collins was thought by some, inaccurately, to be African American; to capitalize on this misperception, his campaign literature tended to omit pictures.

Bill Morris, Dawn's old friend from the Crazy Eight, served as an informal adviser to her campaign. He recommended that she focus on Democratic women with a history of voting and not neglect to campaign back in her old lakefront turf so as not to cede her base to Bowman. Morris also told Dawn to surrender herself to her campaign staff. "This will allow you to be briefed each afternoon and focus all your time and energy to public appearances, fund raising phone calls and your private life."[22] This could be difficult for Dawn, especially because she hated making fund-raising calls.

Dawn's campaign staff drew up an elaborate week-by-week plan of activity running from January 1990 to the March 20 primary, a demanding schedule requiring fund-raising calls and contacts by Dawn, intensive voter contact, including working the el stops and meeting with churches and community groups, and making multiple contacts with the press in an attempt to gain editorial endorsements. The campaign also began work on a series of white papers, starting with "Truth in Budgeting," issued in January 1990. In it, Dawn vowed to put an end to various budgetary gimmicks that make the state budget look balanced when it is not, such as the deferral of payment obligations and questionable revenue forecasting. So that the electorate might know the actual resources available, she proposed reporting a budgetary balance that took account of so-called lapse spending—that is, appropriations from one year that were paid during the first three months of the next fiscal year but ignored in the balance figures issued on June 30 of each year.[23] Although this issue still may not have captured the popular imagination, it did figure in some newspaper endorsements later in the year. During a campaign swing through central and southern Illinois at the end of February, Dawn also proposed more emphasis by the comptroller on monitoring and reporting the status of debts owed the state, better internal accounting and administrative controls throughout state government, oversight of energy consumption and conservation, and an annual review of questionable leases.[24]

According to Chris Meister, her campaign chair, the decision was made early on to approach this low-profile race by direct mail, sending a series of short pieces that people could read as they were sorting their mail (and presumably throwing it away), especially to voters downstate, where Dawn did not have the name recognition she had in Cook County. The other strategic decision, as Morris had recommended, was to sell Dawn to women voters in particular. Her staff developed a plan to contact as many households as possible whose members had voted in the previous two Democratic primaries and that had at least one woman in them. Although the campaign did not have a lot of money, there was enough to do a targeted, well-thought-out and crafted mail program based on the state party voter lists.[25] Dawn continued to make personal visits downstate as well. For example, when the party organization in Madison County (one of the poor, African American, boss-dominated counties around East St. Louis) appeared to be about to endorse Woods Bowman, she flew down and worked the phones with her local allies like Vince Demuzio and captured the endorsement. Ironically, she lost the endorsement of some organizations in Cook County that would have seemed to be naturally hers from past experience. Notably, the Independent Voters of Illinois–Independent Precinct Organization's endorsement went to Bowman.[26]

The primary campaign did not capture much voter interest in Cook County, even after a debate among the four candidates at the City Club in late February at which Dawn tried to explain how important the comptroller's office was in making sure taxpayers got their money's worth. Polls showed that 66 percent of Democratic voters in the county were undecided on the race, with the press surmising that they were "stifling yawns."[27] Bowman attacked Dawn in the press as not interested in the comptroller's office but seeking it because the party wanted Burris to run for attorney general; he pointed out that it had taken her two months to see the need for a racially balanced ticket after Burris entered the race.[28] Dawn replied that there was no way she would campaign statewide for more than a year for an office she did not want.[29]

To the surprise of many, when the time came for the primary on March 20, 1990, Bowman did not turn out to be Dawn's main opposition. In the four-way election, Dawn captured 49 percent of the vote, with Shawn Collins coming in second, with 27 percent; Bowman, 14 percent; and Sarto, 10 percent.[30] Peg Breslin lost the Democratic nomination for treasurer to Pat Quinn, so Dawn was the only woman on the ticket. But with the candidates for both parties now female, it would not be a woman's race anyway.

The 1989 General Election

A week after her primary victory, Dawn closed her campaign office and let all her staff go to save money and effort until the general election campaign in the fall. She returned to teaching and the senate, and she spent her summer revising her textbook on state and local government. By the fall, Dawn had reconstituted her campaign operation, however, this time with Terry Stephan as chair. Stephan had met Dawn in 1985, when she was working on Adlai Stevenson III's second campaign for governor. She remembers, "[Dawn] was unlike anybody I'd ever seen. Sharp as a tack, very serious about what we were doing, flamboyant in her own kind of peculiar way, a lot of fun."[31]

Stephan put together a relatively small staff, consisting of herself, a fund-raiser, a scheduler, an office manager, and a driver; they did not need a press secretary because the press was not interested in the race. They continued to campaign by mail, although Dawn's opponent Sue Suter went on television in September and October, often with negative ads, focusing, for example, on Dawn's opposition to the death penalty, although that had nothing to do with the comptroller's position. Near the end, the Netsch campaign did buy time for a television ad to respond. But Dawn was reluctant to spend money on television and thought it was absurd that a race for a low-profile office would necessitate spending so much.

The two candidates debated once on television as well, sponsored by the League of Women Voters, on October 7, 1990. Suter emphasized her administrative experience at the debate, and Netsch responded with an attack on the backlog of child support cases during the period of Suter's tenure at the Department of Public Aid.[32] As time went on, Dawn's attacks on Suter's record expanded, as she presented reports by the auditor general criticizing Suter's management of the Illinois Department of Rehabilitation Services as well.

Beginning in early October, Dawn also issued a series of policy statements in the form of more white papers—"Economy and Productivity in State Government," proposing measures to cut government waste and inefficiency; "Truth in Local Government Accountability," calling for more accountability from the state in programs it imposed on local governments and an activist role for the comptroller in enabling state and local governments to interact more efficiently and effectively; and "Truth in Borrowing," proposing a comprehensive policy to provide greater accountability and control over state indebtedness. Each white paper was dense and technical—not exactly easy reading for laypeople—and detailed the changes, including new legislation, that would be required to bring about the objectives it presented. The four together made up the Netsch agenda announced at an October 5 press conference.[33] Together they outlined an extremely activist program for an officer whose main function was to pay the state's bills.

A great deal of the campaign, according to Stephan, consisted of scheduling Dawn—getting her out to meet people, especially downstate where she was unknown. At first, Dawn was unhappy about having to spend so much time away from Chicago and Springfield. But by the end of her initial trip to rural areas in Illinois, Stephan describes Dawn as having so much fun that she did not want to leave:

> I was curious when we sent her off the first time, because she was going to be unlike anybody they had ever seen down there. It was as if a spaceship had crashed in a farm field and a strange person got out. But she bowled them over, and she enjoyed it. She had never done that kind of campaigning before, had never really had occasion to go into these small towns and talk to farmers and volunteer firemen. They liked her because she's so genuine, so unpretentious. . . . [Other politicians are] slick, almost interchangeable, and she's different. And she's fun, energetic.[34]

Dawn says she found it pleasant to campaign downstate because people were so welcoming and appreciative of the visit.

Dawn received a lot of support from many of the usual players in Illinois politics. Phil Rock was exceptionally supportive, giving her both moral support and help with fund-raising. Labor unions endorsed her, even those that remained neutral on the race for governor or had endorsed Hartigan's opponent.[35] The mayor was clearly in her corner. Moreover, just being part of the statewide ticket meant that the campaign and Election Day resources of the Chicago and statewide Democratic Party were put to work for Dawn. Almost all of the literature handed out to instruct voters how to vote at the polls included her name on it. Nonetheless, a *Chicago Tribune* telephone survey of Illinois residents at the end of September showed that the race for comptroller was a statistical tie.[36] A new poll, close to the end of October, showed Dawn ahead 27 percent to 24 percent, but 48 percent of the voters were still undecided.[37]

Nonstop activity marked the end of the campaign, including a fly-around of the state during the last weekend, when all the candidates campaigned together in an attempt to hit every media market.[38] Much of the time, they would not leave the airport, where local Democratic officials would hold a rally and the candidates would speak to the press, always with an eye to the time the local news would be on in that market. Proceeding in this fashion, it was possible to cover most of the state in a day and a half—an exhausting task, but one at which Dawn excelled, according to Stephan.

Dawn and her campaign staff did not feel certain of victory by Election Day. When 85 percent of the vote had been counted, however, it showed that she had defeated Suter by a ten-point margin, 55 percent to 45 percent. This result, and Paul Simon's easy reelection as U.S. senator, revealed an enormous amount of ticket splitting by the electorate. Hartigan, at the top of the Democratic ticket, lost by two percentage points to Republican Jim Edgar for governor, and another Republican, George Ryan, was elected secretary of state. Roland Burris became attorney general by a vote of 52 percent to 48 percent. In short, Dawn ran well among the Democrats on the ticket.[39]

Moreover, although Paul Simon's female opponent lost, it was a good year for women candidates throughout the United States; they won half the statewide offices they sought. But positions such as treasurer, comptroller, and lieutenant governor tended to be those deemed appropriate for women, instead of governor or U.S. senator. Interviewed for an article about the obstacles faced by women in politics, Dawn said, "There is still discomfort among some voters about women in high policy positions, almost anything that requires real toughness."[40] Kathy Kleeman, at the Center for the American Woman and Politics at Rutgers University, opined that women faced even more difficulties than that: "There is a fine line that women have to walk. There's the whole question of image—what you wear, your hairstyle, how you shake hands, how you talk. People know what male candidates look like and talk like and act. But with a woman, they don't know yet."[41] They were beginning to find out.

The Transition

Immediately after the election, Dawn put together a transition committee, headed by her old friend and Crazy Eight member Bill Morris. The purpose of the transition committee was to familiarize itself with the workings of the comptroller's office and to translate the commitments Dawn had made to the electorate into a list of things to do after she took office. The Financial Management Subcommittee, charged with coming up with recommendations about the most central tasks of the office, was chaired by Marcus Alexis, an eminent professor of economics at Northwestern, and included eight other people with special expertise, such as Professor Ronald Picur from the College of Business Administration at the University of Illinois at Chicago, Senator Vince Demuzio, Dawn's old Committee on Illinois Government friend Jim Alter, and others. The subcommittee worked for several months, reviewing operations in Springfield and consulting academic and business experts. Although its final report was not submitted until April 1991, an interim report containing the same substantive conclusions was presented to Dawn on January 11, soon after she was sworn in.[42] It examined both the way in which the state managed its cash and how to improve the statewide accounting system.

Long before she received the recommendations of her advisers, however, Dawn was given a series of memoranda from people who had been working in the comptroller's office under Roland Burris; she also met with one of his chief operating officers. She recalls that he told her, "Sit down, I have a few things you need to know. One is we haven't got any money. We are really in terrible shape."[43] Then he told her that the office was equipped with computer technology that was up-to-date several decades earlier. A November 9, 1990, memorandum also warned her of "cash flow" problems, predicting that they would become "virtually unmanageable by the end of February or earlier."[44] Its author explained that the Burris administration had found it necessary to delay certain payments to make ends meet.

Dawn was also supplied by the auditor general's office with a list of the statutory mandates for the comptroller's office, starting from the constitutional provision that "the Comptroller shall be responsible for maintaining the state's fiscal accounts, and order payments into and out of the funds held by the Treasurer" and proceeding through every statutory provision affecting the responsibilities of the office.[45] The Legislative Research Unit provided her with a more user-friendly narrative description of the duties of the office, which discussed, among other things, its preaudit responsibility for examining and verifying all spending requests and its duty to maintain a uniform accounting system for state records, review local government audits, store records, and regulate the care and trust funds of private cemeteries.[46] In short, the duties she had were made clear. How to carry them out, especially under the current fiscal constraints, was the problem.

Burris's former press secretary sent Dawn a memorandum with recommendations about how the comptroller's communications division should be organized.[47] He focused on the monthly fiscal report the comptroller (through her director of fiscal research and staff economist) was required to prepare as an effective media tool, because a press release accompanies the release of each month's report. He advised her about well-timed leaks to the press and ways to use the office to forward the comptroller's own ambitions for higher office, especially when the incumbent was of a different party from the governor and could expose inefficiencies and waste of public funds. This was advice that Dawn was loath to take. She did not see the state's fiscal status as a matter for partisan politics.

The official transition team and its subcommittees provided Dawn with an ambitious program to accomplish when she took office. The Financial Management Subcommittee advised her to improve the comptroller's ability to monitor, project, and manage the state's cash flow in a number of ways, including by tracking payment cycles, which had not been done on a regular basis. It detailed the ways in which the state's true financial status was disguised by presentation of an available balance in the report released at the end of each fiscal year. The experts on the subcommittee also warned her that cash-flow problems were likely to continue for several years, given the recessionary economy with its lower yields of income and sales tax receipts combined with the increased costs of public aid and medical care, thus necessitating measures such as short-term borrowing. They also emphasized the importance of improving the statewide accounting system and upgrading the office's computer technology—not only for the efficient processing of transactions but also for the production of timely and accurate financial information. Because this would be costly, they recommended a timetable by which the system might be enhanced over several fiscal years. They proposed that the comptroller establish a uniform system of accounting that would be used throughout state government and perform financial projections that would be more independent than those of the legislature and governor.[48]

In addition to the substantive tasks of the position, Dawn was required to make decisions about staffing the office and about its internal organization during the transition period. Another subcommittee of her transition team, the Internal Operations Group chaired by attorney George

Muñoz, drafted a report on these issues.[49] This report suggested that the comptroller-elect undertake an analysis of managerial and policy-making positions in the office to properly classify positions that were genuinely policy making and thus could be filled by patronage appointments and positions that should be treated as civil service. Rather than hiring political supporters who were minimally qualified for a job, as appeared to have been done in the past, the subcommittee recommended that Dawn seek the best available talent by working with university placement offices and bringing students in for a trial period as interns. It also suggested that she not fill any existing vacant positions until it was clear that there was a need to do so, that she review the functions of certain specified departments with an eye to economizing, and that she cut staff at the Chicago office. Given that Dawn, like all other state officers, would be required to cut her budgetary requests by a specified percentage to balance the state budget, many of the suggestions were helpful.

Typically, a new comptroller (especially one of a different political party than the previous incumbent, which Dawn was not) would immediately replace large numbers of employees who were classified as policy making. Dawn quickly decided not to engage in wholesale replacement of personnel but rather to retain employees of the office if they were found to be doing a good job in a nonpolitical manner.[50] Thus, even those who were originally hired on the basis of patronage were retained so long as they were performing well in their jobs.

A new comptroller nonetheless requires a number of key personnel on whom she may rely without question to fill the positions at the top of the organizational hierarchy. Dawn solved this problem by recruiting two people who had previously worked with her at the Economic and Fiscal Commission, the bipartisan legislative forecasting agency she had chaired for a number of years. A couple of days after the election, she called Bob Brock, who had worked at the commission for twelve years, and asked him to come to her senate office, where she was meeting with Bill Morris, the head of her transition team. They asked Bob to join the transition team; and when Dawn took office in January 1991, he became her deputy comptroller.[51] Together they succeeded in getting Jim Ofcarcik, also a longtime employee of the Economic and Fiscal Commission, to join them several months later as special assistant to the comptroller. Later they enticed an employee of the Bureau of the Budget to become director of research, even though they assumed he was a Republican. Dawn did not care about political affiliation so long as the person had the right skills for the job.

Linda Fletcher, Dawn's much-trusted secretary at the senate, accompanied her to the new office; and Wendy Cohen, her former legislative assistant, was made deputy chief of staff at the small office of the comptroller in the State of Illinois Building in Chicago. She was the only one of Dawn's longtime political supporters appointed to a position; her task was to serve as Dawn's eyes and ears and to make sure that everything was running smoothly at the Chicago office.[52]

As a general rule, Dawn spent at least three days a week in Springfield and sometimes the entire week, which she always did when the legislature was in session. Although she had continued to teach law on a reduced load throughout her career in the legislature, the arrangement would be impossible now that she had a full-time executive position in state government. Dawn therefore sat down with then dean of the law school Bob Bennett to talk about her future relationship with Northwestern. They decided that she should officially become a professor emerita, allowing her to keep a small office and to return to teaching when she wished.[53]

Comptroller, 1991–1995

In early January 1991, Dawn was sworn in as comptroller of the State of Illinois, with Walter holding the Bible, and she moved into the impressive office in the capitol. The capitol in Springfield is a classical building with an immense dome completed in the late nineteenth century. Its floor plan is based on a modified Latin cross, with four porticoes leading out from the dome area on each of the four floors. The office of the comptroller is on the second floor at the end of the north portico, joined to the dome area by a long marble hallway. One enters the office through an oversized, ornate wooden door into a formal reception area. To the left is another reception area, where Linda Fletcher sat, controlling access to Dawn's office (though she reports that Dawn had a virtually open-door policy for her employees).

The comptroller's office itself matches the grandeur of the building— exceptionally tall ceilings, gilt decorations, an enormous chandelier, and elaborately carved wood on three oversized doors (one into a restroom and one into a storage area). Dawn's large wooden desk faced a marble fireplace on the opposite wall, and a floor-to-ceiling window draped with green velvet overlooked the street below. Dawn spent no money on redecorating the office, as other officeholders had. But into this very traditional setting, with its antique credenzas, side tables, and chairs, Dawn introduced some of the modern art Walter had collected. Robert Indiana's huge painting of a zero hung behind the desk, causing Bob Brock and Jim Ofcarcik to ask, "Dawn, are you trying to send your vendors a message? There's no money, and there's all red ink?" She laughed.[54]

Several other offices and a conference room surrounded the reception area where Fletcher sat, with offices for Brock, Ofcarcik, and Dawn's legislative director. Most of the employees of the comptroller's office—more than three hundred of them—were housed in another building in Springfield, where several shifts of workers wrote all the checks, processed them, and stored them. (Dawn went over to meet those who worked on each shift.) Meetings were held in the conference room outside Dawn's office. A good deal of her time was taken up with meetings and conferences with staff, discussing the cash-flow problems of the day or what to do about a particular issue facing the office with Brock, Ofcarcik, her general counsel Lou Ann Reichle, and her legislative liaison Sharon Corrigan. At other times, legislators or representatives of state agencies or of the governor's office would come in to discuss what needed to be done to take care of one crisis or another. Irate vendors called constantly to ask about when they would be paid, and occasionally Dawn herself would talk to them. The remainder of her time was taken up by looking through financial reports and reports from local government bodies, editing the monthly reports and other communications, responding to inquiries from the press, or going out to talk to groups of citizens about what was happening.[55] The provision of accessible and comprehensible information about state finances to the electorate was a priority for her.

It was only after she took office that Dawn found out how bad things truly were. There simply was not enough in the state's general revenue fund to pay the bills. Certain expenditures had to receive priority under the law, including payroll to state employees, debt financing, and payments to public aid recipients; and basic school aid payments could not be missed or the schools would close down. Beyond these items, the comptroller's office made daily decisions about what would be paid out of the limited monies on hand and in what order, placing holds on numbers of payments to vendors, whose bills were regularly paid months late. Dawn describes her shock at this predicament:

> What I saw when I got there was that what we were doing to people who were vendors or service providers to the state was absolutely outrageous. We were not paying them . . . sometimes for months

and months. And we literally put some people, particularly some of the smaller, independent pharmacies, out of business.

. . . So what I came to realize was that we were borrowing. We were borrowing from the people who provided things to the state. And we could go out and borrow in the market at about half the rate that those folks had to pay in order to be able to finance themselves because we weren't paying their bills on time. And so [although personally opposed to incurring debt to pay for operational expenses] I came to the conclusion that we just simply had to do some short-term borrowing for operating costs, and had a terrible time persuading [Governor] Edgar to that effect.[56]

The state's finances went from crisis to crisis, while the governor tried to protect the state's rating with bond companies by manipulating the balance at the end of the fiscal year. This was done not only by deferring payments but also by lapse spending. While the fiscal year ran from July 1 to June 30, bills would continue to come in for goods and services during the months that followed the June 30 closing of the books. The lapse-spending arrangement provided that bills could be paid within three months after the close of the fiscal year and charged to the prior year's appropriations; of course, the money to pay them came out of the cash on hand, which was for the following year. Thus, when the governor said to Dawn that he needed to show $100 million in the general revenue fund on June 30 for purposes of the state's credit rating, she would simply hold off paying enough bills to leave that amount and have them paid in the lapse period.[57] Governors had been doing this for some time. By 1991 the amount of lapse spending had skyrocketed, so that the official balance sheet bore little relationship to the state's real financial situation. To understand the real situation, one would need to subtract from the balance the amount of money owed, which at one point during Dawn's tenure totaled almost $1 billion. In this way, the state engaged in deficit spending despite the constitutional requirement for a balanced budget. In March 1992, U.S. News and World Report honored this process in an article called "The 10 Worst Economic Moves"—a survey of the most shortsighted financial gimmicks that local governments used throughout the United States. "'Doctoring the Budget Numbers' was the title of Illinois' entry on the dubious list of boneheaded moves."[58]

To make this all work, each year it was necessary to engage in short-term borrowing, loans that would be paid off over the course of the year as revenue came in from tax assessments, the federal government, and other sources. Illinois law required that the state treasurer and the comptroller agree with the governor to authorize any short-term loans. In late July 1992, Netsch and Edgar agreed that it was necessary to borrow $300 million to pay the state's bills. However, Treasurer Pat Quinn refused to agree unless the governor would speed up some payments to the state school districts. Dawn was infuriated, calling this a "political chess game" on Quinn's part. At a press conference, she pounded the podium loudly and "raised her voice to express her frustration about the state falling behind in paying bills."[59] Her anger at Quinn became quite well known, especially after she marched from her office at the State of Illinois Building in Chicago into his office there and let him know in no uncertain terms how she felt about what he was doing to the state and to those to whom the state owed money. Because her voice was raised and the walls paper thin, the episode became famous.[60]

Governor Edgar, responding politically as well, quickly dropped the borrowing plan to place the onus for the state's situation onto Quinn instead of negotiating with him. The upshot was that the short-term loans were delayed for some two months in 1992, further delaying payment to the state's vendors. Quinn did not try this tactic the following year, when he quickly approved a short-term loan of $900 million in July.[61]

Dawn became the official sayer of doom and gloom, as she filed her monthly reports, issued press releases about them, held regular press conferences (jokingly dubbed "Public Finance 101"), and spoke to groups of the public about the situation. In a June 28, 1991, press release, she said, "Plainly and simply, the state's fiscal health is very, very poor as we close the books on fiscal 1991," opining that the state was in a recession, which had decreased its tax revenues.[62] In an August 12 release, she reported that the state had ended the year with a deficit of $295 million and was facing as much as $800 million in lapse period spending, its poorest fiscal condition ever.[63] Another release, the following June 30, reported that fiscal year 1992 was ending with a balance of $2.8 million in the General Revenue Fund, the lowest year-end balance in history, against which there was a backlog of $331 million in unpaid bills.[64] In an August 21, 1992, press release, she complained, "One-shot accounting maneuvers and budgetary sleights of hand in fiscal 1992 helped to disguise a 'structural imbalance.'"[65] The backlog of unpaid bills hit a new record ($858.9 million) at the end of March 1993, according to an April 1 press release, although signs of hope were starting to appear in the form of increases in receipts from sales and income taxes.[66] By July 1, the backlog had been cut to $223.5 million, the lowest since August 22, 1991, largely because the economy was starting to recover.[67]

Needless to say, the role of the Illinois comptroller was laden with tension during those years. Dawn describes it as

> the worst possible job at the worst possible time. It was very tension-laden, very challenging, because we had to figure out what *we* could do to try to make it easier for everybody out there. . . . It was almost like a chess game all the time, moving the various pieces around, who got paid when, because there was never enough money to go around.[68]

It was necessary to sort through the bills and make decisions about payments on a daily basis, with Dawn setting the priorities and her staff executing them. For the first several months, this was the job of Deputy Comptroller Bob Brock, but Jim Ofcarcik took it over when he came to the office from the Economic and Fiscal Commission. Most of his job, he says, consisted of "doing a daily forecast of revenues, what we thought would come in when, and trying to figure out how we would pay, what we would pay, and coordinating with the other parts of the comptroller's office how we would release payments and who would get paid."[69] One goal, he says, was to avoid incurring additional fees or interest for bills that were paid late, and another was trying to stay out of court. This was not always possible, and sometimes Dawn was glad that lawsuits had been filed against her office. For example, welfare recipients had successfully sued in federal court to force the state to pay them even though the legislature was in overtime session and had not passed a budget. State law would have prohibited Dawn from doing so without the federal court order.

At the same time, Dawn had to cut the expenditures of her own office, as the state budget required across-the-board cuts. She implemented measures to save money, even cutting staff positions pursuant to a reorganization (which, of course, occasioned more lawsuits against her). Mostly the office coped with the crisis by every staff member working harder and thus raising overall productivity. People pitched in, at least in part, because they liked working for Dawn. Linda Fletcher describes her sprightly greetings in the morning, her personal concern for each individual and their families. When she was upset, Dawn did not take it out on other people. In addition to her open-door policy, she genuinely listened to her employees and, when she had made the necessary decisions, trusted them to carry out her policy in a competent fashion; she was not a micromanager.[70] She was patient and never lectured anyone. Moreover, Dawn was also clearly pitching in herself by working long days. She was often at the office before others in the morning and long after they had left at night. One gets the sense that she inspired her employees to work harder by sheer example. As Ofcarcik describes it, "Dawn really did set an amazing example for what constituted public service and what people ought to do when you are in a position of public trust." From Dawn, he says, he learned that being a public servant was a high calling—a calling to be "someone who is good at keeping the public trust, at doing the things that . . . need to be done on behalf of people who cannot do it on their own, who need assistance from the state."[71] Similarly, Brock commented, "I don't think I've known anybody in government that cared about good government as much as she does."[72]

Dawn had a special commitment to making financial information, even if gloomy, accessible to the citizens of the state. She tried to liven up many of the rather dull publications that the office put out to make them more readable and thus more likely to be read. The comptroller's monthly report, which previously consisted of ten pages of plain, dull text and numbers, was reformatted to look more like a magazine, with color, pictures, and charts. Each month it also included an article discussing some timely topic, such as the state pension system, the Department of Corrections, elementary and secondary education in the state, and the like. As Brock says,

> She believed that numbers mean something and that you need to write about what the numbers mean. The announcement at the comptroller's office that was done at the time was very, very dry, long-winded, and said nothing. It basically said, "This is up, that's down. . . ." So we set about changing that, and she had a great deal of input into the way the publications were structured and the text. . . . We'd submit the drafts and at first she marked them up a lot.[73]

A glossy pamphlet published in 1993 titled "It's Your Money" shows how well they succeeded in producing a lively, short document to explain the state's finances to its citizens. It is filled with pictures (especially of the many schoolchildren Dawn loved to host at the capitol) and illustrated

with colorful charts and tables. It starts with a multiple-choice test—
"Do You Know Where Your Tax Dollar Goes?"—and uses the answers
to deliver a short course on state finance. It relates almost every item back
to the individual presumed to be reading it, telling, for example, what
their individual share of the state debt is. The booklet is inviting and very
readable.

A particular concern for Dawn, after all her years of teaching state
and local government to law students, was the welfare of the many
small governments in Illinois. As comptroller, she established the Local
Government Advisory Board, which included many members of her
former transition team, such as Bill Morris, Ron Picur, Terry Clark, and
other prominent people. The thirty-member board included academics,
local government officials, private citizens, and certified public accoun-
tants. They were divided into working committees such as the Investment
Guide Review Committee and the Audit Guide Review Committee; the
latter undertook to update the guidebook for local governments about
how to complete their audits, which had last been updated in 1981. Dawn
suggested that the board consider establishing a committee on training as
well, to assist with providing training to local treasurers, which the state
could not then afford to do.[74]

The office of the comptroller has a particularly close relationship with
local governments, which are required to file an annual fiscal report with
the comptroller. Before Dawn's tenure, most of the reports had simply
been piled up in a warehouse. A number of local units had not filed their
reports for some years, and many of the smaller units lacked the funds and
expertise to manage their own finances. Dawn took several steps to address
these problems.[75] First, she instructed her employees to begin to get the
annual reports submitted by local governments onto a computer. Next, she
undertook an extensive reorganization plan for the section of the office
dealing with local government affairs; the goal was both to assist the local
bodies with their required reporting and to provide feedback to them in
the form of analysis and reporting of financial status and indicators.[76] The
newly reorganized section redesigned the annual financial report form to
make it easier to fill out. The section also established the Institute of Local
Government Affairs in cooperation with Southern Illinois University,
which was designed to provide local bodies with both information and
training. Dawn's vision was that the institute could make something out
of all the local government financial information that was simply stored
by the state if her office could get the data into a form in which it could

be analyzed and useful; the institute could then facilitate the sharing of information and ideas among different local bodies. It would help one community to know what others were doing—for example, to compare the costs of running a police department.

Another way in which the comptroller's office and local governmental bodies intersected was through the state's distribution of (or failure to distribute) payments to cities and counties. A certain percentage of the Illinois state income tax is set aside to be distributed to cities and counties on the basis of population, yet this was one of the forms of payment that was held back because of the budgetary crisis. In July 1993, however, when the Mississippi River flooded the area from the Quad Cities to Quincy, Comptroller Netsch took a helicopter trip up and down the flooded river, stopping at a number of small communities as well as at Quincy. When she asked local officials what the state could do to help, they all said, "Get our payments to us!" So Dawn ordered the speedy release of $45.6 million in local government distributive funds. And she regularly argued to the governor and treasurer that the local government distribution should be placed higher on the list of priority payments.[77]

The sorry state of the available computerization handicapped all of the work of the office. According to Brock, when Dawn took office:

> We discovered that cash-flow was handled on the back of an envelope, and then they trashed the records every day. . . . It was effective, but there was no record. We had absolutely no record of anything that happened prior to about the third week of December of 1990. And so I set about trying to computerize things and trying to organize it in such a way that we could track things on a daily basis, and sometimes even on an hourly basis, and that turned out to be the biggest single task we had at the comptroller's office for the four years that Dawn was there.[78]

A great deal of the work of the office had previously been done by hand rather than entered into a computer. According to Brock, "We had at one point rooms full of boxes of unpaid bills. . . . They had to go through boxes by hand to find vouchers that were going to be paid that night."[79] Personal computers in the office were several years old and were hardly used. Moreover, the overall computer system was so antiquated that Dawn kept warning people that if it went down, no one would be paid. Indeed, the main system did go down one night and failed to input any of the cash that comes in regularly for overnight processing. "We ended up with a cash balance in the general revenue fund of [something like] $8.93."[80] Newspaper headlines all over the state proclaimed that the state, with its budget of billions, had only $8 in the bank. Brock was charged with putting together a plan to start modernizing the technology in the office, and he spent most of his time as deputy comptroller on this task.

While she was comptroller, whenever possible, Dawn introduced bills into the legislature intended to improve the working of her office and of state finances, and to fulfill her campaign promises to the electorate. Many of the bills were about issues in which she had long been interested. She had, for example, sponsored a senate bill in 1981, and again in 1990, to define the preaudit duties of the comptroller; her bill included among those duties an obligation to ensure not only that there is an adequate appropriation for a given expenditure but also that the expenditure is substantively legal.[81] Governor Thompson vetoed the bills, as Governor Walker had vetoed a similar bill before him. The issue involved is whether the comptroller has a narrow function, that is, to make sure that any payment is technically correct and within the appropriated budget, or whether he or she has authority to question the substantive legality of vouchers that another agency has approved. A similar bill was introduced into the senate in April 1991, after Dawn became comptroller, allowing the comptroller to conduct an investigation whenever she had reason to question the legality of a payment and to hold up payment for three days while informing the chief executive officer of the agency why this was being done. If the officer filed a responsive affidavit and certified that the transaction was authorized by law, the comptroller was required to make the payment but could continue investigation into its legality.[82] The bill did not become law.

Several instances of this type of questionable payment occurred during Dawn's tenure as comptroller. In 1991, Governor Edgar, under the authority of the hastily passed Governor's First Emergency Budget Relief Act, ordered transfers out of special funds identified only by number into the General Revenue Fund. When Ofcarcik and his staff looked up the numbers, they discovered that the largest single transfer, $21 million, was out of the state pension fund.[83] Dawn had been one of the leading proponents in the legislature for adequate actuarial funding of the seriously underfunded retirement funds that the state held for its employees. Indeed, she had even succeeded in getting a bill passed in 1989 requiring catch-up funding; Governor Thompson signed it before she left the senate. But when Governor Edgar succeeded Thompson, he continued to budget less than the minimum contributions required by law.[84] Thus, when Dawn's staff told her that Edgar was transferring $21 million out of the pension fund into general revenue, she was shocked, but she did not think she had the authority to prevent this from happening.

State employee-participants in the pension funds filed a lawsuit to block the transfer of funds and obtained a temporary restraining order on August 5, 1991. On November 20, 1991, Dawn presented testimony before a U.S. congressional committee about the situation as an example of how a state government was using its pension system to balance its budget.[85] But on May 26, 1992, the Illinois Supreme Court dissolved the restraining order.[86] Only then did Dawn order the movement of $21 million out of the state pension funds into the General Revenue Fund.

Again, in September 1992, Dawn questioned the payment of the final installment of the multimillion-dollar state subsidy to Sears, Roebuck to facilitate its move to the Chicago suburbs after it had threatened to move its headquarters out of state. To Dawn, this was an egregious use of public funds to subsidize a private company, one that was moving away from its downtown location and thereby making it difficult, if not impossible, for its inner-city employees to get to work. She insisted on obtaining assurances that the company was taking steps to ease the transportation problems of its employees before finally releasing the payment at the last minute. But, she says:

> To this day I'm sorry I did that [released the payment]. I wish at the very least I had made a major public fuss . . . a big, public, ugly scene about it. I don't know if it would have done any good, but it might have at least called attention to the fact that a company, which was then of course a terribly profitable company, like Sears was being paid really to hurt a lot of people who had worked for it for years. And not even to build a manufacturing plant. . . . Just to move their headquarters.[87]

This, of course, was not what the comptroller's preaudit function was about; her quarrel was with the deal that the legislature and the governor had struck.

On another occasion, the comptroller's office found that certain Republican legislators had charged items to the state that should have come out of their personal political funds. When her staff brought this to her attention, Dawn went to the Republican leaders and said, "Guys, this is totally inappropriate. I think it behooves you to reimburse the state or else it's going to become public, and that will be very embarrassing for you."[88] They repaid the monies. This is a good example of a payment for which preaudit authority in the comptroller would provide a substantial public benefit.

Continuing with her longtime interest in governmental ethics, Dawn also introduced a legislative package on the subject while she was comptroller.[89] Among other things, her proposal would have extended state ethics laws to executive branch officials and employees and prohibited them from doing business with the state for two years after leaving office. It would also, like the bills she had sponsored as a senator, have provided caps on political contributions and campaign spending limits. The proposals for reform were unsuccessful, just as her earlier efforts had been.

As the next gubernatorial election drew near and it was clear that Dawn would be throwing her hat into the ring, she put together a whole package of legislative reform proposals which she called the BEST Government proposal, an acronym for Budgeting for Economy, Stability, and Truth in Government. A good deal of the legislation she proposed corresponded to promises she had originally made in her "Truth in Budgeting" white paper during her 1990 campaign for comptroller, and some was addressed toward abuses she had seen while in office. One piece of the package, the Illinois Balanced Budget Act, introduced on March 9, 1993, created a commission to provide a balanced budget revenue estimate for each year and provided that the commission's estimate would limit all appropriations from state funds.[90] It also reduced the lapse period, during which one year's expenses could be paid out of the next year's funds, from three months to two months within a year, and from two months to one month in the following year. The Illinois Fiscal and Economic Stability Act introduced the same day would have created a rainy-day fund to cover any budgetary shortfall.[91] In summary, the bills would have forced the legislature to pass balanced state budgets.

Dawn's budgeting proposals were attractive to many Republicans, and they all passed in the house of representatives. However, Republicans in the senate, who had recently won a majority, killed Dawn's reform package in late April 1993, with little discussion and on partisan grounds.[92] Dawn was angry that that her eminently sensible and conservative reforms had become caught up in partisan politics. Various Republican senators had assured her of their support, and one or two of her bills had appeared likely to pass. At that point, however, Governor Edgar called several of the Republican senators in for a talk. He told them not to let Dawn's finance bills leave committee or be called for a vote on the floor, presumably because she was emerging as his opponent for governor. As a result, none of Dawn's proposed bills passed, though in subsequent years the Illinois legislature did reduce the lapse period somewhat and set up a rainy-day fund.[93]

Dawn also prepared an extensive document called "BEST Government Talking Points," about the problems that hidden deficits created during the Edgar administration, and she delivered a summary of them to the Senate Committee on the Executive.[94] The pages read like campaign documents. They are highly critical of fiscal practices under Governor Edgar, such as his diversion of funds from local governments and state pension funds, and they received widespread publicity.

Brock says that the Edgar administration was suspicious of Dawn from the beginning and accused her of playing politics whenever she would issue gloomy reports about the status of the state's finances. There could be a narrow line between transparency in government and criticism of a political opponent. On one occasion, when Edgar accused her of manufacturing the gloomy numbers she had presented, Dawn invited the press to come to the operational offices of the comptroller, where she walked through the rooms with them pointing out the boxes stacked from floor to ceiling. Brock says, "We told them, 'Pull a box out, close your eyes and reach in there and pull out a voucher. That's a real person; that's somebody whose bill should have been paid by now if we did not have cash problems.'"[95] He insists that Dawn always made her decisions about payments on the basis of principled priorities and never let politics enter into it. Yet she was obviously in a prime position to expose the shortcomings of the Edgar administration.

When it became clear that Dawn was going to enter the Democratic primary to become the party's candidate for governor, Brock went in to talk to her late one evening in her office. He asked, "Dawn, why do you want to do this? I'm going to try to talk you out of this." Dawn looked at him solemnly and said, "Somebody's got to change this state. I think I can do that."[96]

—— *Chapter 16* ——

The Race for Governor of Illinois

DAWN HAD WANTED TO run for governor for a long time. She dates her interest to when she was twenty-two years old and working for the League of Women Voters after college. "In high school and college I wanted to be in the U.S. Senate; but when I got interested in state government, I realized you could do more in that role that had a real impact on people's lives, even though you might not be dealing with issues of war and peace."[1] Serving as Governor Kerner's assistant and getting to see the job up close had piqued her interest. She remained interested in eventually becoming governor the entire time she was in state government, from Con Con, when she had written the chapter on the executive in the background papers prepared for the convention, through her service in the legislature and as comptroller. Realistically, however, she knew that it was a long shot.

Preparing to Run

Dawn's increasing frustration as legislator and comptroller with the state and local fiscal situation in Illinois—unfunded pensions, inadequate school funding, overreliance on property tax, and the like—convinced her that she could not hope to address these problems effectively unless she were governor, and so she became increasingly serious about seeking the office. Other people encouraged her to do so. Many of her old friends from the Committee on Illinois Government and law school, like Jim Otis and Hal Shapiro, tried to talk her into running for governor while she was still in the senate. Bill Luking, her former student and longtime supporter, and Sean Heffernan, both of whom were lobbyists in Springfield, told her, "You just *have* to run for governor."[2] Conversations became more serious while Dawn was comptroller, as her frustration continued to grow. "My sense was that [Governor] Edgar was a nice middle-level manager but not a leader. I've always believed that the only way we'll get a dramatic change in school funding is if a governor were willing to expend all of his or her political capital and a lot of time on the issue—traverse the state and convince people that they would not be hurt [by the tax changes necessary]."[3] Her only reluctance to undertake this new challenge stemmed from concern for its impact on her husband, Walter, whose health continued to be poor. Over the years, Walter had said to Dawn that she ought to be governor, but she did not believe he had thought through the consequences. Now they began to have serious conversations about the possibility of her running in 1994.

By September 1992, the Chicago press began to speak of Dawn as a serious candidate for governor; she acknowledged her longtime interest and said that she would make a preliminary decision in December.[4] By November, she was forming an exploratory committee to test the waters, headed by Katherine "Kappy" Laing, a lawyer-lobbyist. Dawn knew Laing from the mid-1980s, when she had been a lobbyist for the City of Chicago under Mayor Harold Washington; and Laing had worked with Dawn on several issues she was sponsoring in the senate. By 1992 Laing had also managed several political campaigns. Dawn thought Laing was smart, and "she knew the landscape, which is terribly important in Illinois, because the landscape is confused at times. She has good sense, and I felt comfortable with her."[5]

Laing remembers getting a phone call from Dawn in November 1992, just after she had started to practice law and was not enjoying it as much as her previous political work and lobbying. Dawn asked whether she could come over to her office at the State of Illinois Building to talk. When Laing arrived, Bill Luking and Sean Heffernan were already there. They told her that Dawn was thinking of running for governor and needed to set up an exploratory committee, and they asked whether she would undertake the task. Laing told them she needed to think about it before giving her answer. But, she recalls, "By the time I got to the street corner, I knew I'd do it. And I knew intuitively that she would win the primary, and that it would be challenging, so I called her as soon as I got back to the office and told her I would do it."[6]

Laing was close to the women in the group that had worked with Dawn on the Illinois Criminal Sexual Assault Act, and she went with them that weekend to their winter retreat at Barbara Engel's house in Michigan. When Laing announced to them that Dawn had asked her to work on exploring a race for governor, she remembers being met with total silence. "You are doing *what?*" they then asked, and voiced their objections: "She has no chance," "She's not a feminist," "She won't raise money," "She doesn't have the common touch." Laing persisted and, despite her friends' initial negative reaction, over the course of the next nine months every one of the group came around. Julie Hamos was the last one to do so, but after early August, she spent a great deal of time working on Dawn's campaign.

The purpose of an exploratory committee is to find out whether a campaign is viable, and the litmus test for viability is whether it can raise money. So Laing's job was first to generate a buzz in the press that would make people say, "Wouldn't it be great if Dawn Netsch ran for governor next year?" She seems to have been successful at this. By February 7, 1993, one of the main political writers for the *Chicago Tribune* published an article with the headline "Voters Gain If Netsch Runs for Governor in '94," detailing Dawn's "vast experience, plain-spoken intellect" and unimpeachable record of integrity, and arguing that her entry into the race would raise the general level of debate about the issues.[7] In March, the press announced that Dawn had formed an exploratory committee with a goal of raising $250,000 by July 1, 1993. A thirty-five-thousand-piece mailing to women's activist groups, North Shore voters, suburban Democrats, and downstate precinct committee members was sent out later that month as part of the fund-raising effort and to gauge reaction to her candidacy.[8]

By early 1993, three other Democratic candidates—Richard Phelan, a wealthy lawyer who had been president of the Cook County Board since 1990, Attorney General Roland Burris, and Treasurer Pat Quinn—were already working on their own campaigns for governor. A fourth, James E. Gierach, also joined the campaign but never had enough support in the polls to be regarded as more than a minor candidate.[9] Gierach was a lawyer and former prosecutor who campaigned on a platform of legalizing drugs to make them easier to regulate and to reduce crime.

A televised forum among Phelan, Quinn, and Netsch was held in mid-April. The media praised Dawn's performance, saying, "While Netsch talked substance, Quinn and Phelan responded in sound bites."[10] The substance of which Dawn spoke was the necessity of raising the state income tax to increase aid for schools and provide property tax relief. To speak openly of raising taxes is usually considered suicide for a political candidate. Most simply say that they will not raise taxes and then proceed to break their pledge to the voters after getting into office, declaring that things were much worse than they thought. By contrast, Dawn was well acquainted with the economics of government in Illinois, and she was determined to be honest with the voters.

In June 1993, Dawn ended any speculation about whether she would seek the office, although she did not formally announce her candidacy until August.[11] The necessity of running against Roland Burris, the first African American candidate for governor, did not deter her this time. She had stepped aside for Burris twice in the past, and her age (she was then sixty-six) did not allow her to wait any longer. Her campaign strategy group set about the task of raising the money necessary for a successful race. At this point, Dawn had no political fund. After 1974 the Republicans had sometimes not even run a candidate against her in her senatorial district; and she did not follow the practice of many politicians of holding a fund-raiser every year whether or not they need the money. The money raised for her campaign for comptroller had been exhausted.

As the activist women at their Michigan retreat had implied in their comments, fund-raising is something Dawn very much dislikes. And she was required to spend as many as four hours a day on it. Laing and her staff would research potential donors and hand Dawn a notebook with information along with the phone. Dawn hated it. Laing recalls that she would say to a potential donor something like this: "'Dave [or whoever], this is Dawn. You know what I'm calling for and I hate it. I need to raise some money.' That was her style of fund-raising. She would tear pages out of the notebook and say 'I don't like doing this.'"[12]

Laing, who was running the exploratory committee out of Walter's studio in the Sandburg Village complex with inadequate phone lines and equipment, decided to appeal to women's political groups in New York, Washington, D.C., and California for assistance. The group Emily's List, which raises money for pro-choice female Democratic candidates for office, was just beginning to grow in strength. In 1994, women were determined to compete for the position of governor in many states—as many as thirty-one women in twenty states planned to run as of late 1993[13]—and Emily's List decided to expand its support from national to gubernatorial races. So Laing and her small staff put together a presentation, including a proposed budget, a staffing plan, and a media campaign, and sent Dawn, who had never identified as a feminist, off to present it. In late June and early July, Dawn made trips to Washington and New York, where she met with leaders of national women's organizations that had raised funds for Carol Moseley Braun and others in the 1992 Year of the Woman election.[14] In July she went to Los Angeles, where she attended a meeting of the National Women's Political Caucus and made contacts with potential fund-raisers and large donors. One of her advisers, Christie Hefner, the chief executive officer of Playboy, set up some of the contacts for her.[15] Yet Dawn continued to tell the press that she "never ran as a 'woman' candidate and never considered myself such."[16]

By the end of June, Dawn had raised $180,551 in six months, short of the $250,000 goal but still substantial. This amount included a small loan from herself and a $50,000 contribution from Ben Heineman, Governor Stevenson's friend and the former chair of the Chicago & North Western Railway whom she had helped convince to head the new Illinois Board of Higher Education when she was working for Governor Kerner.[17] Of her Democratic opponents, Dick Phelan had $1.5 million in his campaign fund as of June 30, Roland Burris had $635,486, and Pat Quinn had $557,513. Most ominously, Governor Jim Edgar had amassed more than $3.5 million for the race.

Despite her comparative lack of funding, Dawn formally announced her candidacy for governor of Illinois on August 9, 1993, at Midway Airport in Chicago, as she began a fly-around of six cities in the state.[18] She declared that her priorities were "balanced budgets, strong schools and fair taxes," calling for a reduction in property taxes and an increase in state funding of public education, paid for by an increase in the state income tax. "No tax is pleasant," she said. "But I'll tell you, I would much rather pay my share in an income tax, which at least means I have an income, than in constantly rising property taxes, which have no relation to my ability to pay."[19] While the press praised her candor, this was a risky strategy, and Dawn needed to connect personally with the voters to get her message across. Given her background and appearance, some questioned whether she would be able to relate well to the ordinary working men and women who pay taxes.[20] This was a problem her campaign advisers recognized and were discussing plans to address. Even before Dawn's announcement speech, Laing made her give a speech to an eighth-grade graduation class. Dawn was furious about having to do this, but it seems to have helped get her to talk more like a political candidate and less like a law professor.[21]

The Battle for the Democratic Nomination

Kappy Laing stayed on as Dawn's campaign manager after the August announcement and began to put together a full campaign staff. She hired a group in Washington to carry out polls, which she then analyzed. The first set of polls taken by the three candidates showed that Burris was decisively ahead, with either Netsch or Phelan running second, depending on the poll, and that a large number of voters were undecided. Dawn's pollster put Burris at 33 percent, herself at 15 percent, and both Phelan and Quinn in single digits.[22] But the campaign did not attract much media attention during September and October.

Laing also hired two fund-raisers, a press person who did not work out and was later replaced by Peter Giangreco and Gail Handleman, Saul Shorr of Philadelphia to film television ads, and a graphic designer whom Walter Netsch fired, later designing the campaign logo himself. Walter's logo was beautiful but, in Laing's opinion, lacked a number of necessary attributes, such as visibility by motorists driving by.[23] In September, Dawn's campaign staff at last moved into a real office—a cavernous space on Grand Avenue that had previously been a clothing factory. Marcia Thompson, who had worked for a long time on the Democratic staff in the senate, became director of issues and research, and an impressive crew of smart people was recruited to develop a platform.

By November, with the help of Emily's List, Dawn had raised a total of $610,282, a substantial improvement over the $180,000 she had at the end of June.[24] Yet a November poll by an independent firm showed that Phelan was gaining strength in Chicago and Cook County, where he led by 41 and 44 percent of those polled, respectively, followed by Burris with 28 and 29 percent, to Dawn's 9 percent (Quinn had essentially dropped out by then to run for reelection as state treasurer).[25] Phelan had chosen a woman, state senator Penny Severns, as his running mate for lieutenant governor, as did Burris, who selected businesswoman Sheila Smith.[26] The governor and lieutenant governor are elected separately in the Illinois primary, but it is conventional for a gubernatorial candidate to select someone to run with as a team. Unconventionally, Dawn decided not to do so but instead left the choice to the voters. Severns had been a protégé of hers, and Dawn felt "disappointed" when Severns agreed to become Phelan's running mate.[27] "Betrayed" might have been a more accurate term, for Dawn had talked to Severns several times, advising her against taking such a step, and she thought Severns had agreed that it would not be a good idea. As Phelan's running mate, of course, she was required to campaign against Dawn, taking swipes at her school-funding program.

The state Democratic Party decided not to endorse a ticket for the March primary.[28] Phelan, as Cook County Board president and the one establishment Democrat in the race, was assured of the support of most of the Chicago Democratic Organization's precinct workers. Although Mayor Daley spoke well of Dawn's plans to fund the schools, he did not openly endorse any candidate. Thus Dawn was running yet again as the candidate whom the Democratic organization did not support. Burris was expected to attract most of the African American vote and had substantial support downstate because he was from Centralia. Dawn picked up predictable endorsements from progressive groups like the National Organization of Women and Independent Voters of Illinois–Independent Precinct Organization, but her usual union support was not forthcoming during the contested primary.[29]

Unflattering newspaper reports began to appear about Dawn's campaign, describing it as having failed "to follow through on a promising start . . . while her opponents are doing a better job of aggressively selling themselves."[30] There were also reports of internal conflicts among Dawn's campaign staff, which Laing confirms:

> From Thanksgiving on, there was a civil war within the campaign; Peter [Giangreco] and Saul [Shorr] were trying to get me fired. It was unbelievably stressful. . . . I also clashed with . . . her staff guy in the comptroller's office. He had wanted to manage her campaign, and he second-guessed decisions. There were major clashes over how money got spent.[31]

Laing also had a number of clashes she describes as "titanic" with the candidate's husband, who would visit or call the campaign office and try to tell the staff what to do, intimidating them. Staff members or other advisers who disagreed with Laing about spending decisions would go around her and appeal directly to Walter Netsch for money to spend on what they thought should be done. Laing tried to protect Dawn from all this, thinking it was stressful enough to be a statewide candidate without being asked to mediate conflicts between her husband and campaign staff.

But Dawn was not the easiest candidate to manage. Her sense of duty made it difficult to get her to leave the comptroller's office, and she was reluctant to come over to the campaign office and raise money in any event. Laing describes having to lure Dawn out of her office by scheduling things she liked to do, such as talking to groups. But when they would sit down to schedule meetings, Dawn "would look at us over her glasses and say 'You're going to kill me.'"[32] Her staff hired an appearance consultant who tried to persuade Dawn to soften her hairstyle and wear earrings. Dawn adamantly refused to change the way she looked, with her bare ears and straight, gray hair often held back by barrettes. The only way Dawn Netsch would run for office was as herself. (Years later, Lisa Madigan, successful candidate for Illinois attorney general in 2002, came to Dawn for advice as she began the race and told her that her advisers wanted her to change her appearance. Dawn said, "Forget it. If you try to be someone you aren't, it shows. But if you want to comb your hair before you go on TV, remember the television lens is a good mirror.")[33]

What Dawn liked to do best was to talk with her issues advisers about developing the policies to present as her platform. She put together a group of public finance experts, such as Ron Picur and John Filan, along with several academics and her advisers Bill Morris and the attorney Ralph Martire, who met together with Marcia Thompson and Hiram Sachs of Dawn's campaign staff, usually over at the University of Illinois at Chicago. Only Thompson and Sachs were paid; the rest were volunteers. Morris says that the policy group would always corner Dawn to start a policy discussion, which she loved, while Laing was trying to get her to make fund-raising phone calls, and "it made Kappy crazy."[34]

The key to what became the Netsch Plan was a so-called tax swap, that is, raising income taxes and reducing property taxes at the same time (the swap part), while increasing the state's contribution to education so that it would approach the goal envisaged in the Illinois Constitution. The constitution states, in a section for which Dawn was responsible at Con Con, "The State has the primary responsibility for financing the system of public education."[35] The state had not been paying anywhere near 50 percent of the cost of education, much of which had been shifted onto local governmental bodies and financed through property taxes. The tax swap was an idea Dawn had been thinking about for a long time, and she gave a blueprint for the policy she wanted to her issues group for them to research and develop the details. According to Morris, "She said, 'Here's what I'm trying to accomplish and here's how I think we can get there'; it had been percolating for years, and she articulated it well."[36] Ralph Martire arranged to work a reduced schedule at his law firm and became deputy issues director for the campaign, working at the headquarters from 5:00 or 6:00 to 10:00 every night, in "a little dungeon-like room where there were research materials and a computer."[37] He, like most of her staff and other volunteers, was totally committed to Dawn as a person rather than just a political operative attached to a candidate, because, he says, the "woman was a phenomenal leader with integrity, brilliance, and compassion."[38]

The research and issues group worked steadily throughout the fall, producing a series of white papers. Unlike other campaigns, which might get by with one page of bulleted points on an issue, Dawn wanted fifteen-plus pages, "thick with substance, footnotes, everything." Once given a particular white paper and briefed on it by her staff, Martire says that Dawn would sometimes reply that she still did not know enough about the issue to go public on it—"she had to understand everything about it and make it her own."[39] Of course, the white papers were too wonkish for the political and communications staff, but they would all be filed and translations into accessible language prepared for the press and public. During the primary season, there were sufficient funds to get almost everything they did out to the public.

Details of Dawn's plan for school funding made their way into the press during January 1994, as she called for raising the individual income tax rate from 3 percent to 4.25 percent and the corporate rate from 4.8 percent to 6.8 percent, diverting $1 billion directly into school funding, reducing property tax levies by $1 billion, and scheduling graduated personal exemptions from the income tax to relieve the impact of the tax increase on low- and middle-income people while still respecting the constitution's requirement of a flat tax rate. The result of her plan would be to increase the state's portion of education funding to 48 percent of the total from its current 34 percent.[40] While her Democratic primary opponents and Governor Edgar all attacked Dawn's proposal to raise taxes, her plan received quite positive responses from the press, which praised her for having "realistically confronted the central problems of state government—insufficient revenues for education and an unfair mix of taxes."[41] Some polls of likely Democratic voters began to show Netsch as having overtaken Phelan, although Burris was still decisively in the lead. Dawn had also raised more than $1 million and was planning a media blitz.[42]

February 1 is the date when candidates in Illinois primary elections typically begin to broadcast ads on television; it is also the day when the networks are required by law to reduce their rates for candidates in the primary election.[43] Dawn's communications staff—specifically Giangreco and Shorr—decided that they needed to do something bold to capture the attention of the public and to take the other candidates by surprise. They had a secret weapon: Walter Netsch was donating $1 million from the sale of his paintings to devote to media coverage. They found out that Phelan had not made a network buy and thus would not be running ads for several weeks. Burris did not plan to begin until February. So the Netsch campaign decided to invest $500,000 and to start to run ads in mid-January, when they had the airwaves to themselves. As an added bonus, it was bitter cold, and most citizens were hunkered down indoors watching television. The decision was tactically brilliant.

The Netsch ad campaign began with a carefully designed series, first introducing the candidate, next establishing her competence and integrity, and then humanizing her. The first ad was a biographical spot, designed to expose Dawn's name to the public and to appeal especially to women in the Democratic Party by impressing on them that here at last was a woman, a pioneer, who was really smart and had something to say. As photos from Dawn's past filled the screen, the voiceover text ran as follows:

> Dawn Clark Netsch. She's a self-made success story. Graduated first in her law school class at Northwestern. A strong pro-choice voice, a pioneer for women who's fighting for equal pay in the workplace. As State Comptroller, she's built a reputation for integrity. Now she's running for Governor . . . and the *Sun-Times* calls her "more knowledgeable about the state's financial condition than any other contender." Democrat Dawn Clark Netsch for Governor. Straight talk—and real solutions for Illinois.[44]

The introduction of Dawn as a straight shooter had begun.

The next spot followed up on this theme and featured Dawn speaking. Two versions of the ad were run—one called "Dishonest," in which she criticized Edgar's inability to balance the budget and to tell the truth about it to the people, and the second called "Investment," with the message that the children of Illinois had paid the price of unbalanced budgets. In both ads, Dawn said emphatically, "If I'm Governor of Illinois, there will be honest budgets. No one else is telling it straight, because there is political risk involved, but the voters want to hear the truth; they are tired of being lied to."[45] The two ads were calculated to lead up to the famous pool ad. They established Dawn as totally competent and totally honest, but she also appeared to be something of a schoolmarm, or as Giangreco put it, a mother telling you to eat your peas. She still needed to be humanized.

Shorr got the idea for the pool ad by talking to Dawn about what it was like growing up. When she told him about having started the canteen for youth in Cincinnati and how she played pool there, he lighted up. His candidate, an academic who talked in paragraphs, had just told him that she played pool! So he took Dawn to a pool hall on Clark Street near El Jardín restaurant, where they shot the ad.[46] Dawn had not played pool for a long time, and so they gave her a period to practice, with an expert giving her pointers about how to make difficult bank and combination shots. "I felt terrible," she says. "I had resisted this thing; I thought it was undignified. I was pretty nervous too."

The thirty-second pool ad shows Dawn first chalking a pool cue and then grinning broadly as she sinks a series of difficult combination shots. "Roland Burris says he won't tell us how he'll fund our schools until after he's elected," a narrator states. "Dawn Clark Netsch is calling 'em like she sees 'em."[47] The ad then calls her a "straight shooter" with a "real plan to restore honesty to the budget and bring reform and solid funding our schools need." The pool ad was an instant success and soon became the talk of the town. Everyone then knew Dawn, and they all asked her how her pool game was or whether she'd like to play. Indeed, she was repeatedly challenged to sink a few shots while out campaigning, to prove that she had really made the shots in the ad; she did so, for example, on February 7 at Vanzo's bar in downstate Edwardsville.[48]

The success of the pool ad upset Dawn, who told the press, "If I had known the effect the commercial would have, I might not have made it. . . . I want my campaign to be about substance. Government is not about fun."[49] When her staff ran another lighthearted Shorr ad, featuring Dawn playing softball and her love of opera, she insisted that it be pulled as "too frivolous."[50] In most people's judgment, however, the pool ad essentially rescued Dawn's campaign and gave prominence to her message. The *Chicago Tribune* reported on February 6, "Written off by political insiders and a few media pundits a month ago, the energetic Netsch has parlayed her reputation as a rare political truthsayer with an inspired advertising strategy to put herself in a position to win the nomination on March 15."[51]

The primary election campaign certainly did not lack a discussion of the issues. In addition to Dawn's plan for funding education, her staff rolled out a series of policy positions throughout the month of February, typically beating the other two candidates to the punch and attracting considerable press. While both Phelan and Burris were running as law-and-order candidates, Dawn released a crime plan with a package of specific proposals to restrict sale and possession of guns of all types. Burris and Phelan were both pushing truth-in-sentencing legislation that would require violent and/or repeat offenders to serve at least 85 percent of their sentences. Dawn agreed with this goal in theory but pointed out that the state did not currently have prisons adequate to accommodate that many inmates and insisted that any such guidelines be linked to available prison space.[52]

Dawn continued to emphasize her plan to fund education through a combined tax increase and reform, embellishing it with suggestions for how to monitor the schools and establish academic performance standards. Phelan simply attacked the tax hike and does not appear to have presented an education plan of his own. Burris announced a "modest" education platform in early February, which he vowed to accomplish without a tax increase, simply by eliminating waste and mismanagement in the state's budget.[53] Dawn quickly responded that, as Burris's successor in the comptroller's office, she knew that he was incapable of cutting a budget and offered figures to show the increased budgets over the many years of his tenure as comptroller.[54]

Next Dawn unveiled her economic plan, which emphasized initiatives to promote the growth of small businesses, especially those headed by women, improvement of communication between small businesses and banks, and better access for small businesses to resources to improve their viability. She vowed to reorganize the Illinois Department of Commerce and Community Affairs to create a one-stop agency for economic development programs and financial and technical services that different agencies provided. Another aspect of her economic plan was to create a statewide computer information network linking universities, businesses, government agencies, and private research and development labs so that they could exchange nonproprietary research.[55] She pointed out the relationship between better education and economic development.

A description of the work that went into producing Dawn's economic plan demonstrates how truly wonkish her campaign was. Ralph Martire, who worked on the Community-Based Economic Development Initiative, explains that they first gathered all the relevant national research, both academic and practical, resulting in mounds of reading. A subcommittee met and divided the research among themselves; after reviewing it, they summarized it in fifteen to twenty pages, noting the pros and cons of various approaches. The next step was to design a policy specific to Illinois:

> What we came up with went through a vetting process by consultants, practitioners, and academics. We usually got some

things wrong, according to the experts, so then we would modify it. Then we'd brief Dawn on it, and she would rip it to shreds. There was no aspect she wasn't familiar with. Dawn would know the substance, and she'd question your footnotes and sources and critique your paper, asking questions like "Is this the best source?" Then you did the Dawn revision. When she signed off, it would go to the political and press people.[56]

The result was a ten-page document titled "An Economic Development Blueprint for the 21st Century," which was released to the press on February 10, 1994, accompanied by a three-page summary press release.

Neither of the other two candidates presented any type of economic plan until less than a week before the March election. Phelan's plan simply called on the state to improve the job training programs it funded, involving businesses in designing the training given.[57] When Burris finally unveiled his economic plan on March 9, it echoed Dawn's.[58] Netsch and Burris had similar visions for health care reform as well, calling for universal coverage and more preventive medical care, but neither offered many specifics about how this could be brought about.[59]

The effect of the Netsch campaign putting out one after another policy initiative was that it effectively controlled the agenda of issues in the primary election. Dawn also moved up in the polls and challenged Burris's lead. A poll in the first week of February 1994 showed that she had doubled her percentage of the vote over the 14 percent she had in the first week of January; Burris was now down to 30 percent, Netsch at 28 percent, and Phelan a distant third at 13 percent.[60] The *Chicago Tribune* attributed this to "her campaign having controlled the agenda and dominated the airwaves since mid-January." Another poll of Illinois voters, which instead asked them about the issues, showed that they favored school-funding reform even if it required an income tax hike, so long as it was accompanied by property tax relief.[61]

Phelan, surprised that his well-financed campaign was not turning in better results, lashed out at Dawn with a series of negative ads. He accused her of voting for property tax increases fifty times while in the senate, and he said that she would raise income taxes 42 percent and that she intended to tax haircuts and laundry. The Netsch campaign called "foul," pointing out that local governments, not the state, levied property taxes; that her tax increase was balanced off by property tax relief and a schedule of graduated income tax exemptions; and that she had not advocated a tax on services.[62] They responded to Phelan's flood of belated television advertisements by running one that accused him of breaking his campaign pledge to cut property taxes as Cook County Board president; he in fact raised them $100 million and created a sales tax costing $200 million. "Aren't you tired of politicians playing dirty pool?" Dawn's ad asks, pointing out that she was the only one of the three candidates who had ever cut a budget (as comptroller) and, continuing the pool theme, was a straight shooter.[63]

As the campaign turned increasingly negative, the first debate among the candidates was held in Springfield on February 22, 1994, and broadcast on the radio. Burris had been reluctant to agree to debates, given his past experience of not excelling in that format, but he finally agreed to participate in three.[64] (One was canceled on the spot as James Gierach, who did not have enough support in the polls to be invited, showed up and demanded to be included.)[65] Dawn described the Springfield debate as "gang up on Dawn."[66] Press reports said that during the first thirty minutes of the hour-long debate, "the phrase '42 percent increase' became a chorus for Netsch's two major opponents." After arguing that families earning $30,000 or more would have to pay more taxes, Burris said to Dawn, "With Walter having to pay $400,000 for campaign commercials, I'm pretty sure you don't understand what $30,000 is."[67] Phelan accused Netsch of planning to "throw a billion dollars at a (school) system that doesn't work."[68] Burris accused her of having cut the comptroller's budget by firing minority employees. Dawn replied to this charge by saying that she had simply not filled the positions vacated by all the patronage employees Burris took along with him to the attorney general's office.[69] Reports of the debate described Burris's "unprecedented effort . . . to use such a public forum to court black voters."[70]

The negative campaigning continued as the candidates toured the state during the last weekend in February. Phelan and Burris continued to attack Dawn about her proposed income tax increase and disagreed with her about the impact of her proposals on the taxpayer.[71] Back in Chicago, Burris accused Dawn of trying to "buy the nomination" with her husband's contributions to her campaign; Dawn's typical response was that at least this saved her from being beholden to special interests.[72] Dawn's campaign still was being run on a shoestring, however, with appeals made to supporters to donate Scotch tape, scissors, and paper, while the press pointed out that Phelan's staff had everything they wanted, but that "the most experienced strategists and the trendiest consultants money can buy will barely heft a candidate out of single digits if voters don't believe him."[73] Desperate, Phelan began to focus when campaigning downstate on the fact that welfare allowed some Illinois citizens not to work while others did. The Netsch campaign accused him of trying to pit one racial group against another and to play on downstate resentment of Chicago.[74]

The candidates' second and final debate took place in Chicago on March 3, 1994, and was televised. Dawn's staff put her through twice-weekly practice sessions, trying to keep her tendency to ramble in check.[75] The press contrasted the March 3 debate with the earlier one in Springfield, saying that it was "as if they had signed a non-aggression pact before taking the stage."[76] Soon after, both major Chicago newspapers endorsed Netsch.[77] More important, she began to pull ahead in the polls. By a poll taken in late February, she and Burris were virtually tied (31 and 32 percent, respectively), and Phelan was essentially out of the running (12 percent). Although Dawn trailed Burris in Chicago and Cook County, she had taken the lead away from him downstate and led him in the so-called collar counties around Chicago.[78] A further poll conducted March 7–8 showed that she had now surpassed Burris and was leading by 34 to 23 percent among likely Democratic voters and by 37 to 24 percent in Cook County itself. The press attributed the surge to her performance in the second televised debate, which 36 percent of Democratic voters said they had watched and judged Dawn to have been the clear winner.[79]

The last week before the primary was a frenzy of activity. On March 9, Dawn went on a fly-around with Giangreco. He reports that it was "the two of us in a single-engine Cessna. It was windier than hell and we took off from Meigs and the plane was wobbling. She was bent over crouched with her fingers in her ears because of some kind of inner-ear thing, and I'm white, about to throw up."[80] When they landed in Rockford, they could barely walk. They proceeded to the Rockford Teamster Hall at 9:30 A.M. and found six television cameras and representatives of all the major newspapers from Chicago and around the state:

> We thought it odd, but it was what the advance guy had set up. He hadn't told anybody that the national billiards champ was from Rockford and there was a pool table there. We've just survived one of the worst flights in our lives. . . . They walk her over to the pool table and everyone crowded around. I'm thinking, we don't want to do this. Dawn cordially says, "Oh, no, I'll just watch you play." He does all these trick shots and [then] intentionally misses

a shot and hands her the pool cue. We have six cameras and the whole press corps. He'd set it up two balls next to each other in the middle of the table. The cameras were running. I'm thinking, if she misses this shot, this will be the spot they run over and over, like Muskie crying. . . . Dawn takes the pool cue, bends over the pool table, pulls back the cue, hits the ball, and—boom!— both balls went into the two corner pockets and the crowd went wild.[81]

The *Chicago Tribune* reported, "It looked like a scene from 'The Hustler.'"[82] Dawn, joking, told her staff, "If I had missed that shot, all you guys would've been out of a job."

The weekend before the election held the obligatory appearances at St. Patrick's Day parades, in the rain, for Phelan and Netsch, while Burris appeared with Jesse Jackson at Operation PUSH headquarters on Saturday and managed to visit a total of six different African American churches or mosques on Sunday.[83] On Tuesday, March 15, the voters went to the polls to select both the Democratic and Republican nominees for governor of Illinois. Edgar sailed to victory in the Republican primary. And Dawn Clark Netsch won 45 percent of the Democratic vote, to 35 percent for Burris and 15 percent for Phelan.

At her victory celebration at the Midland Hotel, Dawn strode through the crowd to the tune of "Here Comes the Sun" and brandished a pool cue over her head triumphantly; only her campaign staff knew how vehemently she had resisted doing so. The photo was all over the media the next day, even if Dawn thought it was gimmicky and without substance. In her victory speech, Dawn proclaimed, "We held an election in Illinois today and the truth won":

> [Voters] were ready for a governor who will take charge, get serious and tell it like it is. I intend to be that governor. I've made a solemn pact with you to change politics in Illinois, to skip the sound bites and the easy answers and to tell it to you straight. With this victory, I think we have already changed politics as usual.[84]

After accepting the concessions of Burris and Phelan, Dawn called for unity among the Democrats to defeat Edgar in the fall.

The fact that Penny Severns had won the slot as Democratic nominee for lieutenant governor created an awkward situation. Her old friend had been acting as Phelan's attack dog just the previous week, declaring that Dawn's tax-and-education proposal could not pass the General Assembly. Dawn immediately said that they had worked on things together in the past and that she expected no problems. As Laing notes, however, "No one would've put up a slate with two women at the top."[85] Activist women were nonetheless delighted by Dawn's victory. They contrasted it with Carol Moseley Braun's election to the U.S. Senate, propelled by women's anger over the Clarence Thomas hearings and the Senate's treatment of Anita Hill. "But this is a greater breakthrough. Netsch's nomination is without baggage. It doesn't come out of anger, hostility. It comes out of power, out of confidence."[86] As the headline put it, her gender was an "afterthought, a bonus."

The Democratic voters of Illinois had listened to Dawn's honesty and supported her. As one reporter put it:

> From start to finish, Dawn Clark Netsch shaped the debate of the 1994 Democratic gubernatorial campaign. Netsch did something unusual in Illinois politics. She talked to the state's residents as grownups. Other candidates listened to focus groups and learned how to be on the right side of controversial issues. Netsch took a risk that Illinois residents could handle the truth about tough issues.[87]

But Jim Edgar was still out there, with his massive political fund intact, while the Democratic candidates had exhausted their resources battling one another.

The General Election

After the primary election, Kappy Laing left the campaign to return to her law practice. She was not replaced until late April, when Jack Reid was hired. Dawn had known about Reid from his work as the downstate organizer for the 1992 Clinton-Gore campaign. Pete Giangreco's wife was pregnant and their baby was born in May, so he took a break for a fairly long period after the primary. Thus, for about two months, the Netsch campaign was understaffed and without a manager. Dawn threw herself into her duties as comptroller for much of the spring.

Jim Edgar, who had spent only a comparatively small portion of his $5 million campaign chest to defeat his negligible primary opponent, did not wait to attack. By the day after the election, he had begun to portray Dawn as an extreme liberal out of touch with the "mainstream," committed to higher taxes and more spending and opposed to the death penalty, which the majority of Illinois citizens supported.[88] He repeated allegations made by Phelan in the primary, to the effect that she favored taxing services like haircuts, although Dawn had not made this part of her tax plan.[89] A report issued by the Legislative Research Unit in Springfield concluded that taxpayers in Cook County outside of Chicago and in the five collar counties would get less from the Netsch tax plan in property tax relief than they would pay in higher taxes, but the plan was good for farmers. Dawn candidly responded, "Moderate- and lower-income people definitely will be paying less; [the] wealthier will be paying more. I don't find that shocking."[90]

Dawn's new opponent had many advantages in addition to his incumbency and vast campaign funds. Jim Edgar, forty-eight years old, was well known and well liked by the voters in Illinois. In Dawn's opinion, he was well liked because he had taken no significant actions during his first term and thus had not offended anyone. Edgar had grown up in Charleston, Illinois, graduated from Eastern Illinois University there, and from 1968 to 1974 had served on the staffs of two legislators in Springfield.[91] After a brief period of service as a legislator himself (two years in the Illinois House of Representatives), Governor Thompson appointed him to his staff in 1979. In 1980, Thompson appointed Edgar secretary of state to fill out the remainder of Alan Dixon's term when Dixon was elected to the U.S. Senate. After two years, Edgar was elected to the office on his own and reelected in 1986. In 1990 he became governor after defeating Democrat Neil Hartigan. His first term, as should already be clear, was marked by fiscal crises, but the economy was improving by 1994. Edgar had promised during his first campaign for governor that there would be no new taxes, and there were not, although he did support making the income tax surcharge permanent. Edgar was a moderate Republican and did not oppose abortion, so he had not raised the ire of feminist groups. An attractive man, he very much looked the part of governor. Illinois voters also found him credible and trustworthy; thus, Dawn did not have a monopoly on those attributes.

Dawn had already laid out many of her policies during the primary election, with the tax swap for education funding at the core. The Netsch Plan had been printed up in glossy thirty-seven-page blue booklets and distributed. As had her opponents in the primary, Edgar immediately and repeatedly emphasized that Dawn's tax proposal amounted to a 42 percent increase, calculated as the percentage increase of 4.25 percent over 3 percent without taking into account the accompanying real estate tax relief and graduated schedule of deductions. During early May, Edgar announced his own education plan, which basically consisted of legalizing riverboat casinos in Chicago and using the casino taxes to help schools pay for improvements without raising taxes.[92] Dawn denounced Edgar's plan, saying that she opposed funding education from gambling proceeds both on moral grounds and because it was an unstable source of revenue.[93] Her aides passed out bologna-and-Swiss-cheese hors d'oeuvres as she campaigned in Wisconsin and blasted Edgar's plan as "a lot of bologna," resting on revenues from gambling operations that had not yet been authorized.[94] She continued to criticize the deficits and underfunding that had characterized his fiscal management, labeling him a "charge-and-spend bureaucrat."[95]

In early June 1994, Edgar's campaign, taking a page from Dawn's own strategy in the primary, launched an early media strike. They paid $700,000 to run two thirty-second television ads across the state for several weeks—negative ads designed to paint Dawn as soft on crime. The first ad, which appeared on June 3, featured a male assailant pointing a pistol at a woman's head and portrayed Edgar as tough on crime while criticizing Dawn for her votes in the legislature against mandatory prison sentences and against life sentences for criminals who committed three felonies (the so-called three-strikes-and-you're-out law).[96] The second ad, appearing a few days after the first, opened with a view of death row cellblocks, with a narrator saying that Dawn Clark Netsch "voted against the death penalty for mass murderers. And she voted against the death penalty for someone convicted of a second, first-degree murder." The ad closed with a picture of the governor's office and the narrator asked, "In death penalty cases in Illinois, the last appeal comes to this desk. Who do you want sitting here?"[97]

Edgar's ad campaign was created by a Republican media consultant, Don Sipple, who produced similar ads during that same election season for California Governor Pete Wilson, who was running against Kathleen Brown, and for George W. Bush, who was running for governor of Texas against the popular incumbent Ann Richards.[98] The similar 1994 media campaigns against three women running for governor have occasioned a good deal of controversy. Some observers have called them sexist because they play into the stereotype that women are weak, subject to attack, and unable to protect themselves or others, and because they insinuate that female governors are soft on crime. Interviewed about them, Dawn commented, "The ads are intended to show rape or assault and to scare the begolly out of people. The message they're trying to convey is, obviously, 'This is going to continue if you elect women.' To suggest to women that somehow they are incapable of dealing with or understanding the importance of violence, it really is insulting."[99] The 1994 ads also echoed the fear and innuendo of the negative "Willie Horton" ads George H. W. Bush had leveled at Michael Dukakis in 1988 as well.

Dawn denounced Edgar's ad campaign as unfair, declaring that she would enforce the death penalty as governor despite her own personal opposition to it, because it was the law. She knew it had wide support among the voters and thus had never introduced a bill to abolish it in her eighteen years in the legislature.[100] But she did not have the money for responsive advertising until after President Clinton came to a Chicago fund-raiser for her in mid-June, adding some $600,000 to her campaign coffers. With that, she had about $1 million and spent a large chunk of it to produce aggressive ads countering Edgar's attacks on her. By then, however, Edgar had raised an additional $1 million, giving him about $6 million in his own fund.[101] By June 30, it was clear that his early definition of the issues, negative ads, and vast resources were paying off. Edgar was shown in the polls to have opened up a two-to-one lead over his challenger. His only problem was that his lieutenant governor, Bob Kustra, was planning to resign to become a radio talk-show host.[102]

Although Kustra later decided to remain with the Edgar campaign, his brief resignation led to a blowup between Dawn and some of her campaign staff. When they heard that Kustra was resigning, Pete Giangreco and Gail Handleman leaked to the press something they had learned about Kustra's wife, implying that her husband resigned from the campaign because she stood to profit from Medicaid reform.[103] They did so without running their decision by Dawn, although they knew that she was adamantly opposed to negative campaigning. Kustra was furious, and so was Dawn when she found out what had happened. En route from Decatur to Springfield by car, she yelled at Giangreco over the phone. He describes the talking-to he received the next day: "She looked at me, grimaced, said nothing. 'I understand you are upset,' I said. She said, 'Bob Kustra is my friend; you never ran this by me.'"[104] Dawn feels the same today about this type of campaigning: "I don't believe that's the way things ought to be, and you have to live with yourself and what you have done. Bob Kustra was a very decent guy and had always been a good friend. I wouldn't go after him just to get a momentary advantage."[105]

The responsive ads produced by the Netsch campaign were ready for release by the end of the first week in July. Suddenly, however, Governor Edgar had emergency quadruple heart-bypass surgery July 7–8. Dawn held a brief news conference to send good wishes to Edgar and his family and canceled her campaign events for a period. "I've been there [with Walter], and I know how difficult it is," she said.[106] Out of respect for the hospitalized governor, Dawn directed her campaign to pull the aggressive response ads that were waiting at the television stations and put a moratorium on television advertising during the governor's recovery from surgery. When they resumed two weeks later, a less confrontational ad substituted for the "hard-hitting" spot that had been planned.[107] This gesture was both very classy and very costly.

Because Dawn's campaign suffered from a lack of funds, her staff took advantage of somewhat gimmicky events, like the bologna described previously, to attract the news media and get free media coverage. The Illinois Education Association, an eighty-five-thousand-member teachers' union that had endorsed Dawn in early July, gave a refurbished yellow school bus to her campaign, and in late July Dawn and her running mate took off in the bus through rural Illinois to explain her tax-swap and school-funding plan directly to the voters. It resembled an old-style whistle-stop campaign. At each stop, grade school children waving Netsch-Severns signs would greet the candidates to the tune of "Here Comes the Sun," and Dawn would give a ten-minute stump speech, simplified from her more typically dense and lengthy policy talks.[108] The bus tour attracted a great deal of attention in both the local and national media.

Within days, however, just as Edgar was recovering enough to restart his campaign, another health disaster hit the Netsch campaign. After receiving biopsy results of a malignant tumor, Penny Severns underwent surgery for breast cancer and was required to suspend campaigning indefinitely for radiation and chemotherapy.[109] Dawn continued on the school-bus tour of the state alone.

In early August, the Netsch campaign finally aired the televised ad it had meant to release in early July, a thirty-second spot by Saul Shorr, who had produced the famous pool ad. The new ad began with the camera moving along a set of railroad tracks, as a photo of Edgar appeared above, with the narrator saying, "For four years, Jim Edgar, you've led Illinois down the wrong track. State finances are a mess. Illinois can't pay its bills. And we've had no real property tax relief." The camera then moved to the faces of children, as the narrator continued, "But even worse, Mr. Edgar, you've cheated the children of Illinois. Because of you, we've slipped to forty-eighth in state support for education. Now, we're even behind Mississippi." It then moved in on a close-up of a child's face, and the narrator asked, "With a record that bad, Mr. Edgar, how can you face the children of Illinois and ask for four more years?"[110] It cost about $750,000 to run the ad in the Chicago area for three weeks; the Netsch campaign also soon began airing ads downstate that noted that school districts there were in dismal financial condition as well.[111] The Edgar campaign came back with ads questioning whether an infusion of money was the remedy for Illinois' educational system and reemphasizing the image of Dawn as a politician eager to raise taxes.

In short, Edgar had money enough to run both positive and negative ads, that is, both ads touting his programs and ads against Dawn, and to respond to attacks at the same time. Dawn did not. She could either try to keep the focus on her own central issue, education funding, or respond to Edgar's attacks on her as soft on crime, which risked allowing him to set the agenda for the campaign. But she could not afford to do both over the costly airwaves. Instead, she appeared with a group of police at the Illinois State Fair and accused Edgar of not showing leadership on fighting crime and for having backed off his previous support of a ban on assault weapons.[112] At the same time, her campaign launched a new ad attacking Edgar for the state's unpaid bills and bad fiscal management. In it, a baseball fan yelled, "He's outta there!" as a player flubbed a play; the booing crowd then applauded as the narrator stated, "Because of Jim Edgar, we rank forty-seventh in financial management [according to *Financial World* magazine]. We're almost in last place."[113]

As the ad buys drained her campaign coffers, the Netsch campaign desperately sought more gimmicks, and perhaps scandals, to grab the public attention. One opportunity that presented itself was a scandal involving the Illinois Tollway Authority, whose executive director, Bob Hickman, was a personal friend of Edgar's. When a double pension plan for top tollway executives and a grand jury investigation into questionable land sales by the tollway were revealed, Hickman quickly resigned and the bonus pension was abolished. Dawn's campaign seized on the opportunity not only to criticize the tollway as "a rogue bureaucracy out of control" but also to call for its abolition and merger with the Illinois Department of Transportation, claiming that this would save both drivers and the state time and money.[114] Over the busy, heavy-driving, Labor Day weekend, the Netsch campaign sent panel trucks onto the tollways bearing signs that read ABOLISH THE TOLLWAY. VOTE NETSCH/SEVERNS. They also parked two such trucks outside the headquarters of the tollway authority to attract press coverage.[115]

In a similarly cost-conscious strategy, Netsch ran radio ads over the holiday weekend, costing only $25,000 and designed to reach motorists in their cars. The radio ad featured honking and traffic noises in the background as the announcer said, "So, you're stuck in traffic on the tollway, just waiting for your turn to drop forty cents in the basket." A sound of coins clinking followed before he continued: "Congratulations. But you'll have to pay that toll a quarter of a million times more to pay for the helicopter trips taken by Governor Edgar's buddy, tollway director Bob Hickman, reportedly to visit his girlfriend in Springfield. And for the $84,000 pension Hickman got after only three years' work." After telling drivers the number of tolls they would need to pay to cover the tollway authority's new headquarters building, the ad concluded with the sound of screeching brakes and the words, "Let's stop Jim Edgar now. It's time to hold Jim Edgar accountable for the tollway scandal."[116] Dawn spent part of the Labor Day weekend calling radio talk shows for more free media appearances.

Around the same time, Dawn finally endorsed the truth-in-sentencing plans that her opponents had touted in the primary, on the grounds that the newly passed federal crime bill would help build new prisons to hold inmates for a longer proportion of their sentences. She also announced a plan to restructure human services, which Edgar claimed was almost identical to his own; and she released more details about her education funding plan, outlining what each school district in the state might expect to receive from it and the average homeowner's property tax reduction.[117] After raising more funds, $57,000 of it in one evening at a rally of gay and lesbian voters, she launched a new set of television ads about "Jim Edgar's tollway scandal."[118] At campaign appearances, Dawn also blamed Edgar on several occasions for crimes that paroled ex-prisoners committed, on the grounds that he had passed a bill allowing early release of prisoners and had cut the number of parole officers, thus placing dangerous people out on the street.[119] In short, after a valiant attempt to redirect attention to the central issues, Dawn, too, was drawn into negative campaigning. Yet Dawn's attacks about the tollway problems—and even revelations that Edgar had used state troopers to mow his lawn—did not appear to make a dent in his popularity.[120] Unless a scandal was major and the candidate directly involved in it personally, voters did not seem to care.

Edgar's own ads became nastier and more negative, proclaiming, "Dawn Clark Netsch wants to abolish the death penalty. And Netsch has a plan to increase the income tax by 42 percent. Instead of telling you her plans, she runs negative ads attacking Jim Edgar's integrity."[121] Going further, an Edgar ad claimed, "Netsch said that if elected governor she would sign legislation to abolish the death penalty" (relying tenuously on a press conference at which Dawn had been asked whether she would sign a bill to abolish the death penalty if, contrary to any realistic expectation, the Illinois legislature should pass one and replied, "You're dreaming. That's not going to happen. . . . I suppose so."). Infuriated, Dawn accused Edgar of spreading falsehoods about her.[122] The force of Edgar's negative advertising about the death penalty was increased by the fact that the second person to be executed in Illinois since 1962 was John Wayne Gacy, who was put to death during the general election campaign. Gacy was a poster child for the death penalty, having raped and murdered thirty-three boys and young men between 1972 and 1978 and then buried them under his house.

Edgar continued to lead, two to one, in all parts of the state except the city of Chicago, but, as a result of the negative campaigning, public opinion of both candidates fell.[123] One journalist commented, "Aside from U.S. Senator Paul Simon, there are no two elected officials in the state with more sterling reputations for integrity and government know-how than Republican Gov. Jim Edgar and his Democratic opponent, state Comptroller Dawn Clark Netsch. . . . Instead of discussing the relative merits of their respective candidacies . . . they [are] doing their best to tarnish each other's reputation."[124]

As September drew to a close, Mayor Daley and other powerful Democrats began to fear that the direction of Dawn's campaign might lead the entire Democratic slate down to defeat, and they called for a summit meeting. On September 28, a strategy session was held, with Michael Madigan, Daley's two top political operatives (Tim Degnan and Jeremiah Joyce), Tom Hynes, Neil Hartigan, Jack Reid, Chris Meister, Peter Giangreco, and Gail Handleman all attending. A number of decisions emerged from the meeting. First, Dawn would refocus her campaign on mobilizing women voters and minorities. Ads featuring Dawn as a history-making first woman and her past advocacy for women's rights were to be produced. More attempts to counter Edgar's tax-hike charges and to portray Dawn as a populist would also appear on television. In addition, the other Democratic leaders pledged to lend more organizational support to her in white "ethnic" precincts and to campaign for her.[125] At the same time, it had become clear that Burris and his operatives were giving covert support to Edgar.[126]

It was a bit late for Dawn to start campaigning as a woman after refusing to do so for so long. Nonetheless, her campaign planned a series of events that featured women, including a fund-raiser at which former vice presidential candidate Geraldine Ferraro appeared, along with Dawn's long-term friends such as Julie Hamos and Jan Schakowsky, who was by then a state legislator.[127] Dawn attacked Edgar for his veto of the family leave bill and his failure to support pay equity for women (the setting of state salaries by equalizing pay among disparate, typically sex-segregated jobs) and pointed to her own record of work on the Equal Rights Amendment, rape reform, abortion, and family leave. However, Edgar himself had a fairly good record on women's issues as well. He was pro-choice, so Dawn was able to attack only his support for laws requiring parental notification of teenagers seeking abortion.[128] Edgar had also paid attention to domestic violence issues and, during the latter part of the campaign, had granted clemency to four battered women who had killed their abusers. Throughout the campaign, his support among women voters remained higher than Dawn's. Some opined that there might have been a gender gap in her favor if she had been able to keep the focus on women's issues, like education and fiscal matters affecting the family, instead of Edgar's preemptive focus on crime.[129]

On October 6, the Netsch campaign released a new pool ad for television. In it, Dawn walked into a crowd in a pool room, and the people shouted, "Look! She's back." The camera panned in on a rack of pool balls with "42%" superimposed, as the announcer said, "No way." Dawn then lined up a difficult shot while the narration continued. "Edgar's not telling us the whole truth. Under the Netsch school plan, low- and middle-income families and seniors will get a tax break. And all property taxes will be cut by 10 percent." As she made the shot, the 42% image broke apart, the crowd cheered, and the narrator said, "So much for 42 percent."[130] But Edgar continued to lead in the polls.

In early October, the Edgar campaign grasped what they saw as a scandal to pin on Netsch. When Dawn and Walter bought a townhouse in Sandburg Village for Walter to use as a studio after his retirement, a clerical error in the tax records had omitted both *e*'s in the address, so that 117 W. Goethe Street looked like 117 W. 60th Street, causing the property tax bills to be sent there, to a railroad yard. Because no tax bill ever arrived, Walter thought the taxes were included in the condominium assessment. This error had been discovered in late 1993, and the Netsches had paid all the unpaid taxes and penalties, with no press coverage until it was revealed in early October 1994 by Joseph Morris, a Republican candidate for the Cook County Board.[131] The Edgar campaign seized on this revelation to run attack ads about the unpaid property tax bill, leading to accusations that Dawn was a tax cheat. Walter Netsch was emotionally devastated by the fact that his mistake was causing such negative press for his wife, and Dawn proclaimed that she would never forgive Edgar for this, saying that the attacks had hurt Walter's health and pointing out that she had held back on television ads during Edgar's convalescence. "Walter made an honest mistake," she said. "To turn it into something that has nothing to do with the campaign and to go after him in that respect is absolutely low."[132]

Netsch and Edgar faced off in their one and only televised debate on October 19, 1994, at 10:35 P.M.[133] Dawn had asked for as many as six debates and presumably would have preferred an earlier time, but Edgar refused, saying that she was just seeking free television time. Dawn used the October 19 debate to hammer home her attacks on Edgar for his financial management of the state and its effect on school funding, while Edgar defended his record, saying that he had inherited the spending and credit problems from the previous administration. The two quarreled about what impact the Netsch Plan would have on the average taxpayer. Edgar continued his attacks on Dawn's record of voting while in the senate against tougher penalties for various crimes. She disputed this while also arguing that the death penalty and other types of tough penalties would not address the crime problem in Illinois without getting to its root causes in the state's failure to adequately support and educate its children.

What attracted the most attention in the press, however, was Dawn's closing argument, in which she said, "Some say that I don't look like a typical candidate, that I'm not polished enough, that I don't talk in ten-second sound bites. Well, they're right. I'd rather take some political risks and tell the truth than look and sound like every other politician. It's time for a governor who's more than just a pretty face."[134] The press initially took this as an attempt to portray Edgar as a "bland, vacuous, hair-sprayed governor."[135]

The not-just-a-pretty-face campaign was, in fact, planned by Dawn's campaign consultants as a way to address, with humor and self-deprecation, the public's perception of her as schoolmarmish. Focus groups had also reacted negatively to her personal appearance. More immediately, the new campaign slogan responded to posters that had recently appeared in downtown Chicago, reading DAWN CLARK NETSCH IS A TAX CHEAT. THE TRUTH IS AS UGLY AS SHE IS. The Edgar campaign denied any connection to the posters, while Dawn and U.S. Senator Paul Simon, himself not a handsome man, held a press conference at the foot of the Abraham Lincoln statue in Grant Park. They joked about the physical appearance of both Simon and Lincoln and reminded the press of Lincoln's witty statement, "I'm not two-faced. Otherwise I wouldn't be wearing the one I'm wearing right now."[136] In addition, the Netsch campaign started to run a television ad in which a woman compared Dawn to "my Aunt Thelma."[137] Campaign buttons reading NOT JUST ANOTHER PRETTY FACE were distributed.

The only other debate held in the gubernatorial campaign was a radio debate before a panel of journalists, which was broadcast from Springfield on October 21. At the debate, Edgar continued to attack Dawn's legislative record on crime bills. Dawn used the opportunity to court female voters. In her opening statement, she said regarding Edgar's campaign focus on the death penalty, "What he's really trying to say to you is that I can't be tough on crime—women can't be tough on crime. Ask any woman. It's women who walk down the street looking over their shoulders. Governor Edgar, you ought to be ashamed of yourself."[138] At a press conference after the debate, Dawn denounced the nationwide pattern of Republican gubernatorial candidates calling their female opponents soft on crime as "at best insensitive. . . . If you want to translate that as sexist," she continued, "you may."

Although at least one commentator thought Dawn's debate performance was superior to Edgar's—indeed, "her strongest performance since winning the Democratic gubernatorial primary in March"—the voters, as reflected in the polls, did not agree.[139] Other commentators bemoaned the media coaching that had turned modern debates into a series of short campaign speeches rather than a reasoned discussion of the issues.[140]

Frenetic activity on Dawn's part marked the last two weeks of the campaign. Because her campaign was hurting for money compared to Edgar's, they relied again on cheap gimmicks to attract the attention of the press—this time, handing out magnifying glasses attached by red ribbons to pieces of paper with tiny writing that asked voters to "take a close look at Edgar's record."[141] Because it is cheaper to charter a plane and fly around the state to hold press conferences at airports in multiple cities than to pay for television time, Dawn traveled a great deal—to the Quad Cities, Rockford, Peoria, and Belleville just in the last two days before the election. While she campaigned on the street in Chicago, Edgar would "glide anonymously through busy streets to a few chosen campaign appearances, letting television news reports and commercials connect him with his public."[142] His campaign had the money to place new television ads at key times to attract the most viewers, such as during Notre Dame football games and the season premiere of *Seinfeld*. In an attempt to even the playing field, Walter made one last donation of $240,000 for media coverage at the end of October.[143] Dawn still feels badly about this, because Walter sold art and sculpture that they both loved for what she knew by then was a losing battle. And all through the latter part of October, Edgar's campaign workers placed phone calls to voters, telling them that Netsch would abolish the death penalty if elected.[144]

Dawn told the press during the last days of the campaign that she had no regrets about having told the electorate what it needed to know, even if that seemed to be leading to defeat.[145] What did sting, however, both then and now, was that so many of the Chicago Democratic Party bosses betrayed her, sending out their precinct workers with palm cards for Edgar at the end of the campaign. Although Mayor Daley, Phil Rock, and the chairs of both the Cook County and state Democratic parties stood by her, large numbers of the older machine committeemen turned against her, including Ed Burke, Richard Mell, Ed Kelly, George Dunne, and many more.[146] Sums of money that had been promised to her campaign, moreover, failed to materialize. After so many years of working for unity within the Democratic Party, Dawn felt this keenly as a betrayal.

Nonetheless, Dawn was realistic about what was happening, both in Illinois and in the country at large. National polls began to show a tsunami taking form, aimed at the Democratic Party in every state and fueled by Newt Gingrich's "Contract with America." Dawn knew by the last weeks that she would lose but tried to focus on keeping up the spirits of her campaign workers without lying to them:

> You can't just say, "I'm going to lose" if you are the lead candidate on the ticket because everyone on the ticket will lose then. Yet I

was darned if I was going to lie to people to their face. I would say, "Who knows what's going to happen on Election Day? It's volatile, things do change." It's a way of not telling a deliberate falsehood but not being so down that people abandon the other Democratic candidates.[147]

Dawn saw less of her in-house campaign staff toward the end and thinks that

> Some of them had not faced reality. . . . When I was where they were, it was more a matter of maintaining an upbeat spirit, even though they knew I knew what was going to happen. What you don't want them to think is that the world is going to fall apart just because they lose the election of someone they believed in. I wanted to keep them from getting cynical, turned off, from walking away from the entire process.[148]

Pete Giangreco says the staff had a party two weeks before the election at Chris Meister's apartment for morale purposes and to prepare the younger volunteers for the loss. "We had all these kids who loved her. We needed to prepare them for what was coming."[149]

What was coming was a landslide. On November 8, 1994, Jim Edgar was reelected by a record margin—64 percent to 34 percent (the remainder went to a Libertarian candidate). Republicans swept all the state offices, took over the Illinois house, and increased their majority in the state senate. The turnout in the city of Chicago was an all-time low, about 46 percent.[150] Netsch's loss was part of a nationwide trend. In what the Republican Party dubbed the "Revolution of '94," Ann Richards lost in Texas to George W. Bush, and Kathleen Brown also lost the race for governor in California. Fifty-four seats in the U.S. House of Representatives changed from Democrat to Republican, resulting in a Republican majority for the first time since 1954. Many incumbents were defeated, including the speaker of the house, Tom Foley. The Republicans took control of the U.S. Senate by winning eight seats away from Democrats. They gained a total of 12 governor seats and 472 state legislative seats, taking control of twenty state legislatures away from the Democrats. So the loss in Illinois was hardly unique.

Dawn spent election night as is traditional, in a hotel suite with her family and close friends until going down to deliver her concession speech to supporters assembled in a ballroom. Someone who was present remembers, "Dawn took it that night with aplomb. If she felt crushed, she didn't act that way around us. She smiled. She joked. She had class. She is not a person who is a defeatist."[151] Dawn gave the concession speech at about 9:30 P.M. on November 8, 1994, still trying to keep up the spirits of her supporters. "Well, doggone it," she said, "we'll just have to try again next time." As she looked out into the crowd, she saw that people were crying. She told them, "Please, no tears or sympathy. I did it my way. I was honest with the voters, and I didn't back down," and she urged them to keep up the fight for school funding, saying, "We may have lost the battle, but the war is still being fought. Regroup and move on. It's worth it, believe me it is worth it."[152] Dawn got up early the next morning to appear on news shows to discuss the election. She remembers:

> Walter Jacobsen had an early morning program and wanted me to be there the next day. I did it the very next morning, live on television. I could talk about it; I knew my life wasn't ended. It was of course an enormous disappointment. It was the thing I had always wanted to do, but it was not to be. . . . What can you do about it? Timing is everything in politics.[153]

One journalist commented that it would have been nice to test Dawn's campaign at a time without the national political turmoil, because, as he said, "Dawn Netsch would rather be Dawn Netsch than be governor. . . . Candidates so intent upon putting candor and personal principle above winning are precisely what lots of voters claim they want to see."[154] Thinking back twelve years later, Giangreco agrees:

> She was very frustrated with how things happened, but at the end she was totally at peace. She'd rather be right than governor, or to make compromises to be governor. . . . I don't think she ever thought winning or losing would define her; she was still going to do whatever she was going to do. . . . It's why she's one of my favorite clients I ever worked for. She taught me that there were more important things than winning. Vision matters. Policy matters. Being willing to stand up and talk about unpopular things matters. It's not just okay if it polls 70 percent.[155]

And, he adds, she was ahead of her time: "Prophets don't always make it to the mountaintop."

Reflections

The Netsch campaign left behind it file boxes full of impressively researched policy papers on a vast number of subjects critical to the state—on agriculture, reforming the welfare system, labor, housing, disability issues, health care, rethinking government, and others—in addition to the mountain of research and policies on taxes and school funding. But, as Ralph Martire comments sadly, "We didn't have the money to get our message out. So our much better position papers never got the hearing with the voters that they could have or should have."[156] Ironically, Governor Edgar adopted many of Dawn's ideas in his second term, calling for education finance reforms quite similar to those in the Netsch Plan (though omitting property tax breaks for businesses). Because Edgar had spent so much time attacking the plan during the campaign, however, he was unable to pass it through the legislature.

What is to be made of this story? Why did someone so knowledgeable and full of creative thought about Illinois government go down to defeat in a landslide only eight months after her big victory in the primary? It cannot just be the difference between Democratic voters and the general electorate, for Edgar attracted a substantial number of Democratic votes in November. Perhaps there was no way a Democrat, whoever was nominated, could have won election against a popular, moderate Republican incumbent in the year of a nationwide Republican tidal wave. It was especially difficult for a candidate who was both a woman and apparently still, after all that time, not part of the local political establishment. And then, of course, there was the string of bad luck, starting with Edgar's heart surgery just as the Netsch campaign had produced television ads to respond to his early attacks on her. Yet there are also underlying lessons to be gleaned about the way political campaigns are funded and run in the United States.

Dawn Clark Netsch had profound and detailed proposals to reform some of the underlying problems in Illinois, but they were complicated to get across to the voters. One newspaper article called them "a policy wonk's fantasy and a disinterested voter's nightmare." By contrast, Edgar stuck to the advice "keep it simple, stupid."[157] Even though they were half-truths, Edgar repeated "42 percent" and "Netsch will abolish the death penalty" so many times that most people believed them to be true. Edgar's crime ads were effective, as well, because they played both into people's fears and also their preconceptions about women. Giangreco remembers it this way:

Jim Edgar was like a robot. He just worked tax increase into every answer, whatever the question, a 42 percent tax increase; he never told you about the swap. The Big Lie, and he just said it over and over and over again. It was very easy for people to understand. And then the next thing was the death penalty; he ran those Willy Horton–esque ads. The first poll went down eight points, then he went negative and it came down thirty some points. We were so far behind that it made it hard to raise money and we couldn't get back on the air to answer. Dawn hated coming back pounding. We tried to do it in the free press, but it was not getting us anywhere; we were buried.[158]

Does this just mean that Jim Edgar ran a better campaign than Dawn Netsch did? It is true that the Netsch campaign was disorganized at times. But Dawn also had principled objections to negative campaigning and about telling anything less than the whole truth. The whole truth is difficult to communicate in sound bites, and Dawn has never been very good at them. In addition, she may have struck many voters as an odd bird, this female law professor who spoke in paragraphs. Bob Creamer, the public interest activist with whom she worked on public utility law reform in the legislature, thinks that voters need to see a political candidate not only as on their side but also as more like them than Dawn appears to be.[159] Although Dawn is warm and communicative one-on-one and people she met and spoke with responded to those qualities, Edgar was able to paint her as "not one of us"—an intellectual, latte-drinking, National Public Radio–listening liberal from the well-to-do North Side. The genius of the pool ad was that it countered this image.

Yet it costs a great deal of money to produce effective television advertising and to flood the airwaves with it. Jim Edgar spent almost $10 million on the 1994 gubernatorial campaign and Netsch some $7 million; but almost half of her total was spent in the primary. In short, Edgar was able to outspend her by a ratio of three to one on television ads in the fall.[160] The way modern political campaigns are carried out—no longer door-to-door, or face-to-face, but by slick advertisements on television—money will almost always be key to success. Thus, until and unless we have genuine public financing of elections, fund-raising from private donors is all important. For a variety of reasons, Dawn had trouble raising adequate funds. Even her customary supporters, like labor unions, preferred to contribute to an incumbent who had been able to help them in the past and might again in the future. Even traditional Democratic funders, like Richard Dennis, Sam Zell, and Irving Harris, did not give money to Dawn. She suspects this is because Edgar's people had let it be known that he would not cooperate with folks who had contributed to her. Moreover, even if one gave substantial sums to Dawn, everyone knew that money could not influence her positions. Her Springfield staff told her that the lobbyists there all said, "Don't give her any money, because she will do nothing for you, no matter what."[161] This leaves a candidate of integrity at a substantial disadvantage.

Many observers have commented that Dawn would have won if she had run later, perhaps because people were more used to a woman as candidate for executive office then and perhaps because the voters had become fed up with a state government that repeatedly encountered the same problems but could not deal with them. Almost without exception, they agree that she would have been an exceptional governor, providing much better leadership than the state has had since then. Paul Green, a political scientist and longtime student of Illinois government, says:

> She certainly is one of the brightest people about government we've had run for office. She understands government from an intellectual point of view, melded with her practical background. . . . We would've come a lot closer to resolving the financial issues that have bugged the state for so long. After that recession, things started to improve, and it would have been interesting to see what would have gotten funded.[162]

—— *Chapter 17* ——

Life After Losing an Election

THE GUBERNATORIAL ELECTION OF 1994 was the first election Dawn Netsch had ever lost, and it was clear that it would be her last. Under circumstances like these—at the age of sixty-eight, after a long life of public service and a humiliating defeat—many politicians would simply disappear into private life. Not Dawn Clark Netsch. From the moment she reemerged as a private citizen, she involved herself in political causes, teaching, and work for a variety of not-for-profit organizations. First, however, she had to complete her term as comptroller.

From the election in early November 1994 through Friday, January 6, 1995, Dawn returned to her work in Springfield. On January 5, she held her last press conference, announcing that it was "the last class session of 'Public Finance 101.'" Releasing one final document to the press, which she called "A Long-Term Look at Short-Term Fixes," she took a parting shot at Governor Edgar's fiscal policies.[1] The refrains were familiar: the state's fiscal situation was not good; short-term fixes like lapse funding had covered up the extent of the budget deficits but had not worked to address the underlying problems. Now it would be someone else's job to deal with them.

In November and December, Dawn and her staff had worked to ensure a smooth transition to the new comptroller, Republican Loleta Didrickson, just as Roland Burris's staff had assisted her in 1990. Didrickson, unlike Dawn, decided to replace most of the upper-level staff in the office, a decision that saddened Dawn: "We had been assured that only the most senior would be replaced; and at the very last minute, 5:00 on a Friday, we got a list of all the people who were not to be protected. They tossed out almost everybody, some who'd been there for a very long time. It was a very bitter day for me."[2] A total of forty-six employees were fired, some with nearly twenty years of experience in their jobs. Dawn told the press that "she did not expect that many to be let go." She added:

> Some of them have been here a long time, and they were not
> political people. . . . It's going to be very difficult for some of
> them. . . . There's a huge amount of talent and experience in that
> group who are being let go. I think that's too bad, because state
> government always needs people who are good and talented and
> interested in what they do.[3]

So Dawn spent some of her last days as comptroller trying to find jobs for
trusted employees who had been laid off.

After this, she desperately needed to rest. She longed to lounge on a
beach in the sun with a good book. Walter, however, had been busy planning a vacation for her, and it was more ambitious than restful. They spent
eighteen days sightseeing, mostly in Germany, in the middle of winter,
with a concert or opera almost every night—sixteen performances in all.[4]

Returning to Chicago, Dawn went back to Northwestern Law School
and took the dean up on his 1990 offer: "If you ever decide to give up that
other life of yours, you can come back and teach."[5] It was too late to start
teaching that semester, but she arranged to begin on a part-time basis in
the fall. She moved into a small office at the school and taught her course
in state and local government for more than a decade thereafter.

In 1996, the new law dean, David Van Zandt, asked Dawn to cochair,
with Professor Stephen B. Presser, the process of producing a strategic
plan for the law school. This was a two-year endeavor, involving extensive consultations with faculty, staff, students, and alumni. The goal
was to examine trends in the legal profession, analyze the law school's
strengths and weaknesses, and come up with a detailed blueprint for the
next five to ten years that would build on current strengths to distinguish
Northwestern from its competitor schools. The result was a twenty-eight-
page glossy brochure setting specific priorities and goals, distributed in
October 1998.[6] This process took up a great deal of Dawn's time, time
spent in endless meetings and conferring with individual members of the
faculty.

Cochair Presser was known as one of the more conservative members
of the law school faculty; Dawn was one of the more liberal. Yet they
managed to work well together through a lengthy and, at times, difficult
process. The law school the dean envisaged as the law school of the future
was not exactly the one Dawn had known and loved in the past. The
school was becoming more business oriented, with joint programs with
the graduate school of business, while Dawn was oriented toward public

service and believed in a broader training in law than the proposed special-izations might provide. The school the dean foresaw was a place to turn out future leaders, primarily ones who corresponded to the needs of large corporate law firms and businesses and thus could be easily placed there on graduation. Dawn wondered why she had been chosen for this task. "I eventually decided I was there to serve the kind of political role—to handle people, count votes, listen to them. I knew the plan was going to differ from my native instincts, but I wanted to make sure that the clinic and public interest law were fully recognized and respected."[7]

Dawn used her organizational and administrative expertise to help draw up an agenda, break it into component parts, and set up subcommit-tees of faculty to study various subjects. When issues were contentious, she visited faculty members to hear them out, employing the skills of diplo-macy and negotiation she had learned during long years in the legisla-ture.[8] She and Presser agree that they worked very well together. Each understood and respected the other's different perspectives: he favored the business, corporate, and big firm goals and she favored public interest and clinical education. They included both in the strategic plan for the school. Presser looks back on their collaboration as particularly fruitful:

> Dawn's politics and mine are completely different (she's a liberal democrat, I'm a conservative republican), and I wondered how we could ever work together when David Van Zandt made us co-chairs of the strategic planning committee. Curiously, it turned out to be a great working relationship—she was always sensitive to the need never to forget that we were training lawyers (she was strong on clinical education), and that we had a duty to promote justice as well as a duty to turn out legal professionals. She and I drafted the law school's mission statement single-handedly, and it was, I think, a marvel of clarity and sharp prose directed toward planning for an institution devoted both to the law and justice. The fact that eventually we got everyone to sign on to the strategic plan (with one abstention) was a tribute probably more to Dawn than to anyone else.[9]

In short, Dawn took the skills she had learned in politics and invested them in the law school that had given her her start.

Dawn's small office at Northwestern, in a modern building that did not exist when she was a law student, overlooks Lake Michigan. The morning light floods in from the east and tends to overheat it. Although there are several chairs, there is no place to sit. Every surface is covered with papers and files. The floor is crowded with boxes holding the files that will not fit into the three tall file cabinets against the wall. Most of the files contain her research notes on the subjects she teaches. There are also books and papers about Illinois politics and finance, and tomes about state and local government, law and public education, the legislative process, and land development. Far from being an archive of the past, the piles reflect Dawn's ongoing interests in all these subjects and continuing activism. There are current magazines about public education and about Chicago and the state of Illinois, along with files on government accountability, government ethics, merit selection of judges, the death penalty, and the call for a constitutional convention placed on the November 2008 ballot, as required every twenty years by the Illinois Constitution.

The room reflects Dawn's many pursuits and passions in other ways as well. Close to her desk are photos from her political past. There she is, standing with Governor Stevenson and Senator Douglas at the Committee on Illinois Government fund-raising party at Stevenson's house, riding on the back of a car in the Gay Pride parade, with Dick Durbin, Bill Clinton, and Justice John Paul Stevens. There is also a picture of the Air Force Academy Chapel Walter designed and a photo of a beloved dog that died recently, the last of the Netsches' many Boston terriers. The shelves and tops of cabinets hold some of the numerous awards Dawn has been given, many of them carved in heavy crystal. They include the 2006 American Constitution Society Legal Legend award, the 2000 John Paul Stevens award, a 1999 award from Personal PAC "for outstanding leadership in support of reproductive rights," a founders award from the Leadership Council for Metropolitan Open Communities, and awards from the City Club and the Chicago Council of Lawyers. A souvenir baseball from the 2005 White Sox World Series championship sits proudly atop a file cabinet, next to political hats and bowls full of political buttons. A book of Stevenson's speeches from 1952 is inscribed by Debs Myers, "To Dawn—my comrade, my friend, a tower of strength by day, a pillar of flame by night," and by Ralph Martin, "To our Dawn, who was so much more than dawn—who was sunshine and brightness and such a big part of this most wonderful time of all our lives."

The file cabinets are crammed. One holds folders filled with research for revisions of her casebook on state and local government, for law school committees on which she has served, and teaching notes. Other drawers contain files on the many groups in which she either participates actively, such as the American Judicature Society, or that she supports and attends more sporadically, like the Chicago Bar Association Committee on Constitutional Law, which she once chaired. Others are filled with file folders marked by names of her numerous friends and political associates throughout the years, many of whom are now dead: Jeanne and Paul Simon, Penny Severns, Vince Demuzio, Grace Mary Stern, Otto Kerner, Harold Washington, Marcia Thompson, Harold Shapiro, Jim Rahl, Victor Rosenblum. Each named folder holds carefully preserved obituaries, funeral programs, newspaper articles, and often the text of a eulogy delivered by Dawn herself, visible signs that the generation to which Dawn belongs is fast disappearing.

All these deaths take their toll on her. When Dawn returned to the law school, her old friend Hal Shapiro was teaching there on an adjunct basis. They continued to joke with one another in the lighthearted way that had marked their long friendship. Shapiro described Dawn in an interview as "one of my best friends," and Dawn loved him fiercely as well. Suddenly, at the end of 2005, he was gone. Dawn grieved intensely and privately. She spoke at the memorial service held for him at the law school a month later. The handwritten draft of her eulogy closes with these words, in her neat handwriting: "We will miss you." And then, in handwriting that appears to be shaky, "*I* will miss you."[10]

The law school certainly does not mark the boundaries of Dawn's world. On returning from Springfield, she again became involved in some groups from her past and extended her commitment to new ones. The Committee on Illinois Government was no longer. Her longtime service on the board of the American Civil Liberties Union had ended, although she remained on the advisory board. But she returned to serve on the board of the Leadership Council for Metropolitan Open Communities at a time of crisis for that organization. The council had fallen on hard times as the early board members, corporate titans like Ben Heineman and Tom Ayers, were replaced by others less able to raise substantial sums of money. A former staff member had embezzled funds. In addition, fair housing was not as salient an issue as it once had been, making it a challenge to raise funds for the thirty-year-old organization. Aurie Pennick, the director, begged Dawn to become treasurer of the council during this critical period. Dawn agreed, and she did so not only by lending her name but also by contributing actively, running the finance committee, working with Pennick on budgets, meeting with funders and auditors, and recruiting a new finance officer for the group. She served as treasurer of the council for more than three years. According to Pennick, it was Dawn's fund-raising and fiscal management skills that pulled the organization out of its acute crisis in the mid-1990s.[11]

Dawn was less active in the council after 2000, becoming a member of the advisory council rather than the board. The group continued to have problems raising money, as it competed with the many good government organizations that had proliferated since it was founded in the 1960s. Although the organization had performed an enormous service in earlier years, other groups were now involved in planning for affordable housing, and law school clinics and private practitioners were taking on housing discrimination suits. The council finally closed in 2006.[12]

In 1997 Dawn had joined the board of Business and Professional People for the Public Interest, a public interest law firm founded in 1970. BPI focuses on issues related to affordable housing, public housing, and public education. When Alexander Polikoff joined BPI, he took with him the *Gautreaux* litigation against the Chicago Housing Authority initiated at the ACLU in the late 1960s. Polikoff describes Dawn as an ideal board member: "Her views are thoughtful; . . . among the board members she is the one you can look to for raising questions. She's a good person to bounce something off if staff are proposing to do something. . . . She asks, 'Have you thought about this? Have you thought about that?'"[13] Dawn's expertise as law professor, legislator, comptroller, and gubernatorial candidate are very important to BPI. The staff consults her on issues of state finance and taxation; they have also discussed with her the possibility of further litigation about school funding in Illinois.

Hoy McConnell, BPI's current executive director, says that Dawn continues to participate actively in all of the group's policy discussions, advancing the quality of discussion enormously. He describes her participation in a special board task force set up to identify the issues BPI should focus its energies on in the future:

> She was a very active participant in that small group. That discussion and her input led us to begin what is one of our very important program initiatives today, that to increase the amount of affordable housing throughout the area, both the preservation of existing housing and creation of new. Her active participation helped us identify this niche for us, and it's been a very good one for us. We've made headway.[14]

In short, Dawn continues actively working for affordable housing in the Chicago metropolitan area even though the Leadership Council is dead. McConnell particularly appreciates that Dawn "helps us keep our feet on the ground, contributing a real-world view." For her part, Dawn enjoys serving on the BPI board and its education committee. Asked what she gets out of it, she replied:

> I learn a lot; I always do. I get to spend time with people that I share a lot of common things with. I also like to be part of a group that's trying to change things that I care about. The groups I work with now all do that. These were my legislative interests, and I can't pursue them as a public official anymore. I can't imagine not being involved.[15]

Proving Peter Tomei's comment at the 1970 Con Con, to the effect that Dawn just never gives up, Dawn has also continued to work for merit selection of judges as a member of the board of the American Judicature Society. The society was founded as a judicial reform group in 1914, and its board is made up of academics, lawyers and nonlawyers, and judges. Dawn had been in close touch with the organization over the years when she was the principal sponsor of merit selection proposals in the senate. After she left Springfield at the beginning of 1995, Fran Zemans, who was then the director of AJS, invited her to be on the board. At that time, the board was huge—more than one hundred members—and an executive committee of about twenty people ran the organization. Dawn soon became a member of the executive committee and later chair of the board.

AJS is primarily a research and policy group rather than an active lobbying group. The staff meet with and advise individuals or groups that want to draw on their expertise about areas included within their mission: the effective administration of justice, judicial selection, judicial independence, the jury system, and judicial ethics. When appropriate, AJS collaborates with organizations working on similar issues. For example, along with others, they spoke out forcefully against several recent constitutional amendments and initiatives aimed at taking away judicial independence in a number of states—the South Dakota constitutional amendment stripping judges of their immunity, for example, and the Colorado initiative to set term limits for appellate judges.[16] AJS also puts out the well-respected journal *Judicature*, which publishes timely and thoughtful articles on judicial administration.

Service on the AJS board was relatively demanding, involving two or more board meetings a year, plus the annual and midyear meetings, at which AJS puts on a substantive program. As chair of the program committee and with limited staff support because of financial constraints, Dawn was responsible, along with AJS staff, for arranging these substantive programs and sometimes spoke on the panels herself. AJS, like the Leadership Council, went through a serious financial crisis in the late 1990s, and for similar reasons—it became difficult to raise money for an eighty-year-old not-for-profit group that was not focused on the latest and most fashionable issue. While Dawn was a board member, the decision was made to move the group's headquarters from Chicago to Des Moines, Iowa, where a generous supporter, Dwight Opperman, had provided a house for it on the campus of Drake University and additional financial support. Several staff members, including the editor of *Judicature,* stayed behind in Chicago after the 2003 move and remain connected electronically. The move has allowed the organization to survive and expand its work.

Dawn chaired the AJS board for a two-year term, serving with Larry Hammond, the president. During this period, a strategic planning process led to the decision to replace the large board with a smaller working board, which oversees finances, audits, strategic plans, and positions taken by the organization, as well as substantive programs. In the restructuring, the position of board chair was eliminated and a national advisory council was created. Dawn continued as a member of this board until 2007 and chaired the program committee after her term as chair was up. Dick Perrault, former executive director of AJS, describes her contributions:

> Dawn knew what the focus of AJS was and had been, its strengths and weaknesses. She always listened to all the good ideas but always came back to merit selection, judicial selection, and judicial ethics as the core. She made certain the board never forgot that was the primary focus of the organization. . . .
>
> She kept insisting that this is our expertise, what we are known for. She kept AJS on track. She did not object to doing some different things if there was money to pay for them. But she always wanted to make sure that whatever we did did not take money from those core issues so we couldn't do what we should be doing.[17]

She was also very good at handling anyone, including the most difficult members of the board. According to Perrault, "Dawn would say, 'Your point is valid, but think about it this other way.' Everyone liked her. She didn't threaten anyone's ego, or tell them how stupid they were." Dawn served on the AJS board until term limits on board membership brought her tenure to an end and then became a member of the honorary board. She felt happy to be relieved of the time commitment until she got a letter informing her that she had been put on the program committee and the strategic planning committee.[18]

In 1997 Dawn was asked to join the board of yet another organization—a brand new one—the Illinois Campaign for Political Reform. ICPR had grown out of a task force on campaign finance in Illinois cochaired by former U.S. Senator Paul Simon and former governor William Stratton. The task force issued a report in 1997 calling for numerous changes in the law governing campaign finance and conduct. ICPR was funded in part by the Joyce Foundation to follow up on the recommendations. Originally a project of the League of Women Voters, it became a separate not-for-profit organization in 2001, aimed at building a coalition to address the impact of money on politics and government in Illinois.

Paul Simon and Bob Kustra, the former lieutenant governor under Jim Edgar, cochaired the first board of the new group, and Abner Mikva and Dawn were active in their support from the outset. Cindi Canary, the executive director of the new organization, was delighted when such a stellar cast of characters agreed to participate in helping to launch the project. Dawn joined the board and was a very active participant from the early days. The group's mission, of course, concerned an issue that had long interested Dawn, who had introduced numerous bills on campaign finance and ethics into the Illinois Senate over the years, with only modest success. Canary recalls:

> Campaign finance was an issue she had spearheaded in the legislature; it was close to her heart. More intuitively or intellectually than anyone she has always understood the linkages between money and politics and public policy. She came with a wealth of knowledge and enthusiasm; she was a mentor, a teacher, an advisor from the get-go. . . .
>
> She has proven to be our best strategist and someone who is just always there, generous of intellect and time.[19]

In the group's early days, when Canary was striving to build the organization and gain recognition for it, Dawn made herself available by telephone for advice on a continuous basis. Just as she had counseled the Committee on Illinois Government many years before, Dawn insisted that it was crucial to back up one's rhetoric with hard data that could not fail to be respected. For this reason, ICPR affiliated with the Sunshine Project at the University of Illinois at Springfield to build a database about campaign contributions and fund-raising.

Dawn also offered moral support and tactical advice. If the group succeeded in raising an issue that exploded in the press, for example, Canary would call Dawn and ask, "What do I do now?" Dawn's experience with legislation, with bringing about incremental change, and with pulling together the support necessary to pass reform bills was extremely helpful. Perhaps the most important thing she did for Canary, though, was to teach her to find her own voice about the issues. Dawn nurtured not only the fledgling organization but also the young woman who directed it.

ICPR took off rapidly. The first bill the organization worked to pass became the Illinois State Gift Ban Act of 1998. Among other things, the new law banned gifts to state officials (with a long list of exceptions that has since been narrowed); banned the use of campaign funds for personal use; barred fund-raising events within fifty miles of Springfield while the legislature was in session; and required the electronic filing of official campaign finance reports for committees that raised at least $25,000 in an election cycle, to be reduced in 2003 to $10,000.[20] The most important achievement, in Canary's opinion, was the provision requiring mandatory electronic filing, because that makes it easy for both newspaper reporters and ordinary citizens to search by computer to discover who has made contributions to whom—and who may be expecting favors.

Dawn and Abner Mikva brought a new issue to ICPR, the issue of campaign contributions to judges. Although both favored appointment of judges based on merit, such a system was not realistically on the horizon in Illinois. Under the circumstances, Dawn thought it was important to begin to track contributions to judicial campaigns. Throughout the country, interest groups such as medical associations, business groups, and trial lawyers had begun to invest heavily in judicial campaigns, raising substantial concerns about the potential effect of contributions by people or groups litigating a case in front of a judge. Since about 2000, elections to the Illinois Supreme Court have become increasingly expensive and hard fought. Using Dawn's knowledge and contacts from her long involvement with AJS, ICPR began to focus on the problems, to gather data and to document them, and to develop a proposal for limited public financing of judicial elections. Dawn thought it would be possible to get the legislature to focus on this issue as a first step in campaign finance reform, because judicial campaigns take money away from the legislators' own campaigns and the legislators are generally not interested in protecting judges from limits on campaign finance. After ICPR focused substantial attention on the issue, Barack Obama introduced the Supreme Court Campaign Reform Act into the senate in early 2004. As of 2009, it had still not passed both houses of the legislature.

ICPR also branched out into a broader focus on governmental ethics. The group drafted a comprehensive ethics package, circulated it to its board members for comment, and then began to meet with legislators in Springfield about the issue in 2003. Lobbying in Springfield for the reforms, Canary constantly drew on Dawn for advice, because Dawn knew the players in the legislature and was astute at distinguishing integral parts of the bill from provisions on which compromise was possible or necessary. Ultimately, a compromise version of ethics reform legislation was worked out between the house and the senate, but Governor Rod Blagojevich exercised an amendatory veto of it, supposedly because it did not go far enough.

Blagojevich, a Democrat, was elected governor of Illinois in 2002, and both Dawn Netsch and Abner Mikva served on his transition team, cochairing the Public Integrity Working Group. Thus, Dawn and a few others were responsible for the ideas that went into the new governor's ethics program, including campaign finance limits and measures to address gifts to public employees, contracts awarded to campaign contributors (popularly referred to as "pay to play"), and revolving-door problems (state officials who go to work for the very groups they have been regulating as soon as they leave state government and are thus subject to conflicts of interest). The bill that emerged from the legislature in 2003 was a watered-down version of the reforms the governor proposed.

Dawn and Mikva tried to head off the governor's veto.[21] They wrote Blagojevich a letter urging him to sign the bill as passed by the legislature because it was the best they could get at that time and could be improved in the future. Nonetheless, Blagojevich vetoed the legislation, and he did so without any advance notice. He also openly insulted the legislators by saying that they lacked the courage of their convictions. The legislators and other executive officers reacted with fury. The new governor had not built trust with members of the legislature, and there were major tensions between him and other executive officials, including the new attorney general, Lisa Madigan.

When everything unraveled, Dawn decided that it was important for her to step in. No one trusted Governor Blagojevich, but Dawn Netsch was still well respected in all quarters. Dawn concluded that it was crucial to get all the constitutional executive officers united in support of the ethics legislation that would regulate the executive branch; she therefore proceeded to determine the concerns each of them had about the current version. She and Canary met with Madigan to find out what her office did not like in the bill. Dawn also talked with Dan Hynes, the comptroller; Judy Baar Topinka, the treasurer; and Jim Burns, the secretary of state's inspector general, to see what problems each of their offices had with the bill. She encountered difficulty, however, getting an appointment with the governor himself. When his office did not cooperate in setting up a meeting, Dawn asked his scheduler to tell Blagojevich that "the last thing he needs right now is for two of the people he most respects on ethical issues [herself and Mikva] to tell the newspapers that he won't even meet with us on the subject."[22] He met with them the next day.

This intervention resulted in an ethics bill backed by all of the executive officers and legislative leaders—a strong, though far-from-perfect, piece of executive branch ethics legislation and a substantial improvement over what had existed before. This legislation, the State Officials and Employees Ethics Act of 2003, prohibits government employees from accepting jobs with companies they had regulated or to which they had awarded contracts worth more than $25,000 for a year after leaving state employment. Among other things, it also removes many exemptions from the State Gift Ban Act, requires ethics training for all state employees, and strengthens the ban on using state employees for political work. For enforcement, the new law requires each executive officer to appoint an executive inspector general (EIG) to review ethics complaints within his or her office. The act also established an Executive Ethics Commission to determine appropriate action in any cases brought forward by the EIGs and created the position of legislative inspector general and the Legislative Ethics Commission to enforce its provisions in the legislative branch.

The new bill was passed during the fall veto session, and the governor signed it at a ceremony on December 9, 2003, at the State of Illinois Building in Chicago. Dawn was at the signing ceremony, of course, and Governor Blagojevich gave her credit for bringing about the successful passage of the legislation. Handing her the pen, he said, "This is for the one who most deserves it. We couldn't have done it without Dawn Clark Netsch."[23] Dawn's one regret was that her friend Paul Simon died suddenly that day and did not live to see this victory in an area where he had contributed so significantly.

The deaths continued to mount up. In 2007 Dawn's brother Keith, the last of her small family from Cincinnati, died. She flew out to Nevada to speak at his memorial service. By far the greatest loss came in June 2008, when her husband, Walter, died. Walter's health had declined over a long period, though he remained fiercely engaged intellectually. His vascular problems grew worse until his leg was cold and discolored. Emergency surgery was performed using veins in his legs to bypass the clogged arteries, which worked for a while but then had to be repeated. The first of two amputations came in 2000, and Walter was bound to a wheelchair. Their house of many levels was sublimely ill suited to a wheelchair, so Walter designed an elevator that was added in one corner. This allowed him to go from his room and study on the lowest level to the kitchen and dining room area, and thus to have access to some parts of the house he designed and loved. A caretaker was hired so that Dawn could get out during the day to work, but any trips out of town became difficult. Dawn rushed home at the end of each day to make dinner. Repeated medical crises also kept Dawn at Walter's hospital bed and then making elaborate arrangements so that he could return home.

By 2008 Walter was bedridden and required around-the-clock care, as it had become physically impossible for Dawn alone. On June 15, he died. Dawn and a few close friends and family buried his ashes (mixed with those of a couple of his beloved dogs) in Graceland Cemetery on the north side of Chicago. At the end of a brief service, they all left daisies, Walter's favorite flower, at the base of a gingko tree he had planted in 1992.

A memorial service was held the next month at the Arts Club in downtown Chicago, before an overflow crowd. Walter's former colleagues from Skidmore, Owings and Merrill assisted with the displays of his work and a slide show of photos of Walter and his work. A string quartet played Barber and Shostakovich. Craig Hartman, his close friend from Skidmore who had arranged the firm's contributions to the memorial, Walter's nephew, and a number of architects spoke about him as a person and an architect. But everyone agreed that the best speech was the last, given by Dawn herself. It was the speech of a lifetime, after a lifetime of speeches.

Because it reveals so much about Walter as a person and his relationship with Dawn, a lengthy excerpt is in order:

> We should acknowledge Walter wasn't always the easiest person to work with—whether it was on the drafting tables at Skidmore or in the battles to protect and extend the parks and green spaces that he so loved. Nor was it always easy for those who spent nonwork time with him—his friends, his caretakers, even his wife of forty-four years.
>
> He was intense, demanding, impatient. In fact, in recent years he rather relished describing himself as a "curmudgeon." But the impatience was always for a reason, and it was quickly replaced with a warm sigh, a laugh, and his most abiding quality—generosity. . . . He was, as so many have said, larger than life.[24]

She then described Walter's civic activities, his commitment to the civil rights movement, his love of teaching, art, music, and politics—attributing the last not to her own involvement but to the fact that "he knew it made a difference in how the world turns, and he had a responsibility for making it turn the right way." She concluded, "Walter experienced so many medical and physical challenges over the last several years but he was tough; he did not give up; he kept fighting for life just as he had for good architecture. He has earned his rest." Then she quoted Corinthians 13, about faith, hope, and love, which ends, "Love bears all things, believes all things, hopes all things, endures all things." She added, "Beauty endures also and, Walter, you have given us so much of that. But love endures beyond all else, and you have given me that." It was a fitting coda to a remarkable partnership of love between two extraordinary people.

Dawn, now alone, continues to live an active and politically engaged life in her ninth decade. She sits on the board of *Illinois Issues* magazine. Officeholders and candidates regularly call on her for advice and help. Many Democratic candidates running for political office seek Dawn's endorsement. She puts in frequent appearances at fund-raisers, both for political campaigns and for the public interest groups in her many areas of interest. She still rides in the Gay Pride parade each year, now traveling with the group in the Gay and Lesbian Hall of Fame, of which she has long been a member. These days her parade car displays a sign that reads: DAWN CLARK NETSCH—I'M NOT RUNNING FOR ANYTHING. She was overjoyed by Barack Obama's campaign for president and his victory.

From time to time, Dawn still enters the Illinois political arena when she deems it necessary. When the question whether to call a constitutional convention was placed on the ballot in November 2008, Dawn became active—as she had in 1988—advocating against holding a convention. The 1970 constitution was still relatively new and deserved a longer period of testing. Although it was not perfect, it represented the best Dawn thought possible to get if a convention were held—and the state might end up with a document that was much worse. At a time when the state budget was so stretched, moreover, holding a constitutional convention could be very expensive.

The movement for a new Con Con became quite loud in 2008, however, largely because people were fed up with the continuous battles between Governor Blagojevich and the legislature and the legislative stalemates that resulted; they thought, inaccurately, that a new constitution might remedy the situation. Pat Quinn, the grandstanding treasurer when Dawn was comptroller, wanted to introduce the devices of recall and popular initiative into the constitution, so that propositions could be placed on the ballot for the electorate to vote on directly, as in California. Dawn thought this was the last thing Illinois needed and was convinced that any convention held under the current circumstances would result in a worse document than the 1970 charter.[25] So the fall of 2008 found Dawn's calendar crowded with speeches, meetings, and media interviews in a flurry of activity to defeat the call for a constitutional convention. On November 4, 2008, the call for a convention was decisively defeated.[26]

Dawn has also remained active in the continuing struggle for government ethics reform in Illinois. When the Illinois General Assembly finally passed a pay-to-play bill prohibiting political contributions by state contractors to the officeholder awarding the contract in 2008, Governor Blagojevich used the amendatory veto to rewrite the entire bill, as he had done with several other bills. Dawn and Cindi Canary met with the governor's staff. As the author of the amendatory veto provision of the 1970 constitution, Dawn told them that this was a serious misuse of the amendatory veto; it was not intended as a way to pass a bill that had not been subjected to scrutiny in committee and without any negotiations over the new provisions the governor had inserted.[27]

The Illinois house voted almost immediately to override Blagojevich's veto of the pay-to-play bill. But it was only after Obama was recruited to call Emil Jones, the president of the senate and a Blagojevich ally, that Jones agreed to ask the senate to consider the question. In late September

2008, that chamber also voted by an overwhelming margin to override the governor's veto, and thus the original bill became law on January 1, 2009.

The great irony of Dawn's work on ethics reform with the Blagojevich administration, of course, is that Blagojevich himself apparently was taking advantage of every possible opportunity to profit personally from his office. In December 2008, the United States Attorney accused him of trying to sell the remainder of Barack Obama's Senate term to the highest bidder.[28] Refusing to resign, on December 30, he appointed Roland Burris to fill the seat for the remainder of Obama's term, over the objections of political leaders in both Washington and Springfield.[29] The Illinois legislature then removed Blagojevich from office by impeachment, making Lieutenant Governor Pat Quinn the new governor.[30] In April 2009, Blagojevich was indicted for a broad scheme of corruption "to exercise and preserve power over the government of the State of Illinois for the financial and political benefit of" himself and his family.[31] While privately wondering at the sudden elevation of Roland Burris and Pat Quinn, Dawn's public response was to take advantage of the publicity focused upon the state and redouble her efforts to press for reform of governmental ethics in Illinois. In short, she has remained very much in the middle of the political fray.

What is particularly interesting, after having been one of the guys for much of her life, is the extraordinary amount of support Dawn gives to women, especially to those who want to follow her into the political arena. In the many speeches she has given since the early 1990s on the topic of women in politics, Dawn has increasingly emphasized the benefits of the perspective women bring to the legislature or other offices. "The fact is," she said in one speech, "in Illinois, it took the leadership of women legislators in the 1980s to initiate action on issues of pay equity, teen pregnancy, day care, cocaine babies, family and medical leave and many others. On issues of public policy, women are three times more likely than men to make the welfare of women and children a top legislative priority." (One should add reform of the rape laws to the list of women's legislative achievements in Illinois.) Although she is reluctant to generalize, Dawn also believes that women are "less militaristic on issues of war and peace than men [and] more likely to favor protecting the environment, racial equality, and laws that control social vices such as drugs and gambling."[32] Women also, she said in another speech, approach the political process differently: "Women are more likely to bring citizens into the process.

Women are more likely to opt for government in public view rather than government behind closed doors. Women are more responsive to groups previously denied full access to the policymaking process."[33]

Yet Dawn notes that women face many problems entering politics, most especially problems raising the money necessary to run for office:

> Women and minorities . . . are generally not part of the traditional network of political giving. Moreover, a substantial portion of campaign funding comes from PACs [political action committees, or groups organized to elect political candidates]. PACs give overwhelmingly to incumbents. So it is especially difficult for a nonincumbent, which is most women and minorities.[34]

Having concluded that old-boy networks and incumbency are the problems, Dawn has long been active in trying to address these roadblocks. She thinks back to the days of all-men's clubs and the fact that her younger self was not offended by them. Now she says:

> Over time I came to realize that as long as this pattern was taking place, it was harming women professionals because they were being excluded from full participation. The fact that boys wanted to be with boys I never found offensive. . . . . It's when it begins to be not just their camaraderie but to impinge on the careers, credibility, and participation of women professionals that there is a problem.[35]

Men have networks that have always existed; women have to build them. Dawn was therefore part of the group that discussed setting up an official network for women professionals in Chicago. She was on the first board of the Chicago Network, a group specifically dedicated to forming a network of women to support one another, and she remains a member. She is also a big supporter of Emily's List, the organization that raises money for pro-choice Democratic women candidates.

The only way to address the incumbency obstacle, of course, is to get more women into political office. Dawn was a founding member of the board of the Illinois Women's Institute for Leadership, which aims to encourage and train women to participate effectively in politics and government in Illinois. Interested women may apply, and a class of about fourteen or fifteen are chosen each year. The first class was in 2002.

Members of the class attend programs throughout the year, led by legislators in Springfield and Washington. Dawn speaks to each year's group on the history of women and politics and on the important third branch of government, the judiciary. Someone like Pete Giangreco does a program on handling the media as a public figure.[36] The group also attends classes about how to conduct a political campaign, and they interact with experienced politicians and legislators to learn about both public policy and their own career paths.[37] Some of the graduates are beginning to be elected to office. Deborah Shore, for example, was elected a commissioner of the Metropolitan Water Reclamation District of Greater Chicago in 2006.

When asked why she devotes so much time to these efforts, Dawn replies:

> Because I am a woman. . . . Women tend to be more ethical in public office. . . . They are not as hidebound by partisan labels; they are more willing and able to cross party lines and coalesce around issues and priorities. . . . They tend to be more concerned about the safety net . . . and less about the tax consequences than men. . . . Women are less antigovernment than men; they see government not as the problem but as the solution.[38]

In other words, when all is said and done, Dawn wants more women in politics both because they are women and because they will further many of the goals she has spent her life working for.

Women candidates typically beat their way to Dawn's door—both for blessing and for support—and she gives it. Jan Schakowsky, now a member of the U.S. Congress, says that Dawn was a role model for her and that she goes to her for advice: "She's been a very good friend and very supportive, a rock there for me. . . . Women all go ask her advice. . . . And at all the women's events I go to, Dawn is there, and she is acknowledged, because she still is an important player. You just say her name and the whole place erupts."[39] Lisa Madigan, who may be the next woman to run for governor of Illinois, came to see Dawn before the general election in 2002, even though Dawn had supported her old friend John Schmidt, who opposed Madigan in the primary election for attorney general. Dawn not only supported her by giving advice based on her personal experience but also served on Madigan's transition committee after she won.

When Dawn Netsch entered the Illinois Senate in 1973, there were three women there and eight women in the house. By 2008 (before the

November election), there were thirteen women in the state senate and thirty-five in the house, as well as three representing Illinois in the U.S. House of Representatives.[40] The women who have followed her path know that they owe her a debt of gratitude. Cindi Canary has perhaps stated this best:

> [Dawn] will continue to have a strong influence on the policy debate that's going on even if she is not at the center of the stage, because her voice is heard through those of us she has mentored. Her voice is continuing to resonate. . . . She has really shared of herself, particularly to younger women, and has planted the seeds and confidence for another generation of women who share similar values to learn how to speak out and be strong in a process that can be a bit of a bloodbath.[41]

The same may be said for the men Dawn has brought into the political process or mentored there, like Paul Vallas and others. Virtually everyone who has worked for Dawn has continued to be involved in politics and government, including those who worked in her frustrating campaign for governor.

What is striking about this political life is its consistency. People who have known Dawn for a long time say that she is the same today as she was fifty years ago. She continues to fight for reforms she believes are important, such as merit selection, campaign reform, tax reform, and adequate funding for education, despite repeated defeats. She really just never gives up.

ACKNOWLEDGMENTS

So many thanks are due to all those who helped in the creation of this book. First and most especially, I thank Dawn Clark Netsch. Although a very private person, Dawn opened up her life and all her papers to me without any restrictions other than her insistence on accuracy. Despite her reluctance to be the subject of a biography, it has been a wonderful collaboration. I am grateful also to the numerous people—almost sixty of them—who allowed me to interview them for this project. Not a single person declined my request for an interview. The universal response was one of pleasure at being asked, no matter how busy they were. The names of all those who answered this call are listed in the bibliography.

Credit is due to Len Rubinowitz, Wendy Cohen, and Karen Shields, who came up with the idea for a biography of Dawn Clark Netsch and persisted in their conviction that one should be written until author, publisher, and funds were found to turn their idea into reality. Those who contributed financially to this project include Wendy Cohen; Richard D. Cudahy; Kappy Laing; Karen Shields; the Northwestern Alumnae Association, who gave me a seed grant; and Walter Netsch, who supported the travel and personnel necessary to complete it.

I would also like to thank the two institutions that supported me while I researched and wrote this biography. Northwestern University School of Law provided me with research assistants over a two-year period and with grants to do summer research, as well as able assistance from librarians and other staff. Specifically, I thank John Lanham, David Kraut, and Tehseen Ahmed for their excellent research assistance, which extended in some cases to making their way through disorganized files both in Chicago and in Springfield and to interviewing some of the cast of characters. My faculty assistant at Northwestern, Tim Jacobs, was exceptionally helpful in ways too numerous to list here. Marcia Lehr, my library liaison while at Northwestern, was incredibly supportive and resourceful in tracking down sources that were not always easy to locate. I also thank Cornell Law School, which has enthusiastically supported this project since I moved there in 2007. Julie Jones of the Cornell Law Library did amazing detective work to find obscure sources. My faculty assistant Anne Cahanin transcribed interviews, scanned photos, and helped in numerous other ways. Rebecca Vernon's research assistance in the summer and fall of 2008 and fall of 2009 is also much appreciated. I am also grateful for Sheri Englund's expert editing.

And, as always, thanks are due to Ben Altman, whose continuing support of me and my many and varied projects is of inestimable value.

NOTES

Preface
1. Michael Holland, interview by Cynthia Bowman, Dec. 28, 2006.

Chapter 1: Growing Up in Cincinnati
1. According to the 1928 U.S. Statistical Abstract, Table 39, the estimated 1927 Cincinnati population was 412,200. For information about the greater Cincinnati area, see Henry Graff, "Cincinnati Profile," in *Cincinnati: A Guide to the Queen City and Its Neighbors* (Cincinnati, Ohio: Wiesen-Hart Press, 1943), xix.

2. Graff, *Cincinnati*, 39, xxi–xxii.

3. Ibid., xix–xx. A talented writer, Henry Graff later became a prominent American historian at Columbia University.

4. Dawn Clark Netsch, interview by Cynthia Bowman, May 2, 2006. Unless otherwise identified, information in this chapter relies on this May 2 interview.

5. Newspaper clipping, courtesy of Keith Clark, Carson City, Nevada.

6. Netsch, interview, May 2, 2006.

7. Dawn Clark Netsch, interview by Cynthia Bowman, Aug. 4, 2006.

8. Keith Clark Jr., interview by Cynthia Bowman, Aug. 2, 2006.

9. Ibid., Aug. 2, 2006.

10. Graff, *Cincinnati*, 305.

11. Robert McGrath, interview by Cynthia Bowman, Aug. 7, 2006.

12. *Et Cetera*, Feb. 23, 1944, Netsch Papers.

13. "Foxhole, Inc., to Open Soon as Canteen for Teen-Agers," n.d., unidentified newspaper article, Netsch Papers.

14. Robert A. Burnham, "The Cincinnati Charter Revolt of 1924: Creating City Government for a Pluralistic Society," in *Ethnic Diversity and Civic Identity: Patterns of Conflict and Cohesion in Cincinnati since 1820*, ed. Henry D. Shapiro and Jonathan D. Sarna (Urbana: University of Illinois Press, 1992), 202.

15. Murray Seasongood, *Local Government in the United States: A Challenge and an Opportunity* (Cambridge, Mass.: Harvard University Press, 1933), 16–19. Seasongood was a participant in the events he describes and later mayor of Cincinnati.

16. Burnham, "Cincinnati Charter Revolt," 203–4, 213.

Chapter 2: Northwestern University
1. Robert McGrath, interview by Cynthia Bowman, Aug. 7, 2006.

2. Dawn Clark Netsch, interview by Cynthia Bowman, May 10, 2006. Unless otherwise identified, information in this chapter is from this interview.

3. Frances Eschbach Kinney, interview by Cynthia Bowman, June 15, 2006.

4. Harold F. Williamson and Payson S. Wild, *Northwestern University: A History 1850–1975* (Evanston, Ill.: Northwestern University, 1976), 211, 242–43.

5. Melville J. Herskovits, "The Social Science Units of the Northwestern University Liberal Arts Program," *Journal of General Education* 1 (1947): 216–20.

6. Wendy Leopold, "Herskovits: A Leader in Study of African Heritage," *Northwestern Observer,* Oct. 23, 1995, 3; Leopold, "Perspectives on the Beginning," *Program of African Studies News and Events* 8.3 (Spring 1998): 2; *Northwestern Perspective* 9.3 (Spring 1996): 14.

7. Carla Reiter, "Visionary of Africa," *Northwestern Perspective* 9, no. 3 (Spring 1996): 15–17.

8. Quoted in Reiter, "Visionary of Africa," 15.

9. Jean F. Herskovits, "Remarks at the Celebration of the Centenary of the Birth of Melville J. Herskovits, Northwestern University," Oct. 26, 1995, Netsch Papers.

10. Quoted in Jennifer Liss, "NU Celebrates African Studies Program Founder," *Daily Northwestern,* Oct. 27, 1995, 5.

11. *Daily Northwestern,* Oct. 10, 1945, 1; Apr. 4, 1946, 1; Apr. 10, 1946, 1.

12. Williamson and Wild, *Northwestern University,* 238–39.

13. *Daily Northwestern,* Jan. 24, 1947, 4.

14. *Daily Northwestern,* Jan. 28, 1947, 4; Jan. 29, 1947, 2; Jan. 30, 1947, 4.

15. "Quibblers Club Takes Stand on Negro Housing Policy," *Daily Northwestern,* Feb. 5, 1947, 2.

16. "Does Quota Exist Here?" *Daily Northwestern,* Feb. 6, 1947, 4.

17. "SGB: Act on Housing Now," *Daily Northwestern,* Feb. 12, 1947, 1; "Housing Petition Is Student Weapon," *Daily Northwestern,* Feb. 12, 1947, 2.

18. "Dean Defends School Policy on Housing," *Daily Northwestern,* Feb. 14, 1947, 1, 3.

19. "IHC to Launch Poll on Housing," *Daily Northwestern,* Feb. 13, 1947, 1.

20. Jim Davis, "NU Housing Poll Draws 'Color-Line,'" *Daily Northwestern,* Feb. 20, 1947, 1, 2.

21. "SGB Modified Negro Housing Stand," *Daily Northwestern,* Feb. 21, 1947, 1, 3.

22. "Poll: 58 Per Cent for Open House," *Daily Northwestern,* Feb. 21, 1947, 4.

23. "University Supports Plan for International House," *Daily Northwestern,* May 6, 1947, 4; "NU Buying Int'l House Residence," *Daily Northwestern,* July 18, 1947, 1.

24. "International House Opens for 16 Women Students," *Daily Northwestern,* Sept. 30, 1947, 5.

25. "Snyder Denies That Race Problem Exists at NU," *Daily Northwestern,* Mar. 31, 1948, 1.

26. Gunnar Myrdal, *An American Dilemma: The Negro Problem and Modern Democracy* (New York: Harper, 1944); Junfu Zhang, "Black-White Relations: The American Dilemma," *Perspectives* 1, no. 4 (Feb. 29, 2000), available at http://www.oycf.org/; Ralph Ellison, *"An American Dilemma:* A Review" (1944), in *Shadow and Act* (New York: Random House, 1953), 303–17.

27. Dawn Clark, paper on *An American Dilemma* [1947 or 1948], Netsch Papers.

28. "UNO Outlines Procedure," *Daily Northwestern,* Feb. 8, 1946, 2.

29. See Williamson and Wild, *Northwestern University,* 244; "Senator Talks to Final UN Session," *Daily Northwestern,* Apr. 26, 1946, 1; "World Recognizes Problems: Bunche," *Daily Northwestern,* Apr. 26, 1946, 2.

30. "Houses Will Represent 66 United Nations," *Daily Northwestern*, Jan. 29, 1946, 1.

31. "Campaign to Begin for UNO," *Daily Northwestern*, Feb. 6, 1946, 1; "UNO Elects Haiman Chairman," *Daily Northwestern*, Feb. 13, 1946, 1.

32. "Pan-American, Small Nations Form UNO Blocs," *Daily Northwestern*, Feb. 12, 1946, 1.

33. "UNO Member Nations Will Air Problems at General Assembly," *Daily Northwestern*, Feb. 26, 1946, 1, 3.

34. "Mock UN Votes Eventual Federal World Government," *Daily Northwestern*, Apr. 26, 1946, 2.

35. Eugene G. Schwartz, *American Students Organize: Founding the National Student Association After World War II* (Westport, Conn.: Praeger, 2006), 135.

36. The Constitution of the U.S. National Student Association, bylaws I and II, in *American Students Organize*, 1110.

37. Schwartz, *American Students Organize*, 195.

38. *Daily Northwestern*, Mar. 2, 1948, 4.

39. George Likeness, "MPC Chairman's Duties Are Listed," *Daily Northwestern*, Apr. 2, 1948, 2.

40. George Likeness, "MacArthur Backers Organize," *Daily Northwestern*, Apr. 14, 1948, 1.

41. "MPC Heads Deny Illegal Nomination," *Daily Northwestern*, Apr. 16, 1948, 1.

42. George Likeness, "Houses Form MPC Bloc for Honest Campaign," *Daily Northwestern*, Apr. 15, 1948, 1.

43. George Likeness, "Eight-House Power Bloc Disintegrates," *Daily Northwestern*, Apr. 20, 1948, 1.

44. *Daily Northwestern*, Apr. 16, 1948, 1.

45. George Likeness, "MPC Board Refuses to Move Stassen Talk," *Daily Northwestern*, Apr. 21, 1948, 1.

46. "Mock Convention Opens Tonight," *Daily Northwestern*, Apr. 23, 1948, 1.

47. George Likeness, "Time Forces Stassen, Vandenberg Deadlock," *Daily Northwestern*, Apr. 27, 1948, 1.

48. "Flexible Deadline Would Have Helped," *Daily Northwestern*, Apr. 27, 1948.

49. Quoted in "Dawn Clark Relaxes After MPC Weekend," *Daily Northwestern*, Apr. 23, 1948, 1.

50. Werner W. Schroeder to Dawn Clark, June 2, 1948, Netsch Papers.

Chapter 3: The Law

1. Scott W. Lucas to Kenneth Colegrove, May 26, 1948, Netsch Papers; Kenneth Colegrove to Elbert D. Thomas, May 15, 1948, Netsch Papers; Kenneth Colegrove to Scott W. Lucas, May 15, 1948, Netsch Papers.

2. Kenneth Colegrove to Dawn Clark, May 14, 1948, Netsch Papers.

3. Kenneth Colegrove to Anna Lord Straus, May 15, 1948, Netsch Papers.

4. Kay J. Maxwell, *The League of Women Voters Through the Decades*, available at http://www.lwv.org/.

5. Dawn Clark Netsch, interview with Cynthia Bowman, June 16, 2006.

6. Dawn Clark to Jo Abraham and Herbert Abraham, Dec. 18, 1948, Netsch Papers.

7. Stevenson-for-Governor Committee to Dawn Clark, Nov. 8, 1948, Netsch Papers.

8. Adlai E. Stevenson to Dawn Clark, Nov. 8, 1948, Netsch Papers.

9. Dawn Clark to Paul H. Douglas, Nov. 6, 1948, Netsch Papers.

10. Paul H. Douglas to Dawn Clark, Nov. 19, 1948, Netsch Papers.

11. Dawn Clark to Jo Abraham and Herbert Abraham, Dec. 18, 1948, Netsch Papers.

12. Jo Abraham to Dawn Clark, Dec. 21, 1948, Netsch Papers.

13. Dawn Clark to Jo Abraham and Herbert Abraham, Dec. 18, 1948, Netsch Papers.

14. Harold C. Havighurst to Dawn Clark, Mar. 14, 1949, Netsch Papers.

15. Dawn Clark to Harold C. Havighurst, Mar. 30, 1949, Netsch Papers.

16. Dawn Clark Netsch, interview by Cynthia Bowman, June 26, 2006.

17. Harold Shapiro, interview by Joe Harper, Jan. 22, 2005, transcript in possession of author.

18. Jack Coons, interview by Cynthia Bowman, Aug. 1, 2006.

19. Ibid.

20. "Dawn Clark Top Freshman Scholar," *Northwestern Reporter* 4 (May 1951): 3.

21. James J. Richards, interview by Cynthia Bowman, July 28, 2006.

22. Coons interview, Aug. 1, 2006.

23. See, e.g., Karen Berger Morello, *The Invisible Bar: The Woman Lawyer in America: 1638 to the Present* (Boston: Beacon Press, 1986), 100–105; Cynthia Fuchs Epstein, *Women in Law,* 2nd ed. (Urbana: University of Illinois Press, 1993), 60–70.

24. Willard Wirtz, interview by Cynthia Bowman, Nov. 4, 2006.

25. Marilyn Coons, interview by Cynthia Bowman, Aug. 1, 2006.

26. Dawn Clark Netsch, interview by Cynthia Bowman, June 22, 2006.

27. Dawn Clark, report concerning Greyhound post houses, Netsch Papers.

28. Netsch interview, June 16, 2006.

29. Richards interview, July 28, 2006.

30. Netsch interview, June 16, 2006.

31. Coons interview, Aug. 1, 2006.

32. Netsch interview, June 22, 2006.

33. Shapiro interview, Jan. 22, 2005.

34. Netsch interview, June 26, 2006.

35. Dawn Clark Netsch and Harold D. Shapiro, "100 Years and Counting," *Northwestern University Law Review* 100 (2006): 1.

Chapter 4: Adlai Stevenson, 1952

1. John G. Laylin to Dawn Clark, Dec. 18, 1951, Netsch Papers; Dawn Clark to John G. Laylin, Jan. 3, 1952, Netsch Papers.

2. John G. Laylin to Dawn Clark, Jan. 7, 1952, Netsch Papers.

3. Dawn Clark to John G. Laylin, Mar. 1, 1952, Netsch Papers.

4. Edward Burling Jr. to Dawn Clark, Mar. 14, 1952, Netsch Papers.

5. For detailed information about Adlai E. Stevenson I, see Jean H. Baker, *The Stevensons: A Biography of an American Family* (New York: W. W. Norton, 1996), 86–181.

6. John Bartlow Martin, *Adlai Stevenson* (New York: Harper & Brothers, 1952), 38.

7. Porter McKeever, *Adlai Stevenson: His Life and Legacy; A Biography* (New York: William Morrow, 1989), 19.

8. Martin, *Adlai Stevenson*, 39; McKeever, *Adlai Stevenson*, 24.

9. McKeever, *Adlai Stevenson*, 44–45.

10. See McKeever, *Adlai Stevenson*, 62–64, 72–106.

11. Ibid., 119–20.

12. Ibid., 130–31, 146–47, 171.

13. Ibid., 128–30.

14. Ibid., 150–68.

15. Ibid., 134–37, 156–57.

16. Quoted in McKeever, *Adlai Stevenson*, 171.

17. Jerry N. Hess, "Oral History Interview with Judge Carl McGowan, July 27, 1970," Harry S. Truman Library and Museum, 12–17, available at http://www.trumanlibrary.org/.

18. McKeever, *Adlai Stevenson*, 194–95.

19. Adlai E. Stevenson, *Major Campaign Speeches of Adlai E. Stevenson, 1952* (New York: Random House, 1953), 10.

20. McKeever, *Adlai Stevenson*, 263.

21. Ibid., 212. *Major Campaign Speeches of Adlai E. Stevenson, 1952* was No. 12 on the *New York Times* nonfiction best-seller list on August 30, 1953, and had been on the list for nineteen weeks.

22. Martin, *Adlai Stevenson*.

23. Dawn Clark Netsch, interview by Cynthia Bowman, June 28, 2006.

24. Connie Chadwell Koch, interview by Cynthia Bowman, Jan. 4, 2007.

25. Stevenson 1956 campaign materials described in this section are found in Netsch Papers.

26. Herman Wouk, "Why I Switched to Stevenson" (campaign literature, unpublished), Netsch Papers.

27. Adlai Stevenson, *Speeches of Adlai Stevenson*, with a foreword by John Steinbeck and a brief biography of Adlai Stevenson by Debs Myers and Ralph Martin (New York: Random House, 1952).

28. McKeever, *Adlai Stevenson*, 210.

29. Volunteers for Stevenson, "Throw a Party!" Netsch Papers.

30. Volunteers for Stevenson, "Why We're Volunteers for Stevenson," Netsch Papers.

31. Stevenson, *Major Campaign Speeches*, 311–12.

32. McKeever, *Adlai Stevenson*, 256–57.

33. Ibid., 262.

34. Netsch interview, June 28, 2006.

35. Willard Wirtz, interview by Cynthia Bowman, Nov. 4, 2006.

36. Debs Myers to Dawn Clark, postmarked Jan. 29, 1953, Netsch Papers.

Chapter 5: Covington & Burling, 1952–1954

1. Karen Berger Morello, *The Invisible Bar: The Woman Lawyer in America, 1638 to the Present* (Boston: Beacon Press, 1986), 203–4.

2. Erwin O. Smigel, *The Wall Street Lawyer: Professional Organization Man?* (New York: Free Press, 1964), 46–47.

3. See, e.g., Judith S. Kaye, "Women Lawyers in Big Firms: A Study in Progress Toward Gender Equality," *Fordham Law Review* 57 (1988): 112n6.

4. Dawn Bradley Berry, *The 50 Most Influential Women in American Law* (Los Angeles: RGA Publishing, 1996), 215; Morello, *Invisible Bar,* 207.

5. Berry, *50 Most Influential Women,* 265 (Ferraro, Reno); Judith Richards Hope, *Pinstripes and Pearls: The Women of the Harvard Law School Class of '64 Who Forged an Old-Girl Network and Paved the Way for Future Generations* (New York: Scribner, 2003), 155, 175 (Schroeder, Dole).

6. Kaye, "Women Lawyers in Big Firms," 112n6.

7. Howard Kane, interview by Cynthia Bowman, June 28, 2006.

8. Howard C. Westwood, *Covington & Burling, 1919–1984* (Washington, D.C.: Covington & Burling, 1986), 161–62.

9. Virginia Watkin, interview by Cynthia Bowman, Nov. 4, 2006.

10. Ibid.

11. Dawn Clark Netsch, interview by Cynthia Bowman, June 28, 2006.

12. Dalehite v. United States, 346 U.S. 15, 42 (1953).

13. University of Texas, "Texas City Disaster," The Handbook of Texas Online, available at http://www.tshaonline.org/index.html.

14. Watkin interview, Nov. 4, 2006.

15. Dawn Clark Netsch, interview by Cynthia Bowman, July 7, 2006.

16. Alicia J. Campi, Immigration Policy Center, "The McCarran-Walter Act: A Contradictory Legacy on Race, Quotas, and Ideology," June 2004, available at http://www.immigrationpolicy.org/index.php?content=pr0604.

17. Netsch interview, July 7, 2006.

18. Netsch interview, June 28, 2006.

19. Netsch interview, July 7, 2006.

20. Mrs. R. L. Remke to Dawn Clark, June 7, 1954, Netsch Papers.

21. Netsch interview, June 28, 2006.

22. Ibid.

23. Harold Shapiro to Dawn Clark, Feb. 12, 1953, Netsch Papers.

24. Dawn Clark Netsch, interview by Cynthia Bowman, June 26, 2008.

Chapter 6: Back to Chicago and the Committee on Illinois Government

1. Joseph C. Goulden, *The Benchwarmers: The Private World of the Powerful Federal Judges* (New York: Weybright & Talley, 1974), 117–18.

2. James D. Nowlan, *Glory, Darkness, Light: A History of the Union League Club of Chicago* (Evanston, Ill.: Northwestern University Press, 2004), 101–8.

3. Daniel Walker, *Rights in Conflict: Chicago's Seven Brutal Days, A Report to the National Commission on the Causes and Prevention of Violence* (New York: Grosset & Dunlap, 1968), ix.

4. See John Schultz, *The Chicago Conspiracy Trial* (New York: Da Capo Press, 1993), 60–80.

5. United States v. Dellinger, 472 F.2d 340, 386 (7th Cir. 1972). The contempt citations were reversed in *In re* Dellinger, 461 F.2d 389 (7th Cir. 1972).

6. Dawn Clark Netsch, interview by Cynthia Bowman, July 7, 2006.

7. Ibid.

8. Jim Otis, interview by Cynthia Bowman, July 21–22, 2006.

9. Committee on Illinois Government, *The Stratton Record: A Look at the Facts,* June 1954, Netsch Papers.

10. Walter P. Dahl to Members of the Committee on Illinois Government, memorandum, Oct. 5, 1954, Netsch Papers.

11. Committee on Illinois Government, "A Definitive Outline," Netsch Papers.

12. George Thiem, *The Hodge Scandal* (New York: St. Martin's Press, 1963).

13. Otis interview, July 21–22, 2006.

14. James W. Clement, memorandum, Oct. 1, 1956, Netsch Papers.

15. Committee on Illinois Government, "Proposals for Changes in State Government Growing out of the Hodge Scandal," Oct. 20, 1956, Netsch Papers.

16. Abner Mikva, interview by Cynthia Bowman, June 19, 2006.

17. Dawn Clark, "Mental Health Fund," July 12, 1956, Netsch Papers; "Tinley Park State Hospital," Aug. 14, 1956, Netsch Papers; "Community Level Mental Health Services," Aug. 16, 1956, Netsch Papers; "Personnel," Sept. 5, 1956, Netsch Papers.

18. "Paschen Hits Stratton on Mental Care," *Chicago Daily News,* May 1, 1956; George Tagge, "Sachs, Wright Meet and Talk Rebel Politics," *Chicago Daily Tribune,* May 2, 1956.

19. Fred K. Hoehler to Dawn Clark, Aug. 8, 1958, Netsch Papers; Howard R. Sacks to Jim Clement, memo, redirected to "Miss P. Dawn Clark," Aug. 8, 1958, Netsch Papers.

20. Committee on Illinois Government, *A Democratic Challenge* (pamphlet, 1958), 3–7, Netsch Papers.

21. Dawn Clark Netsch, interview by Cynthia Bowman, July 12, 2006.

22. Reproduction by author of original invitation in Netsch Papers.

23. Jim Alter, interview by Cynthia Bowman, June 28, 2006.

24. Nancy Stevenson, interview by Cynthia Bowman, July 6, 2006.

25. Adlai Stevenson III, interview by Cynthia Bowman, July 6, 2006.

Chapter 7: Starting to Take On the Machine

1. Willard Wirtz, interview by Cynthia Bowman, Nov. 4, 2006.

2. Porter McKeever, *Adlai Stevenson: His Life and Legacy: A Biography* (New York: William Morrow, 1989), 379–80.

3. Dawn Clark Netsch, interview by Cynthia Bowman, June 28, 2006.

4. Dawn Clark Netsch, interview by Cynthia Bowman, July 12, 2006.

5. Dawn Clark Netsch, interview by Cynthia Bowman, July 7, 2006.

6. Stevenson 1956 campaign materials described in this section are found in Netsch Papers.

7. Dawn Clark to Ken Hechler, telegram, Oct. 28, 1956, Netsch Papers.

8. Netsch interview, June 28, 2006.

9. Ibid.

10. Netsch interview, July 7, 2006.

11. Netsch interview, June 28, 2006.

12. Netsch interview, July 7, 2006.

13. Joseph R. Julin to E. W. Tatge, Dec. 6, 1956, Netsch Papers; E. W. Tatge to Joseph R. Julin, Dec. 10, 1956, Netsch Papers.

14. William L. Cary to Dawn Clark, Dec. 17, 1956, Netsch Papers.

15. Netsch interview, July 7, 2006.

16. Richard Rhodes, interview by Cynthia Bowman, June 20, 2006.

17. Dave Nelson, quoted in Rhodes interview, June 20, 2006.

18. See "Market Power and the Antitrust Laws: 'New' Old Section 7 of the Clayton Act," *Yale Law Journal* 66 (July 1957): 1251–66.

19. Rhodes interview, June 20, 2006.

20. Netsch interview, July 7, 2006.

21. Ibid.

22. Schiller-Banks Democratic Club Constitution, draft, Netsch Papers.

23. "Mrs. Roosevelt, Sen. Gore Speakers for DFI Convention May 23–24," *Illinois Democrat,* Apr. 1958, Netsch Papers.

24. Walter Netsch, interview by Cynthia Bowman, Dec. 19, 2005.

25. Edward Schreiber, "'Paddy' Runs Scared in 43d Race," *Chicago Tribune,* sec. 1, Feb. 2, 1959.

26. Edward Schreiber, "Paddy's Foe: A Social Registerite," *Chicago Tribune,* sec. 1, Jan. 16, 1959.

27. Schreiber, "'Paddy' Runs Scared."

28. Editorial, "City Needs Men like Fisher," *Chicago Daily News,* Feb. 10, 1959.

29. McKeever, *Adlai Stevenson,* 438–52.

30. Jim Alter, interview by Cynthia Bowman, June 28, 2006.

31. Dawn Clark Netsch, interview by Cynthia Bowman, July 17, 2006.

32. Ibid.

33. Ibid.

34. Bill Barnhart and Gene Schlickman, *Kerner: The Conflict of Intangible Rights* (Urbana: University of Illinois Press, 1999), 113.

35. Netsch interview, July 12, 2006.

Chapter 8: Springfield and Governor Kerner

1. See John M. Allswang, *A House for All Peoples: Ethnic Politics in Chicago, 1890–1936* (Lexington: University Press of Kentucky, 1971); Alex Gottfried, *Boss Cermak of Chicago: A Study of Political Leadership* (Seattle: University of Washington Press, 1962).

2. Bill Barnhart and Gene Schlickman, *Kerner: The Conflict of Intangible Rights* (Urbana: University of Illinois Press, 1999), 25, 38, 43, 60.

3. Ibid., 99.

4. Ibid., 108.

5. Ibid., 110.

6. Dawn Clark Netsch, interview by Cynthia Bowman, July 14, 2006.

7. Dawn Clark Netsch, interview by Cynthia Bowman, July 20, 2006.

8. Barnhart and Schlickman, *Kerner,* 127–28.

9. Ibid., 130.

10. Dawn Clark Netsch, interview by Cynthia Bowman, July 27, 2006.

11. Barnhart and Schlickman, *Kerner,* 109, 125.

12. Ibid., 133.

13. Ibid., 125–26.

14. Netsch interview, July 20, 2006.

15. Jim Otis, interview by Cynthia Bowman, July 21–22, 2006.

16. Hon. James B. Moran, interview by Cynthia Bowman, July 11, 2006.

17. Otis interview, July 21–22, 2006.

18. Moran interview, July 11, 2006.

19. Illinois Veto Messages, 73rd Biennium (1963), 73–74 (Senate Bill 1753, Aug. 30, 1963), papers in personal collection of James Otis. See also D. J. R. Burckner, "Teamsters Endorse Kerner, End Holdout," *Chicago Sun-Times,* Oct. 10, 1964.

20. Otis interview, July 21–22, 2006.

21. Netsch interview, July 14, 2006.

22. Barnhart and Schlickman, *Kerner,* 141.

23. Ibid., 152, 143.

24. Otis interview, July 21–22, 2006.

25. Netsch interview, July 14, 2006.

26. The facts about the charges against Otto Kerner, though contested at trial, are taken from the Seventh Circuit opinion affirming his conviction. United States v. Isaacs, 493 F.2d 1124 (7th Cir. 1974). For more detail and information about conflicting versions, see Barnhart and Schlickman, *Kerner,* 262–327; Hank Messick, *The Politics of Prosecution: Jim Thompson, Marje Everett, Richard Nixon and the Trial of Otto Kerner* (Ottawa, Ill.: Caroline House Books, 1978).

27. Netsch interview, July 14, 2006.

28. Dawn Clark Netsch, character affidavit on behalf of Otto Kerner, deceased, Oct. 17, 2000, Netsch Papers.

Chapter 9: Walter Netsch

1. Nancy Stevenson, interview by Cynthia Bowman, July 6, 2006.

2. The information about Walter Netsch's life is taken from interviews with both Dawn Clark Netsch (multiple interviews by Cynthia Bowman) and Walter Netsch (one interview by Cynthia Bowman, Dec. 19, 2005, and one by Peter Matuszek, Jan. 22, 2005), as well as from Betty J. Blum, "Oral History of Walter Netsch," Department of Architecture, Art Institute of Chicago (1997), available at http://digital-libraries.saic .edu/; Northwestern University Library, *Walter A. Netsch, FAIA: A Critical Appreciation and Sourcebook* (Evanston, Ill.: Northwestern University Press, 1998).

3. See "Air Force Academy Chapel," http://www.greatbuildings.com/.

4. Martin Felsen and Sarah Dunn, "Field Theory: Walter Netsch's Design Methodology," in *FAIA: A Critical Appreciation and Sourcebook* (Evanston, Ill.: Northwestern University Press, 1998), 73–78.

5. Dawn Clark Netsch, interview by Cynthia Bowman, July 27, 2006.

6. Dawn Clark Netsch, interview by Cynthia Bowman, July 17, 2006.

7. Walter Netsch, interview by Peter Matuszek, Jan. 22, 2005, transcript in possession of author.

8. Walter Netsch, interview by Cynthia Bowman, Dec. 19, 2005.

9. Netsch interview, July 17, 2006.

10. Kay Clement, interview by Cynthia Bowman, June 29, 2006.

11. Jim Otis, interview by Cynthia Bowman, July 21–22, 2006.

12. Description of the around-the-world trip is drawn from Dawn Clark Netsch, interview by Cynthia Bowman, Oct. 8, 2007.

Chapter 10: Teaching Law

1. Herma Hill Kay, "The Future of Women Law Professors," *Iowa Law Review* 77 (1991): 8–12.

2. Jack Heinz, interview by Cynthia Bowman, June 4, 2007.

3. Dawn Clark Netsch, interview by Cynthia Bowman, July 28, 2006.

4. Jack Coons, interview by Cynthia Bowman, Aug. 1, 2006.

5. Daniel R. Mandelker, Dawn Clark Netsch, Peter W. Salsich Jr., Judith Welch Wegner, Sandra M. Stevenson, and Janice C. Griffith, *State and Local Government in a Federal System*, 6th ed. (Newark, N.J.: Matthew Bender, 2006).

6. Dawn Clark Netsch, interview by an unidentified Northwestern law student supervised by Professor Leonard Rubinowitz (2005), transcript in possession of author.

7. Joyce A. Hughes, "Dawn Clark Netsch" (unpublished), July 12, 2006, in possession of author.

8. This document and other Committee on Illinois Government documents described in this paragraph are found in Netsch Papers.

9. Jay Miller, interview by Cynthia Bowman, June 20, 2007.

10. Dawn Clark Netsch, interview by Cynthia Bowman, July 13, 2007.

11. Leslie J. Reagan, *When Abortion Was a Crime: Women, Medicine, and Law in the United States, 1867–1973* (Berkeley: University of California Press, 1997), 237.

12. Doe v. Scott, 321 F. Supp. 1385, 1388 (N.D. Ill. 1971).

13. Alexander Polikoff, *Waiting for Gautreaux: A Story of Segregation, Housing, and the Black Ghetto* (Evanston, Ill.: Northwestern University Press, 2006); Leonard S. Rubinowitz and James E. Rosenbaum, *Crossing the Class and Color Lines* (Chicago: University of Chicago Press, 2000).

14. Netsch interview, July 13, 2007.

15. See Philippa Strum, *When the Nazis Came to Skokie: Freedom for Speech We Hate* (Lawrence: University Press of Kansas, 1999).

16. Information about the early years of the Leadership Council of Metropolitan Open Communities is based on Aurie Pennick, interview by Cynthia Bowman, Jan. 8, 2007.

17. Village of Arlington Heights v. Metropolitan Housing Development Corp., 429 U.S. 252 (1977).

18. Dawn Clark Netsch, interview by Cynthia Bowman, Jan. 10, 2007.

19. Jeri S. Dodson, "She Speaks Her Mind," *Decatur Herald and Review*, sec. 3, Aug. 23, 1970.

20. Dawn Clark Netsch, interview by unidentified Northwestern law student, 2005.

Chapter 11: Con Con

1. James Banovetz and Thomas Kelty, "Illinois Home Rule and Taxation: A New Approach to Local Government Enabling Authority," *Northern Illinois University Law Review* 8 (1988): 709n2.

2. State of Illinois, Report of the Constitution Study Commission (created by the 74th General Assembly), Feb. 1967, 10, Netsch Papers.

3. State of Illinois, Constitution Study Commission, "Illinois Constitutional Revision: A Bibliography" (unpublished, Nov. 1968).

4. George D. Braden and Rubin G. Cohn, *The Illinois Constitution: An Annotated and Comparative Analysis, Prepared for the Illinois Constitution Study Commission* (Urbana: Institute of Government and Public Affairs, University of Illinois, 1969).

5. Joseph P. Pisciotte, "How Illinois Did It," *National Civic Review* 58, no. 7 (1969): 291–96. See also Elmer Gertz and Joseph P. Pisciotte, *Charter for a New Age: An Inside View of the Sixth Illinois Constitutional Convention* (Urbana: University of Illinois Press, 1980), 22–35; Samuel K. Gove and Thomas R. Kitsos, *Revision Success: The Sixth Illinois Constitutional Convention* (New York: National Municipal League, 1974), 14–19.

6. Dawn Clark Netsch, notes for speeches about Con Con, Netsch Papers.

7. Samuel K. Gove and Victoria Ranney, eds., *Con-Con: Issues for the Illinois Constitutional Convention: Papers Prepared by the Constitution Research Group* (Urbana: University of Illinois Press, 1970).

8. Dawn Clark Netsch, "The Executive," in Gove and Ranney, *Con-Con*, 148–49.

9. Ibid., 156–67.

10. Ibid., 179–80.

11. See, e.g., Dawn Clark Netsch, "The Governor Shall . . . ," *Chicago Bar Record*, Oct. 1968, 28–36.

12. University of Illinois Bulletin, *The Illinois Constitution: Final Report and Background Papers*, ed. Lois M. Pelekoudas (Urbana, Ill.: Institute of Government and Public Affairs, 1962).

13. Dawn Clark Netsch, interview by Cynthia Bowman, Aug. 11, 2006.

14. Dawn Clark Netsch to George Dunne, June 13, 1969, Netsch Papers.

15. George Dunne to Dawn Clark Netsch, June 13, 1969, Netsch Papers.

16. Dawn Clark Netsch, notes for June 19, 1969, presentation at Democratic Party Headquarters, Netsch Papers.

17. Dawn Clark Netsch, interview by Cynthia Bowman, June 8, 2006.

18. See Weisberg v. Powell, 417 F.2d 388 (7th Cir. 1969).

19. Dawn Clark Netsch, interview by Cynthia Bowman, June 22, 2006.

20. Gove and Kitsos, *Revision Success*, 162.

21. Ibid., 35, 37.

22. Ibid., 170.

23. Gertz and Pisciotte, *Charter for a New Age*, 70.

24. Ibid., 49–52.

25. Gove and Kitsos, *Revision Success*, 60.

26. Samuel W. Witwer, *Con Con Diary: Reflections of Samuel W. Witwer* (Wichita, Kan.: Hugo Wall School of Urban and Public Affairs, Wichita State University, 1997), 16.

27. Jeri S. Dodson, "She Speaks Her Mind," *Decatur Herald and Review*, sec. 3, Aug. 23, 1970.

28. Editorial, *Chicago Tribune*, sec. 1, Jan. 3, 1970.

29. Witwer, *Con Con Diary*, 86–87.

30. Dawn Clark Netsch, interview by Cynthia Bowman, June 16, 2006.

31. Joyce D. Fishbane and Glenn W. Fisher, *Politics of the Purse: Revenue and Finance in the Sixth Illinois Constitutional Convention* (Urbana: University of Illinois Press, 1974), 33–34.

32. Thorpe v. Mahin, 250 N.E.2d 633 (Ill. 1969).

33. Fishbane and Fisher, *Politics of the Purse*, 56–57.

34. Ibid., 59.

35. Ibid., 73.

36. Ibid., 75

37. Ibid., 84.

38. Ibid., 98–99.

39. John M. Karns Jr. and Dawn Clark Netsch, Sixth Illinois Constitutional Convention, Committee on Revenue and Finance Proposal No. 2, *Report of the Committee on Revenue and Finance Supporting Recommended Revenue Article Including Dissenting Statements and Minority Proposals*, June 16, 1970, i, Netsch Papers.

40. Ibid., 68.

41. Fishbane and Fisher, *Politics of the Purse*, 111.

42. Client Follow-Up Co. v. Hynes, 390 N.E.2d 847 (Ill. 1979).

43. Gove and Kitsos, *Revision Success*, 118.

44. Gertz and Pisciotte, *Charter for a New Age*, 98.

45. Ibid., 100; Witwer, *Con Con Diary*, 16, 106.

46. Witwer, *Con Con Diary*, 258–59.

47. Ann Lousin, interview by Cynthia Bowman, June 23, 2006.

48. Netsch interview, June 8, 2006.

49. Witwer, *Con Con Diary*, 256, 268, 273.

50. Netsch interview, June 8, 2006.

51. Witwer, *Con Con Diary*, 333.

52. Gertz and Pisciotte, *Charter for a New Age*, 314–15.

53. Illinois General Assembly, Legislative Research Unit, Sixth Illinois Constitutional Convention, *Record of Proceedings*, vol. 2, *December 8, 1969–September 3, 1970*, 4669–70.

54. "Address to the People," Netsch Papers.

55. Dawn Clark Netsch, notes for explanatory talk on 1970 constitution, Sept. 9, 1970, Netsch Papers.

56. Dawn Clark Netsch to Dear Friend, Nov. 1970, Netsch Papers.

57. The speech to the Law Club and other speeches given by Dawn Clark Netsch during the campaign to pass the 1970 constitution are found in Netsch Papers.

58. Dawn Clark Netsch, interview by Cynthia Bowman, June 22, 2006.

59. Netsch interview, June 8, 2006.

60. Gove and Kitsos, *Revision Success*, 135.

61. JoAnna M. Watson, "Analysis of the Vote at the Election for the 1970 Illinois Constitution," *Illinois Government* (Feb. 1971): 34; Edward S. Gilbreth, "Cook County Puts It Over!" *Chicago Daily News*, Dec. 16, 1970.

62. Ann Lousin, "The 1970 Illinois Constitution: Has It Made a Difference?" *Northern Illinois University Law Review* 8 (1988): 588.

63. Ibid., 608

64. Ibid., 620; Watson, "Analysis of the Vote," 2–3; Nancy Ford, "From Judicial Election to Merit Selection: A Time for Change in Illinois," *Northern Illinois University Law Review* 8 (1988): 673.

65. Lousin, "1970 Illinois Constitution," 615.

66. See Jack R. Van Der Slik, "Reconsidering the Amendatory Veto for Illinois," *Northern Illinois University Law Review* 8 (1988): 753–77.

Chapter 12: Taking On the Machine, Act 2

1. Dawn Clark Netsch, interview by Cynthia Bowman, Aug. 11, 2006.

2. Daniel Walker, *Rights in Conflict, Report to the National Commission on the Causes and Prevention of Violence* (New York: Grosset, 1968).

3. Dawn Clark Netsch, interview by Cynthia Bowman, July 20, 2006.

4. Ibid.

5. Ibid.

6. Michael Holland, interview by Cynthia Bowman, Dec. 28, 2006.

7. James Houlihan, interview by Cynthia Bowman, July 5, 2006.

8. Houlihan interview, July 5, 2006.

9. Holland interview, Dec. 28, 2006.

10. Netsch interview, Aug. 11, 2006.

11. Ibid.

12. All 1972 Netsch campaign literature described in this section is found in Netsch Papers.

13. Rita McLennon, interview by Cynthia Bowman, June 16, 2007.

14. Netsch interview, Aug. 11, 2006.

15. John Elmer, "CIGs May Win Control of Assembly," *Chicago Tribune*, Mar. 23, 1972.

16. "Mrs. Netsch's Foe Withdraws," *Chicago Tribune*, sec. B, Sept. 21, 1972.

17. McLennon interview, June 16, 2007.

18. "Sen. Netsch Will Seek Reelection," *Chicago Tribune*, Nov. 12, 1973.

19. Henry Hanson, "Netsch vs. Levy Race a Classic," *Chicago Daily News*, Feb. 20, 1974.

20. Leonard Aronson, "'Bossism' Key Issue for Netsch, Levy," *Chicago Today*, Feb. 14, 1974.

21. Hanson, "Netsch vs. Levy."

22. "Have They Lied Enough to Steal the Election from Senator Dawn Clark Netsch?" Netsch Papers.

23. Sheldon Hoffenberg, "Levy Says He's More Independent of Daley Than Netsch Is of Walker," *Lerner Booster*, Feb. 20, 1974.

24. Eleanor Randolph, "It's Sen. Netsch 1, Levy 1 After Round 2 of Slugfest," *Chicago Sun-Times*, Feb. 10, 1974.

25. Ibid.

26. Frank Zahour, "Sen. Netsch Trades Barbs with Levy," *Chicago Tribune*, sec. B, Mar. 11, 1974.

27. Edward S. Gilbreth, "Six Senators Defend Netsch Voting Record," *Chicago Daily News,* Mar. 18, 1974.

28. Edward S. Gilbreth, "Netsch, Levy Battle Dips to 'Lie' Stage," *Chicago Daily News,* Mar. 18, 1974.

29. Thomas Powers, "Massive Security Planned at Polls," *Chicago Tribune,* sec. A, Mar. 18, 1974.

30. Leonard Aronson, "Netsch Survives Daley Assault," *Chicago Today,* Mar. 20, 1974, 14.

31. Michael Sneed, "Chicago Won't Be the Same: Netsch," *Chicago Tribune,* Mar. 20, 1974.

32. Eleanor Randolph, "Sen. Netsch Exults over Beating High-Power Challenge," *Chicago Sun-Times,* Mar. 21, 1974.

33. Burnell Heinecke, "New Force in Senate—They Call Themselves the Crazy 8," *Illinois Issues,* Jan. 1976, 23.

34. Bill Morris, interview by Cynthia Bowman, Dec. 21, 2006.

35. Neil Mehler, "Dem Bloc Angered at Partee 'Secrecy,'" *Chicago Tribune,* Nov. 29, 1974.

36. Morris interview, Dec. 21, 2006.

37. Philip Rock, interview by Cynthia Bowman, Jan. 11, 2007.

38. Press release, Feb. 3, 1977, Netsch Papers.

39. *Chicago Tribune,* sec. B, Feb. 11, 1977.

40. Charles N. Wheeler III, "Souped Up State Senator Soaks 3," *Chicago Sun-Times,* Feb. 16, 1977.

41. Dawn Clark Netsch, interview by Cynthia Bowman, Dec. 22, 2006.

42. John Elmer and William Griffin, "Springfield Picks Up the Pieces," *Chicago Tribune,* sec. A, Feb. 20, 1977.

43. Dawn Clark Netsch, interview by Cynthia Bowman, May 31, 2006.

44. Morris interview, Dec. 21, 2006.

45. David Axelrod, "The Son Also Rises," *Chicago Tribune,* sec. F, Sept. 12, 1982.

46. Dawn Clark Netsch, interview by Cynthia Bowman, Aug. 8, 2006.

47. "Behind the Blizzard of Bills—the Uncommon Seven," *Chicago Tribune,* sec. A, June 22, 1975.

48. Ed McManus, "Young Richie Faces a Fight," *Chicago Tribune,* sec. A, Dec. 9, 1975.

49. Axelrod, *Son Also Rises.*

50. Ibid.

51. Netsch interview, Aug. 8, 2006.

52. Illinois Mental Health and Developmental Disabilities Code, P.A. 80-1414, 405 I.L.C.S. 5/1-100 et seq., effective Jan. 1, 1979.

53. Netsch interview, May 31, 2006.

54. Netsch interview, Aug. 8, 2006.

55. F. Richard Ciccone, "Daley, Independents Playing Ball?" *Chicago Tribune,* Sept. 29, 1977.

Chapter 13: Legislative Losses and Gains

1. Barbara Salins and Frank Zahour, "State Senate OKs Prescription Ads," *Chicago Tribune,* May 17, 1975.

2. Dawn Clark Netsch, interview by Cynthia Bowman, May 31, 2006.

3. Ibid.

4. Dawn Clark Netsch, interview by Cynthia Bowman, Aug. 8, 2006.

5. Bob Creamer, interview by Cynthia Bowman, May 6, 2006.

6. John Schrag and R. Bruce Dodd, "Legislators Clear Utility Reform in Deadline Hustle," *Chicago Tribune,* sec. 1, July 1, 1985.

7. "Bill Would Cut Electric Tariff," *Chicago Tribune,* Mar. 4, 1986.

8. Dawn Clark Netsch, interview by Cynthia Bowman, Oct. 26, 2008.

9. "Ethics Vote on the Record," *Chicago Tribune,* June 29, 1973; "Votes to Remember," *Chicago Tribune,* Mar. 4, 1974.

10. Daniel Egler and Larry Sandler, "Senate OKs Student Test Plan," *Chicago Tribune,* May 27, 1981.

11. Tim Franklin and Daniel Egler, "Elected School Board Bill OK'd," *Chicago Tribune,* May 2, 1987.

12. Illinois Code of Fair Campaign Practices, 10 I.L.C.S. 5/29B-5.

13. Justice Ben F. Overton, "Trial Judges and Political Elections: A Time for Reexamination," *University of Florida Journal of Law and Public Policy* 2 (1988–89): 20; M. L. Henry Jr., *Characteristics of Elected Versus Merit-Selected New York City Judges, 1977–1992* (Fund for Modern Courts), 9–16.

14. McCourt proposal, submitted Jan. 31, 1979, H.R.J.—Constitutional Amendment 35, supported by the Illinois State Bar Association; see John C. Mullen and Thomas A. Clancy, "The McCourt Bill: A Practical Merit Selection Plan," *Illinois Bar Journal,* Sept. 1977, 12.

15. Cullerton proposal, introduced Apr. 19, 1984, H.B. 3230, 83rd Gen. Assem. (Ill. 1983 and 1984), Netsch Papers.

16. See, e.g., Netsch-Kustra bills, S.J. Res.—Constitutional Amendment 30, 84th Gen. Assem. (Ill. 1985 and 1986), Netsch Papers; S.J. Res.—Constitutional Amendment 7, 85th Gen. Assem. (Ill. 1987 and 1988), Netsch Papers.

17. "A Merit Bill—For Real," *Chicago Tribune,* sec. A, Apr. 25, 1977.

18. David Axelrod and Robert Enstad, "Remap Plan Imperils Netsch," *Chicago Tribune,* sec. A, Sept. 24, 1981.

19. "Mr. Madigan's Remapping Hobby," *Chicago Tribune,* sec. B, Dec. 12, 1981.

20. "Court Orders New Remap," *Chicago Tribune,* Dec. 25, 1981.

21. David Axelrod, "Rock Certain He'll Lead Senate Again," *Chicago Tribune,* sec. E, Jan. 7, 1981.

22. Daniel Egler, "Senate President Rock Narrowly Wins 4th Term," *Chicago Tribune,* Jan. 10, 1985; Daniel Egler, "Rock Adds 6th Leader to His Senate Team," *Chicago Tribune,* sec. A, Feb. 6, 1985.

23. Philip Rock, interview by Cynthia Bowman, Jan. 11, 2007.

24. Daniel Egler, "Rock Re-elected After Bargaining," *Chicago Tribune,* Jan. 16, 1987.

25. Philip Lentz, "Senate Will Hear Thompson Tax Bid," *Chicago Tribune,* sec. B, May 3, 1983.

26. Philip Lentz, "State Tax Hike Passes," *Chicago Tribune*, July 1, 1983.

27. Dawn Clark Netsch, interview by Cynthia Bowman, Dec. 19, 2006.

28. Daniel Egler, "Senate Rejects 'Sin Tax' Hike," *Chicago Tribune*, June 23, 1989; Philip Lentz, "Taxing Issues Raise Political Dust Cloud," *Chicago Tribune*, Chicagoland, July 4, 1983.

29. *Crain's Chicago Business*, Oct. 16, 1989, 2.

30. Daniel Egler and Rick Pearson, "Democrats Scuttle GOP Tax Cap Plan," *Chicago Tribune*, Chicagoland, May 4, 1990.

31. Christopher Wills, "Safety Measure Advances," *St. Louis Post-Dispatch*, sec. A, May 18, 1990.

32. Daniel Egler and Rick Pearson, "A Legacy Delayed," *Chicago Tribune*, Perspective, Mar. 11, 1990.

33. Daniel Egler and Rick Pearson, "All About the T-word," *Chicago Tribune*, Perspective, May 13, 1990.

34. Daniel Egler, "Tax-accountability Bill Killed," *Chicago Tribune*, May 2, 1990; Janet Neiman, "Voter Nod Seen for Tax-delinquency Measure," *Crain's Chicago Business*, Sept. 3, 1990, 26.

35. Dawn Clark Netsch, *4th District Newsletter*, Aug. 1988, Netsch Papers.

36. Dyer v. Blair, 390 F.Supp. 1291 (N.D. Ill. 1975).

37. "E.R.A. Loses in Senate," *Chicago Tribune*, sec. A, May 4, 1973.

38. Dorothy Collin, "People," *Chicago Tribune*, Mar. 9, 1975.

39. Dawn Clark Netsch, undated speech on the ERA, Netsch Papers.

40. Jane Fritsch, "6,000 March on Capitol for ERA," *Chicago Tribune*, May 17, 1976.

41. Dawn Clark Netsch, interview by Cynthia Bowman, Sept. 29, 2008.

42. Rock interview, Jan. 11, 2007.

43. Unless otherwise identified, information in this section is taken from a group interview by Cynthia Bowman with Polly Poskin, Julie Hamos, Tina Tchen, Barbara Engel, and Linda Miller, June 30, 2006, at the offices of the Skadden, Arps law firm in Chicago (hereafter Rape Reform Group interview).

44. Netsch interview, May 31, 2006.

45. Hamos, Rape Reform Group interview.

46. Ibid.

47. Ibid.

48. Miller, Rape Reform Group interview.

49. Hamos, Rape Reform Group interview.

50. *Record of Proceedings in the Illinois Senate*, June 27, 1983, 352 (Netsch).

51. Ibid., 370 (Bloom).

52. *Proceedings*, June 27, 1983; July 1, 1983, 98 (Rock).

53. *Proceedings*, June 27, 1983, 101 (Bruce).

54. Ibid., 92 (Netsch).

55. *Proceedings*, Nov. 2, 1983, 17 (Demuzio).

56. Joseph R. Tybor and Mark Eissman, "City Rape Convictions Soar," *Chicago Tribune*, Nov. 24, 1985.

57. Pub. Act 88-421.

58. Pub. Act 93-958.

59. Dawn Clark Netsch, interview by Cynthia Bowman, Dec. 28, 2006.

60. Michael Bauer, interview by Cynthia Bowman, Dec. 26, 2006.

61. Dawn Clark Netsch, interview by Cynthia Bowman, July 17, 2006.

62. Edie Gibson, "Family Leave on the Table," *Chicago Tribune*, TempoWoman, Sept. 13, 1987.

63. Jennifer Halperin, "Plan Offers Workers Time Off," *Chicago Tribune*, News, May 1, 1989.

64. "Thompson Vetoes Measure on Right to Unpaid Leave," *St. Louis Post-Dispatch*, News, Sept. 12, 1989.

65. Daniel Egler, "Required Health Insurance Opposed," *Chicago Tribune*, Business, Jan. 18, 1990.

66. Daniel Egler and Paul Wagner, "Family Leave Bill Advances," *Chicago Tribune*, Chicagoland, May 17, 1990.

67. Family and Medical Leave Act of 1993, 29 U.S.C. 28, §§ 2601 et seq.

68. Dawn Clark Netsch, notes for speech to Illinois Association of Graduate Programs in Public Administration, May 13, 1986, Netsch Papers.

69. Rock interview, Jan. 11, 2007.

Chapter 14: Life Outside the Legislature

1. Dawn Clark Netsch, notes for speeches on behalf of President Carter, 1980, Netsch Papers.

2. Information about the impact of the Chicago blizzard of 1979 on the transit system is available at Chicago-L.org, "The Blizzard of 1979," http://www.chicago-l.org/mishaps/blizzard79.html.

3. Dawn Clark Netsch, interview by Cynthia Bowman, July 17, 2007.

4. "Dawn Clark Netsch: The Aristocratic Political Hustler Representing Chicago's Independent 13th District," *Illinois Issues*, Jan. 1981, 27.

5. Dawn Clark Netsch, interview by Cynthia Bowman, July 27, 2007.

6. Dawn Clark Netsch, interview by Cynthia Bowman, Aug. 8, 2006.

7. Netsch interview, July 27, 2007.

8. Netsch interview, Aug. 8, 2006.

9. Dawn Clark Netsch, interview by Cynthia Bowman, Aug. 2, 2006.

10. Paul M. Green, "The Primary: Some New Players—Same Old Rules," in *The Making of the Mayor: Chicago 1983*, ed. Melvin G. Holli and Paul M. Green (Grand Rapids, Mich.: Eerdmans Publishing, 1984), 37.

11. Netsch interview, July 27, 2007.

12. Robert Cross, "A Man Who Dreams of Classic Parks," *Chicago Tribune*, Tempo, July 6, 1986; Harry Golden Jr., "Aldermen Walk, Stall Appointee," *Chicago Sun-Times*, May 31, 1986.

13. See Florence Hamlish Levinsohn, "Hidden Treasures," *Chicago Tribune*, Sunday Magazine, Mar. 22, 1987.

14. Michael Gillis, "Netsch Quits Park Board," *Chicago Sun-Times*, Dec. 19, 1989.

15. See, e.g., Michael Gillis, "Netsch Stalks out of Parks Meeting," *Chicago Sun-Times*, June 27, 1989.

16. John Kass, "Netsch Quits Park Board, Says It Ignored His Views," *Chicago Tribune*, Chicagoland, Dec. 19, 1989.

17. "Remarks by Edward Uhlir at the Memorial Service for Walter Netsch on July 7, 2008, at the Arts Club of Chicago," Netsch Papers.

18. Kass, "Netsch Quits Park Board."

19. Kay Clement, interview by Cynthia Bowman, June 29, 2006.

20. Walter Netsch, interview by Cynthia Bowman, Dec. 19, 2005.

21. "Dawn Clark Netsch: The Aristocratic Political Hustler Representing Chicago's Independent 13th District," *Illinois Issues,* Jan. 1981, 27.

22. Walter Netsch interview, Dec. 19, 2005.

23. Clement interview, June 29, 2006.

24. Rita McLennon, interview by Cynthia Bowman, June 16, 2007.

25. Clement interview, June 29, 2006.

26. Walter Netsch interview, Dec. 19, 2005.

27. Information in this chapter about Walter Netsch's health is drawn from Dawn Clark Netsch, interview by Cynthia Bowman, Aug. 4, 2006.

28. Clement interview, June 29, 2006.

29. Dawn Clark Netsch, interview by David Kraut, June 20, 2006, transcript in possession of author.

30. Michael Holland, interview by Cynthia Bowman, Dec. 28, 2006.

Chapter 15: Comptroller

1. Philip Lentz, "State Democrats Get Early Start as Jockeying Begins for 1986," *Chicago Tribune,* sec. 4, Nov. 18, 1984.

2. Steve Neal, "'86 Statewide Election Draws Politicians into Battle Early," *Chicago Tribune,* Chicagoland, Apr. 18, 1985.

3. Richard J. Durbin to Dawn Clark Netsch, June 17, 1985, Netsch Papers.

4. Greg Hinz, "Dawn of New Age," *Lerner Booster,* Aug. 7, 1985.

5. Quoted in Hinz, "Dawn."

6. Bill Tapella to Dawn, the committee, memorandum, n.d., Netsch Papers.

7. R. Bruce Dold and Steve Neal, "Democratic Unity Falling into Place," *Chicago Tribune,* News, Nov. 12, 1985; Tim Franklin and Daniel Egler, "Women Democrats Press for Spot on State Ticket," *Chicago Tribune,* News, Nov. 23, 1985.

8. Quoted in Franklin and Egler, "Women Democrats."

9. See, e.g., Steve Daley, "Burris Leans Toward Running for Governor," *Chicago Tribune,* News, Feb. 10, 1989.

10. Greg Hinz, "Welsh in Running for Chief Attorney," *Skyline,* sec. 1, Apr. 6, 1989.

11. Irv Kupcinet, "Kup's Column," *Chicago Sun-Times,* June 1, 1989.

12. Thomas Hardy, "Race On to Replace Hartigan," *Chicago Tribune,* sec. 2, July 28, 1989; Patrick E. Gauen, "Sen. Netsch Declares Candidacy," *St. Louis Post-Dispatch,* News, July 28, 1989.

13. Dawn Clark Netsch, interview by John Lanham, July 25, 2006, transcript in possession of author.

14. Quoted in R. Bruce Dold and Matt O'Connor, "Netsch Won't Drop Out of Race," *Chicago Tribune,* sec. 2, Aug. 16, 1989; see also Fran Spielman, "Netsch Proposes Ethics Unit for Attorney General's Office," *Chicago Sun-Times,* Aug. 16, 1989.

15. Thomas Hardy, "Netsch Joins Comptroller Race," *Chicago Tribune,* DuPage, Oct. 31, 1989.

16. Netsch interview, July 25, 2006.

17. Daniel Egler, "State Democrats Slate Women for 2 Offices," *Chicago Tribune,* News, Nov. 29, 1989.

18. Daniel Egler, "Comptroller Race Shapes Up for GOP," *Chicago Tribune,* sec. 2C, Dec. 6, 1989.

19. Chris Meister, interview by Cynthia Bowman, Dec. 21, 2006.

20. R. Bruce Dold, "Comptroller's Race in the Doldrums," *Chicago Tribune,* Chicagoland, Feb. 22, 1990.

21. Dold, "Comptroller's Race."

22. Bill Morris to Dawn Clark Netsch, memorandum, Jan. 19, 1990, Netsch Papers.

23. Dawn Clark Netsch, *Truth in Budgeting: A White Paper, Attachment III: The Budgetary Balance,* Jan. 1990, Netsch Papers.

24. Pete Ellertsen, "Netsch Wants Panel Formed to Review State Bureaucracy," *State Journal-Register* (Springfield, Ill.), Feb. 28, 1990.

25. Meister interview, Dec. 21, 2006.

26. "Bowman Given Liberal Voter Group's Backing over Netsch," *Chicago Tribune,* Chicagoland, Jan. 7, 1990.

27. R. Bruce Dodd, "Comptroller's Race in the Doldrums," *Chicago Tribune,* Chicagoland, Feb. 22, 1990.

28. Woods Bowman campaign, "Does Sen. Netsch Really Want to Be Comptroller?" press release, Feb. 26, 1990, Netsch Papers.

29. Ellertsen, "Netsch Wants Panel."

30. Kathleen Best, "Hopefuls Vie in Illinois Primary," *St. Louis Post-Dispatch,* Mar. 21, 1990.

31. Terry Stephan, interview by Cynthia Bowman, Dec. 29, 2006.

32. Sharman Stein and Thomas Hardy, "Rest of State Ticket Has Debatable Sunday," *Chicago Tribune,* Chicagoland, Oct. 8, 1990.

33. Dawn Clark Netsch Campaign Committee, press release, Oct. 5, 1990, Netsch Papers.

34. Stephan interview, Dec. 29, 2006.

35. Thomas Hardy, "Big Union Neutral on Governor," *Chicago Tribune,* Chicagoland, Sept. 19, 1990; Thomas Hardy, "Teachers Group Backs Edgar," *Chicago Tribune,* Chicagoland, Sept. 24, 1990.

36. Thomas Hardy and Tim Jones, "Voters Cool to 4 Lower-Ticket State Races," *Chicago Tribune,* Chicagoland, Oct. 9, 1990.

37. Thomas Hardy, "Ryan Cuts into Lead of Burris," *Chicago Tribune,* News, Oct. 30, 1990.

38. Stephan interview, Dec. 29, 2006.

39. Thomas Hardy and Tim Jones, "Edgar Squeaks Past Hartigan," *Chicago Tribune,* News, Nov. 7, 1990.

40. Quoted in Tim Jones, "Women Find 2 Strikes Against Them in Politics," *Chicago Tribune,* Chicagoland, Nov. 25, 1990.

41. Quoted in Jones, "Women Find."

42. Interim Report to Comptroller-Elect Dawn Clark Netsch from Transition Team Financial Management Subcommittee, Jan. 11, 1991, Netsch Papers; Final Report to Comptroller Dawn Clark Netsch from Transition Team Financial Management Subcommittee, Apr. 1991, Netsch Papers.

43. Netsch interview, July 25, 2006.

44. Tom Dodegge, intraoffice memorandum, Nov. 9, 1990, in "Summary of Significant Transition Issues," Netsch Papers.

45. Lee Malany to Dawn Clark Netsch, letter and enclosure, Dec. 4, 1990, Netsch Papers.

46. Karen Fahrion, Legislative Research Unit, Illinois General Assembly, memorandum on the role of the comptroller, Nov. 12, 1985, Netsch Papers.

47. Rick Davis to Dawn Clark Netsch, memorandum, Nov. 28, 1990, Netsch Papers.

48. Final Report to Comptroller Dawn Clark Netsch from Transition Team Financial Management Subcommittee, Apr. 1991, 4–30, 33–35, Netsch Papers.

49. Transition Team—Internal to Comptroller Netsch Transition Committee, memorandum, Jan. 11, 1991, Netsch Papers.

50. Bob Brock, interview by John Lanham, Aug. 10, 2006, transcript in possession of author.

51. Ibid.

52. Wendy Cohen, interview by Cynthia Bowman, July 19, 2006.

53. Dawn Clark Netsch, interview by Cynthia Bowman, Aug. 4, 2006.

54. Jim Ofcarcik, interview by John Lanham, Aug. 10, 2006, transcript in possession of author.

55. Netsch interview, July 25, 2006.

56. Ibid.

57. Ibid.

58. "Magazine Blasts Illinois Budget Process," *State Journal-Register* (Springfield, Ill.), Mar. 2, 1992.

59. Jay Fitzgerald, "Netsch Raps Quinn for Killing Loan Plan," *State Journal-Register* (Springfield, Ill.), July 30, 1992.

60. Netsch interview, July 25, 2006.

61. Toby Eckert, "State Plans to Borrow $900 Million," *Peoria (Ill.) Journal Star*, sec. A, July 22, 1993.

62. Comptroller, press release, June 28, 1991, Netsch Papers.

63. Comptroller, press release, Aug. 12, 1991, Netsch Papers.

64. Comptroller, press release, June 30, 1992, Netsch Papers.

65. Comptroller, press release, Aug. 21, 1992, Netsch Papers.

66. Comptroller, press release, Apr. 1, 1993, Netsch Papers.

67. Comptroller, press release, July 1, 1993, Netsch Papers.

68. Netsch interview, July 25, 2006.

69. Ofcarcik interview, Aug. 10, 2006.

70. Linda Fletcher, interview by John Lanham, Aug. 9, 2006, transcript in possession of author.

71. Ofcarcik interview, Aug. 10, 2006.

72. Brock interview, Aug. 10, 2006.

73. Brock interview, Aug. 10, 2006.

74. Information about the Local Government Advisory Board in this paragraph is drawn from the agenda and minutes of the board's orientation meeting held on July 22, 1993, Netsch Papers.

75. Netsch interview, July 25, 2006.

76. Office of the Comptroller, Local Government and Fiscal Programs Division, Plan of Reorganization, Oct. 16, 1992, Netsch Papers.

77. Netsch interview, July 25, 2006.

78. Brock interview, Aug. 10, 2006.

79. Ibid.

80. Netsch interview, July 25, 2006.

81. Senate Democratic Bill Analysis concerning S.B. 1848, Apr. 25, 1990, Netsch Papers.

82. S.B. 668, amending the State Comptroller Act, 87th Gen. Assem., 1991–92 Reg. Sess. (Ill. Apr. 10, 1991).

83. Ofcarcik interview, Aug. 10, 2006.

84. Netsch interview, July 25, 2006.

85. Testimony to the Joint Economic Committee and House Select Committee on Aging, Nov. 20, 1991, attached to Comptroller, press release, Nov. 20, 1991, Netsch Papers.

86. People *ex rel.* Robert Sklodowski v. State, 642 N.E.2d 1180 (Ill. 1994).

87. Netsch interview, July 25, 2006.

88. Ibid.

89. Comptroller, press release, Feb. 11, 1993, Netsch Papers.

90. Illinois Balanced Budget Act, H.B. 1623, 88th Gen. Assem., 1993–94 Reg. Sess. (Ill. Mar. 9, 1993).

91. Illinois Fiscal and Economic Stability Act, H.B. 1624, 88th Gen. Assem., 1993–94 Reg. Sess. (Ill. Mar. 9, 1993).

92. Bill O'Connell, "Senate Committee Kills Budget-Reform Package," *Peoria (Ill.) Journal Star,* sec. A, Apr. 29, 1993.

93. Dawn Clark Netsch, interview by Cynthia Bowman, Sept. 29, 2008.

94. BEST Government Talking Points, Netsch Papers.

95. Brock interview, Aug. 10, 2006.

96. Ibid.

Chapter 16: The Race for Governor of Illinois

1. Dawn Clark Netsch, interview by Cynthia Bowman, Dec. 15, 2006.

2. Ibid.

3. Ibid.

4. Thomas Hardy, "Madigan's '94 Slate Has More Than Himself Going Against It," *Chicago Tribune,* Perspective, Sept. 6, 1992.

5. Dawn Clark Netsch, interview by Cynthia Bowman, Dec. 19, 2006.

6. Kappy Laing, interview by Cynthia Bowman, Dec. 18, 2006.

7. Thomas Hardy, "Voters Gain If Netsch Runs for Governor in '94," *Chicago Tribune,* Perspective, Feb. 7, 1993.

8. Thomas Hardy, "Netsch Fundraiser to Test Waters for Plan to Enter Governor's Race," *Chicago Tribune,* Chicagoland, Mar. 9, 1993.

9. Philip Franchine, "Gierach Will Continue Crashing Debates," *Chicago Sun-Times,* Feb. 20, 1994.

10. Steve Neal, "Netsch Is Showing Leadership on Taxes," *Chicago Sun-Times,* Apr. 16, 1993.

11. Steve Neal, "Netsch Aims to Be 1st Woman Governor," *Chicago Sun-Times,* June 7, 1993.

12. Laing interview, Dec. 18, 2006.

13. Thomas Hardy, "Sex and Race Still Count When It's Election Time," *Chicago Tribune,* Chicagoland, Aug. 8, 1993.

14. Thomas Hardy, "Netsch and Phelan Staking Claim to Women's Vote in '94," *Chicago Tribune,* Chicagoland, July 7, 1993.

15. Kathleen Best, "'The Year of the Woman Governor'; That's the Goal in 19 States but Raising Money Enough for All May Be Daunting," *St. Louis Post-Dispatch,* sec. B, July 11, 1993.

16. Thomas Hardy, "A Surplus of Promise: Count Comptroller Dawn Clark Netsch as One of the Stronger Prospects for Governor Next Year," *Chicago Tribune,* Tempo, July 19, 1993.

17. Bernard Schoenburg, "Edgar Raised $1.6 Million for Campaign, Report Says," *St. Louis Post-Dispatch,* Illinois, Aug. 5, 1993.

18. "Netsch 2nd to Join Race for Governor," *Chicago Tribune,* News, Aug. 9, 1993.

19. Thomas Hardy, "Netsch Enters Governor's Race, Supports Tax Hike for Education," *Chicago Tribune,* Chicagoland, Aug. 10, 1993.

20. Thomas Hardy, "Netsch Dares What Few Have Done Before—Runs on Tax-Raising Pledge," *Chicago Tribune,* Perspective, Aug. 15, 1993.

21. Laing interview, Dec. 18, 2006.

22. Steve Neal, "New Polls Give Burris Edge in Race to Challenge Edgar," *Chicago Sun-Times,* Sept. 15, 1993.

23. Laing interview, Dec. 18, 2006.

24. Thomas Hardy and Rob Karwath, "Group Gives Netsch Help on Funding," *Chicago Tribune,* Chicagoland, Nov. 3, 1993.

25. Steve Neal, "Phelan Leads Edgar's '94 Challengers," *Chicago Sun-Times,* Nov. 17, 1993.

26. Thomas Hardy, "Netsch Forgoes Running Mate in Primary," *Chicago Tribune,* Chicagoland, Nov. 23, 1994; Patrick E. Gauen, "Second Woman on Ticket with Illinois Hopeful," *St. Louis Post-Dispatch,* sec. C, Nov. 30, 1993.

27. Gauen, "Second Woman."

28. Thomas Hardy and Rick Pearson, "No Old-Time Slate for Democrats," *Chicago Tribune,* Dec. 1, 1993.

29. Thomas Hardy, "Democratic Candidates Rev Up Campaign Engines," *Chicago Tribune,* Chicagoland, Dec. 6, 1993; Steve Neal, "Netsch, Oberman Thwart Challenge, *Chicago Sun-Times,* Jan. 18, 1994.

30. Mark N. Hornung, "Netsch's Campaign Is Disappointing," *Chicago Sun-Times,* Nov. 24, 1993.

31. Laing interview, Dec. 18, 2006.

32. Ibid.

33. Netsch interview, Dec. 19, 2006.

34. Bill Morris, interview by Cynthia Bowman, Dec. 21, 2006.

35. Illinois Constitution, art. 10.

36. Morris interview, Dec. 21, 2006.

37. Ralph Martire, interview by Cynthia Bowman, Jan. 8, 2007.

38. Ibid.

39. Ibid.

40. Thomas Hardy, "Netsch Gambles on Tax Hike: She Risks Candidacy on School Funding Plan," *Chicago Tribune*, Jan. 20, 1994.

41. See, e.g., "Risky Netsch Plan Is Correct on Taxes," Editorial, *Chicago Sun-Times*, Jan. 21, 1994; see also "Calling the Question on State Finances," *Chicago Tribune*, Editorial, Jan. 23, 1994.

42. Steve Neal, "Netsch Is Gaining Momentum," *Chicago Sun-Times*, Jan. 13, 1994; Steve Neal, "Burris Parlays Name, Popularity into Lead," *Chicago Sun-Times*, Jan. 16, 1994.

43. Jean Latz Griffin, "Netsch and Pappas Hope TV Ads Sharpen Images," *Chicago Tribune*, Chicagoland, Jan. 26, 1994.

44. "Illinois: Poll Shows Burris on Top of Dem Rivals," *Hotline*, Jan. 18, 1994.

45. "Illinois: Netsch Releases Two New Ads," *Hotline*, Jan. 25, 1994.

46. Peter Giangreco, interview by Cynthia Bowman, Dec. 22, 2006.

47. Mark Brown and Jim Merriner, "Phelan Unveils TV Spots; Netsch Ads Attack Burris," *Chicago Sun-Times*, Jan. 27, 1994; Thomas Hardy and Joseph Kirby, "Hofeld, Oberman Get Personal in Radio Debate," *Chicago Tribune*, Chicagoland, Jan. 28, 1994.

48. Patrick E. Gauen, "Netsch Takes Cue, Gains Recognition," *St. Louis Post-Dispatch*, sec. B, Feb. 8, 1994.

49. Joseph A. Kirby, "OK, Everybody out of the Pool, Netsch Begs," *Chicago Tribune*, Chicagoland, Feb. 4, 1994.

50. Jean Latz Griffin, "Netsch Campaign Pulls Lighthearted New TV Ad Featuring Opera, Softball," *Chicago Tribune*, Chicagoland, Feb. 18, 1994.

51. Thomas Hardy, "Netsch Flexes Muscles in Truth and Advertising," *Chicago Tribune*, Perspective, Feb. 6, 1994.

52. Joseph A. Kirby, "Netsch Calls for Assault Rifle Ban," *Chicago Tribune*, Chicagoland, Feb. 1, 1994.

53. Flynn McRoberts and Rick Pearson, "Burris Fires Shot at Netsch; He Unveils Plan for Education," *Chicago Tribune*, Chicagoland, Feb. 8, 1994.

54. Joseph A. Kirby and Flynn McRoberts, "Burris Bashed for Past Budgets; Netsch Points to Comptroller Office Spending Hikes," *Chicago Tribune*, Chicagoland, Feb. 9, 1994.

55. Joseph A. Kirby, "Netsch Seeks State Aid to Small Firms," *Chicago Tribune*, Chicagoland, Feb. 11, 1994.

56. Martire interview, Jan. 8, 2007.

57. Flynn McRoberts and Jean Latz Griffin, "Phelan Takes a Daffy Turn in Campaign," *Chicago Tribune*, Chicagoland, Mar. 8, 1994.

58. Flynn McRoberts and Christi Parsons, "Burris Unveils Economic Plan; His Proposal Echoes in Part That of Opponent Netsch," *Chicago Tribune*, Chicagoland, Mar. 10, 1994.

59. Peter Kendall, "Burris, Netsch Put Out Same Diagnosis," *Chicago Tribune*, Chicagoland, Feb. 14, 1994.

60. Thomas Hardy, "Netsch Closing In on Burris," *Chicago Tribune*, Feb. 13, 1994.

61. Peter Kendall, "Voters Like Shifting Taxes for Schools," *Chicago Tribune*, Feb. 1, 1994.

62. Thomas Hardy and Flynn McRoberts, "Netsch Calls New Phelan Ad Misleading," *Chicago Tribune*, Chicagoland, Feb. 20, 1994.

63. Scott Fornek and Jim Ritter, "Netsch, Phelan Trade Shots—Democratic Governor Race Takes Negative Turn," *Chicago Sun-Times*, Feb. 21, 1994.

64. Steve Neal, "Burris Takes a Chance by Debating," *Chicago Sun-Times*, Jan. 28, 1994.

65. Christi Parson and Joseph A. Kirby, "Uninvited to Democrat Debate, Long-Short Gierach Steals Show," *Chicago Tribune*, News, Feb. 19, 1994.

66. Peter Kendall and Rick Pearson, "Burris, Phelan Hammer at Netsch Tax-Hike Plan," *Chicago Tribune*, Feb. 23, 1994.

67. "Illinois: Burris and Phelan 'Gang Up' on Netsch in Debate," *Hotline*, Feb. 23, 1994.

68. Tim Landis and Diana Wallace, untitled, Gannett News Service, Feb. 22, 1994.

69. Kendall and Pearson, "Burris, Phelan Hammer."

70. Thomas Hardy, "Burris Remains Up Front; Leader in Polls Solid in Debate," *Chicago Tribune*, Chicagoland, Feb. 24, 1994.

71. Joseph A. Kirby and Christi Parsons, "3 Democrat Hopefuls Concur on State Taxes; but Netsch's Figures Are Disputed," *Chicago Tribune*, Chicagoland, Feb. 27, 1994.

72. Ray Long, "Netsch Wins Endorsement in Phelan Country," *Chicago Sun-Times*, Feb. 28, 1994; Joseph A. Kirby and Susan Kuczka, "Netsch Receives a $250,000 Donation from Her Husband," *Chicago Tribune*, Chicagoland, Feb. 24, 1994.

73. Christi Parsons, "Suave or Just Scraping; Funding Disparity Shows in Gubernatorial Campaigns," *Chicago Tribune*, Chicagoland, Feb. 28, 1994; Thomas Hardy, "Big Money Can't Erase Phelan's Phlip-Phlops," *Chicago Tribune*, Perspective, Feb. 27, 1994.

74. Christi Parsons, "Phelan Finds Welfare Reform Is an Issue That Strikes a Chord Downstate," *Chicago Tribune*, Chicagoland, Mar. 1, 1994.

75. Joseph A. Kirby and Flynn McRoberts, "Candidates in Training for Word-Class [*sic*] Democratic Primary Bout," *Chicago Tribune*, Chicagoland, Mar. 3, 1994.

76. Thomas Hardy, "Democrats Keep the Gloves on in Debate," Chicagoland, *Chicago Tribune*, Mar. 4, 1994.

77. "For the Democrats: Dawn Netsch," *Chicago Tribune*, Editorial, Mar. 6, 1994; "For Netsch in Dem Gubernatorial Race," *Chicago Sun-Times*, Mar. 11, 1994.

78. Thomas Hardy, "Netsch Is Closing In on Burris," *Chicago Tribune*, Mar. 6, 1994.

79. Thomas Hardy, "Netsch Pulling Away from the Pack; Debate Seen as Turning Point in Poll," *Chicago Tribune*, Mar. 10, 1994.

80. Giangreco interview, Dec. 22, 2006.

81. Ibid.

82. Joseph A. Kirby and Andrew Fegelman, "Democratic Governor Hopefuls Take Best Shot," *Chicago Tribune*, Chicagoland, Mar. 9, 1994.

83. Christi Parson and Flynn McRoberts, "Burris Says He Senses Washington 'Fervor,'" *Chicago Tribune*, Chicagoland, Mar. 13, 1994; Joseph A. Kirby and Flynn McRoberts, "Parade's Nearly Over in Campaign for Governor," *Chicago Tribune*, Mar. 14, 1994.

84. Thomas Hardy and Peter Kendall, "Netsch, Rostenkowski Win," *Chicago Tribune*, Mar. 16, 1994.

85. Laing interview, Dec. 18, 2006.

86. Mary Schmich, "For Many Voters, Gender Was a Thought, but an Afterthought, a Bonus," *Chicago Tribune*, Chicagoland, Mar. 18, 1994.

87. Steve Neal, "Netsch Set Agenda in Dem Primary," *Chicago Sun-Times*, Mar. 14, 1994.

88. Mark Brown and Daniel J. Lehmann, "Edgar Wastes No Time, Goes Right After Netsch," *Chicago Sun-Times*, Mar. 16, 1994.

89. Steven R. Strahler, "Dawn to Jim: Rack 'Em Up," *Crain's Chicago Business*, Mar. 21, 1994.

90. Doug Finke, "Netsch's Tax Plan Would Help Downstate Counties, Study Says," *St. Louis Post-Dispatch*, Illinois, Mar. 24, 1994.

91. Biographical material about Jim Edgar is drawn from Robert P. Howard, *Mostly Good and Competent Men* (Springfield, Ill.: Institute for Public Affairs, 1999), 325–35.

92. Eric Krol, "Edgar's Education Answer; Governor Pledges $1 Billion, Hopes for More from Casinos," *Chicago Tribune*, News, May 6, 1994.

93. Thomas Hardy, "Edgar School Plan Rides on Riverboats," *Chicago Tribune*, News, May 11, 1994.

94. Patrick E. Gauen, "Netsch Goes on Offensive; Candidate Criticizes Edgar Education Plan," *St. Louis Post-Dispatch*, News, June 2, 1994.

95. Rick Pearson, "Edgar, Netsch Jostle on Pension Plans," *Chicago Tribune*, Chicagoland, Apr. 19, 1994.

96. Tim Novak, "Edgar Lands 1st Punch: Ad Calls Netsch Soft on Crime," *St. Louis Post-Dispatch*, News, June 4, 1994; Jim Merriner, "Edgar Ads Take Aim at Netsch's Record on Crime," *Chicago Sun-Times*, June 12, 1994.

97. Jim Merriner, "2nd Edgar Ad Attacks Netsch on Crime Issue," *Chicago Sun-Times*, June 9, 1994.

98. Thomas Hardy, "Edgar-Netsch Race Sizzles Early," *Chicago Tribune*, Chicagoland, June 12, 1994.

99. Richard L. Berke, "The 1994 Campaign: Women," *New York Times*, Oct. 3, 1994.

100. Merriner, "2nd Edgar Ad."

101. Steve Neal, "Big Guns Give Guv Big Bucks," *Chicago Sun-Times*, June 17, 1994.

102. Thomas Hardy, "Edgar Has 'Free Choice' for No. 2," *Chicago Tribune*, Metro Northwest, June 30, 1994.

103. Jim Merriner, "Lt. Gov. Rejoins Race," *Chicago Sun-Times*, July 19, 1994.

104. Giangreco interview, Dec. 22, 2006.

105. Netsch interview, Dec. 22, 2006.

106. Thomas Hardy, "Edgar's Health Is Issue Now and for Fall Campaign," *Chicago Tribune*, News, July 9, 1994.

107. Thomas Hardy, "Netsch to End Cease-Fire of Her TV Ads," *Chicago Tribune*, Chicagoland, July 22, 1994.

108. Christi Parsons, "Netsch Starts Rolling on Downstate Swing," *Chicago Tribune*, Chicagoland, July 26, 1994.

109. Zay N. Smith, "Severns Treated for Cancer," *Chicago Sun-Times*, July 30, 1994.

110. Steve Neal, "New Netsch Ads Paint 'Do-Nothing' Edgar," *Chicago Sun-Times*, Aug. 7, 1994.

111. Terry Wilson, "Netsch Stepping Up Fundraising," *Chicago Tribune*, Chicagoland, Aug. 8, 1994; Jean Latz Griffin, "Ad Gurus Unleash Attacks," *Chicago Tribune*, News, Aug. 15, 1994.

112. Thomas Hardy, "Netsch Rips Edgar on Anti-Crime Bill," *Chicago Tribune*, Chicagoland, Aug. 19, 1994.

113. Jean Latz Griffin, "Netsch's New Ad Takes a Swing at Edgar on State's Unpaid Bills," *Chicago Tribune*, Metro DuPage, Aug. 23, 1994.

114. Joseph A. Kirby, "Netsch Calls Toll Authority Unnecessary," *Chicago Tribune*, News, Aug. 25, 1994.

115. Rick Pearson, "Tollway Chief Loses His Cool as Netsch Turns Up the Heat," *Chicago Tribune*, News, Sept. 3, 1994.

116. Jean Latz Griffin, "Netsch Ads Take Tollway to Rip Edgar," *Chicago Tribune*, Metro DuPage, Sept. 2, 1994.

117. Peter Kendall and Rick Pearson, "Crime Becomes Key Issue for Edgar, Netsch," *Chicago Tribune*, Chicagoland, Aug. 30, 1994; Joseph A. Kirby and Susan Kuczka, "Netsch Plan Draws Fire from Edgar," *Chicago Tribune*, Metro Southwest, Sept. 8, 1994; Roderick Kelley, "Netsch School Plan: More Money Locally," *State Journal-Register* (Springfield, Ill.), Local, Sept. 8, 1994.

118. Jean Latz Griffin, "Netsch's New TV Ads Rip 'Edgar's Tollway Scandal,'" *Chicago Tribune*, Chicagoland, Sept. 13, 1994.

119. Kevin McDermott, "Edgar Termed a 'Barney Fife' for Stance on Crime Issues," *State Journal-Register* (Springfield, Ill.), Local, Sept. 13, 1994; Joseph A. Kirby and Rick Pearson, "Netsch, Edgar Trade Accusations on Crime," *Chicago Tribune*, Chicagoland, Oct. 24, 1994.

120. Jean Latz Griffin and Joseph A. Kirby, "Use of Troopers Perks Up 2 Contests," *Chicago Tribune*, Chicagoland, Sept. 21, 1994; Rick Pearson, "Netsch Fails to Make Inroad by Riding Tollway Problems," *Chicago Tribune*, News, Sept. 26, 1994; Hanke Gratteau and Ray Gibson, "Scandal Fails to Take a Toll on Edgar Bid," *Chicago Tribune*, Perspective, Oct. 2, 1994.

121. Rick Pearson and Jean Latz Griffin, "State Agency Report Knows Who Boss Is," *Chicago Tribune*, Chicagoland, Sept. 14, 1994.

122. Peter Kendall, "Netsch, Edgar Ads Assailed," *Chicago Tribune*, Metro Northwest, Sept. 26, 1994; Peter Kendall and Susan Kuczka, "Netsch Left Dangling by Death-Penalty Twist," *Chicago Tribune*, News, Oct. 3, 1994.

123. Thomas Hardy, "Netsch Attacks Fail to Dent Edgar's Lead," *Chicago Tribune*, News, Sept. 22, 1994.

124. Thomas Hardy, "Edgar, Netsch Muddy Their Clean Reputations," *Chicago Tribune*, Perspective, Sept. 18, 1994.

125. Dorothy Collin and Thomas Hardy, "Netsch to Refocus Campaign Pitch," *Chicago Tribune*, Chicagoland, Sept. 29, 1994.

126. "Illinois: Edgar Gets 'Covert Help' from Burris Operatives," *Hotline*, Sept. 29, 1994.

127. Ray Long and Michael Gillis, "A Rallying Cry to Women: Vote," *Chicago Sun-Times*, Nov. 5, 1994.

128. Rick Pearson, "Netsch Slams Edgar on Abortion Policy," *Chicago Tribune*, Chicagoland, Mar. 25, 1994.

129. Jean Latz Griffin and Thomas Hardy, "Edgar's Winning Showdown at Gender Gap," *Chicago Tribune*, News, Oct. 5, 1994.

130. Jean Latz Griffin and Joseph A. Kirby, "Netsch's Newest TV Ads Take Some Pool Shots at Edgar," *Chicago Tribune*, Chicagoland, Oct. 6, 1994.

131. Kevin McDermott, "Both Sides Try to 'Spin' Tax Lapse," *State Journal-Register* (Springfield, Ill.), Local, Oct. 11, 1994.

132. Ray Long, "Netsch Calls Edgar Ads on Tax Bill Dirty Pool," *Chicago Sun-Times*, Oct. 28, 1994.

133. Thomas Hardy, "Netsch Needs Big Debate Victory," *Chicago Tribune*, Metro Lake, Oct. 19, 1994.

134. Jim Merriner and Ray Long, "Netsch Jokes, Edgar Jabs," *Chicago Sun-Times*, Oct. 20, 1994.

135. Rick Pearson and Dorothy Collin, "Netsch Uses Debate to Put New Face on Election," *Chicago Tribune*, News, Oct. 20, 1994.

136. Phillip J. O'Connor, "Netsch, Simon Condemn 'Ugly' Campaign Poster," *Chicago Sun-Times*, Oct. 20, 1994.

137. Merriner and Long, "Netsch Jokes, Edgar Jabs."

138. Michael Gillis, "Netsch Calls Edgar Tactics Sexist," *Chicago Sun-Times*, Oct. 23, 1994; Rick Pearson and Joseph A. Kirby, "Netsch Gets Gender-Specific in Debate, Accusing Edgar of Sexism," *Chicago Tribune*, News, Oct. 22, 1994.

139. Steve Neal, "Netsch Wins Battle; Edgar Winning War," *Chicago Sun-Times*, Oct. 21, 1994; Thomas Hardy, "Debates Fail to Lift Netsch; Edgar Keeps Commanding Lead with Just 2 Weeks to Go," *Chicago Tribune*, News, Oct. 25, 1994.

140. Charles M. Madigan, "TV Debates: Turn On, Tune In, Learn Zilch," *Chicago Tribune*, Perspective, Oct. 23, 1994.

141. Bernard Schoenburg, "Edgar and Netsch: A Tale of Two Campaigns," *State Journal-Register* (Springfield, Ill.), Local, Oct. 30, 1994.

142. Patrick E. Gauen and Tim Novak, "Netsch Stays with 'Straight Shooting,'" *St. Louis Post-Dispatch*, sec. A, Nov. 6, 1994.

143. Ray Long, "Spouse Kicks In $240,000 for Netsch Ads," *Chicago Sun-Times*, Oct. 29, 1994.

144. Bernard Schoenburg, "Netsch Campaign Calls Edgar Phone Bank Questions 'Dirty,'" *State Journal-Register* (Springfield, Ill.), Local, Oct. 19, 1994.

145. Gauen and Novak, "Netsch Stays with 'Straight Shooting.'"

146. Steve Neal, "Democrats Jumping Ship for Edgar," *Chicago Sun-Times,* Nov. 2, 1994.

147. Dawn Clark Netsch, interview by Cynthia Bowman, Jan. 12, 2007.

148. Netsch interview, Jan. 12, 2007.

149. Giangreco interview, Dec. 22, 2006.

150. Thomas Hardy and Dorothy Collin, "Netsch Swept Aside by GOP Tide," *Chicago Tribune,* News, Nov. 9, 1994.

151. Martire interview, Jan. 8, 2007.

152. Hardy and Collin, "Netsch Swept Aside"; Jim Merriner, "Edgar Clobbers Netsch," *Chicago Sun-Times,* Nov. 9, 1994; Patrick E. Gauen and Tim Novak, "GOP's Tidal Wave Crushes Democrats; Edgar Wins," *St. Louis Post-Dispatch,* sec. A, Nov. 9, 1994.

153. Netsch interview, Jan. 12, 2007.

154. Pat Gauen, "Candidate Follows High Road, Though Buried in Landslide," *St. Louis Post-Dispatch,* Illinois, Nov. 14, 1994.

155. Giangreco interview, Dec. 22, 2006.

156. Martire interview, Jan. 8, 2007.

157. Joseph A. Kirby and Rick Pearson, "Campaign Has Illuminating Power of a 2-Watt Bulb," *Chicago Tribune,* Perspective, Nov. 6, 1994.

158. Giangreco interview, Dec. 22, 2006.

159. Robert Creamer, interview by Cynthia Bowman, May 6, 2006.

160. Thomas Hardy, "Edgar Victory Will Have Been Gift-wrapped," *Chicago Tribune,* News, Nov. 6, 1994.

161. Netsch interview, Jan. 12, 2007.

162. Paul Green, interview by Cynthia Bowman, Jan. 10, 2007.

Chapter 17: Life After Losing an Election

1. Rick Pearson, "Netsch Sounds a Warning," *Chicago Tribune,* Jan. 6, 1995.

2. Dawn Clark Netsch, interview by Cynthia Bowman, Dec. 28, 2006.

3. Quoted in Doug Finke, "46 Being Fired by New Comptroller," *State Journal-Register* (Springfield, Ill.), Dec. 30, 1994.

4. Dawn Clark Netsch, interview by Cynthia Bowman, Aug. 4, 2006.

5. Dawn Clark Netsch, interview by Cynthia Bowman, Jan. 12, 2007.

6. Northwestern Law School, "Strategic Plan for Northwestern University School of Law," available at http://www.law.northwestern.edu/difference/Strategic_Plan.pdf.

7. Netsch interview, Jan. 12, 2007.

8. Netsch interview, Aug. 4, 2006.

9. Stephen B. Presser, e-mail message to author, June 19, 2006.

10. Dawn Clark Netsch, "Harold Shapiro," [eulogy], Netsch Papers.

11. Aurie Pennick, interview by Cynthia Bowman, Jan. 8, 2007.

12. Dawn Clark Netsch, interview by Cynthia Bowman, July 13, 2007.

13. Alexander Polikoff, interview by Cynthia Bowman, July 19, 2007.

14. Hoy McConnell, interview by Cynthia Bowman, July 19, 2007.

15. Netsch interview, July 13, 2007.

16. Dawn Clark Netsch, interview by Cynthia Bowman, Oct. 8, 2007.

17. Dick Perrault, interview by Cynthia Bowman, Dec. 20, 2007.

18. Netsch interview, Oct. 8, 2007.

19. Cindi Canary, interview by Cynthia Bowman, June 11, 2007.

20. Ed Wojcicki, "Still the Wild West? A 10-Year Look at Campaign Finance Reform in Illinois," Paul Simon Public Policy Institute Occasional Papers, 2006, available at http://opensiuc.lib.siu.edu/ppo_papers/5.

21. Netsch interview, Dec. 28, 2006.

22. Ibid.

23. Ibid.

24. Dawn Clark Netsch, "Walter," [eulogy], July 7, 2008, Netsch Papers.

25. Dawn Clark Netsch, interview by Cynthia Bowman, Oct. 8, 2007.

26. "Referendum Results," *Chicago Tribune*, News, Nov. 6, 2008.

27. Dawn Clark Netsch, interview by Cynthia Bowman, Sept. 27, 2008.

28. Monica Davey, et al., "Governor Accused in Scheme to Sell Obama's Seat," *New York Times*, Dec. 10, 2008.

29. Monica Davey, "Defiant Governor Names Successor to Obama," *New York Times*, Dec. 31, 2008.

30. Malcolm Gay and Susan Saulny, "Blagojevich Is Removed by Illinois Senate, 59-0," *New York Times*, Jan. 30, 2009.

31. Monica Davey and Susan Saulny, "Blagojevich Indictment Lays Out Broad 'Enterprise' of Corruption," *New York Times*, Apr. 2, 2009.

32. Dawn Clark Netsch, speech given at panel, "Women in Politics in the '90s—Breaking the Good Old Boy Network," Illinois Park and Recreation State Conference, Jan. 9, 1992, Netsch Papers.

33. Dawn Clark Netsch, speech to American Civil Liberties Union, Peoria, Ill., Apr. 2, 1993, Netsch Papers.

34. Dawn Clark Netsch, speech to Illinois State Bar Association Sixth Annual Minority and Women Attorneys' Conference, John Marshall Law School, Chicago, May 13, 1995, Netsch Papers.

35. Dawn Clark Netsch, interview by Cynthia Bowman, July 17, 2007.

36. Ibid.

37. For information about the Illinois Women's Institute for Leadership, see http://www.iwilinfo.org/.

38. Netsch interview, July 17, 2007.

39. Jan Schakowsky, interview by Cynthia Bowman, Dec. 20, 2006.

40. Center for American Women and Politics, "Illinois Fact Sheet," available at http://www.cawp.rutgers.edu/.

41. Canary interview, June 11, 2007.

SELECTED BIBLIOGRAPHY

Bibliographical note: *On leaving government service, Dawn Clark Netsch donated her official papers to the Illinois State Historical Library, now known as the Abraham Lincoln Presidential Library, in Springfield, Illinois. The numerous boxes of materials have never been cataloged but are available for review. Netsch also has many papers, clippings, letters, photos, and other documents in her personal collection in Chicago. She gave the author and her research assistants access to all these documents, which have been referred to throughout as "Netsch Papers." The interviews conducted in the course of this project have almost without exception been tape-recorded; some of them have been transcribed as well. The tapes and transcripts are in the possession of the author.*

Interviews

Jim Alter, June 28, 2006, in his home, Chicago, Illinois, by Cynthia Bowman

Michael Bauer, December 26, 2006, in his home, Chicago, Illinois, by Cynthia Bowman

Robert Brock, August 10, 2006, in his office at the Department of Human Services, Springfield, Illinois, by John Lanham

Cynthia Canary, June 11, 2007, at offices of Illinois Campaign for Political Reform, Chicago, Illinois, by Cynthia Bowman

Keith Clark Jr., August 2, 2006, in his home, Carson City, Nevada, by Cynthia Bowman

Kathryn A. Clement, June 29, 2006, in her home, Chicago, Illinois

Wendy Cohen, July 19, 2006, at Northwestern University School of Law, Chicago, Illinois, by Cynthia Bowman

Jack Coons and Marilyn Coons, August 1, 2006, in their home, Berkeley, California, by Cynthia Bowman

Robert Creamer, May 6, 2006, in his office, Chicago, Illinois, by Cynthia Bowman

Barbara Engle, June 30, 2006, at offices of Skadden, Arps, Chicago, Illinois, by Cynthia Bowman

Linda Fletcher, August 9, 2006, at Office of the Comptroller, Springfield, Illinois, by John Lanham

Peter Giangreco, December 22, 2006, in his office, Evanston, Illinois, by Cynthia Bowman

Paul Green, January 10, 2007, in his office at Roosevelt University, Chicago, Illinois, by Cynthia Bowman

Julie Hamos, June 30, 2006, at offices of Skadden, Arps, Chicago, Illinois, by Cynthia Bowman

John Heinz, June 4, 2007, at Northwestern University School of Law, Chicago, Illinois, by Cynthia Bowman

Michael H. Holland, December 28, 2006, at Northwestern University School of
    Law, Chicago, Illinois, by Cynthia Bowman
James Houlihan, July 5, 2006, in office of the Cook County assessor, Chicago,
    Illinois, by Cynthia Bowman
Howard Kane, June 28, 2006, in his office at DLA Piper law firm, Chicago, Illinois,
    by Cynthia Bowman
Frances Eschbach Kinney, June 15, 2006, in her home, Evanston, Illinois, by
    Cynthia Bowman
Connie Chadwell Koch, January 4, 2007, in her home, Washington, D.C., by
    Cynthia Bowman
Kathryn Laing, December 18, 2006, at Northwestern University School of Law,
    Chicago, Illinois, by Cynthia Bowman
Ann Lousin, June 23, 2006, at Northwestern University School of Law, Chicago,
    Illinois, by Cynthia Bowman
William H. Luking, December 29, 2006, at Northwestern University School of
    Law, Chicago, Illinois, by Cynthia Bowman
Ralph Martire, January 8, 2007, at his office at the Center for Tax and Budget
    Accountability, Chicago, Illinois, by Cynthia Bowman
E. Hoy McConnell II, July 19, 2007, at offices of Business and Professional People
    in the Public Interest, Chicago, Illinois, by Cynthia Bowman
Robert McGrath, August 7, 2006, Cincinnati, Ohio, by Cynthia Bowman
Rita A. McLennon, June 16, 2007, at home of Cynthia Bowman, Chicago, Illinois,
    by Cynthia Bowman
Chris Meister, December 21, 2006, in his office at Office of the Comptroller,
    Chicago, Illinois, by Cynthia Bowman
Abner J. Mikva and Zoe Mikva, June 19, 2006, at their home, Chicago, Illinois, by
    Cynthia Bowman
Jay A. Miller, June 20, 2007, at his home, Wilmette, Illinois, by Cynthia Bowman
Linda Miller, June 30, 2006, at offices of Skadden, Arps, Chicago, Illinois, by
    Cynthia Bowman
Hon. James B. Moran, July 11, 2006, in his chambers, Federal Building, Chicago,
    Illinois, by Cynthia Bowman
Bill Morris, December 21, 2006, in his office, D. A. Davidson & Co., Chicago,
    Illinois, by Cynthia Bowman
Dawn Clark Netsch, repeated interviews, November 2005–October 2008, in her
    home and at Northwestern University School of Law, Chicago, Illinois
Walter A. Netsch, December 19, 2005, in his home, Chicago, Illinois, by Cynthia
    Bowman
Walter A. Netsch, January 22, 2005, in his home, Chicago, Illinois, by Peter
    Matuszek
James Ofcarcik, August 10, 2006, in his office at the Department of Transportation,
    Springfield, Illinois, by John Lanham
James T. Otis and Margaret B. Otis, July 21–22, 2006, in their home, Hanover,
    Illinois, by Cynthia Bowman
Aurie A. Pennick, January 8, 2007, in her office at the Field Foundation, Chicago,
    Illinois, by Cynthia Bowman

Richard F. Perrault, December 20, 2007, in his home, Lombard, Illinois, by Cynthia Bowman

Alexander Polikoff, July 19, 2007, at offices of Business and Professional People for the Public Interest, Chicago, Illinois, by Cynthia Bowman

Polly Poskin, June 30, 2006, at offices of Skadden, Arps, Chicago, Illinois, by Cynthia Bowman

Richard Rhodes, June 20, 2006, in his law office, Chicago, Illinois, by Cynthia Bowman

Hon. James J. Richards, July 28, 2006, in his chambers, Munster, Indiana

Philip J. Rock, January 11, 2007, in his office at Rock, Fusco, and Associates, Chicago, Illinois, by Cynthia Bowman

Victor Rosenblum, December 29, 2005, in his home, Evanston, Illinois, by Cynthia Bowman

Leonard S. Rubinowitz, December 27, 2007, in his home, Evanston, Illinois, by Cynthia Bowman

Jan Schakowsky, December 20, 2006, in her legislative office, Chicago, Illinois, by Cynthia Bowman

Harold Shapiro, no date, by Joe Harper

Andy Shaw, July 11, 2006, at Northwestern University School of Law, Chicago, Illinois, by Cynthia Bowman

Karen G. Shields, July 19, 2006, at Northwestern University School of Law, Chicago, Illinois, by Cynthia Bowman

Terry Stephan, December 29, 2006, at Northwestern University School of Law, Chicago, Illinois, by Cynthia Bowman

Adlai E. Stevenson III and Nancy A. Stevenson, July 6, 2006, in their home, Chicago, Illinois, by Cynthia Bowman

Christina Tchen, June 30, 2006, at offices of Skadden, Arps, Chicago, Illinois, by Cynthia Bowman

Virginia Watkin, November 4, 2006, in her home, Washington, D.C., by Cynthia Bowman

Willard Wirtz, November 4, 2006, in his home, Washington, D.C., by Cynthia Bowman

Books and Articles

Allswang, John M. *A House for All Peoples: Ethnic Politics in Chicago 1890–1936.* Lexington: University Press of Kentucky, 1971.

Art Institute Department of Architecture. *Oral History of Walter Netsch.* Chicago: Art Institute of Chicago, 1997.

Baker, Jean H. *The Stevensons: A Biography of an American Family.* New York: W. W. Norton, 1996.

Banovetz, James, and Thomas Kelty, "Illinois Home Rule and Taxation: A New Approach to Local Government Enabling Authority." *Northern Illinois University Law Review* 8 (1988): 709–30.

Barnhart, Bill, and Gene Schlickman. *Kerner: The Conflict of Intangible Rights.* Urbana: University of Illinois Press, 1999.

Braden, George D., and Rubin G. Cohn. *The Illinois Constitution: An Annotated and Comparative Analysis, Prepared for the Illinois Constitution Study Commission.* Urbana: University of Illinois Institute of Government and Public Affairs, 1969.

Burnham, Robert A. "The Cincinnati Charter Revolt of 1924: Creating City Government for a Pluralistic Society." In *Ethnic Diversity and Civic Identity: Patterns of Conflict and Cohesion in Cincinnati Since 1820,* ed. Henry D. Shapiro and Jonathan D. Sarna. Urbana: University of Illinois Press, 1992.

Carroll, Susan J., ed. *The Impact of Women in Public Office.* Bloomington: University of Indiana Press, 2001.

"Dawn Clark Netsch: The Aristocratic Political Hustler Representing Chicago's Independent 13th District." *Illinois Issues,* Jan. 1981, 27.

Epstein, Cynthia Fuchs. *Women in Law,* 2d ed. Urbana: University of Illinois Press, 1993.

Felsen, Martin, and Sarah Dunn. "Field Theory: Walter Netsch's Design Methodology." In *FAIA: A Critical Appreciation and Sourcebook,* by Northwestern University Library, 73–78. Evanston, Ill.: Northwestern University Press, 1998.

Fishbane, Joyce D., and Glenn W. Fisher. *Politics of the Purse: Revenue and Finance in the Sixth Illinois Constitutional Convention.* Urbana: University of Illinois Press, 1974.

Ford, Nancy. "From Judicial Election to Merit Selection: A Time for Change in Illinois." *Northern Illinois University Law Review* 8 (1988): 665–708.

Gertz, Elmer, and Joseph P. Pisciotte. *Charter for a New Age: An Inside View of the Sixth Illinois Constitutional Convention.* Urbana: University of Illinois Press, 1980.

Gottfried, Alex. *Boss Cermak of Chicago: A Study of Political Leadership.* Seattle: University of Washington Press, 1962.

Goulden, Joseph C. *The Benchwarmers: The Private World of the Powerful Federal Judges.* New York: Weybright & Talley, 1974.

Gove, Samuel K., and Thomas R. Kitsos. *Revision Success: The Sixth Illinois Constitutional Convention.* New York: National Municipal League, 1974.

Gove, Samuel K., and Louis H. Masotti, eds. *After Daley: Chicago Politics in Transition.* Urbana: University of Illinois Press, 1982.

Gove, Samuel K., and James D. Nowlan. *Illinois Politics and Government: The Expanding Metropolitan Frontier.* Lincoln: University of Nebraska Press, 1996.

Gove, Samuel K., and Victoria Ranney, eds. *Con-Con: Issues for the Illinois Constitutional Convention: Papers Prepared by the Constitution Research Group.* Urbana: University of Illinois Press, 1970.

Graff, Henry. "Cincinnati Profile." In *Cincinnati: A Guide to the Queen City and Its Neighbors,* by Writers' Program (Ohio), xix–xxiii, 3–142. Cincinnati: Wiesen-Hart Press, 1943.

Granger, William, and Lori Granger. *Fighting Jane: Mayor Jane Byrne and the Chicago Machine.* New York: Dial Press, 1980.

Henry, M. L., Jr., *Characteristics of Elected Versus Merit-Selected New York City Judges, 1977–1992.* New York: Fund for Modern Courts, 1992.

Herskovits, Melville J. "The Social Science Units of the Northwestern University Liberal Arts Program." *Journal of General Education* 1 (1947): 216–20.

Holli, Melvin G., and Paul M. Green, eds. *The Making of the Mayor: Chicago 1983*. Grand Rapids, Mich.: Eerdmans Publishing, 1984.

Howard, Robert P. *Mostly Good and Competent Men*. Springfield, Ill.: Institute for Public Affairs, 1999.

Illinois General Assembly, Legislative Research Unit, Sixth Illinois Constitutional Convention. *Record of Proceedings: December 8, 1969–September 3, 1970*. 7 vols.

Kay, Herma Hill. "The Future of Women Law Professors." *Iowa Law Review* 77 (1991): 5–18.

Kaye, Judith S. "Women Lawyers in Big Firms: A Study in Progress Toward Gender Equality." *Fordham Law Review* 57 (1988): 111–26.

Leopold, Wendy. "Herskovits: A Leader in Study of African Heritage." *Northwestern Observer*, Oct. 23, 1995, 3.

Lousin, Ann. "The 1970 Illinois Constitution: Has It Made a Difference?" *Northern Illinois University Law Review* 8 (1988): 571–650.

Mandelker, Daniel R., Dawn Clark Netsch, Peter W. Salsich Jr., Judith Welch Wegner, Sandra M. Stevenson, and Janice C. Griffith. *State and Local Government in a Federal System*, 6th ed. Newark, N.J.: Matthew Bender, 2006.

Martin, John Bartlow. *Adlai Stevenson*. New York: Harper & Brothers, 1952.

McKeever, Porter. *Adlai Stevenson: His Life and Legacy; A Biography*. New York: William Morrow, 1989.

Messick, Hank. *The Politics of Prosecution: Jim Thompson, Marje Everett, Richard Nixon and the Trial of Otto Kerner*. Ottawa, Ill.: Caroline House Books, 1978.

Morello, Karen Berger. *The Invisible Bar: The Woman Lawyer in America; 1638 to the Present*. Boston: Beacon Press, 1986.

Mullen, John C., and Thomas A. Clancy. "The McCourt Bill: A Practical Merit Selection Plan." *Illinois Bar Journal*, Sept. 1977, 12–19.

Myrdal, Gunnar. *An American Dilemma: The Negro Problem and Modern Democracy*. New York: Harper & Brothers, 1944.

Netsch, Dawn Clark. "The Executive." In *Con-Con: Issues for the Illinois Constitutional Convention: Papers Prepared by the Constitution Research Group*, ed. Samuel K. Gove and Victoria Ranney, 144–82. Urbana: University of Illinois Press, 1970.

———. "The Governor Shall . . ." *Chicago Bar Record*, Oct. 1968, 28–36.

Netsch, Dawn Clark, and Harold D. Shapiro. "100 Years and Counting." *Northwestern University Law Review* 100 (2006): 1–23.

Northwestern University Library. *Walter Netsch: FAIA: A Critical Appreciation and Sourcebook*. Evanston, Ill.: Northwestern University Press, 1998.

O'Connor, Len. *Clout: Mayor Daley and His City*. Chicago: Contemporary Books, 1975.

Overton, Ben F. "Trial Judges and Political Elections: A Time for Re-examination." *University of Florida Journal of Law and Public Policy* 2 (1988–89): 9–23.

Pisciotte, Joseph P. "How Illinois Did It." *National Civic Review*, 58, no. 7 (1969): 291–96.

Polikoff, Alexander. *Waiting for Gautreaux: A Story of Segregation, Housing, and the Black Ghetto.* Evanston, Ill.: Northwestern University Press, 2006.

Rakove, Milton L. *We Don't Want Nobody Nobody Sent: An Oral History of the Daley Years.* Bloomington: Indiana University Press, 1979.

Reagan, Leslie J. *When Abortion Was a Crime: Women, Medicine, and Law in the United States, 1867–1973.* Berkeley: University of California Press, 1997.

Reiter, Carla. "Visionary of Africa." *Northwestern Perspective* 9, no. 3 (Spring 1996): 15–17.

Royko, Mike. *Boss: Richard J. Daley of Chicago.* New York: Dutton, 1971.

Rubinowitz, Leonard S., and James E. Rosenbaum. *Crossing the Class and Color Lines.* Chicago: University of Chicago Press, 2000.

Schultz, John. *The Chicago Conspiracy Trial.* New York: Da Capo Press, 1993.

Schwartz, Eugene G. *American Students Organize: Founding the National Student Association After World War II.* Westport, Conn.: Praeger Publishers, 2006.

Seasongood, Murray. *Local Government in the United States: A Challenge and an Opportunity.* Cambridge, Mass.: Harvard University Press, 1933.

Stevenson, Adlai E. *Major Campaign Speeches of Adlai E. Stevenson, 1952.* New York: Random House, 1953.

Stevenson, Adlai. *Speeches of Adlai Stevenson,* with a foreword by John Steinbeck and a brief biography by Debs Myers and Ralph Martin. New York: Random House, 1952.

Strum, Philippa. *When the Nazis Came to Skokie: Freedom for Speech We Hate.* Lawrence: University Press of Kansas, 1999.

Thiem, George. *The Hodge Scandal.* New York: St. Martin's Press, 1963.

Travis, Dempsey J. *"Harold": The People's Mayor.* Chicago: Urban Research Press, 1989.

University of Illinois Bulletin. *The Illinois Constitution: Final Report and Background Papers,* ed. Lois M. Pelekoudas. Urbana, Ill.: Institute of Government and Public Affairs, 1962.

Van Der Slik, Jack R. "Reconsidering the Amendatory Veto for Illinois." *Northern Illinois University Law Review* 8 (1988): 753–79.

Walker, Daniel. *Rights in Conflict: Chicago's Seven Brutal Days, A Report to the National Commission on the Causes and Prevention of Violence.* New York: Grosset & Dunlap, 1968.

Watson, JoAnna M. "Analysis of the Vote at the Election for the 1970 Illinois Constitution." *Illinois Government* (Feb. 1971): 34.

Westwood, Howard C. *Covington & Burling 1919–1984.* Washington, D.C.: Covington & Burling, 1986.

Williamson, Harold F., and Payson S. Wild. *Northwestern University: A History 1850–1975.* Evanston, Ill.: Northwestern University, 1976.

Witwer, Samuel W. *Con Con Diary: Reflections of Samuel W. Witwer.* Wichita, Kan.: Hugo Wall School of Urban and Public Affairs, Wichita State University, 1997.

Wojcicki, Ed. "Still the Wild West? A 10-Year Look at Campaign Finance Reform in Illinois." Paul Simon Public Policy Institute Occasional Papers, 2006. http://opensiuc.lib.siu.edu/ppo_papers/5.

Newspapers

Chicago Daily News
Chicago Sun-Times
Chicago Tribune
Crain's Chicago Business
Daily Northwestern
The Hotline
Lerner Booster
New York Times
Peoria (Ill.) Journal Star
St. Louis Post Dispatch
State Journal-Register (Springfield, Ill.)

Cases

Dalehite v. United States, 346 U.S. 15 (1953).
Doe v. Scott, 321 F. Supp. 1385 (D.C. Ill. 1971).
Client Follow-Up Co. v. Hynes, 390 N.E.2d 847 (Ill. 1979).
Thorpe v. Mahin, 250 N.E.2d 633 (Ill. 1969).
United States v. Dellinger, 472 F.2d 340 (7th Cir. 1972), *rev'd, In re Dellinger*, 461 F.2d 389 (7th Cir. 1972).
United States v. Isaacs, 493 F.2d 1124 (7th Cir. 1974).
Village of Arlington Heights v. Metropolitan Housing Development Corp., 429 U.S. 252 (1977).
Weisberg v. Powell, 417 F.2d 388 (7th Cir. 1969).

INDEX

ABOUT THE AUTHOR

Cynthia Grant Bowman is the Dorothea S. Clarke Professor of Law at Cornell University Law School in Ithaca, New York. For eighteen years, she taught at Northwestern University School of Law, where she was Dawn Clark Netsch's colleague. Bowman has written and lectured extensively about patronage politics in Chicago and legal issues concerning women, including common-law marriage and cohabitation, child sex abuse, domestic violence, and sexual harassment. Her current research focuses on feminist legal theory, women and the legal profession, and family law.